Lonely Planet Publications
Melbourne | Oakland | London

Mat Oakley

Singapore

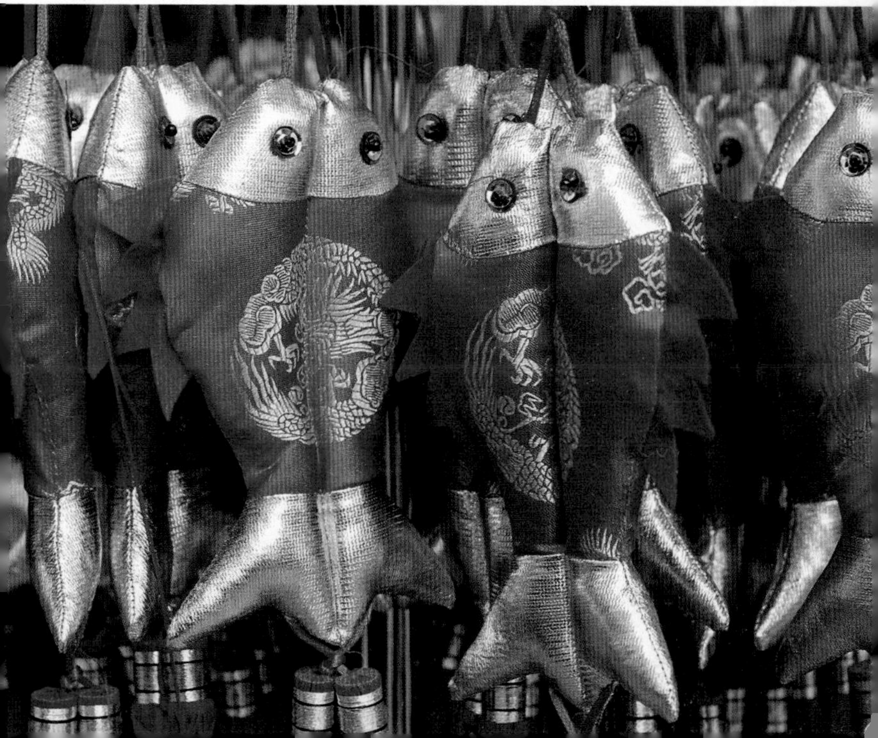

The Top Five

1 Orchard Road
Lose yourself in this shoppers' paradise (p63)

2 Chinatown
Soak up the vibrant culture, cuisine and history (p56)

3 Night Safari & Zoo
Get up close and personal with all kinds of species (p78)

4 Sentosa & Cable Car
Enjoy the spectacular view from the cable car (p85)

5 Jurong BirdPark
Take in a variety of exhibits and simulated ecosystems (p82)

Contents

Published by Lonely Planet Publications Pty Ltd
ABN 36 005 607 983

Australia Head Office, Locked Bag 1, Footscray, Victoria 3011, ☎ 03 8379 8000, fax 03 8379 8111, talk2us@lonelyplanet.com.au

USA 150 Linden St, Oakland, CA 94607, ☎ 510 893 8555, toll free 800 275 8555, fax 510 893 8572, info@lonelyplanet.com

UK 72–82 Rosebery Ave, Clerkenwell, London, EC1R 4RW, ☎ 020 7841 9000, fax 020 7841 9001, go@lonelyplanet.co.uk

Printed by SNP Security Printing Pte Ltd, Singapore

The Author

Mat Oakley

The son of a Scouse git and an aspic jelly-eating Yorkshire woman, Mat was born in the English town of Watford, whose residents are famous for not wanting to live in Watford anymore. After stints living in Laos, Thailand, Australia and Fiji, he has spent the last 18 months in Singapore with his girlfriend and a couple of badly behaved Fijian cats. Besides paddling and walking at the MacRitchie Reservoir, pedalling on Pulau Ubin, eating *sambal stingray* at Newton Circus and drinking *mojitos* at the Post Bar, his most memorable Singapore experience was standing in the Penny Black with a local branch of the Liverpool Supporters' Club watching the 2005 European Cup Final.

Although he had passed through Singapore countless times, when he had the chance to actually explore the city he found it was full of surprises: 'the Singapore River by water taxi, good cheap food from a myriad of cultures and history that can sometimes be hidden by the steel and glass'.

MAT'S TOP SINGAPORE DAY

An early morning stroll through the Botanic Gardens, or by one of the reservoirs, listening to the birds and watching the mist clear, followed by a *roti canai* and *kopi* for breakfast. A stroll down Orchard Rd, wandering under the trees and browsing through the quirkier malls before the crowds move in, a walk through Chinatown, checking out the antique shops and the teahouses. Onto the MRT and down to Sentosa to spend a couple of hours lazing under a tree on Siloso beach with a Coastes pizza. Late afternoon, a gentle bike ride along the beach in East Coast Park, capped off with a beer, then across town to Dempsey Rd for a bottle at The Wine Network, washed down with either a curry at Samy's Curry Restaurant or a plate of stingray at a hawker centre. Late evening cocktails at the Post Bar, a stroll past the colonial buildings on the north bank of the Singapore River, watching the bumboats sputter past, then up to Arab St for a *shisha* pipe, some mint tea and a plate of olives. Finally, a mosquito-free night's sleep, with the windows open.

PHOTOGRAPHERS

Phil Weymouth

Australian born, Phil moved with his family to Iran in the late 1960s and called Tehran home until the revolution in 1979. He studied photography in Melbourne, returned to the Middle East to work as a photographer in Bahrain, then spent several years working for an Australian rural media company. He now runs a freelance photojournalism business based in Melbourne.

LONELY PLANET AUTHORS

Why is our travel information the best in the world? It's simple: our authors are independent, dedicated travellers. They don't research using just the Internet or phone, and they don't take freebies in exchange for positive coverage. They travel widely, to all the popular spots and off the beaten track. They personally visit thousands of hotels, restaurants, cafés, bars, galleries, palaces, museums and more – and they take pride in getting all the details right, and telling it how it is. For more, see the authors section on **www.lonelyplanet.com**.

Introducing Singapore

It's popular to dismiss Singapore as a kind of Asia Lite – blandly efficient and safe, a boringly tasteless, disciplinarian and unadventurous place where citizens are robbed of their cherished freedom to spit on the street and chew gum. Utter nonsense.

Singapore is in fact one of the most enjoyable cities in Southeast Asia. As you zoom in from one of the world's best airports along the lushly tree-shaded expressway or on the zippy MRT train line, you'll quickly realise this is no traffic-snarled Bangkok. And as you stroll through the fashion emporiums of Orchard Rd, poke around antique shops in Chinatown or take a walk around one of the dozens of beautiful city parks, you'll know the city bears no comparison to crime- and poverty-ridden Manila or Jakarta.

Then, as you are drinking and dancing until dawn in the city's pubs and clubs, or sipping a cocktail surrounded by the colonial elegance of a Raffles Hotel veranda, think of your fellow travellers in Bangkok, who are being turfed onto the street at midnight.

There's no law that says an Asian city can't be well run. It may have been a long and difficult haul from swampy colonial outpost and notorious den of vice to powerhouse industrial nation, but those who say that Singapore has lost its soul along the way couldn't be more wrong.

Few cities in Southeast Asia can boast Singapore's fascinating ethnic brew. Where else in the world can you dip into the cultures of China, India and Muslim Malaysia all in one day, against a backdrop of ultra-modern Western commerce? Not only has Singapore's history of migration left a rich cultural and architectural legacy that makes wandering the streets an absorbing delight, it has created one of the world's great eating capitals.

Food is the national obsession – and it's not difficult to see why. Sitting out under the stars at a bustling hawker centre with a few bottles of Tiger beer and diving into an enormous array of Asian dishes is one of the iconic Singaporean experiences. *Sambal stingray*, *char kway teow*, oyster omelette, chicken rice, clay-pot seafood, fish head curry, beef *rendang*...the list is as long as it is delicious.

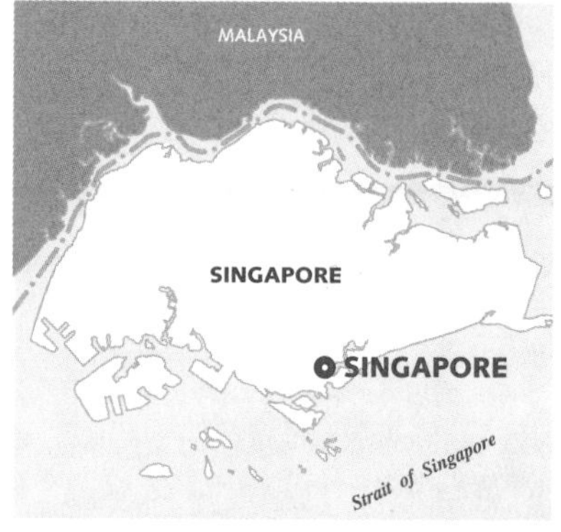

And, of course, if your credit card hasn't already taken a battering in the shops, the city's restaurants are some of the most stylish and innovative in the region.

If there's one thing more stylish than the bars and restaurants, it's the boutiques that

LOWDOWN

Population 4.4 million

Time zone GMT + 8hr

3-star room $110

Cup of kopi 60¢

Caffe latte $3.40

MRT ticket $2.30 (with a $1 refund)

Fine for littering $1000

Number of city food stalls (approximation) 11,500

have made Singapore a byword in Asia for extravagant shopping. Away from the Gucci and Louis Vuitton onslaught of Orchard Rd, however, there are bargains to be found on everything from clothes to electronics – and a range of art and antique shops that few Asian cities can match.

But Singapore is not all about shopping and eating. Nor is the notion of Singapore as completely urbanised anything more than popular myth. Adventure activities include diving with sharks at Underwater World on Sentosa, mountain biking around Bukit Timah, leopard-spotting at Singapore Zoo's magical Night Safari, waterskiing or wakeboarding on the Kallang River, go-karting and rock climbing. And if you want to retreat from civilisation completely, the centre of the island retains large tracts of forest where the only sound you can hear is the monkeys swinging through the trees. In fact, Singapore is one of only two cities in the world that still retains a patch of primary rainforest, in the form of Bukit Timah Nature Reserve.

It's a fascinating place – and a remarkable achievement. No-one is denying that Singaporeans have had to sacrifice some level of freedom in their island's rise from racially divided, resource-starved port town. But you get the feeling that if Western development aid had ever matched Singapore's strides in poverty reduction, education, infrastructure and health care, they'd be patting themselves on the back and saying that political freedom was a small sacrifice to make.

Besides, it's not all strait-laced conformity. You don't have to look far to find echoes of the island's colourful, rakish past, or evidence of a thriving and creatively unfettered artistic community. Singapore's soul is alive and well – and it is unique.

ESSENTIAL SINGAPORE

- Night Safari & Zoo (p78)
- Jurong BirdPark (p82)
- Hawker centre meal (see Top 10 Hawker Centres, p106)
- Concert at the Esplanade (p134)
- Shopping on Orchard Rd (p156)

City Life

City Life

SINGAPORE TODAY

Singapore is a city preoccupied with its future. Despite the decades of success, there's a sense that many Singaporeans know deep down how precarious it all is, how easily it could all fall apart. The Asian financial crisis in 1997 and the SARS scare of 2002 left the island with an acute sense of vulnerability.

Now that India and China are awake and stretching their economic muscles, Singaporeans know, and the government never loses an opportunity to let them know, that the country needs to reinvent itself to avoid falling behind. Newspapers are full of the 'Next Big Thing' that will propel the economy through the 21st century. In the late '90s the government announced that IT was Singapore's future. When that bubble burst, they turned their attention to the booming biomedical engineering sector and nanotechnology. Years of spoon-feeding seem to have left Singapore dangerously short of risk-taking entrepreneurs and the fear is that in the ruthlessly globalised world, today's mollycoddled young do not have the toughness to compete.

HOT CONVERSATION TOPICS

You can try anything from US foreign policy to global warming, but nothing will get Singaporeans as excited as the discovery of a new place to eat. The location, analysis and comparison of foods is a major topic of daily discussion. Tell a Singaporean you had a particularly fantastic oyster omelette, for example, and you will be subjected to a thorough interrogation concerning the location of the stall, price and precise qualities of the oysters, omelette and chilli sauce (referred to simply as 'chilli'). You will likely then be informed where, in fact, the best oyster omelettes in Singapore can be found.

The only other thing likely to spark such an animated discussion is English Premier League football, a national obsession that is debated, probed and scrutinised with as much fervour as it is in Britain, just with a slightly different vocabulary ('Wah lau, Gary Neville damn sotong one lor!').

But Singaporeans do have a serious side too of course, and despite the sensitive nature of politics in the country, they are quick to air their opinions on everything from casinos to politicians to that universal favourite: the declining state of the country.

The answer, it appears, is to cast Singapore as a 'hub', attracting high-value global enterprise to take advantage of the country's location, educated workforce, social stability and comfortable lifestyle. You'll see the word everywhere in the media. Singapore is an Aviation Hub, an Education Hub, a Medical Hub, a Bioengineering Hub, a Multimedia Hub.

But Singaporeans are also concerned that in the desperate rush to stay ahead, they will lose the strong sense of values (see Culture, p12) that helped bring them this far.

Conversely, the country's relative affluence has afforded many younger Singaporeans the luxury of indifference to the material imperatives that drove their parents and grandparents. The old adage that Singaporeans are driven by The Five Cs – car, condo, career, credit card and cash – still has a ring of truth, but is not nearly as accurate as it used to be.

CITY CALENDAR

Any time's a good time to go to Singapore. There are cultural events and festivals all year round, from fashion to film to food. Because Singapore is home to so many ethnic communities, you can hardly step outside without bumping into a festival. The less spectacular, less visible aspects of traditional culture are still practised too, and even the casual visitor will notice the numerous little street shrines, with their incense sticks, offerings and pyramids of oranges, that are inserted into the most unexpected corners.

Practically on the equator, Singapore is constantly hot (the temperature never drops below 20°C) and humid and gets fairly steady year-round rainfall. The wettest months are supposedly November to January, when it's also a little less hot, while the driest are May to July, but in reality there is little distinction between the seasons. Similarly, there is no high and low tourism season as such, though during local school holidays (see p202) and major cultural festivals the streets become noticeably more crowded.

The most spectacular festival is Thaipusam, occurring in the Hindu month of Thai (January or February), followed by Chinese New Year (also in February) and Deepavali (October or November). If eating is one of your major concerns, March and April are good times to visit to coincide with the Singapore Food Festival; for shoppers, visit in June and you'll catch the month-long Great Singapore Sale.

The **Singapore Tourism Board** (www.stb.com.sg) puts out a useful pamphlet every year detailing all the events – cultural, religious and sporting – coming up that year.

JANUARY & FEBRUARY

HARI RAYA HAJI

Animals are ritually slaughtered and given to the poor at mosques on this holy day in early January, commemorating the annual pilgrimage to Mecca.

PONGGAL

A four-day harvest festival celebrated in mid-January by southern Indians, especially at the Sri Mariamman Temple (p58) on South Bridge Rd.

CHINESE NEW YEAR

Dragon dances and pedestrian parades mark the start of the New Year between late January and mid-February. Families hold open house, unmarried relatives (especially children) receive *ang pows* (gifts of money in red packets), businesses clear their debts and everybody says *'Gung hei faat choi'* (I hope that you gain lots of money). Chinatown is lit up, especially Eu Tong Sen St and New Bridge Rd, and the 'Singapore River Hongbao Special' features *pasar malam* (night market) stalls, variety shows and fireworks.

CHINGAY

www.chingay.org.sg

Singapore's biggest street parade occurs on the 22nd day after Chinese New Year. It's a multicultural event, held along Orchard Rd, with flag bearers (balancing 6m- to 12m-long bamboo flag poles), lion dancers, floats and other cultural performers.

THAIPUSAM

Held between late January and mid-February, Thaipusam is one of the most dramatic Hindu festivals, in which devotees honour Lord Subramaniam with acts of amazing masochism. Hindus march in a procession from Sri Srinivasa Perumal Temple (p62) on Serangoon Rd to Chettiar Hindu Temple (p55) on Tank Rd carrying *kavadis* (heavy metal frames decorated with peacock feathers, fruit and flowers). The *kavadis* are hung from followers' bodies with metal hooks and spikes that are driven into their flesh. Other devotees pierce their cheeks and tongues with metal skewers *(vel)*, or walk on sandals of nails.

MARCH & APRIL

GOOD FRIDAY

A candlelit procession bearing the figure of the crucified Christ takes place at St Joseph's Catholic Church (Map p230; Victoria St).

SINGAPORE INTERNATIONAL COMEDY FESTIVAL

Nightly performances of stand-up, cabaret and comedy theatre from both local and overseas acts in late March/early April.

SINGAPORE FASHION FESTIVAL

Not quite Paris, but as close as you'll probably get in Southeast Asia, this features a fortnight of shows in late March/early April from local designers as well as prominent international names.

QING MING FESTIVAL

On All Souls' Day (4 or 5 April), Chinese traditionally visit the tombs of their ancestors to clean and repair them and make offerings. Singapore's largest temple complex, Kong Meng San Phor Kark See Monastery (p78), in the centre of the island, is the place to be.

Statues at Sri Srinivasa Perumal Temple (p62)

WORLD GOURMET SUMMIT

www.worldgourmetsummit.com

The two-week World Gourmet Summit from mid-April is a gathering of top international chefs and gourmet events.

SINGAPORE INTERNATIONAL FILM FESTIVAL

www.filmfest.org.sg

Well-established film festival running in the last two weeks of April that culminates in the Silver Screen Awards. In 2005 the festival featured around 300 films from 40 countries.

APRIL & MAY

VESAK DAY

Buddha's birth, enlightenment and death are celebrated by various events in early May, including the release of caged birds to symbolise the setting free of captive souls. Temples such as Sakaya Muni Buddha Gaya Temple (p61) in Little India throng with worshippers.

SEVENS SINGAPORE

www.singaporesevens.com.sg

About the only time you'll see rugby in Singapore – a two-day tournament in the world Rugby Sevens calendar renowned for its party atmosphere and heavy drinking.

MAY & JUNE

BIRTHDAY OF THE THIRD PRINCE

During this Chinese festival in late May, the child-god is honoured with processions, and devotees go into a trance and spear themselves with spikes and swords. Celebrations are held at various temples and on Queen St, near Bencoolen St.

GREAT SINGAPORE SALE

www.greatsingaporesale.com.sg

Orchard Rd is decked with banners, and merchants are encouraged by the government to drop prices in an effort to boost Singapore's image as a shopping destination. The sale is held for one month from the end of May to the beginning of July.

DRAGON BOAT FESTIVAL

www.sdba.org.sg

Commemorating the death of a Chinese saint who drowned himself as a protest against government corruption, this festival (held between late May and late June) is celebrated with boat races at East Coast Park.

SINGAPORE ARTS FESTIVAL

www.singaporeartsfest.com

Organised by the National Arts Council, this is Singapore's premier arts festival with a world-class programme of art, dance, drama and music through the month of June.

JULY & AUGUST

SINGAPORE FOOD FESTIVAL

www.singaporefoodfestival.com

Celebrating the national passion, this month-long festival in July (though it has been known to switch months) has special offerings at everything from hawker centres to top-end restaurants.

SINGAPORE NATIONAL DAY

On 9 August a series of military and civilian processions and an evening firework display celebrate Singapore's independence, gained in 1965. This is held on alternate years at the Padang (p52) and National Stadium (Map pp224–5). Various national day festivals and the prime minister's national day rally speech are held later in the month.

WOMAD

www.womadsingapore.com

Marking the end of National Day celebrations, this festival of world music usually takes place at Fort Canning Park (p51).

FESTIVAL OF THE HUNGRY GHOSTS

The souls of the dead are released for this one day of feasting and entertainment on earth. Chinese operas and other events are laid on for them (head to Chinatown) and food is put out – the ghosts eat the food's spirit but leave the substance for mortal celebrants. The festival is usually held sometime in August.

SEPTEMBER & OCTOBER

BIRTHDAY OF THE MONKEY GOD

T'se Tien Tai Seng Yeh's birthday is celebrated twice a year (September and February) at the Monkey God Temple (Map pp224–5) on Seng Poh Rd near the Tiong Bahru Market. Mediums pierce their cheeks and tongues with skewers and go into a trance, during which they write special charms in blood.

MOON-CAKE FESTIVAL

Celebrated on the full moon of the eighth lunar month (falling between mid-September and early October), this is also known as the Lantern Festival. Moon cakes are made with bean paste, lotus seeds and sometimes a duck egg.

NAVARATHRI

In the Tamil month of Purattasi (between mid-September and early October), the Hindu festival of 'Nine Nights' is dedicated to the wives of Siva, Vishnu and Brahma. Young girls are dressed as the goddess Kali; this is a good opportunity to see traditional Indian dancing and singing. Chettiar Hindu Temple (p55), Sri Mariamman Temple (p58) and Sri Srinivasa Perumal Temple (p62) are the main areas of activity.

ARTSINGAPORE

www.artsingapore.net

A fair of contemporary Southeast Asian art in late September.

OCTOBER & NOVEMBER

PILGRIMAGE TO KUSU ISLAND

Tua Pek Kong, the god of prosperity, is honoured by Taoists in Singapore who make a pilgrimage to the shrine on Kusu during the month of October.

DEEPAVALI

Rama's victory over the demon king Ravana is celebrated with the 'Festival of Lights', with tiny oil lamps outside Hindu homes and lights all over Hindu temples. Little India is ablaze with lights during the month of October.

THIMITHI (FIRE-WALKING CEREMONY)

Hindu devotees prove their faith by walking across glowing coals at the Sri Mariamman Temple (p58). This festival is usually in late October.

SINGAPORE BUSKERS FESTIVAL

This festival boasts Southeast Asia's largest showcase of street performing talent, from acrobats, artists, magicians and contortionists to the inevitable jugglers and mimes. The Singapore Buskers Festival takes place in November principally along Orchard Rd/Marina Sq and the Singapore River.

DECEMBER

HARI RAYA PUSA

The major Muslim events are connected with Ramadan, the month during which Muslims cannot eat or drink from sunrise to sunset. In the evenings food stalls are set up in Singapore's Arab St district near the Sultan Mosque (p63). Hari Raya Pusa marks the end of the month-long fast with three days of celebration; in the Malay areas, Geylang Serai (p66) is draped in lights.

CHRISTMAS

Orchard Rd celebrates Christmas with extravagant shopfront displays and even more extravagant lights.

WAH LAU, YOU VERY BLUR ONE, LOR!

Perhaps the first thing many visitors will notice, after the city's immaculate cleanliness, is that Singaporeans speak English fluently, often so fluently you can barely understand a word they are saying. This baffling dialect, which is basically English peppered with Malay, Hokkien and Tamil slang and spoken in a distinctive sing-song manner, is proudly known as Singlish.

Singlish mortifies the government, which runs the sternly named Speak Good English campaign and even banned a song with Singlish lyrics, Fried Rice Paradise, from the radio. It's a futile effort, akin to banning Cockney or trying to stop Australians adding an '-ie' to the end of each other's names. Whatever your opinion of it, Singlish is a rich vernacular in its own right and, if language is the ultimate manifestation of a national identity, ought to be celebrated rather than discouraged. For Singlish tips and phrases, see p208.

Happily the government has quietly admitted defeat. Now it is redirecting its energies towards encouraging people to develop a kind of spare accent; an intelligible English-speaking voice that they can pull out of their pockets whenever they need to speak to a foreigner.

CULTURE

IDENTITY

As prosperous Singapore forges ahead into the 21st century, it is keenly examining its own unique identity and what it means to be a Singaporean. The government is eager to define the Singaporean identity, especially in its promotion of Asian values, and to downplay the widely held belief that Singaporeans are only concerned about making money and being number one (see Everything Also Must Grab, opposite).

The government's neo-Confucian ideals are based on subservience to family and society, hard work and the desire to succeed. This dovetails with the government's authoritarian notions of 'Asian democracy', which argue that Western pluralism and democracy are decadent luxuries that Singapore cannot afford. Though that was unarguably true in the past, many feel that Singaporean society has evolved and matured (or become apathetic!) to the point where 'dangerous' points of view can be aired freely without threatening social order.

ETHNIC GROUPS

Chinese	76.7%
Malay	14%
Indian	7.9%
Other	1.4%

Traditional Chinese culture is promoted and there are political restrictions, yet Singapore enjoys diverse and growing cultural expression. Visitors and foreign residents, particularly non-Caucasian, are often surprised by the level of inquisitiveness, particularly where 'identity' is concerned.

Having said that, Singaporeans are also not afraid to laugh at their own social quirks – the surest sign of all that there is some kind of shared national identity.

Despite the astonishing pace of change, or maybe because of it, many traditional customs, festivals and ceremonies survive and even flourish. The most notable example, perhaps, is feng shui, which is still an important force in the construction industry (see The Art of Geomancy, below).

One City, Many Peoples

As each race flowed into the growing Singapore, it was given its own place within the city. They're still there – to a greater or lesser extent – and a visit to Singapore is a chance to take a tour of three Asian cultures in one day. Chinatown (p56) may have been over-polished, but there are still corners (the market at Chinatown Complex and around Sago Lane) where a whiff of the old Singapore lingers. And even the cleaned-up parts are vibrant and attractive.

THE ART OF GEOMANCY

Feng shui, the Chinese technique of manipulating or judging the environment, dictates much of what you see in Singapore – from the five-fingered shape of the Suntec City mall to the angle of the Hyatt Regency Hotel's front doors. Pronounced 'fung shway', and literally meaning 'wind-water', the art of geomancy taps into unseen currents swirling around the surface of the earth, caused by dragons that sleep beneath the ground. The energy, it is believed, travels on the wind and stops when it reaches water, which symbolises wealth. Hence the importance attached to water features, from the smallest home to the largest development.

If you want to build a house or a high-rise hotel or find a site for a grave, then you call in a feng shui expert. It is said that Lee Kuan Yew regularly consulted feng shui experts when in power, and his luck declined when he insisted on continuing with badly sited land reclamation.

Feng shui tours (adult/child $38/18), taking in a visit to a feng shui centre and trips to buildings like Suntec City to see how the principles have been implemented, are available on weekdays. Contact **Holiday Tours & Travel/Tour East** (☎ 6738 2622) or **SH Tours** (☎ 6734 9923).

Check out the highly colourful www.geomancy.net for information, contacts, personal feng shui calculators, wedding date selections and some feng shui reviews of buildings in Singapore.

EVERYTHING ALSO MUST GRAB

Kiasu, a Hokkien word meaning 'afraid to lose', entered Singapore's popular lexicon via the Mr Kiasu cartoon character, whose philosophies include: Always must win; Everything also must grab; Jump queue; Keep coming back for more; Look for discounts; Never mind what they think; Rushing and pushing wins the race; and Winner takes it all! all! all!

And are Singaporeans *kiasu*? At the risk of generalising, it's true that they are competitive and a bargain will never pass a Singaporean by. Retailers know this well and are constantly offering FOC (free of charge) gifts or 'limited edition' goods to attract shoppers. This can go too far, as was the case in 2000 when blows were exchanged between Singaporeans who had been queuing to receive limited-edition Hello Kitty dolls from McDonald's.

As a visitor there's no need for you to be swept up in such consumer madness (unless you want to), which is rare anyway. In fact, Singapore's reputation for rudeness is largely exaggerated (it certainly doesn't come close to Hong Kong). Even so, the government runs concerted courtesy campaigns that have, to some extent, paid dividends. Queuing is generally well observed, people give up their train seats to the elderly, and if you are lost or in trouble you can always count on Singaporeans to stop what they are doing to help you out, if you ask them.

Singapore also considers itself a charitable nation. Volunteer programmes are widespread and people pride themselves on giving to good causes. (After the 2004 tsunami disaster, two young men in singlets, shorts and thongs/flip-flops turned up at one charity drop-off point with $200,000 in cash. They said they had won it, but refused any publicity.)

However, it is true that the not-altogether-sincere Western concepts of 'please' and 'thank you' are not widely observed, which irritates some foreigners. Don't be surprised if the drinks auntie at the hawker centre shuffles up to your table and barks 'wa you wan!?', then throws your change on the table; it's just that no-nonsense Chinese charm.

Little India (p59) has more than a whiff of the subcontinent, where tatty shops sell *bhangra* (Punjabi folk music and dance) and Bollywood DVDs, while hundreds of eateries serve food from Nepal in the north to Tamil Nadu in the south. On weekends, thousands of male Tamil and Bangladeshi workers flock there to eat, chat, shop and send money home.

Historically, the Malays settled in Geylang (p65) and Katong (p66), east of the city. There are still some laid-back, Malay-style corners there, and while the Malay Village feels pretty phoney, the nearby streets still have old Asian charm.

Away from the tourist hotspots, though, this kind of ghettoisation is a thing of the past. Ever since race riots shook the city in 1964, Singapore has taken pains to engender racial harmony. Singaporeans celebrate Racial Harmony Day on 21 May, the anniversary of the riots. Other government initiatives abound, and multiracial and multireligious harmony is a cornerstone of the city-state.

In fact, Singapore effectively became independent because of racial tensions. Fearful of the rising economic power of the immigrant Chinese, the young Malaysian Federation gave special status to native-born ethnic Malays. In 1965 the predominantly Chinese Singapore was kicked out of a federation with which it was at odds anyway. Now all races are pointedly equal. Besides, racial tensions don't make for a booming economy.

In each of the thousands of Housing Development Board blocks, there are quotas for the different races. It's a noble idea, but it has a downside: when it comes to selling, there are fewer buyers for an Indian- or Malay-owned flat (which must be sold to an Indian or a Malay, to maintain the quota), and this basic market force drives down the price.

Each race has its own self-help organisations, in the shape of the Chinese clans, Mendaki for the Malays and Sinda for the Indians. Even the few thousand Eurasians have their own clubhouse.

Apartment building, Tiong Bahru (p58)

THE PERANAKANS

'Peranakan' means half-caste in Malay, which is exactly what the Peranakans are: descendants of Chinese immigrants who from the 16th century onwards settled in Singapore, Melaka and Penang and married Malay women. The term does not in fact strictly denote Chinese – there were also 'Peranakan Yahudi' (Jews), 'Ceti Peranakan' (Hindus from southern India) and 'Peranakan Yawi' (Arabs).

The culture and language of the Chinese Peranakans is a fascinating melange of Chinese and Malay traditions. The Peranakans took the name and religion of their Chinese fathers, but the customs, language and dress of their Malay mothers. They also used the terms 'Straits-born' or 'Straits Chinese' to distinguish themselves from later arrivals from China, who they looked down upon.

Other names you may hear for these people are Babas or Nonyas, after the Peranakan words for male *(baba)* and female *(nonya)*. The Peranakans were often wealthy traders and could afford to indulge their passion for sumptuous furnishings, jewellery and brocades. Their terrace houses were gaily painted, with patterned tiles embedded in the walls for extra decoration. When it came to the interior, Peranakan tastes favoured heavily carved and inlaid furniture.

Peranakan dress was similarly ornate. Nonyas wore fabulously embroidered *kasot manek* (slippers) and *kebaya* (blouses worn over a sarong), tied with beautiful *kerasong* brooches, usually of fine filigree gold or silver. Babas, who assumed Western dress in the 19th century, reflecting their wealth and contacts with the British, saved their finery for important occasions such as the wedding ceremony, a highly stylised and intricate ritual dictated by *adat* (Malay customary law).

The Peranakan patois is a Malay dialect but one containing many Hokkien words – so many that it is largely unintelligible to a Malay speaker. The Peranakans also included words and expressions of English and French, and occasionally practised a form of backward Malay by reversing the syllables. There are very few monolingual Peranakans left – and they are very old – and fewer than 5000 people in Singapore now speak the language at all.

Western culture has largely supplanted Peranakan traditions among the young, and the language policies of the government are also accelerating the language's decline. As the Peranakans are considered ethnically Chinese, children study Mandarin as their mother tongue in schools. Many also marry within the broader Chinese community, resulting in the further decline of the Peranakan patois.

Peranakan culture is far from dead in modern Singapore, though. The **Peranakan Association** (☎ 6255 0704; www.peranakan.org.sg) reports growing interest in Peranakan traditions as Singaporeans discover their roots. The distinctive Peranakan cuisine is also popular across the island (see p33). To find out more about how Peranakans once lived, visit the Armenian St branch of the Asian Civilisations Museum (p50).

Has it worked? There is certainly no danger of race riots, but a 2004 survey by the National University of Singapore Political Association suggested racial quotas on public housing had not encouraged more interaction. Only 7.4% of residents talked to neighbours of a different race daily, while 44.3% almost never did. At school, despite initiatives to help them mix, students mostly sit with others from their linguistic group. While all the men pull together during their two years of compulsory national service, old racial distinctions reassert themselves after. Each race has its own cultural characteristics – and other races inevitably have their opinions about them. Even within races, Singaporeans draw distinctions between Hokkien-speaking, Mandarin-speaking and Straits Chinese, or between northern Bengalis and southern Malayalis.

Having said that, most Singaporeans have friends of other races. As in other countries, youth culture mixes races more comfortably than its parents or grandparents did. Many of the emerging new wave of rock bands (see p133), for example, feature both Chinese and Malays.

The challenge now is to create a Singaporean culture while preserving the cultures of the different races. The best approach so far has been to repeatedly proclaim racial tolerance and harmony as a very Singaporean characteristic.

Religion

The variety of religions found in Singapore reflects the diversity of races living here. The Chinese mainly follow Buddhism and Shenism (deity worship), though some are Christians. Malays are overwhelmingly Muslim. Most of Singapore's Indians are Hindus, but many are Muslim, and there are also Sikhs, Parsis, Christians and Buddhists.

Despite increasing Westernisation and secularism, traditional religious beliefs are still held by the large majority. Singaporeans overwhelmingly celebrate the major festivals associated with their religions, though religious worship has declined among the young and the higher-educated, particularly the English-educated. In the Chinese community, for example, almost everyone will celebrate Chinese New Year.

The government is wary of religion and has abolished religious instruction in schools with the stated, and apparently successful, aim of avoiding religious intolerance and hatred.

The government's stated philosophy is Confucian, which is not a religion as such but a moral and social model. Its ideal society is based on the Confucian values of devotion to parents and family and loyalty to friends, and the emphasis is on education, justice and good government. Everyone, regardless of their religious beliefs, is expected to uphold these central principles.

Social Graces

The days when arriving travellers could be denied entry to Singapore for having long hair or dressing like a hippy are long gone, but you will still get scant respect if you walk around looking like you have just emerged from the jungle or a Thai beach. Singapore may have the ideal climate for dressing down, but Singaporeans dress smartly, particularly in the central city, and you will stick out even more than usual if you look scruffy. Out in the 'heartlands', however, shorts and thongs (flip-flops) are the uniform of choice.

Singapore has strict laws defining appropriate public behaviour. Spitting, littering, urinating in public, chewing gum (unless it's nicotine gum on prescription!), jaywalking or even failing to flush the toilet are all misdemeanours that can land you with a fine. In practice, this doesn't happen as often anymore, but the renowned Singaporean 'policeman within' generally keeps these menaces in check.

Laws aside, there are few social restrictions in Singapore (even overt public affection is becoming more common), but one small, everyday piece of etiquette is worth noting: when handing something to a Chinese person, or taking something from them, do so with both hands. It shows respect. For Indians and Malays, it's common to hand something over with the right hand while cupping your left hand underneath your elbow.

LIFESTYLE

The average middle-class Singaporean can look forward to a long life: 84 years for a woman and 79 years for a man. They'll most likely be married and have no more than two children (the average number of children per woman is only 1.05). Their monthly income, if both of them are working, will be about $4500, a large chunk of which will go towards paying off the loans on their $300,000 Housing Development Board flat and perhaps the family car.

This average can be misleading, however, as there are still plenty of people here who subsist on a relatively low income of a little over $1000 a month.

SHUT YOUR MOUTH

In November 2003 a police sergeant was jailed for two years after accepting oral sex from a consenting 16-year-old girl (who later turned out to be 15, however). The incident sparked a flurry of calls for the government to review a law that stated: 'Whoever voluntarily has carnal intercourse against the order of nature with any man, woman or animals shall be punished with imprisonment for life…', which was deemed by the Court of Appeal in 1997 to mean, among other things, oral sex that does not lead to sexual intercourse.

Apparently, in making its decision, the court had referred to cases in England and India dating back to 1817, in which the victims of these unnatural acts were young boys and buffalo.

Some letter-writers in the local media pointed out that the law only seemed to punish men and cited a case in which a vengeful wife performed oral sex on her cheating husband and then reported him to the police, as an example of how it might be abused.

In response to this outpouring of public dismay, in January 2004 the government promised to decriminalise oral sex between men and women, but retain the ban for homosexual acts.

VISITING CHINESE HOMES

A few simple rules that should ease any visit to a Chinese home:

- Take a gift. If it's a celebration, give food, fruit, money, everyday items. It doesn't have to be fancy, but giving pairs of things symbolises good luck (except if the person is sick). If you want to wrap it, using red paper will be especially welcome. The host will not open the gift in front of you, as this is considered very rude.
- If offered a gift, always accept and never open it in front of the giver.
- You will likely be offered a drink. Accept, receive it with both hands and take a few sips.
- If it's a wedding, birthday or Chinese New Year, it's customary to give a 'red packet', a small, decorated red envelope, containing a little money.
- At Chinese New Year, it's customary when you arrive to present your host with a pair of mandarin oranges, which symbolise wealth. They will give a pair to you in return.
- If hosting, see your guests to the door and watch them until they disappear. Turning your back after saying goodbye is considered rude.

Singaporeans on the whole follow the modern urban patterns of hard work and long hours, which can leave minimal time for the extended families that often share one home (though this, too, is changing).

It also, apparently, leaves little time for sex. Surveys repeatedly place Singaporeans low on the libido list and as the birth rate (particularly the Chinese birth rate) falls, there is now a concerted effort by the government to provide financial incentives to get couples back in the sack and making babies again.

FASHION

Singaporeans are smart and fashionable, which means you'll have no trouble finding every major designer label under the sun. But they are not the most adventurous dressers. The most popular single item of clothing is probably the polo shirt. Occasionally you'll see a teenager in a gothic/punk outfit on the MRT or wandering the malls, but in terms of daring street fashion that's about the limit. Most young people stick with the usual jeans/T-shirt combos, imitation American hip-hop gear and skimpy skirt/top outfits, while the T-shirt/singlet, bermudas and thongs (flip-flops) look is almost a Singaporean heartlands uniform. Hair fashions are equally conservative. This is certainly no Tokyo.

Gadgets form a key part of a fashionable outfit and mobile phones, iPods and handhelds are often prominently displayed and constantly fiddled with.

For a couple of weeks in late March/early April, the Singapore Fashion Festival, while no match for Milan, Paris or London, puts on some impressive shows from local and international designers. In October Singapore Fashion Week showcases the local industry, with exhibitions, awards and shows from local luminaries like M)phosis, Daniel Yam, Allure and GG>5, as well as rising stars.

SPORT

There's not much in the way of live spectator sport in Singapore, unless you count watching English Premier League football on television. The local 10-team S.League football competition, which runs from March to October, is fairly well supported and features dozens of overseas players. The victory of the national team in the regional Tiger Cup in 2004 gave a much needed boost to local football.

DRAGON BOAT RACING

A popular weekend workout with expats and locals alike is a furious paddle in a dragon boat – it's a great way to sweat off your Friday-night hangover! Groups meet at the Water Sports Centre (Map pp224–5), Stadium Lane, a short walk from the Singapore Indoor Stadium at Kallang. The **British Chamber of Commerce Dragon Boat Team** (www.britishdragonboat.com) meets every Saturday between 3.30pm and 4pm; bring $10, a change of clothes and some water (you don't need to be British, or even an expat, to join in). Refreshments are provided afterwards. Competitions are held occasionally on the Boat Quay stretch of the Singapore River.

SPEAKING OUT IN SINGAPORE

As any opposition politician or crusading journalist can tell you, criticising the Singaporean government can be hazardous to your liberty and murderous on your bank balance. The government, keen to be seen as 'democratic', established **Speakers' Corner** (Map p230; Hong Lim Park, cnr New Bridge Rd & Upper Pickering St) in 2000, but the various restrictions on what you can speak about (nothing controversial or potentially libellous – just about anything in Singapore!) have led to its failure.

Opposition politician Chee Soon Juan found himself hauled through the courts in 2004–05 for libelling Minister Mentor Lee Kuan Yew and Senior Minister Goh Chok Tong. He was eventually fined around $500,000.

Still, as a glance at the letters page of the *Straits Times* will show, Singaporeans are becoming more daring about speaking out (in 2005 one young student even referred to the government as a 'dictatorship' in a public forum with Lee Kuan Yew, for which he earned himself a stern rebuke). However, people who do make a prominent show of dissent, or even those who appear to undermine the social order, are regularly given short shrift by the conservative media.

The popular website **Talking Cock** (www.talkingcock.com), which satirises the government, sometimes quite scathingly, has strangely been spared the official rod and permitted to make fun of ministers and their policies.

There are regular calls for more artistic freedom – which seems to be happening. The trouble is that no-one knows when the government might decide it's all gone too far and clamp down again, as they did with gay parties (see p125) in 2005.

Once a year in April, the Sevens Singapore tournament, part of the global IRB Rugby Sevens championship, takes place at the National Stadium.

At the time of writing, there was also talk of reintroducing motor racing to the country in the form of the newly created A1 championship. Singapore held the Grand Prix in 1973, but Lee Kuan Yew (to his regret he says) banned it shortly after, fearing that it would promote dangerous driving.

MEDIA

The press in Singapore (which is almost entirely owned by the gigantic Singapore Press Holdings) knows its limits most of the time and holds off from any damaging criticism of the government. News coverage, especially in the *Straits Times*, is heavily geared towards reinforcing the social order and national interests. There is also a lively lifestyle media and the shelves of newsagents are brimming with men's and women's magazines (including *Cosmopolitan*) with their customary brand of sensational sex cover lines, as well as what's-on publications and special-interest magazines.

Local television, which is divided into English, Chinese, Tamil and Malay language stations, features a mixture of local and imported dramas (which are sometimes heavily censored) and American-style news shows. There is a notable fondness for weepy, heartbreak true-life re-enactment programmes among local producers.

Of all the media, radio is probably the biggest risk-taker and is certainly the medium that lands itself in hot water with the authorities most frequently. However, the music stations are still dominated by bland, identikit DJs with American accents.

See the Directory for a run-down on local newspapers and magazines (p204), television (p205) and radio (p204).

THE SPACE ENCROACHER

One public figure who does seem to get away with a variety of published gripes is DJ and writer Chris Ho – or X'Ho, as the self-styled Ginsberg, Burroughs and Johnny Rotten of Singaporean letters prefers to be known.

Ho's books *Skew Me, You Rebel Meh?* and *Attack of the SM Space Encroachers* bring together columns from the *Big O* magazine, plus new commentaries. It's hit-and-miss stuff, covering Ho's pet peeves on censorship and the stereotypical ugly slow-mo Singaporean. Beneath it all, though, lies Ho's deep affection for his country. As Ho says, 'No-one writes better hate mail to Singapore than I do. What can I say? It's an astonishing love.'

Aside from DJ-ing at the ultra-trendy Liquid Room, X'Ho also has a website at www.xhosux.com.

ECONOMY & COSTS

It's a tiny island with few natural resources – not even its own water supply – so how come Singapore is so well off?

The answer is a smart government, which took maximum advantage of the country's position as a trading crossroads to establish Singapore as the world's largest port (though now second behind Rotterdam) and a major manufacturing centre. Its status as a hub (you'll hear that word a lot) also made it an ideal location for petroleum and petrochemical refining, drilling rig manufacture, and ship building and repair. Stand on one of Sentosa's beaches, look west and you'll see just how huge this industry is. Singapore has 11 refineries and in terms of capacity is the world's third-largest petroleum refiner after Rotterdam and Houston.

Its reputation for low corruption, stable currency, low inflation and low interest rates also helped Singapore become a key Asian financial centre.

As a result of this dynamic success, Singapore has one of the highest living standards and home ownership levels in the world. It guarantees its citizens decent housing, health care, high standards of education and superannuation. While there are no unemployment payments or programmes, unemployment is negligible and Singapore still imports thousands of workers in both skilled and unskilled jobs.

With the exception of a few major troughs in the '80s, Singapore recorded a phenomenal growth rate averaging around 9% in its first 30 years as an independent state, but a series of setbacks in the last decade or so has given the country a nasty jolt. The Asian financial crisis in the mid to late 1990s and a recession from 2001 to 2003 put the brakes on, then the outbreak of SARS (severe acute respiratory syndrome) gave the country a huge scare, as tourist arrivals and consumer spending plummeted.

Manufacturing, for so long the engine room of Singapore's success, is in decline, due in large part to the rapid growth of China and India. Tourism numbers are also lagging behind other major Asian destinations. The government is now trying to remodel the economy and build up sectors like biomedical engineering and multimedia to ensure the country's future. Massive investments in tourism are also in the pipeline.

For the visitor, Singapore is probably Southeast Asia's most expensive destination, but compared with the West, things like food, accommodation and clothes are still cheap. It's no longer the electronics paradise it once was, but prices are also generally lower than in Western countries.

For a stay in a three-star hotel, with three modest meals, perhaps a restaurant splurge, a bit of sightseeing and a few drinks, count on spending $250 a day, though obviously this can go both a lot lower and a lot higher. It is possible to live very cheaply in Singapore and visitors with families might want to take note of the free museum entry periods (see Singapore on the Cheap, p47).

HOW MUCH?

Litre of petrol $1.46

Litre of bottled water 90¢

Bottle of hawker centre Tiger beer $5

Souvenir T-shirt $5

Plate of chicken rice $4

Movie ticket $9

Five-star room $300+

No-star room $40

iPod $528

Tailored suit $200+

GOVERNMENT & POLITICS

In theory, Singapore has a democratically elected government based on the Westminster system. In practice, however, the electoral laws are biased in favour of the ruling People's Action Party (PAP), which has been in power since independence – and in effect the government is more like the board of a rather socially conscious corporation. Most Singaporeans accept the status quo that has enriched them and raised them from third world to first in two generations, but a few dissenting voices continue.

The current unicameral parliament has 84 elected members, with nine of the MPs from single-member constituencies and the 75 others from group representation constituencies, which are supposed to ensure the representation in parliament of members of the Malay, Indian and other minority communities. A side effect of having several MPs for a single seat is to make it harder for opposition parties to field enough candidates to contest the seat. Voting in elections is compulsory. Governments are elected for five years, but a ruling government can dissolve parliament and call an election at any time.

The PAP argues that since it listens to all opposition and is happy to take on good ideas no matter where they originate, there is less need for political plurality. Since the vast majority of MPs belong to PAP, the government has created a system that allows it to appoint an opposition. Nonconstituency members of parliament (NCMPs) are appointed to parliament if fewer than four opposition members are elected. Nominated MPs (NMPs) comprise nine prominent citizens who are appointed to give nonpartisan views.

Singapore also has a popularly elected president (SR Nathan at the time of writing). The position is largely ceremonial.

The government shows signs of wanting to involve the population more in its decision-making process. A year-long debate on whether Singapore should open a casino involved everyone from religious and grassroots leaders to charities and social services. Eventually, the government opted to open two 'integrated resorts', big tourist attractions in which casinos are a small part. And it has promised safeguards to deal with the possible social fallout of increased gambling.

There's a strong push to engage the youth, who are often stigmatised as being politically apathetic. Suggestions have been invited for what to put in a new youth centre off Orchard Rd – although some politicians believe that using it as a venue for political debate won't make much headway.

The legal system is also based on the British system. The judiciary's independence is enshrined in the constitution, but many judges are appointed on short tenure and their renewal is subject to party approval. Rulings that have gone against the government have been followed by new laws enacted by parliament to ensure the government's victory. Singapore's Internal Security Department keeps records of its citizens, and there is widespread (albeit unverifiable) fear of losing jobs, promotional opportunities or contracts through criticism of the government.

Rather than being heavy-handed politically, though, the government is inclined to use the courts against anyone it considers guilty of defamation. It almost always wins, as opposition politicians such as JB Jeyaretnam and Chee Soon Juan and publications such as the *Economist* found to their cost.

ENVIRONMENT

Singapore stands out as an environmentally enlightened country. Strict laws control littering and waste emissions, and though industry in the past may have developed with a relatively free hand, Singapore is now much more environmentally aware.

THE LAND

The main island of Singapore is 42km long and 23km deep, and sits a degree above the equator. There are a further 63 outlying islands, some industrial, some military, some for pleasure and some little more than wave-washed rocks. Altogether, Singapore has a landmass of 700 sq km, and is growing through land reclamation (see The Growing Island, p20).

The other main islands are Pulau Tekong, which is gazetted as a military area but planned to be semiresidential; the largely rural Pulau Ubin; and Sentosa, Singapore's rapidly developing fun park.

Around half the main island of Singapore is built up and the rest is given over to parkland, reservoirs, some small farms, some large military areas and a bit of jungle. It's a flat island, easy for walking. Bukit Timah (Hill of Tin) is the highest point at 166m. The central area has most of Singapore's forest and open areas. The western part is a sedimentary area of low-lying hills and valleys, while the southeast is mostly flat and sandy. Singapore is connected to Peninsular Malaysia by two causeways, in the north and the west.

GREEN SINGAPORE

Singapore has 1006 species of fungi, 2697 species of plants, 364 species of birds, 451 species of crabs and shrimps, and 935 species of insects. But the most common wildlife you'll spot in nature reserves and parks are long-tailed macaques, squirrels and geckos. The more eagle-eyed and fortunate may see flying lemurs, reticulated pythons, black-bearded flying lizards and the very rare anteater.

A host of birds – including the greater racket-tailed drongo, striped tit-babbler and white-bellied sea eagle – are more often heard than seen. But cheeky mynah birds and occasional flocks of parakeets enliven the branches, and flashes of yellow or blue show you've just missed a golden oriole or a kingfisher.

The Singapore Green Plan 2012 was launched in 2002, a 10-year blueprint for environmental sustainability, focusing on waste management, clean air, water supply and ecology. The island, always spotless and well organised, is becoming even cleaner and greener. A second botanic gardens is slated for the new Marina Bay development.

Around 300 hectares is nature reserve, and growing interest in ecology has seen new bird sanctuaries and parkland areas gazetted by the government. Ordinary people play their part, too: plans to reclaim land at Chek Jawa, a low-tide nature reserve on Pulau Ubin (p181), were indefinitely delayed following a rare public outcry.

But while the island tackles environmental issues at home, it has no control over its neighbours. From June to September, forest fires in Indonesia can bring brown skies, and on bad days a haze hangs over the island, a gloomy reminder of its environmentally vulnerable position in the region.

THE GROWING ISLAND

It's a long time since Beach Rd was anywhere near the sea. The island state has increased its landmass from 581 sq km at independence in 1965 to 700 sq km today. This is nothing new: Singapore's first land reclamation project was during Raffles' time when earth was removed from a hill to fill a swamp.

Reclamation has drastically changed the geography around the city centre, particularly in the Marina Bay area where more than 550 hectares have been added. In the Tanah Merah and Changi airport area in the east, and Tuas in the west, land is creeping into the sea. Some reclamation projects have trodden on the toes of Malaysia next door.

One of the most ambitious projects was the joining up of seven islands to make Jurong Island, now the biggest island after Singapore itself. The new land is mainly used for oil storage.

URBAN PLANNING & DEVELOPMENT

As fast as the island grows, the population grows faster, and the challenge is to fit them all in. Even so, new towns like Punggol and Jurong West still have vacant flats, as people aren't rushing to live there until the infrastructure is better. A $20-billion transport system is being developed. The MRT network will more than double in size, but suffers from a catch-22 situation. Some of the new stations won't open until there are more people in the neighbourhoods they service; and people are unwilling to move there until the MRT is open. Owning a car is something most Singaporeans aspire to, but is still the preserve of the wealthy few, thanks to heavy registration fees.

The amount of land gazetted for housing and work is set to rise. Building upwards is still the favoured solution, where possible, as not all the land can be developed. Water catchment areas already take up 40% of the land and flight paths lead to height restrictions in areas like Changi and Tampines.

For an overview – literally – of the island, go to the Urban Redevelopment Authority (URA) Gallery (p59) for interactive exhibits and a huge scale model of the island state.

Arts & Architecture

Arts & Architecture

Singapore's cultural variety is its greatest strength, so over the course of a year, performances will include everything from Chinese opera to Indian classical dance to British pantomime. International ballet troupes, touring theatre companies from the West, and major international pop artists drop by regularly.

It's not a free-for-all and there are taboos when it comes to advocating alternative lifestyles, but shows are more likely to close because of poor ticket sales than government interference.

Shoppers pick up local art and sculptures from the region, although it's a fraction of the price if you go to the source and buy in Hanoi or Bali. Creative locals are encouraged to express themselves in more economically viable ways, such as computer-generated animation for George Lucas' new studio, which opened in Singapore in 2005.

A mix of architectural styles makes wandering the streets an eclectic delight, with Indian temples in Chinatown, and the brand new Foster Partners–designed Supreme Court looming like a spaceship over the old colonial quarter. Art and architecture go hand in hand, as the spiky, endearing Esplanade shows, and many colonial buildings are reinventing themselves as arts venues, such as the Arts House at the Old Parliament House.

Music and dance performances, such as the Womad (World of Music and Dance) festival and Ballet under the Stars in Fort Canning Park, are often held in open spaces and shopping malls to appeal to a wider audience. The annual Arts Festival (June/July) ranges from larky street theatre to impenetrably avant-garde.

The government has sought to boost art in a number of ways. It has introduced an Arts Education Programme administered by the **National Arts Council** (NAC; www.nac.gov.sg) in schools, and established arts schools at both the National University of Singapore and Nanyang Technological University.

LITERATURE

Singapore has experienced a literary boom and many young novelists are hard at work writing (in English) about Singapore. The late Goh Sin Tub has a place in Singapore's heart for his cosy tales of local life, such as *12 Best Singapore Stories*. No-one has emerged to take over as the Voice of Singapore, but lawyer and author Philip Jeyaretnam is one of the leading lights. Look for *Raffles Place Ragtime* and *Abraham's Promise*.

Tan Hwee Hwee's entertaining books *Foreign Bodies* and *Mammon Inc* illuminate cultural confusions and compromises Generation X Singaporeans contend with. Catherine Lim, whose outspokenness once troubled the government, is another highly regarded writer. Her books, such as *Following the Wrong God Home* and *The Bondmaid*, are mostly about relationships with Singapore as backdrop.

TOP FIVE SINGAPORE FICTION

- *Tigers in Paradise* (Philip Jeyaretnam, 2004) Selected works.
- *Juniper Loa* (Lin Yutang, 1963) A young immigrant leaves his love behind in China.
- *Tangerine* (Colin Cheong, 1996) A Singaporean struggles in Vietnam.
- *Playing Madame Mao* (Lau Siew Mai, 2000) Magical realism during purge of communists.
- *Mammon Inc* (Tan Hwee Hwee, 2001) Affectionate satire of big business and the Singapore way.

PAINTING

The School of Singapore hasn't established itself in the same way as those in Indonesia and Vietnam – apart from the Nanyang School of the Sixties, which went on to found the Nanyang School of Fine Art. Among its founders, collagist Goh Beng Kwan is still working hard today. Artists Tan Swie Hian, Heman Chong and Francis Ng all took part in the Venice Biennale in 2003. Tan also became the first Singaporean to receive the World Economic Forum Crystal

Award in 2003. Ong Kim Seng is a well regarded local watercolourist while Chua Ek Kay works beautifully in Chinese ink.

The MICA Building (Ministry of Information, Communication and the Arts) has a handful of galleries, while boutique galleries like Red Sea Gallery on River Valley Rd and Utterly Art on South Bridge Rd showcase art from the region.

The grand old man of pottery is Iskandar Jalil, who fell foul of the authorities when his ancient kiln turned out to flout planning regulations (though admirers gave him a newer, safer one).

TOP FIVE ART GALLERIES

- **Singapore Art Museum** (p53) Eclectic Asian.
- **Gajah Gallery** (p143) Chic Asian.
- **Red Sea Gallery** (p144) Well-priced Vietnamese.
- **Utterly Art** (p146) Modern local.
- **Opera Gallery** (p159) Expensive European.

SCULPTURE & PUBLIC ART

Sculpture Sq (Map p230), on Middle Rd, was launched in 1999, and public art is springing up everywhere. While New York's Wall St has the bull, Singapore's financial district has the vast, chubby *Bird* by Colombian artist Fernando Botero. More exciting are the People of the River sculptures along the Singapore River (see The Sculpture Trail, below). They show scenes from Singapore's history, from the little boys jumping joyously into the river, to the pigtailed Chinese businessman negotiating with a 19th-century colonial over the price of a bale of cotton.

The new MRT North East Line, which opened in 2003, has some interesting murals. Husband and wife team Milenko and Delia Prvacki illuminated Dhoby Ghaut station with intricate, swirling murals, while Outram Park has bas-reliefs of local scenes by Teo Eng Seng that look scarily as if people have been imprisoned in plaster while playing soccer or shopping. Two of the city-state's leading sculptors are both blind: Victor Tan and Chng Seok Tin, who won the Cultural Medallion, Singapore's highest artistic award.

MUSIC & DANCE

The Singapore rock scene is surprisingly lively. Local bands such as Electrico and Ugly in the Morning have produced solid first albums, while the next wave of bands like rockers Ronin, nu-electric Zircon.Gov Pawn Starz and punk-poppers Pug Jelly are showing greater staying power than most young wannabes. Going lighter, pianist Jeremy Monteiro and his sister, Clarissa, keep the Singapore flag flying proudly on the international jazz scene.

The excellent Singapore Symphony Orchestra (SSO), established in 1979, was Singapore's first professional orchestra and now holds more than 100 performances a year at the Esplanade.

The well-respected Singapore Chinese Orchestra, set up in 1997, has about 20 performances of traditional and symphonic Chinese music yearly, as well as Indian, Malay and Western.

There are over 30 dance companies and societies. The nation's leading dance company, Singapore Dance Theatre, puts on about 28 performances a year – the annual Ballet under

THE SCULPTURE TRAIL

Start at Raffles Pl (Map pp234–5) and tick off the following sculptures:

1. Aw Tee Hong's boat-shaped *Struggle for Survival* at the south end of Raffles Pl.
2. The Singapore streetscape *Progress & Advancement* by Yang Ying-Feng at the north end of Raffles Pl.
3. Henry Moore's *Reclining Figure* in front of the OCBC Centre on South Canal Rd.
4. The surreal *Homage to Newton* by Salvador Dalì in the atrium of the UOB Plaza on Chulia St.
5. Fernando Botero's giant, fat *Bird* on the river in front of UOB Plaza.
6. The family of tiny *Kucinta* cats on the left-hand side of Cavenagh Bridge.
7. The river-diving boys of *First Generation* by Chong Fat Cheong, on the right-hand side of Cavenagh Bridge.

the Stars season at Fort Canning Park draws an audience of 10,000. Odyssey Dance Theatre represented Singapore at the Asean Festival of Arts, while groups such as EcNad and Ah Hock & Peng Yu all add to a growing scene. The minority groups are well represented with Bhaskar's Arts Academy and the Nrityalaya Aesthetics Society for Indian dance, and Sri Warisan Som Said Performing Arts for contemporary and traditional Malay dance.

CHINESE OPERA

In Singapore, *wayang* (Chinese opera) is derived from the Cantonese opera, which is seen as a more music-hall mix of dialogue, music, song and dance. What the performances lack in literary nuance, they make up for in garish costumes and crashing music. Scenery is virtually non-existent, but action is all-important. Performances can go for an entire evening, with the audience drifting in and out, eating and chatting. It's usually easy for the uninitiated to follow the gist of the action. The acting is stylised and the music searing to Western ears, but seeing a performance – or at least part of it – is worthwhile.

Street performances are held during important festivals such as Chinese New Year, the Festival of the Hungry Ghosts and the Festival of the Nine Emperor Gods – head to Chinatown for the best chance of seeing performances.

CINEMA & TV

In 1997, a Singaporean film was shown at Cannes, giving cinema in the island nation a boost: Eric Khoo's *12 Storeys* was selected for the Un Certain Regard section of the 50th Cannes Film Festival. Like his first film, *Mee Pok Man*, it's set in the Singaporean 'heartlands' and covers 24 hours in a typical Housing Development Board (HDB) block. In 2005, it happened again. Khoo's *Be With Me*, three intertwined love stories featuring a blind and deaf woman, opened the Cannes' Directors Fortnight, receiving a standing ovation.

Singapore cinema has seen dawns like this before. Local movies gained international attention with *Medium Rare*, based on the strange but true story of a psychopathic occultist hanged in 1988 for murder. *Bugis Street* (1995) was criticised as being melodramatic and clichéd – and grossed $1 million. It was beaten by *I Not Stupid*, Jack Neo's heartrendingly funny look at the hothouse education system.

TOP FIVE SINGAPOREAN FILMS TO WATCH

- *I Not Stupid* (Jack Neo, 2002) A harsh but funny insight into the school system.
- *Chicken Rice War* (CheeK, 2001) Romeo and Juliet rewritten with food sellers.
- *Money No Enough* (Jack Neo, 1998) Why not to borrow money from loansharks.
- *Mee Pok Man* (Eric Khoo, 1995) A noodle seller loves and abducts a hooker.
- *Be With Me* (Eric Khoo, 2005) Three disparate love stories weave together.

In 1998 the Singapore Film Commission was established, to 'nurture, support and promote' Singaporean talent in the film industry by dispensing grants, loans and scholarships, conducting training and supporting film-related events. The **Singapore International Film Festival** (www.filmfest.org.sg) is held every April, and the **Singapore Film Society** (www.sfs.org.sg) also screens more than 150 international features a year, many themed into festivals.

Singaporean TV has little to keep you indoors, apart from endless local soaps, lifestyle magazine shows, copycat American-style competition series like *Singapore Idol* and *Eye For A Guy*, and 'true-life' re-enactment dramas.

THEATRE

Professional English-language theatre is barely 20 years old. Reports of its death are premature, but it struggles, despite a passionate core of actors and directors. Visitors are more likely to see imported shows with exclamation marks in the title such as *Oliver!* and *Mamma Mia!* at the Esplanade or Victoria Theatre. Local hero Dick Lee has written a few successful crowd-pleasers, such as *Forbidden City: Portrait of an Empress* about the life of Empress Dowager Tzu His.

Singapore theatre has gone to the other extreme, with challenging, sometimes risky pieces. Creative, inventive luna-id Theatre specialises in plays by overseas playwrights that 'contain universal relevance'. Necessary Stage aims for 'challenging indigenous and innovative theatre that touches the heart and mind'. Other companies such as Wild!Rice veer from the inspired *Emily of Emerald Hill* to the patchy farce *Boeing Boeing* and gay angst *Landmark: Asian Boys 2*. All up, buying a theatre ticket in Singapore is a lottery that can leave you wondering how such a small island can create such inspired drama, or why you didn't go to the movies instead.

ARCHITECTURE

Away from the ranks of HDB blocks, gleaming skyscrapers of the central business district (CBD) stand side by side with the charming restored shophouses, all ornate and human scale, and the grandeur of colonial era buildings, particularly around the Padang.

Colonial architecture (left)

COLONIAL

Irishman George Drumgoole Coleman, who became Singapore's town surveyor and superintendent of public works in 1826, is the pre-eminent colonial architect. He was a skilful adapter of the Palladian style (Doric columns, high ceilings, wide verandas) to suit the tropical climate. His buildings include the Armenian Church (p54), Caldwell House in Chijmes (p50) and Old Parliament House (p52); he was also responsible for the city's original central road network.

Other colonial buildings of note from the mid-1800s include St Andrew's Cathedral (p54) and the Cathedral of the Good Shepherd (p54), as well as the Thian Hock Keng Temple (p58) and the Hajjah Fatimah Mosque (p60).

SHOPHOUSES

Before HDB flats, the definitive Singaporean building was the shophouse. They're still scattered around Chinatown, Little India, Kampong Glam, a couple of pockets near Orchard Rd, and Geylang and Kallang, east of the city centre. They were designed with a shop or business on the lower floor and accommodation upstairs. Often projecting over the footpath is a canopy, known as a five-foot-way. This was Stamford Raffles' idea; he wanted to ensure pedestrians were protected from the sun and rain. But shopkeepers had other ideas and before long they all became extensions of the shops inside.

The first shophouses dating from 1840 are plain, squat, two-storey buildings. In the shophouses vernacular, these are known as Early, and are followed by First Transitional, Late, Second Transitional and Art Deco–style. Classical elements such as columns are often used on the façades along with beautiful tiles and bright paint – the Chinese, Peranakans and Malays all favour lively colours. The shophouses are cleverly designed around a central courtyard, which creates a through-draft keeping the houses cool.

BUNGALOWS

Not the single-storey retirement homes of the West, bungalows here are named after Bangalore-style houses and are usually two storeys high. Most are 'black and whites' after the mock-Tudor exposed-beam style adopted from 1900 to the late 1930s, and are much sought after by expatriates chasing colonialism's glory days three generations ago. You'll find many black and whites (with expats inside) lurking in the leafy residential areas off Orchard Rd (Map pp226–7) such as along Nassim Rd and the stretch of Scotts Rd near the

TOP FIVE MODERN BUILDINGS

- **Supreme Court** (Map p230) Foster Partner's contributions to the Singapore skyline tend to involve large silver discs, which are prominent on both the Expo Station near Changi airport, and now on the gleaming, ultra-modern new Supreme Court, which opened in June 2005.
- **Esplanade** (p51) Designed by Briton Michael Wilford and affectionately known as the Durians, this bulbous, spiky double concert hall intends to be the iconic equivalent of Sydney's Opera House. It might just make it, standing out as a breath of creativity in a safely designed city.
- **National Library** (Map p230) The Esplanade took a while to garner many passionate supporters, but so far that hasn't happened with the new National Library on Victoria St. The much-loved warm 1960 redbrick building has been replaced with a modern 16-storey tower that stops people in their tracks with its ugliness. But it's five times larger than the old one, with state-of-the-art facilities and cements Singapore's reputation as a seat of learning and research.
- **Parkview Square** (Map p232) A study in 1930s Art Deco kitsch, Parkview Sq, designed by American James Adam, is a Gotham City–style throwback, with a cathedral-domed entryway, terraced courtyard, a phalanx of statues of notable men of history, plus eight bronzed colossi kneeling at the building's corners.
- **The Gateway** (Map p232) The clean lines of The Gateway provide a stark contrast to the frivolity of Parkview Sq. These sleek glass and steel twin towers, designed by IM Pei as identical parallelograms, appear two-dimensional no matter what angle you glance at them.

Sheraton Towers hotel. They also cluster in the exclusive parks such as Alexandra Park and Ridley Park, where you can practically taste the gin slings and elegantly discreet liaisons.

Down at Mountbatten Rd in Kallang (Map pp224–5) are examples of both the highly decorative Victorian bungalow and the concrete Art Deco bungalows dating from the 1920s and '30s, typically with flat roofs, curved corners and a strong horizontal design.

HDB FLATS

Only in Singapore could you walk safely through a tower-block estate at night and find a cold drinks vending machine full, working and un-vandalised. While public high-rise housing estates are being torn down elsewhere, in Singapore they work. They have to: land is limited, so the government had little choice but to build upwards. The state-run Housing Development Board (HDB) is locked into a mammoth construction project, erecting areas of well-built, well-maintained and affordable housing. So far, they have built close to a million units.

HDB 'towns' such as Toa Payoh, Pasir Ris and Tampines provide homes for nearly 84% of the population. The new, 50-storey Pinnacle@Duxton, in Chinatown, will be the largest HDB project of all. HDB developments have markets, schools, playgrounds, shops and hawker centres hardwired into them; the older ones (from the '60s and '70s) have mature trees keeping them shady and (relatively) attractive. Many blocks also have 'void deck', empty areas on the ground floor that allow a breeze to circulate, and where old men play chess in the shade.

The MRT system makes it simple to visit the HDB heartlands. Just jump on a train and pop up somewhere like Toa Payoh. You won't see stunning architecture, but you will get a glimpse of what life is like for most Singaporeans.

MODERN

The area around Bras Basah Rd (Map p230) is filling up with new establishments, all showcasing extraordinary design and a pointer to the more experimental line Singapore is taking with its cityscape. The new Singapore Management University (Map p230) looks chunky and functional, while Lasalle–SIA College of the Arts (Map p230) is building a remarkable, crystalline building, designed to look as if a block of ice has been dropped and shattered into six parts. These new buildings can take time to get used to and public opinion is fiercely divided.

In the CBD is a cluster of gleaming towers by famous Japanese architects including Kurokawa Kisho's 66-storey Republic Plaza (Map pp234–5), and Tange Kenzo's OUB Centre (Map pp234–5) and UOB Plaza (Map pp234–5). Tange also designed the URA Centre in Chinatown (Map pp234–5); find out about the future of Singapore's built environment here.

Food

Food

Few cities in the world can match Singapore for food. The choice is staggering. Within a few hundred metres, there might be a hawker centre selling $4 Singaporean, Peranakan, Chinese and Malay specialities, a food court with Japanese, Korean and Thai stalls, a coffee shop serving up barbecued seafood and laksa, an Indian shophouse making wafer thin *roti pratha* and chicken curry, and an air-conditioned French restaurant where a bottle of wine costs more than a maid's monthly wage. And that's not counting the endless titbits and snacks.

It's hard to know whether this multitude inspired Singapore's food obsession, or whether the obsession inspired the multitude. Either way, Singaporeans are obsessed with eating. They think nothing of driving right across the island to sample a renowned *sambal stingray*, and whenever a new food fad hits town, they will happily queue for an hour to get their hands on it. Food is a major topic of discussion and debate; everyone has an opinion on what's the best this and where to get the best that. Maybe it's a substitute for politics – but then if you had this much fantastic food on your doorstep you'd probably be serious about it too.

As a major crossroads in Asia, Singapore's food culture has evolved as successive waves of migrants moved, settled and adapted to their new environment. Without distinctive produce of its own, local varieties of homeland staples have been slower to develop, but there are dishes that can truly be called Singaporean; chilli crab, fish-head curry and *yusheng* (Chinese raw fish salad) are three prominent examples.

Whether you hunt down the finest hawker fare or prefer flipping your credit card in fancy restaurants, if you don't leave Singapore puffing your cheeks and rubbing a full belly, you've missed out.

For an encyclopaedic guide to Singapore's food, read Lonely Planet's *World Food Malaysia & Singapore*.

CULTURE

ETIQUETTE

The drill at a hawker centre/food court/coffee shop is to bag a seat first (reserve it with either a non-valuable item or a person – a packet of tissues is the local favourite), then wander off to survey the various options. You can buy any number of dishes from any number of stalls and sit wherever you like; the vendors will usually find you and bring you the food. Don't worry if there are no free tables; it's quite normal to share with a complete stranger. Just ask if the seats are taken and offer a nice smile. Usually there are no menus, but signs on the stall will list their specialities. Dishes usually come in small, medium or large. Two small dishes will amply feed two people.

At hawker centres you pay when you order. Usually your food will be brought over to you (they'll tell you to go and sit down), but sometimes you have to take a tray and transport it to a table yourself, after collecting your chopsticks, or fork and spoon, and filling a little dish with whatever sauce takes your fancy. Food court stalls will often display a sign saying 'self-service', which means you have to carry your own food to your table, not dish it up yourself. In most coffee shops and hawker centres, someone will come to your table and take your drinks order. You pay them when they deliver the drinks. In food courts, it's more common to go and order your own drinks from a special stall.

CHINESE BANQUET ETIQUETTE

If by some lucky chance you are invited to a Chinese banquet, wait to be seated by the host (never just plonk yourself down, as the seating arrangement is highly significant) and observe the following chopstick rules:

- Never reach over someone else to pick up food.
- Never leave your chopsticks poking upright out of the rice.
- Don't hit your chopsticks against an empty bowl.
- Don't dilly-dally and hover your chopsticks over the food. Decide, plunge, grab, retreat.

Some hawker centres, notably Newton Circus (the one most popular with visitors), have wandering touts who try to grab you when you arrive, sit you down and plonk menus in front of you. You are not obliged to order from them.

If you are eating Indian or Muslim food, remember that they will only use their right hand to eat – the left is considered unclean.

WHERE TO EAT

Aside from the standard Western-style restaurants and cafés, Singapore has several local species of eating venue, principally the hawker centre, food court and coffee shop.

The term 'hawker' was once used to describe food vendors who moved their wares around in mobile carts, stopping and setting up their burners wherever there were customers. Of course, such itinerant behaviour was unacceptable in modern Singapore and virtually all hawkers are now stockaded into hawker centres, which, admittedly, makes life easier for everyone.

A visit to Singapore isn't complete without taking a meal at one of these vibrant, colourful places. There are usually a wide variety of different local cuisines on offer and the atmosphere is often raucous. However, the food is uniformly good. If it wasn't, the stalls would go out of business very quickly.

Food courts are subtly different from hawker centres and generally refer to indoor or covered markets, often found in air-conditioned shopping malls. There's usually a wider variation of cuisines – sometimes even a curious version of Western food, usually featuring a 'mixed grill'. Prices are marginally higher, though some very swanky food courts are springing up where prices are almost at restaurant levels.

Traditional coffee shops, sometimes called *kopi tiam* (*tiam* is Hokkien for 'shop'), are another Singaporean institution. These are open shopfront cafés, usually with a handful of stalls inside, patrolled by an 'auntie' or 'uncle' who takes your drinks order after you've bought your food.

Hawker centres and food courts are scrupulously inspected for hygiene. Look for the 'ABC' signs, representing an annually awarded grading based on excellence in cleanliness and food hygiene ('A' is the highest award). A long queue in front of a particular stall will also be an indication of what's good to try. Some also have special stickers indicating that they offer healthier options, low in oil, salt and other substances.

CUISINES

CHINESE

With Chinese food, the more people you can muster for the meal the better, because dishes are traditionally shared so that all can sample the greatest variety. A corollary of this is that a Chinese meal should be balanced. A *yin* (cooling) dish, such as vegetables, most fruits and clear soups, should be matched by a *yang* (heating) dish, such as starchy foods and meat.

The best-known and most popular style of Chinese cooking is Cantonese, despite the majority of Singaporean Chinese not being of Cantonese descent. Cantonese food, noted for the variety and freshness of its ingredients, is usually stir-fried with just a touch of oil to ensure that the result is crisp and fresh. Typical dishes include won ton soup, chow mein, spring rolls, *mee* (noodles) or *congee* (rice porridge). At the expensive end of the spectrum are shark's-fin and bird's-nest dishes.

One of the most famous Cantonese specialities is dim sum (literally 'little heart'), small snack-type dishes, often dumplings. Dim sum, also known as yum cha, is usually eaten at lunchtime or as a Sunday brunch, in large, noisy restaurants where the dishes are whisked around the tables on trolleys or carts; take what you like as they come by.

The most popular Hainanese dish is chicken rice – simply steamed fowl, rice cooked in chicken stock, a clear soup and slices of cucumber; it's practically the Singaporean national dish. Flavour it with ginger, soy or chilli sauce and have yourself a delicious meal for around $5 or less. Another popular Hainanese dish is steamboat, an Oriental variation on a Swiss

Typical hawker stall in the Chinatown Complex (p108)

fondue, where you have a boiling stockpot in the middle of the table, into which you dip pieces of meat, seafood or vegetables.

Many of Singapore's Chinese are Hokkien or Hakka, originally from the southern provinces of China. Simple ingredients are a feature of Hakka food. The best-known Hakka dish is *yong tau foo*, bean curd stuffed with minced meat. Another popular dish is *hokkien mee*, or Singapore noodles. It's made of thick egg noodles cooked with pork, seafood and vegetables, and a rich sauce. *Hokkien popiah* (unfried spring rolls) are also delicious and fun to roll yourself.

If you're looking for something more fiery, try Sichuan (or Szechwan) food – garlic and chillies play their part in dishes like diced chicken and hot-and-sour soup. Beijing cuisine also has more robust flavours and is usually eaten with noodles or steamed buns. The most famous dish is Beijing (or Peking) duck – specially fattened ducks basted in syrup and roasted on a revolving spit. The crispy skin is served as a separate first course.

From the area around Shantou in China, Teochew is a style noted for its delicacy and natural flavours. Seafood is a speciality, and a popular food-centre dish is *char kway teow* – broad noodles, clams and eggs fried in chilli and black-bean sauce.

Food from Shanghai is, to some extent, a cross between northern and Cantonese cuisines, combining the strong flavours of the north with the ingredients of Canton. Only a few places in Singapore serve it, though.

Chinese Food Glossary

ah balling	glutinous rice balls filled with a sweet paste of peanut, black sesame or red bean and usually served in a peanut- or ginger-flavoured soup
bak chang	local rice dumpling filled with savoury or sweet meat and wrapped in leaves
bak chor mee	noodles with pork, meat balls and fried scallops
bak choy	variety of Chinese cabbage that grows like celery, with long white stalks and dark-green leaves
bak kutteh	local pork rib soup with hints of garlic and Chinese five spices
char kway teow	Hokkien dish of broad noodles, clams and eggs fried in chilli and black-bean sauce
char siew	sweet roast-pork fillet
cheng ting	dessert consisting of a bowl of sugar syrup with pieces of herbal jelly, barley and dates
choi sum	popular Chinese green vegetable, served steamed with oyster sauce
congee	Chinese porridge

Hainanese chicken rice	a local speciality; chicken dish served with spring onions and ginger dressing accompanied by soup and rice
hoisin sauce	thick seasoning sauce made from soya beans, red beans, sugar, vinegar, salt, garlic, sesame, chillies and spices; sweet-spicy and tangy in flavour
ka shou	fish-head noodles
kang kong	water convolvulus, a thick-stemmed type of spinach
kway chap	pig intestines cooked in soy sauce; served with flat rice noodles
kway teow	broad rice noodles
lor mee	local dish of noodles served with slices of meat, eggs and a dash of vinegar in a dark-brown sauce
mee pok	flat noodles made with egg and wheat
popiah	similar to a spring roll, but not fried
spring roll	vegetables, peanuts, egg and bean sprouts rolled up inside a thin pancake and fried
won ton	dumpling filled with spiced minced pork
won ton mee	soup dish with shredded chicken or braised beef
yu char kueh	deep-fried dough; eaten with congee
yusheng	salad of raw fish, grated vegetables, candied melon and lime, pickled ginger, sesame seeds, jellyfish and peanuts tossed in sweet dressing; eaten at Chinese New Year
yu tiao	deep-fried pastry eaten for breakfast or as a dessert

INDIAN

Essentially, Indian cuisine can be classified into two broad categories: South Indian and North Indian.

South Indian food tends to be hot, with the emphasis on vegetarian dishes. The typical South Indian dish is a thali (rice plate), often served on a large banana leaf. On this leaf is placed a large mound of rice, then scoops of various vegetable curries and a couple of papadams for good measure. South Indian vegetarian food is traditionally eaten with your right hand, not utensils. Using the tips of your fingers, knead the curries into the rice and eat away.

Other vegetarian dishes include *masala dosa*, a thin pancake which, when rolled around spiced vegetables with some *rasam* (spicy soup) on the side, is about the cheapest light meal you could ask for. An equivalent snack meal in Indian halal (Muslim) restaurants is *murtabak*, made from paper-thin dough filled with egg and minced mutton and lightly grilled with oil. A *roti canai* – made from *murtabak* dough, which you dip into a bowl of *dhal* or curry – is a very popular and filling breakfast.

Another favourite Indian halal dish is biryani. Served with a chicken or mutton curry, the dish takes its name from the saffron-coloured rice it is served with.

North Indian cuisine is most commonly associated with tandoori food, which takes its name from the clay tandoor oven in which meat is cooked. The meat is marinated overnight in a yogurt-and-spice mixture.

Although rice is also eaten in North India, it is not the ubiquitous staple it is in the south. More common are delicious Indian breads such as naan (leavened bread baked inside a clay oven), chapati (griddle-fried whole-wheat bread), *paratha* (bread made with ghee and cooked on a hotplate) and roti.

Indian Food Glossary

achar	vegetable pickle
fish-head curry	red snapper head in curry sauce; a famous Singapore-Indian dish
gulab jamun	fried milk balls in sugar syrup

idli	steamed rice cake served with thin chutneys
keema	spicy minced meat
kofta	minced meat or vegetable ball
korma	mild curry with yogurt sauce
lassi	yogurt-based drink, either sweet or salted
mulligatawny	spicy beef soup
pakora	vegetable fritter
paratha	bread made with ghee and cooked on a hotplate
pilau	rice fried in ghee and mixed with nuts, then cooked in stock
raita	side dish of cucumber, yogurt and mint, used to cool the palate
rasam	spicy soup
roti john	fried roti with chilli
saag	spicy chopped-spinach side dish
sambar	fiery mixture of vegetables, lentils and split peas
samosa	fried pastry triangle stuffed with spiced vegetables or meat
tikka	small pieces of meat and fish served off the bone and marinated in yogurt before baking
vadai	fried, spicy lentil patty, served with a savoury lentil sauce or yogurt

MALAY & INDONESIAN

The cuisines of Malaysia and Indonesia are similar. Satay – tiny kebabs of chicken, mutton or beef dipped in a spicy peanut sauce – is ubiquitous. Other common dishes include *tahu goreng*, fried soya bean curd and bean sprouts in a peanut sauce; *ikan bilis*, anchovies fried whole; *ikan assam*, fried fish in a sour tamarind curry; and *sambal udang*, fiery curried prawns.

Ayam goreng is fried chicken and *rendang* is curried meat in coconut marinade. Nasi goreng (fried rice) is widely available, but it is as much a Chinese and Indian dish as Malay, and each style has its own flavours. *Nasi lemak* is coconut rice served with fried *ikan bilis*, peanuts and a curry dish.

The Sumatran style of Indonesian food bends much more towards curries and chillies. *Nasi padang*, from the Minangkabau region of West Sumatra, consists of a wide variety of hot curries served with rice. *Mee rebus*, noodles in a rich soya-based sauce, is a Javanese dish that is also widely available in food centres.

Malay & Indonesian Food Glossary

ais kacang	similar to *cendol* but made with evaporated milk instead of coconut milk; it is also spelt 'ice kacang'
belacan	fermented prawn paste used as a condiment
belacan kankong	green vegetables stir-fried in prawn paste
cendol	local dessert made from a cone of ice shavings filled with red beans, *attap* (sweet gelatinous fruit of the attap palm) and jelly, then topped with coloured syrups, brown-sugar syrup and coconut milk
gado gado	cold dish of bean sprouts, potatoes, long beans, *tempeh*, bean curd, rice cakes and prawn crackers, topped with a spicy peanut sauce
itek manis	duck simmered in ginger and black-bean sauce
itek tim	a classic soup of simmered duck, tomatoes, green peppers, salted vegetables and preserved sour plums
kari ayam	curried chicken
kaya	a toast topping made from coconut and egg

kecap	soy sauce, pronounced 'ketchup' (we got the word from them, not the other way around)
kepala ikan	fish head, usually in a curry or grilled
kueh mueh	Malay cakes
lontong	rice cakes in a spicy coconut-milk gravy topped with grated coconut and sometimes bean curd and egg
mee siam	white thin noodles in a sourish and sweet gravy made with tamarind
mee soto	noodle soup with shredded chicken
nasi biryani	saffron rice flavoured with spices and garnished with cashew nuts, almonds and raisins
nasi minyak	spicy rice
pulut kuning	sticky saffron rice
o-chien	oyster omelette
rojak	salad made from cucumber, pineapple, yam bean, star fruit, green mango and guava, with a dressing of shrimp paste, chillies, palm sugar and fresh lime juice
sambal	sauce of fried chilli, onions and prawn paste
soto ayam	spicy chicken soup with vegetables, including potatoes
tempeh	preserved soya beans, deep-fried

PERANAKAN

As descendants of early Chinese immigrants who married Malay women, the Peranakans (see p14) also developed a unique cuisine that blends Chinese ingredients with Malay sauces and spices. It is commonly flavoured with shallots, chillies, *belacan* (Malay fermented prawn paste), peanuts, preserved soybeans and galangal (a gingerlike root). Thick coconut milk is used to create the sauce that flavours the prime ingredients.

In the past decade there has been a resurgence of interest in Peranakan cuisine, which was once confined to the home, with a number of restaurants now specialising in this unusual blend; see Eating (p100) for some good examples.

COOKERY COURSES

If you fancy trying out some local dishes for yourself, then there are several cookery courses visitors can join. The best are offered by **At-Sunrice** (Map p230; ☎ 6336 3307; www.at-sunrice.com; Fort Canning Centre, Fort Canning Park; Dhoby Ghaut MRT).

These half-day courses start with a guided tour of the park's spice garden and then move into the teaching kitchens for hands-on experience making local dishes such as laksa, chilli crab and chicken rice. The featured cuisines vary from week to week. A two-component course, consisting of two morning classes in which chefs demonstrate various dishes, costs $60. A three-component course, featuring a hands-on cooking class with lunch, costs $100. The tutors are excellent and you'll get to enjoy your efforts at the end with a meal on the centre's terrace. There are kids' classes in the school holidays, and for those who are professionally inclined, a three-week full-time Asian Culinary Arts course costs US$3250.

Raffles Culinary Academy (Map p230; ☎ 6412 1256; www.raffleshotel.com/dining/culinaryacad.php; 2nd level, Raffles Hotel Arcade; City Hall MRT) offers a wide variety of day-long cookery classes for groups of up to 20 people costing $70 to $90 per person. Very few are hands-on, but you will get lunch or dinner at the end.

The Asian fusion restaurant **Coriander Leaf** (Map p230; ☎ 6732 3354; www.corianderleaf.com; 3A Merchant Ct, River Valley Rd, Clarke Quay; Clarke Quay MRT) also runs courses, where keen cooks can learn a mix of South Asian, Southeast Asian, Middle Eastern, Mediterranean and fusion dishes and cooking techniques.

Popular classes tailored for enthusiastic beginners are offered by **Cookery Magic** (Map p236; ☎ 6348 9667; www.cookerymagic.com; Haig Rd, Katong; Paya Lebar MRT), run by the amiable Ruqxana, who teaches a huge range of popular Indian, Malay, Indonesian, Chinese and Singaporean classics to small groups in her own home. Classes cost $50 to $60 per person. She also runs special weekend classes, kids' cooking classes and market tours – and even special kampong cooking trips to the island of Pulau Ubin.

Diners at the Chinatown Complex (p108)

Typical dishes include *otak-otak*, a wonderful sausage-like blend of fish, coconut milk, chilli paste, galangal and herbs, wrapped and cooked in a banana leaf; *ayam buah keluak*, chicken stewed with dark nuts imported from Indonesia to produce a rich earthy sauce – make sure you eat the filling stuffed in the nut shell; and *itek tim*, a classic soup of simmered duck, tomatoes, green peppers, salted vegetables and preserved sour plums.

Also don't miss out on slurping the distinctive Peranakan laksa (noodles in a savoury coconut-milk gravy with fried tofu and bean sprouts) or *mee siam* (Thai-inspired rice vermicelli in a spicy-sour gravy) at most food centres.

Peranakan Food Glossary

carrot cake	omelette-like dish made from radishes, egg, garlic and chilli; also known as *chye tow kway*
papaya titek	type of curry stew
satay bee hoon	peanut sauce–flavoured noodles
shui kueh	steamed radish cakes with fried preserved radish topping
soup tulang	meaty bones in a rich, spicy, blood-red tomato gravy

OTHER

The huge variety of cuisines marks Singapore as a truly international city. Everything is available, from the familiar Thai, Japanese, Korean, Italian, Mexican, French and Middle Eastern to the more unusual African or Russian. Some cuisines have their own geographical epicentres, like the Golden Mile Food Centre for Thai food, or the Arab St area for Middle Eastern.

DESSERTS

The lurid mini-volcanos you'll often see at food centres are *ais kacang* (pronounced 'ice kachang'), a combination of a mound of shaved ice, syrups, evaporated milk, fruit, beans and jellies. *Cendol* is similar, consisting of coconut milk with brown sugar syrup and green jelly strips topped with shaved ice. Both taste terrific, or rather a lot better than they look. Also worth trying is *ah balling*, glutinous rice balls filled with a sweet paste of peanut, black sesame or red bean and usually served in a peanut- or ginger-flavoured soup.

Head to Little India to experiment with Indian sweets: *burfi*, *ladoo*, *gulab jamun*, *gelabi*, *jangiri*, *kesari* and *halwa*, to name a few, are made with ingredients that include condensed milk, sesame and syrups.

Nonya (Peranakan) desserts are typified by *kueh* (colourful rice cakes often flavoured with coconut and palm sugar) and sweet, sticky delicacies such as miniature pineapple tarts that are sold everywhere in small plastic tubs with red lids. The magnificent *kueh lapis*, a laborious layer cake that involves prodigious numbers of eggs, is a must-try.

One notable popular Singaporean oddity is the ice-cream sandwich, dished out by mobile ice-cream vendors and enjoyed by young and old alike. This consists of a thick slab of ice cream folded into a slice of bread, though sometimes it's served between the more traditional wafer slices.

TROPICAL FRUIT

Singapore is a great place to inspire and indulge a passion for tropical fruit. In food centres you can have a personalised fruit salad made up on the spot.

Large and oval, the durian is the region's most infamous fruit, renowned for its phenomenal smell, a stink so powerful that first-timers are often forced to hold their noses while they taste. In fact, durians emanate a stench so redolent of open sewers that you'll see signs in hotels and on public transport all over Singapore warning that durians are expressly forbidden entry. It's definitely an acquired taste, like overly ripe cheese, but locals go crazy over them.

Rambutans, the size of a small tangerine, are covered in soft red spines. You peel the skin to reveal a close cousin to the lychee; cool and mouthwatering flesh around a central stone.

The dark-purple outer skin of the mangosteen breaks open to reveal pure white segments shaped like orange segments, but with a sweet-sour flavour that has been compared to a combination of strawberries and grapes.

Jackfruit, also known as *nangka*, is an enormous watermelon-sized fruit covered by a green pimply skin. When opened it breaks up into a large number of bright orange-yellow segments with a slightly rubbery texture and a delicately sweet flavour.

Sometimes known as soursop or white mango, the custard apple has a warty green outer covering and is ready to eat when it begins to look slightly off. Inside, the creamy white flesh has a deliciously thirst-quenching flavour with a hint of lemon.

Pomelo looks like a huge orange or grapefruit, although the skin is generally greenish. The flavour is similar to a grapefruit, although the texture is tougher and drier.

Dragonfruit, a prehistoric-looking oval pink fruit covered with large, rubbery spurs and about the size of a (deformed) grapefruit, is popular. Originally from Vietnam, it is now grown in Malaysia and is readily available for about 40¢ each (or $1 each in tourist areas!). Sliced open and peeled, it reveals a delicious, sweet, soft white flesh speckled with black seeds.

DRINKS

In Singapore's heat and humidity it's important to keep up your fluid intake. Bottled mineral water is widely available and cheap, as are a mouthwatering variety of fruit juices, particularly the ubiquitous lime juice, a sweet, sour, magnificently refreshing drink that acts as a perfect counterbalance to spicy, oily foods. Most food courts have a specialist drinks stall offering a huge variety of freshly squeezed juices for $2 to $3. There are some unusual drinks, too. Try soy milk (flavoured and natural), chrysanthemum tea and coconut water – sometimes straight from the coconut. There's no excuse for drinking fizzy soft drinks in Singapore.

Unless you go to one of the many chain cafés for your lattes and iced mochas, coffee – or *kopi* – is drunk strong and sweet. There are several variations: *kopi* (coffee with sweet condensed milk), *kopi-o* (with sugar but no milk), *kopi-c* (with sugar and evaporated milk) or *kopi peng* (iced coffee). Tea drinkers should substitute 'kopi' with 'teh' to get the same results. *Teh tarik*, a rich, frothy sweet tea that is 'pulled' by drawing it from one cup to another, is a popular drink at Malay stalls.

Beer is also widely available and you can usually get it at hawker centres or food courts, as well as restaurants. However, alcohol in Singapore is expensive: expect to pay around $5 for a can at a food centre, $5 to $6 for a large bottle at a hawker centre or up to $15 for a pint in a city pub. This is because of hefty government duties on alcohol ($9.50 per litre of alcohol for wine and $2.70 for beer). The local brew is Tiger. Guinness and ABC stout are also popular – mainly because the locals believe it has medicinal value. Foreign beers are becoming increasingly popular with trendy professionals and you'll find Erdinger, Kilkenny, Heineken, Bodingtons, Stella Artois, the Belgian white beer Hoegaarden and many others in fashionable pubs, though expect to pay premium prices. In supermarkets, local and Thai beers are considerably cheaper.

Foreigners (or at least those foreigners who haven't tried Beer Lao yet) regularly cite Tiger as their favourite Asian beer. First brewed in 1932 as a joint venture with Heineken, it's a crisp, refreshing lager that goes perfectly with spicy Singaporean food and is still far and away the most popular beer in the country. If you're flying in or out, make a point of picking up some duty free cans of Tiger Classic, a wonderful, strong, dark brew made with crystal malt. For some mystifying reason, it's not sold in Singapore.

In Chinatown you'll come across large, polished metal urns (although sometimes just vacuum flasks) at the front of traditional medical halls. Tonic herbal teas (around $1 per serve) are usually dispensed from these urns. Some teas are sweet; others are unbelievably bitter. All are supposed to be good for you.

History

History

THE RECENT PAST

One day, son, all this will be yours.

In 2004, Lee Hsien Loong – Prime Minister Goh Chok Tong's deputy prime minister and minister for defence, as well as Lee Kuan Yew's son – took over the top job, unopposed. Goh took over Lee Snr's role of senior minister, while the founder of the nation now bears the title of Minister Mentor.

Lee Jr faces challenges as great as those his father dealt with. Racial tensions still bubble under the surface, despite all the policies and good will tackling them. China looms large on the horizon, and the challenge is to find a role that will discourage the new economic giant from eating Singapore for breakfast. The younger generation, which has grown up in times of plenty, doesn't feel so tied to the country and sees greater opportunities overseas. Many of the brightest have left, although strong family ties and appeals to patriotism work hard to slow the brain drain.

Statue of Sir Stamford Raffles (p49)

A shrewd political alliance with the US, allowing US forces to base themselves on the island, and now a Free Trade Agreement, has caused anti-US terrorists to look askance at this island once dismissed as a 'little red dot' for its left-wing leanings. A home-grown threat was contained after a video detailing a planned attack on an MRT station was apparently found in the bombed-out home of an Al Qaeda leader in Afghanistan.

Finally, the younger Lee is working to gain popular support. His father and Goh are both hard acts to follow – one a father to the nation, the other a friendly uncle. Lee Hsien Loong's former reputation for being aloof is changing, and he is developing a more approachable persona.

FROM THE BEGINNING

Malay legend has it that long ago, a Sumatran prince visiting the island of Temasek saw a strange animal that was identified to him as a lion. The good omen prompted the prince to found a city on the spot of the sighting. He called it Singapura (Lion City).

TIMELINE

300
Chinese maps mark island as Pu-Luo-Chong

1365
Island is called Temasek (Sea Town) and is a trading post in Sumatran Sriwijayan empire

From the arrival in 1819 of Stamford Raffles – officially declared Singapore's founder in the 1970s in order to 'neutrally' settle rival claims by local Malays and Chinese – to the present, Singapore's past has been continually moulded to fit political and economic demands. Nevertheless, beneath the serene surface of gentrified colonial-era buildings lies an intriguing tale of the rise and fall of local empires, European colonial 'great games' and the enduring legacy of 19th-century British rule.

EARLY EMPIRES

Chinese traders en route to India had plied the waters around what is now Singapore from at least the 5th century AD. Some sources claim that in 1292 Marco Polo visited a flourishing city where Singapore now stands (though the Venetian's only sure report is of the city of Malayu – now called Jambi – on Sumatra).

What is certain, however, is that Singapore was not the first of the great entrepôt cities in the region. By the 7th century, Sriwijaya, a seafaring Buddhist kingdom centred on Palembang in Sumatra, held sway over the Strait of Malacca (now Melaka); by the 10th century it dominated the Malay peninsula as well. At the peak of Sriwijaya's power, Singapore was at most a small trading outpost.

Raids by rival kingdoms and the arrival of Islam spelled the eclipse of Sriwijaya by the 13th century. Based mainly on the thriving pirate trade, the sultanate of Melaka quickly

RAFFLES REMEMBERED

Sir Stamford Raffles, cultural scholar, Singaporean colonist, naturalist and founder of the London Zoo, died at his home in Hendon, North London, the day before his 45th birthday in 1826, probably from a brain tumour. Having fallen out with the East India Company, his death was ignored by London society, and it was eight years before his marble statue, commissioned by friends and family, was placed in Westminster Abbey.

Meanwhile, in Singapore, you can hardly go anywhere without being reminded of the man. Apart from the famous hotel, the Raffles City complex, a hospital, school and fancy club, he's also remembered in addresses such as Raffles Pl and Stamford Rd. The original Singaporean bronze statue of Raffles, unveiled in the Padang on 29 June 1887, now stands in front of Victoria Theatre and Concert Hall with the white stone replica round the corner on Empress Pl, supposedly where Sir Stamford first set foot on the island.

Raffles himself was an extraordinary man, in many ways at odds with the British colonial mould. While he was a firm believer in the British empire as a benevolent force, he also preached the virtues of making Singapore a free port. He opposed slavery and proclaimed 'unenforced' limitations on indentured labour, under which 'coolies' would be forced to work off the cost of their passage from China for 'no more than two years'. Raffles was also a sympathetic student of the peoples of the region.

His character was probably a result of his humble upbringing. He began his working life at 14 as a clerk for the giant East India Company, but was a tireless self-improver, a trait he never lost. In 1805, he was appointed as part of a group to cement the emerging British interests in Penang. Within six years, through several promotions, he had become the governor of Java, where his compassionate leadership won him enduring respect. From there he travelled to Sumatra, where he became governor of Bencoolen on the island's southern coast.

Intent on securing a strategic base on the Malaka Strait, he set up a British trading post in Singapore in 1819, where he laid out a town plan that still exists today.

His life was struck by tragedy, however. While in Southeast Asia he lost four of his five children to disease, his massive natural history collection in a ship fire and his personal fortune in a bank collapse. The East India Company refused him a pension and, after his death, his parish priest refused him a headstone because he disagreed with his anti-slavery stance.

His achievements as a statesman have often obscured his brilliance as a naturalist. He made an intricate study of the region's flora and fauna and though much of his work was lost, it is still honoured at the National University of Singapore, which maintains the Raffles Museum of Biodiversity Research (p83) in his honour.

1500s
First record of island's name as Singapura (Lion City) in Malay

1824
Singapore ceded to British Empire; first census puts Singapore's population at 10,000

acquired the commercial power that was once wielded by Sriwijaya. It was a cosmopolitan, free-port emporium that valued money above any notions of cultural imperialism.

COLONIAL GREAT GAMES

The Portuguese took Melaka in 1511, while the equally ardent Dutch founded Batavia (now Jakarta) to undermine Melaka's position, finally wresting the city from their European competitors in 1641. In the late 18th century, the British began looking for a harbour in the Strait of Melaka to secure lines of trade between China, the Malay world and their interests in India. Renewed war in Europe led, in 1795, to the French annexation of Holland which prompted the British to seize Dutch possessions in Southeast Asia, including Melaka.

After the end of the Napoleonic Wars, the British agreed to restore Dutch possessions in 1818, but there were those who were bitterly disappointed at the failure of the dream of British imperial expansion in Southeast Asia. One such figure was Stamford Raffles, lieutenant governor of Java. Raffles soon procured permission to found a station to secure British trade routes in the region and was instructed to negotiate with the sultan of nearby Johor for land.

RAFFLES ARRIVES

When Raffles landed at Singapore in early 1819, the empire of Johor was divided. When the old sultan had died in 1812, his younger son's accession to power had been engineered while an elder son, Hussein, was away. The Dutch had a treaty with the young sultan, but Raffles threw his support behind Hussein, proclaiming him sultan and installing him in residence in Singapore.

In Raffles' plans the sultan wielded no actual power but he did serve to legitimise British claims on the island. Raffles also signed a treaty with the more eminent *temenggong* (senior judge) of Johor and set him up with an estate on the Singapore River. Thus, Raffles acquired the use of Singapore in exchange for modest annual allowances to Sultan Hussein and the *temenggong*. This exchange ended with a cash buyout of the pair in 1824 and the transfer of Singapore's ownership to Britain's East India Company.

The Dutch were unimpressed, but in an 1824 Anglo-Dutch treaty that carved up spheres of influence in Asia, Singapore remained the property of Britain. In 1826 Singapore, Penang and Melaka became part of the Straits Settlements, controlled by the East India Company in Calcutta but administered from Singapore.

THE CITY EMERGES

Raffles' first and second visits to Singapore in 1819 were brief, and he left instructions and operational authority with Colonel William Farquhar, formerly the Resident (chief British representative) in Melaka, now Resident of Singapore. But, three years later, when Raffles returned to run the then-thriving colony he found his ambitious plans were not being carried out.

Raffles initiated a town plan that included levelling one hill to form a new commercial district (now Raffles Pl) and erecting government buildings around another, Forbidden Hill (now Fort Canning Hill). The plan also embraced the colonial practice, still vaguely operative in Singapore today, of administering the population according to neat racial categories. The city's trades, races and dialect groups were divided into kampongs (villages): Europeans were granted land to the northeast of the government offices, though many soon moved out to sequestered garden estates in the western suburbs; Chinese, who included Hokkien, Hakka, Cantonese, Teochew and Straits-born, predominated around the mouth of the Singapore River; Indians (Hindu) were centred in Kampong Kapor and

1867	1887
Straits Settlements (Singapore, Penang and Melaka) becomes British Crown Colony; huge wave of immigrants arrives as prosperity soars	Raffles Hotel opens for business

Serangoon Rd; Gujarati and other Muslim merchants were housed in the Arab St area; Tamil Muslim traders and small businesses operated in the Market St area; and the Malay population mainly lived on the swampy northern fringes of the city, where the Sultan Mosque was also located.

HOW THE EAST WAS WON

Recognising the need for cooperation with Chinese communities, Raffles also sought registration of the *kongsi* (clan organisations for mutual assistance, known variously as ritual brotherhoods, secret societies, triads and heaven-man-earth societies). Labour and dialect-based *kongsi* would become increasingly important to Singapore's success in the 19th century, as overseas demand for Chinese-harvested products such as pepper, tin and rubber – all routed through Singapore from the Malay peninsula – grew enormously. Singapore's access to *kongsi*-based economies in the region, however, depended largely on revenues from an East India Company product that came from India and was bound for China – opium.

Farquhar had established Singapore's first opium farm for domestic consumption, and by the 1830s excise and sales revenues of opium accounted for nearly half the administration's income, a situation that continued for a century after Raffles' arrival. But the British Empire (which has been called the world's first major drug cartel) produced more than Chinese opium addicts; it also fostered the Western-oriented outlook of Straits-born Chinese.

In the 19th century, women were rarely permitted to leave China; thus, Chinese men who headed for the Straits Settlements (after 1867, the Crown Colony) of Singapore were likely to marry Malay women. These creole Baba Chinese (the term 'Peranakan' is now preferred in Singapore) found an identity in the Union Jack, British law and citizenship. The British could count on those Peranakan (also see p14) with capital and a local family to stay in Singapore, while other traders were considered to be less reliable.

The authorities needed all the help they could get, for while revenues and Chinese labourers poured in until the early 1930s, Singapore was continually plagued by bad sanitation, water-supply problems, man-eating tigers and piracy.

Despite a massive fall in rubber prices in 1920, the ensuing decade saw more boom times. Immigration soared and millionaires were made overnight. In the 1930s and early 1940s, politics dominated the intellectual scene. Indians looked to the subcontinent for signs of

THE LEE DYNASTY

If one person can be held responsible for the position Singapore finds itself in today, it is Lee Kuan Yew. Born 16 September 1923, this third-generation Straits-born Chinese was given the name Harry Lee (hence his nickname among older expats of Uncle Harry) and brought up to be, in his own words, 'the equal of any Englishman'. His education at the elite Raffles Institution and later Cambridge (from which he graduated in 1949 with a first-class honours degree in law) equipped him well to deal with both colonial power and political opposition when Singapore took control of its own destiny in the 1960s. Often tagged as 'authoritarian', particularly in the Western media, Lee showed remarkable drive and vision (and, yes, a hint of bossiness) in dragging this fraught, divided port city up by its pyjama bottoms and making it a success.

Despite resigning as prime minister in 1990 (after 31 years in the job), as Minister Mentor Lee keeps an eye on his successors – and his comments on various issues frequently flag future government policy.

Now that his son, the more demure but equally sharp Lee Hsien Loong, has taken the reins, the vision of Singapore's future for which Lee Kuan Yew has worked tirelessly looks secure, at least for the next couple of decades.

'Even from my sickbed,' said Lee in 1988, 'even if you are going to lower me into the grave and I feel that something is wrong, I'll get up.'

1942–45	1946
Japanese occupy Singapore and rename it Syonan (Light of the South)	Singapore becomes a Crown Colony

the end of colonial rule, while Kuomintang (Nationalist) and Communist Party struggles in the disintegrating Republic of China attracted passionate attention. Opposition to Japan's invasions of China in 1931 and 1937 was near universal in Singapore.

JAPANESE RULE

Singaporean Chinese were to pay a heavy price for opposing Japanese imperialism when General Yamashita Tomoyuki pushed his thinly stretched army into Singapore on 15 February 1942. For the British, who had set up a naval base near the city in the 1920s, surrender was sudden and humiliating.

Blame for the loss of Singapore fell on everyone from British prime minister Winston Churchill, who failed to divert sufficient forces from the war in Europe to defend Singapore, to squabbling British commanders and the wholesale desertion of Australian troops under the divisive command.

Displays at the Changi Prison Museum & Chapel (p75)

Japanese rule was harsh in Singapore, which was renamed 'Syonan' (Light of the South). Yamashita had the Europeans and Allied POWs herded onto the Padang; from there they were marched away for internment. Many of them were taken to the infamous Changi prison. Chinese Communists and intellectuals, however, were executed and Malays and Indians were also subject to systematic abuse. As the war progressed, inflation skyrocketed. Food, medicines and other essentials became in short supply, so much so that near the end of the war, people were dying of malnutrition and disease.

The war ended suddenly with Japan's surrender on 14 August 1945, and Singapore was passed back into British control.

DO MENTION THE WAR

The impact of WWII on Singapore cannot be underestimated: check out the number of memorials and museum displays around the island. In many ways, Singapore's wartime experiences have been used by politicians to galvanise Singaporeans into taking control of their own destiny and guarding against aggressors and dissidents.

All Singaporean men between the ages of 18 and 40 must perform military service for no less than two years. This is just part of Singapore's overall Total Defence programme, which aims to promote internal cohesion and readiness against any invasion or calamity.

To see how seriously this is taken, pop along to the Singapore Discovery Centre (p84) and soak up the many displays singing the praises of the Singapore armed forces and Total Defence. For a glimpse of the sacrifices made by ordinary Singaporeans during WWII in the protection of the island, visit Reflections at Bukit Chandu (p83), which focuses on one doomed attempt to hold the Japanese at bay. The Kranji War Memorial (p78) pays tribute to the Allied troops who died fighting in Southeast Asia during WWII, while the Civilian War Memorial (Map p230; commonly called the 'chopsticks memorial'), opposite Raffles City, similarly recognises civilian casualties. For most visitors, especially Australasian ones, Changi Prison Museum & Chapel (p75) will be the place where the lingering ghosts of WWII are felt most keenly.

1959
People's Action Party (PAP), led by Lee Kuan Yew, wins election; Lee is made prime minister

1963–65
Singapore included in new federation of Malaysia, Singapore booted out of Malaysian Federation and becomes an independent nation

SIBLING RIVALRY: SINGAPORE–MALAYSIA RELATIONS

Ever since 1965, when Singapore was unceremoniously kicked out of its short-lived union with Malaysia, relations between the two countries have been warmish at best, pretty chilly at worst.

But now both countries are under new management, there has been a distinct thawing of relations. While Lee Kuan Yew and Dr Mahathir regularly scored political points off each other, Lee Hsien Loong and new Malaysian premier Abdullah Badawi have found it more expedient to get along. In 2005 they finally reached agreement on land reclamation issues in the Straits of Johor, although there are still niggling unresolved issues such as dual territorial claims over a small island in the Singapore Strait, payment for water (Singapore gets 40% of its water from Malaysia but plans to be self-sufficient in water by 2061 when the current agreement runs out) and Malaysian Railways land-holdings on Singapore (railway bridges are actually Malaysian owned). There are also petty restrictions on Malay citizens operating freely within Singapore's commercial sector, and vice versa, and only now after 40 years the two countries are considering raising the ban on each other's newspapers. However, the two nations are more united by common interests than divided by differences. Talk of reunification does resurface occasionally in the press on both sides of the Strait, but appears highly unlikely, at least in the foreseeable future.

POST-WAR ALIENATION

The British were welcomed back to Singapore after the war, but their right (and ability) to rule was now in question. Plans for limited self-government and a Malayan Union were drawn up, uniting the peninsular states of British Malaya with Crown possessions in Borneo. Singapore was excluded, largely because of Malay fears of Chinese Singapore's dominance.

Singapore's destitute state provided support for the Malayan Communist Party, whose mainly Chinese freedom fighters had emerged as heroes of the war. The Communist General Labour Union also had a huge following, and in 1946 and 1947 Singapore was crippled by strikes.

The island moved slowly towards self-government. The socialist Malayan Democratic Union was the first real political party, but it boycotted Singapore's first elections in 1947. After early successes, the Communists realised they were not going to gain power under the colonial government's political agenda and began a campaign of armed struggle in Malaya. In response, British authorities declared the Malayan Emergency in 1948. The Communists were outlawed and a bitter guerrilla war was waged on the peninsula for 12 years. There was no fighting in Singapore, but left-wing politics languished under the political repression of Emergency regulations.

SINGAPORE'S MALAYSIAN SPLIT

By the early 1950s the Communist threat had waned and left-wing activity was again on the upswing, with student and union movements at the forefront of the political activity. One of the rising stars of this era was Lee Kuan Yew. The socialist People's Action Party (PAP) was founded in 1954, with Lee as secretary-general. A shrewd politician, Lee appealed for support to both the emerging British-educated elite and to radicalistic passions. The party included a Communist faction and had an ambitious post-Raffles plan of its own: strong state intervention to industrialise Singapore's economy.

Under arrangements for internal self-government, PAP won a majority of seats in the new Legislative Assembly in 1959, and Lee Kuan Yew became the first Singaporean to hold the title of prime minister, which he held when Singapore joined the Malay Federation in the early 1960s. It lasted only two years and in 1965 Singapore was booted out of the federation and left to fend for itself as the Republic of Singapore. Despite Lee Kuan Yew's public tears and real fears at the messy divorce, both peninsular Malays and Singapore's Chinese were mostly relieved that the marriage of convenience was over.

1971
British forces leave Singapore

1989
Lee Kuan Yew steps down as prime minister and is succeeded by Goh Chok Tong

BUILDING THE NEW SINGAPORE

Making the most of one-party rule, the PAP, under Lee's paternal control, began moulding its multiracial citizens and fragile state into a viable entity. Industrialisation paid off, and ambitious infrastructure, defence, health, education, pension and housing schemes were pursued. Housing and urban renovation, in particular, have been the keys to the PAP's success (by the mid-1990s, the city-state had the world's highest rate of home ownership).

Singapore's leaders sought order and progress in the regulation of social behaviour and identity. This involved banning chewing gum and smoking in public (enforced with fines), installing cameras and automatic locks in lifts to catch public urination, setting up state-sponsored matchmaking venues, and offering financial incentives to well-educated (mostly Chinese) women to have more children.

Under Lee, high economic growth rates supported political stability, which was further ensured by exiling or jailing dissidents, banning critical publications and controlling public speech and the media. Though this has been relaxed slightly in recent years, few dare to voice serious challenges to the government.

1995

Singapore-based trader Nick Leeson brings down Barings Bank

2004

Goh Chok Tong steps down as PM, replaced by Lee Kuan Yew's son, Lee Hsien Loong

Sights

Sights

ITINERARIES

One Day

Start the day with coffee and *kaya* toast at **Ya Kun Kaya Toast** (p116), then wander along **Orchard Road** (p63) before the crowds move in. Take the MRT to **Chinatown** (p56), browsing through the arts and antiques and visit the excellent **Heritage Centre** (p57), before sampling the famous chicken rice at **Tian Tian** (p109). Then head up to **Boat Quay** (p55) admiring the **sculptures** (see The Sculpture Trail, p23) and crossing the Cavenagh Bridge to the **Asian Civilisations Museum** (p50). Round that off with a **boat trip** (p48) along the Singapore River and harbour, then take the MRT up to Little India for a slap-up curry feed. Then finish your evening off with a cocktail in the **Bar & Billiard Room** (p53) at Raffles Hotel. If you still have energy, head to **Attica** (p131) to club with the beautiful people, or have a quieter drink at **Alley Bar** (p125).

Three Days

Peace and quiet dominate day two. Head down to **Sentosa Island** (p85) on the cable car and spend your morning at **Underwater World** (p87) and **Fort Siloso** (p86), before wandering along Siloso Beach to have lunch at **Trapizza** (p120) or **Coastes** (p120). Then take a cab up to the **Singapore Zoo** (p78), spending a few hours among the polar bears, white tigers and primates, before taking on the magnificent Night Safari next door. After that's over, head down to **Lau Pa Sat hawker centre** (p109) for a cheap feed, then have an abrupt change of scene and sample the magnificent *mojitos* at the **Post Bar** (p130) in the elegant Fullerton Hotel nearby.

NEIGHBOURHOODS (see also Map Section p221)

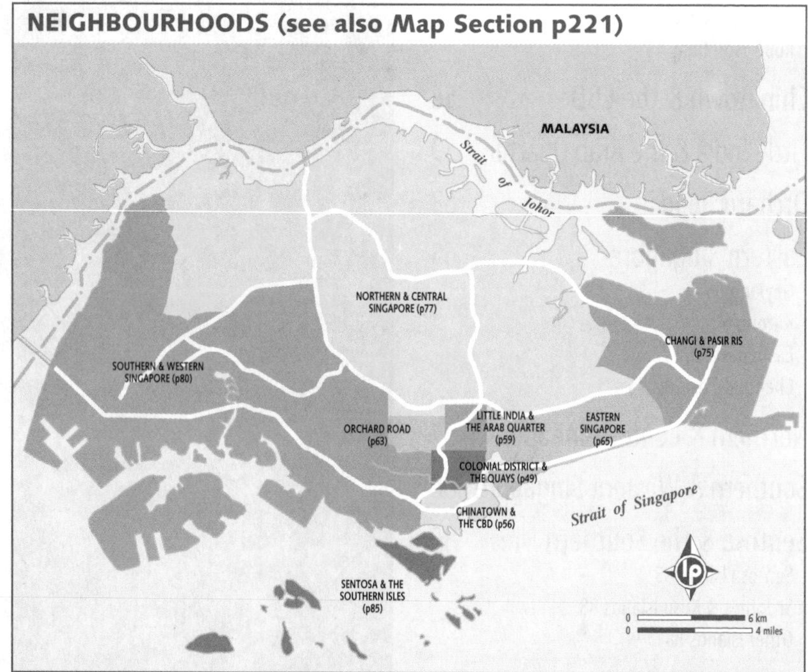

SINGAPORE ON THE CHEAP

Here are our top 10 tips for making your tourist dollar go further:

- Visit the Asian Civilisations Museum (p50), Singapore Art Museum (p53) and Singapore Philatelic Museum (p55) on Friday evenings from 6pm to 9pm, when entry is free.
- Eat and drink in hawker centres – where you can get a meal for $3 and a large beer for $5.
- Take advantage of the happy hours in bars, usually from 5pm to 8pm or 9pm, or go on Ladies Night (Tuesday or Wednesday), when drinks can even be free.
- Go for a stroll in the Singapore Botanic Gardens (p64) or a hike in the Bukit Timah (p77) or Central Catchment (p78) Nature Reserves.
- On Sentosa (p85), kick back on the beaches.
- Board an MRT train and do a loop of the island, checking out the suburbs as you go.
- Stroll down to the Esplanade complex (p51) – there are often free performances on Friday afternoons.
- Garner good luck by walking clockwise three times around the Fountain of Wealth (Map p230) – the world's largest fountain – at Suntec City.
- Hop on the ferry to Pulau Ubin (p181) for $2 and explore this last rural corner of Singapore.
- Have lunch at the superb Annalakshmi vegetarian restaurant (p102), where the waiters are volunteers and you pay what you like.

On day three, head for the **Botanic Gardens** (p64) for a serene breakfast at **Au Jardin** (p114), before walking it off among the trees and lakes. Then scuttle off to Little India for some shopping and temple-spotting (see p92) and lunch at the **Banana Leaf Apolo** (p111). Following this, head over to **East Coast Park** (p75) for a relaxing afternoon by the sea. Return to the Swissôtel, The Stamford in the city and shoot up 70 floors to have dinner at **Equinox** (p104), which boasts the best views in the city.

ORGANISED TOURS

A huge variety of tours can be booked at travel agents, the desks of the big hotels or through individual operators such as those listed in the tourism board's *Singapore Official Guide*. As well as general city tours, which whizz you around the major sights in three to four hours and cost $25 to $35, there are a number of specialised operators, offering more detailed tours of the various ethnic districts, WWII sites, Chinese opera and even feng shui (see The Art of Geomancy, p12).

The Singapore Tourism Board offices have full details and brochures of all tours and can also make bookings for you.

ORIGINAL SINGAPORE WALKS

☎ 6325 1631; www.singaporewalks.com; adult $18-22, child $12-16

Very popular and very entertaining, these 2½-hour strolls around the lesser-known parts of the Colonial District, Kampong Glam, Little India, Chinatown and WWII sites, take in everything from mosques and palaces to old brothels, opium dens and graveyards. No pre-booking necessary; check the itinerary and turn up at the meeting spot.

SHOP & EAT TOURS

☎ 6738 2622; adult $35-41, child $18-24

A convenient way to delve into Singapore's twin national obsessions. These tours take you where the locals eat and shop, covering the gastronomic treasures of Little India and Kampong Glam, popular 'heartland' bargain mines like Toa Payoh and more upmarket enclaves like Holland Village. At three to five hours long, they are a little brief, but provide an excellent starting point for your own explorations.

TIGER BREWERY Map pp222-3

☎ 6860 6483; 459 Jalan Ahmed Ibrahim; admission free; bus 182 from Boon Lay MRT

The hi-tech home of Asia-Pacific Breweries offers free tours of the factory for lovers of Singapore's favourite product. The tour begins with a short film recounting the history of the brew, which dates back to the early 1930s, then moves on to the brewery, which is a marvel in itself. The guides try to get this over and done with as quickly as possible because they know why you're really there – the final leg of the tour when you get to spend an hour or so in the factory bar. Pre-booking is required and tours need at least 10 people, but it's quite possible to tag along with another group if you don't have the numbers.

Special Interest Tours

DIANA CHUA

☎ 9489 1999; dime@pacific.net.sg; tours per hr $80
Diana Chua is an official Heritage Guide who comes recommended for walking (or driving, if you prefer) tours of Singapore's historical areas, including Chinatown and Katong.

GERALDENE LOWE-ISMAIL

☎/fax 6737 5250, 6737 9489; geraldenestours@hotmail.com; tours per hr $80
Singapore-born Geraldene Lowe-Ismail has been leading walking tours of Singapore for nigh on 40 years. She is a mine of information and her tours give you a unique insight into Singapore's history and culture. You may be able to join a group to reduce costs. She is also able to tailor tours to suit your particular interests. In addition to English, she conducts tours in Italian.

SUBARAJ RAJATHURAI

☎/fax 6787 7048; serin@swiftech.com.sg
For bird-watching and nature tours, try Subaraj Rajathurai. His enthusiastic and knowledgeable guidance has long been highly regarded.

River Cruises

One of the best ways to get a feel for central Singapore and its history is to take a river cruise. Bumboat cruises depart from several places along the Singapore River including Clarke Quay, Raffles Landing and Boat Quay, as well as Merlion Park and the Esplanade Jetty on Marina Bay. These cruises generally run between 8.30am and 10.30pm.

Two companies operate glass-top boats and bumboats up and down the river (for atmosphere, the chugging bumboats are by far the most preferable). The trips may be short, but they pack in a surprisingly comprehensive view of the city's architectural variety.

At night, the bumboats are festooned with red Chinese lanterns and the whole experience becomes quite romantic.

SINGAPORE EXPLORER

☎ 6339 6833; www.singaporeexplorer.com.sg; adult/child glass-top boat $15/6, bumboat $12/6
Besides the standard tours with voicetrack commentaries, glass-top boats can be hired out for evening dinner cruises – even more romantic than a bumboat with lanterns!

SINGAPORE RIVER CRUISES

☎ 6336 6111; www.rivercruise.com.sg; adult/child 30min tour $12/5, 45min $15/8
Offers two tour lengths: one goes as far as Clarke Quay, while the longer tour takes in Robertson Quay as well, which is not really worth the extra 15 minutes.

Harbour Cruises

A host of operators run harbour cruises that depart from Clifford Pier (Map pp234–5), just east of Raffles Pl. Companies offer *towkang* (Chinese junk) cruises as well as a number of lunch and dinner cruises. Most do the rounds of the harbour, involving a lot of time passing oil refineries, then give you a look at Sentosa and the southern islands of St John's, Lazarus and Kusu. The short stop at Kusu is worthwhile and you will get some good views of the city and harbour.

DUCKTOUR

☎ 6333 3825; www.ducktours.com.sg; adult/child $33/17
If you're not too embarrassed to be seen in a bright yellow amphibious buggy – and that's quite a big 'if' – this combination city and harbour tour can be fun for some, a boundless purgatory for others. The Duck, an ex-US military craft used in the Vietnam War, begins its journey at Suntec City, pootles around the Colonial District to a tinny, endlessly looped soundtrack, then goes for a splutter around the harbour, by which time you might feel like throwing yourself into the water. Best to go with kids, so you can look like you were forced into it.

FAIRWIND TROPICAL JUNK

☎ 6533 3432; Clifford Pier; adult/child day cruise US$13/7, starlight cruise US$23/11
A 2½-hour tour aboard a colourful Chinese junk with gleaming red sails, the day cruise leaves at 10.15am and 3pm daily. There is also a starlight cruise lasting 2½ hours; it leaves at 6pm and includes buffet dinner.

COLONIAL DISTRICT & THE QUAYS

Eating p102; Shopping p142; Sleeping p165

An urban treasure-trove of pristine colonial buildings, galleries, museums, massive shopping centres, parks and three riverside entertainment strips, this is the heart of Singapore. Nowhere else do you get as vivid a picture of Singapore as an organic city, where old courthouses and churches now welcome boozers and gluttons, men on trishaws offer you rides outside glassy megamalls and everywhere you look there is the loud echo of British rule.

COLONIAL DISTRICT & THE QUAYS TOP FIVE

- Taking in a free performance at the **Esplanade – Theatres on the Bay** (p51)
- Sipping a cocktail at the bar in the **Raffles Hotel** (p52)
- Visiting the Hindu-Buddhist gallery at the **Asian Civilisations Museum** (p50)
- Enjoying the peace and quiet in **Fort Canning Park** (p51)
- Catching a **bumboat ride** (opposite) down the river

The mark of Sir Stamford Raffles remains indelibly stamped on this district. His statue watches over the Singapore River and his house is still perched on a hill in the lush green oasis of Fort Canning Park. And the edifices of colonialism still surround the Padang, where British high society once converged to play cricket and exchange gossip. It's here you'll find the famous Raffles Hotel, a string of old churches, the old and new parliament houses, the art and history museums and, dragging the area into the present, the dazzlingly contemporary 'durians', otherwise known as Esplanade – Theatres on the Bay.

It's not all culture and history of course. A short walk from the columns and the statues are the three revitalised quays – Clarke, Boat and Robertson – where sweating labourers once loaded and unloaded goods from the riverside warehouses. These days they are buzzing nightspots, with endless restaurants, bars and clubs lining the newly clean river, and the traditional belching bumboats now ferry tourists rather than sacks of rice (see opposite). The entire riverfront strip from Marina Bay right up to Kim Seng Rd is earmarked for a massive makeover in an attempt to turn the Singapore River into Asia's biggest waterfront playground. Watch this space.

Aside from Orchard Rd, this area is the Singapore everybody knows, the city's showpiece, where despite decades of often unsentimental demolitions, upgrades and makeovers, a uniquely Singaporean character remains.

Orientation

The grid layout of the district makes it easy to navigate. From City Hall MRT station underneath the towering Raffles City mall/hotel complex, the area to the south has most of the colonial treasures, including the Padang, St Andrew's Cathedral, City Hall, the Parliament building and Asian Civilisations Museum (which is actually closer to Raffles Place MRT). From there you can cross the elegant Cavenagh Bridge to Boat Quay and follow the river to Clarke Quay, then along to Robertson Quay or north to climb the steep steps up to Fort Canning Park.

One block north of City Hall MRT you'll find Raffles Hotel and its famous old bars. Another short walk east will land you at the Chijmes entertainment compound. The area is also walking distance from Waterloo St.

TRANSPORT

Unless you're lucky enough to be staying in the pricey Colonial District, your point of reference will be City Hall MRT, which is an easy walk from all the main attractions in the Padang area. For the Asian Civilisations Museum and Boat Quay, the closest stop is Raffles Place MRT. If it's too hot to walk, the following buses can ease the pain. Bus 2 takes you down Victoria St and Hill St. Buses 51, 61, 63 and 80 go along North Bridge Rd. For Beach Rd, hop on bus 100, 107 or 961. Along Bras Basah Rd, get on bus 14, 16, 77 or 111.

At night, the best guaranteed taxi spots are the Clarke Quay rank on River Valley Rd and at the Elgin Bridge next to the Jazz at Southbridge pub on South Bridge Rd. Elsewhere, it can be a lottery.

SINGAPORE FOR KIDS

Singapore is heaven for kids – in fact you might find yourself dragging them screaming to the airport when it's time to leave (unless they are dragging you screaming from Orchard Rd). The city packs a huge number of family-friendly activities into its small area, with enough variety to please children of every temperament, as long as they can cope with the heat. Here are a few suggestions:

- Have breakfast with an orang-utan at the zoo (p78), or combine a zoo and night safari trip. Get up close to the birdlife in Jurong BirdPark (p82) and sealife at Underwater World (p87) and Dolphin Lagoon (p87) on Sentosa.
- Have a fun lesson in science at the Singapore Science Centre (p84), check out the huge Omni-Theatre (p83), then go chuck snowballs or hurtle down the slope on inner tubes at neighbouring Snow City (p85).
- Take the cable car across to the theme-park attractions of Sentosa Island (p85) or the MRT up to NTUC Lifestyle World at Pasir Ris, where the Escape Theme Park (p76) and Wild Wild Wet water park (p77) will keep them occupied all day.
- Unpack the skateboard and get down to the National Youth Centre Skate Park and Youth Park (Map pp226–7) near Somerset MRT off Orchard Rd.
- Rollerblade or bicycle along East Coast Park (p75) where there's another water fun park, Big Splash.
- Frolic in the leaping, dancing fountain at Parco Bugis Junction (p155), a cooling experience for kids of all ages.
- Sign up for a kids' cooking course at At-Sunrice (see Cookery Courses, p33), where they can produce delights like Hansel and Gretel Cinnamon Egg Tarts.
- Check out the fabulous Christmas light displays at the Orchard Rd malls (p156) from October to the end of December.
- Board the DUCKtour (p48), an amphibious craft that tours the city streets before plunging into the harbour. Go on, you know you want to.
- Introduce them to a bit of tropical nature at one of Singapore's reserves – Bukit Timah (p77), MacRitchie (p78) or Sungei Buloh (p80) – where they can see cavorting monkeys and, if you're lucky, huge monitor lizards that'll scare them witless.
- Take them to a farm (see Down on the Farm, p84).

ASIAN CIVILISATIONS MUSEUM
Map p230

☎ 6332 7798; 1 Empress Pl; adult/child $5/2.50; ⏲ 1-7pm Mon, 9am-7pm Tue-Sun, 9am-9pm Fri; Raffles Place MRT

This is a must! This jewel in the National Heritage Board's bevy of museums is split across two locations, both worth visiting. This most recent wing occupies the grand Empress Place building (1865) named in honour of Queen Victoria. You enter through a series of images projected onto walls, floors and finally a slatted curtain, which you walk through to enter the galleries. The Hindu-Buddhist gallery is perhaps the highlight, with beautifully lit displays including a stunning 18th-century Burmese Buddha head and a large bronze drum. Elsewhere you'll find exquisite examples of porcelain, textiles, lacquerware, costumes and huge traditional procession statues. There are also regular touring and programmed exhibitions. Tours in English run at 11am and 2pm most days.

The **Armenian St branch** (Map p230; ☎ 6332 3015; 39 Armenian St; adult/child $3/1.50; ⏲ 9am-5.30pm Tue & Thu-Sun, 9am-9pm Wed; City Hall MRT) is housed in the beautifully restored Tao Nan School, dating from 1910. Included here are permanent displays on Peranakan culture, Chinese ceramics and Buddhist artefacts.

CHIJMES Map p230

30 Victoria St; City Hall MRT

Singapore never lets something like religion get in the way of a good development. This former Convent of the Holy Infant Jesus is now a shrine to worldly indulgence in the form of a swish restaurant, bar and shopping complex. The Anglo-French Gothic chapel (1903) at the centre of the complex has been beautifully preserved and wedding celebrations are still held there. Here you'll also find Caldwell House (1841), designed by George Coleman (see p25) and the original residence of the French nuns who set up the school that once existed on the site.

CIVIL DEFENCE HERITAGE GALLERY Map p230

☎ 6332 2995; 62 Hill St; admission free; ⏲ 10am-5pm Tue-Sun; City Hall MRT

The Civil Defence Heritage Gallery, which is devoted to firefighting and civil defence

Outside a café, Chijmes (opposite)

in Singapore, will be of interest to few. This gallery is based in the handsome red-brick and white-plaster Central Fire Station, built in 1908, which is still in use today.

ESPLANADE – THEATRES ON THE BAY Map p230

☎ 6828 8222; www.esplanade.com; 1 Esplanade Dr; City Hall MRT

Nicknamed, quite aptly, 'the durians' (after the pungent, spiky fruit), the twin silver hedgehog domes of this $600-million arts complex couldn't be more of a contrast to the colonial ensemble of the Padang. Love it or hate it (and we love it), the Esplanade complex has become the poster boy of contemporary Singapore, a shining example of the artsy, creative side of the island state.

As well as twin auditoriums that are both visually and acoustically spectacular (they both rest on rubber pads to soak up external noise and vibrations), there are several very good restaurants here. Also worth looking out for are the regular free performances outside the buildings, which are advertised either on the theatre's website or in the monthly what's on guide.

The building itself was the product of Singapore's recognition that it needed iconic buildings to keep pace with the competitive international tourist industry – a kind of Asian Sydney Opera House.

Despite their fruity nickname, or comparisons with Madonna's infamous bra, the theatre complex's twin glass domes, covered in spiky metal sunshades, do not take their design reference from tropical fruit or celebrity breasts, but from the natural geometries of nature and traditional Asian reed weavings. Varying angles and geometrics make the roofline morph and mutate across the building 'the way feathers on a bird's neck gradually change in size and orientation', according to the project's director Vikas Gore.

Situated on reclaimed land along the waterfront, the project was built with public money and had been in the pipeline since the 1970s. It wasn't commissioned until 1993 and construction didn't start until 1996. The controversial exterior is made from 7139 variously angled aluminium shades that maximise the natural light while shielding the glass roof from the sun; by night, internal lighting makes the building glow a cool green. The interior has the hushed, slightly awestruck atmosphere you get in truly special buildings. Some Singaporeans grumble about the expense, but this was worth every dollar.

FORT CANNING PARK Map p230

Dhoby Ghaut MRT

The only natural high spot in the district, Fort Canning Park was once known as Bukit Larangan (Forbidden Hill) and it has a shrine to Sultan Iskander Shah, the last ruler of the ancient kingdom of Singapura.

When Stamford Raffles arrived, the only reminder of the Sultan's long-gone kingdom was an earthen wall that stretched from the sea to the top of Fort Canning Hill. Raffles built his modest thatch-roofed residence atop the hill in 1822, and it later became Government House until the military replaced it with Fort Canning in 1860, named in honour of Viscount Canning, first viceroy of India.

Little is left of the hill's historic buildings, but even after climbing up the exhausting steps it's a wonderfully cool retreat from the hot streets below and the park is designed with little pathways and quiet corners so that at times you'd hardly know you were in a city.

A couple of Gothic gateways lead into the pleasant park, where gravestones from the old Christian cemetery are embedded in the brick walls. There's also a **spice garden** here, on the site of Raffles' original botanical garden. Guided tours can be arranged through the **At-Sunrice Cooking Academy** (see Cookery Courses, p33), based in the monumental **Fort Canning Centre**, the former barracks building dating from 1926. Plants and trees are mostly labelled if you just want to wander around yourself for a pinch-and-sniff.

Inside the spice garden is an archaeological dig, where under a wooden roof you can see the Javanese artefacts from the 14th-century Majapahit empire that have been uncovered there.

The park hosts several outdoor events each year including Womad and Ballet under the Stars and the occasional outdoor movie festival.

Also on Fort Canning Hill is the **Battle Box** (☎ 6333 0510; 51 Canning Rise; adult/child $8/5; 10am-6pm Tue-Sun), Singapore's largest underground military operations complex during WWII. This warren of 26 rooms and tunnels now houses a fascinating hi-tech exhibition on the fall of Singapore in 1942. You can gaze through binocular-like lenses to view holographic figures tapping out Morse messages; the Japanese codes are still etched on the walls. However, this place often seems understaffed and since you can only go on guided tours you may find yourself waiting half an hour for the next tour.

PADANG & AROUND Map p230

City Hall MRT

The open field of the Padang is where flannelled fools play cricket in the tropical heat, cheered on by the Singapore Cricket Club members in the pavilion. At the opposite end of the field is the Singapore Recreation Club, set aside for the Eurasian community. Cricket is still played on the weekends but segregation is, officially, no longer practised. The Padang was a centre for colonial life and a place to promenade in the evenings – and one corner of the field known as Scandal Point was notorious as the spot where the post-match chatterers would gather to swap the latest rumours and society scandals.

It was also here that the invading Japanese herded the European community together before marching them off to Changi prison. Apart from the reconstructed monstrosity that is the Singapore Recreation Club (it looks like something made from kids' building blocks), the Padang is ringed by a handsome collection of colonial buildings and assorted monuments, all of which can be taken in on a leisurely stroll (see p96).

At the Padang's southern end, the **Victoria Theatre & Concert Hall** (1862), once the town hall, is now used for cultural events. **Parliament House** (1827) is Singapore's oldest government building. Originally a private mansion, it became a courthouse, then the Assembly House of the colonial government and, finally, the Parliament House for independent Singapore.

Along St Andrew's Rd, the **Supreme Court**, built in 1939, is a relatively new addition and was the last classical building to be erected in Singapore. It replaced the Grand Hotel de L'Europe, which once outshone the Raffles as Singapore's premier hotel. Situated next door and even newer is the Foster Partners–designed **Supreme Court** (p26), which was opened in June 2005.

City Hall, with its classical façade of Corinthian columns, is located next to the Supreme Court and dates from 1929. It was here that Lord Louis Mountbatten announced Japanese surrender in 1945 and Lee Kwan Yew declared Singapore's independence in 1965. Completing the colonial trio is **St Andrew's Cathedral** (see Places of Worship, p54).

RAFFLES HOTEL Map p230

☎ 6337 1886; www.raffleshotel.com; 1 Beach Rd; City Hall MRT

Go on, don't be shy. Raffles Hotel is a Singaporean institution and, though it may be a cliché, no trip is complete without a look inside to soak up the genteel, historical atmosphere and perhaps relax in one of the hotel's famous bars for a cocktail (a Singapore Sling if you must, but we think they taste like cough medicine).

Viewing the regal edifice that stands today, it's hard to believe that Raffles Hotel started life as a 10-room bungalow. It was opened in December 1887 by the Sarkies brothers, immigrants from Armenia and proprietors of two other grand colonial hotels, the Strand in Yangon (Rangoon) and the Eastern & Oriental in Penang.

The hotel's heyday began with the opening of the main building in 1899, the same one that guests stay in today. Raffles soon became a byword for oriental luxury ('A legendary symbol for all the fables of the Exotic East', went the publicity blurb) and was featured in novels by Joseph Conrad and Somerset Maugham. The famous Singapore Sling was first concocted in the hotel's Long Bar in 1915.

By the 1970s, however, Raffles had become a shabby relic and seemed destined to go the way of Raffles Institution, the elite school that stood on Bras Basah Rd until it was demolished to make way for Raffles City. Fortunately the government designated the building a national monument in 1987, and in 1991 it was reopened after an expensive restoration project that has seen the hotel all but swallowed up by a fancy shopping and dining arcade.

If you can't afford to stay, the hotel lobby is open to the public. (Dress standards apply; so no shorts or sandals. Tennis shoes are allowed, but please don't!) High tea is served in the Tiffin Room. Drinks can be taken at any of its bars. The Long Bar is the most famous, but far better is the Bar & Billiard Room. (By the way, that famous tiger was shot under this building, not the billiard table.)

Hidden away on the 3rd floor of the Raffles Hotel Arcade, the **Raffles Hotel Museum** (admission free; ⌚ 10am-7pm) is worth hunting out. Here you'll find a fascinating collection of memorabilia including photographs and posters from bygone eras and a fine city map showing how Noel Coward could once sip his gin sling and stare out at the muddy sea from the hotel veranda.

SINGAPORE ART MUSEUM Map p230

☎ 6332 3222; 71 Bras Basah Rd; adult/child $3/1.50; ⌚ noon-6pm Mon, 9am-6pm Tue-Thu, Sat & Sun, 9am-9pm Fri; City Hall or Dhoby Ghaut MRT

Two blocks west of Raffles Hotel is this fine museum based in the former St Joseph's Institution, a Catholic boys' school that closed down in 1987.

The reconstruction by local architect Wong Hooe Wai fuses historical charm with a strong contemporary feel. Features include Filipino artist Ramon Orlina's abstract glass window in the former school chapel and US artist Dale Chihuly's sea anemone–like blown-glass installations, which incidentally can also be seen at the **Chihuly Lounge** (p127) in the Ritz-Carlton Millenia hotel.

The 13 galleries focus on Singaporean and regional artists, with exhibitions ranging from classical Chinese calligraphy to contemporary works examining issues of Asian identity and the modern Singaporean experience, as well as temporary overseas exhibitions. Afterwards, it's worth stopping for coffee in the museum's genteel café, **Dôme**.

SINGAPORE HISTORY MUSEUM

Map p230

93 Stamford Rd; Dhoby Ghaut MRT

The Singapore History Museum was closed for renovations at the time of writing, but was due to open in 2006. Filling the gap is a temporary innovative exhibition called

TOP FIVE PARKS

Singapore has approximately 50 public parks – and that doesn't include the nature reserves. And these parks are not just patches of grass slotted between the concrete either – the majority are immaculately shaped and manicured, imaginatively designed and filled with facilities like bike tracks, fitness trails, playgrounds, fish ponds and even cafés. Many are also linked by Park Connectors, bike trails that thread through the city allowing runners and cyclists to travel long distances untroubled by cars. Listed here, in no particular order, are our five favourite parks:

- **East Coast Park** (p75) A huge 11km stretch of seafront and one of the best places to ride a bike in Singapore, provided you miss the weekend crowds.
- **Fort Canning Park** (p51) A hilltop oasis right in the city, with historical sites, peaceful paths and excellent views.
- **Pasir Ris Park** (p76) Another large, peaceful seafront park in eastern Singapore, where the highlight is a pristine mangrove reserve complete with boardwalks and an observation tower. Lots of facilities for kids, plus a beachfront restaurant complex.
- **Mt Faber Park** (p82) On the steep hill just across the water from Sentosa, Mount Faber is covered with secondary rainforest and affords some spectacular views across the city and the Singapore Strait.
- **Bishan Park** (p78) One of the largest in Singapore, spread over two halves, dissected by Ang Mo Kio Ave 1. Much quieter than East Coast, with a long bike trail, large ornamental lakes, a skate park, an outdoor café and even an equipped dog run. One entrance is opposite the Kong Meng San Phor Kark See Monastery.

Rivertales (☎ 6332 3659; Riverside Point, 30 Merchant Rd; adult/child $2/1; ⏰ 1-7pm Mon, 9am-7pm Tue-Thu, Sat & Sun, 9am-9pm Fri). It's a worthwhile trip, featuring a murder mystery, a 3-D show charting Singapore's rise from seedy port town and a memorable short film called *The Old Man and the River*, which sees the river's history through the eyes of an elderly road sweeper.

PLACES OF WORSHIP

Be respectful when you visit the following places of worship by observing proper dress etiquette. Sleeveless shirts and shorts are frowned upon. In mosques and Indian and Sikh temples, shoes should be removed before entering. Males and married women should cover their heads in synagogues and everyone must cover their heads in Sikh temples.

At Chinese temples there are no communal services except for funerals. However, the community comes together to observe popular holidays, and noisy parades are held on special occasions. Call the numbers listed here to check service times.

Churches

Singapore's oldest church – and one of its oldest buildings full-stop – is the little **Armenian Church** (Map p230; ☎ 6334 0141; 60 Hill St). Designed by eminent colonial architect George Coleman, the neoclassical-style building dates from 1836 and is dedicated to St Gregory the Illuminator. In its grounds lie the graves of several Sarkies (but not the brothers of Raffles Hotel fame) and Agnes Joaquim, the Armenian who discovered the island's first hybrid orchid, now the national flower. Inside is a painting of the Last Supper.

Coleman also designed the original **St Andrew's Cathedral** (Map p230; ☎ 6337 6104; 11 St Andrew's Rd) in 1837 but this was demolished after lightning damage and rebuilt between 1856 and 1862 in its current form. The outside walls were daubed with a mixture of eggs, sugar, lime and coconut husks, which accounts for their gleaming quality. An interesting, ironic, historical footnote is that this house of God was erected by the hands of the sinful or, to be precise and less melodramatic, convict labourers from India.

Singapore's oldest Catholic church (consecrated in 1846) is the **Cathedral of the Good Shepherd** (Map p230; ☎ 6337 2036; 4 Queen St), the product of the unification of the diverse Spanish, Portuguese and French parishes, whose priests were sick of having nowhere suitably reverential to hold their services.

Mosques

The focus for Singapore's Muslim community is the grand Sultan Mosque (p63) in the heart of Kampong Glam. Nearby on Beach Rd is the Malabar Mosque (p61), or Blue Mosque, which is inlaid with more than 20,000 eye-catching lapis lazuli tiles. Further up Beach Rd is the Hajjah Fatimah Mosque (p60), named after its Malaka-born female benefactor, who married a Bugis Sultan.

Chinese Temples

Chinese temples abound in Singapore. The oldest and most important of them is the beautifully restored Thian Hock Keng Temple (p58) in Chinatown. On Waterloo St, Kuan Im Thong Hood Cho Temple (p61), also known as Kuan Yin Temple, is one of the most popular and is always teeming with visitors and flower sellers.

Singapore's largest temple complex is Kong Meng San Phor Kark See Monastery (p78), a short bus ride from Bishan MRT station. The ornate Siong Lim Temple & Gardens (p79), near Toa Payoh MRT station, are also worth visiting.

Hindu Temples

Chinatown's Sri Mariamman Temple (p58) is Singapore's best known, busiest and oldest Hindu temple.

Over in Little India are the Sri Veeramakaliamman Temple (p62) and the Sri Srinivasa Perumal Temple (p62), both on Serangoon Rd. This second temple is also the starting point for the Thaipusam procession to the Chettiar Hindu Temple (opposite), close to Fort Canning Park and Clarke Quay.

Sikh Temples

It took over 30 years for the **Central Sikh Temple** (Map p232; ☎ 6299 3855; 731 Serangoon Rd), near Boon Keng MRT, to make it off the drawing board and into reality, but this simple domed building, opened in 1986, won a government design award.

Synagogues

The **Maghain Aboth Synagogue** (Map pp224-5; ☎ 6337 2189; 24 Waterloo St), built in 1878, is the oldest of Singapore's two synagogues and the only one still used for services.

SINGAPORE PHILATELIC MUSEUM

Map p230

☎ 6337 3888; www.spm.org.sg; 23B Coleman St; adult/child $2/1; 9am-6pm Tue-Sun; City Hall MRT

The Singapore Philatelic Museum is unlikely to thrill anyone except, of course, stamp collectors; however, it does have its moments. The museum is housed in the attractive former Methodist Book Room Building dating from around 1895, and holds a well-presented collection of rare and not-so-rare stamps from Singapore and around the world; some of the artwork and design is impressive. Kids will enjoy designing stamps and other interactive displays.

BOAT QUAY

Once crowded with hundreds of bumboats, Boat Quay was the location of the city's leading *towkays* (Chinese business chiefs) and remained busy right up to the 1960s. By the mid-1980s, many of the shophouses were in ruins, business having shifted to hi-tech cargo centres elsewhere on the island. Boat Quay was declared a conservation zone by the government and its revival into an entertainment district began. Given the raucous character of Boat Quay today, some might say that the revival has been too successful, but there's no doubting that when viewed from across the river or from high up in one of the city's skyscrapers, the whole brightly painted and lit strip makes for a dazzling scene.

THE WORLD'S PORT OF CALL

Anyone who flies into Singapore, or stands on the island's southern or East Coast beaches, cannot fail to notice that there are an awful lot of very large ships out there. Singapore is the world's largest transhipment point. Every day more than 400 vessels pass through the country's four container terminals at Tanjong Pagar, Keppel, Brani and Pasir Panjang, accounting for 17% of the world's transhipment traffic. There are 200 shipping lines operating here, with connections to 600 ports in 123 countries. It's a staggering technical and logistical operation and not surprisingly the security operation there is massive (they even have gamma ray scanners to inspect containers, due in large part to pressure from the US), but you can get a good look at the Keppel terminal from the cable car that runs to Sentosa and Mt Faber.

CLARKE QUAY

This quay, named after Singapore's second colonial governor, Sir Andrew Clarke, was developed like Boat Quay into a dining and shopping precinct in the early 1990s and has recently undergone another, highly distinctive, renovation that has cemented its status as one of Singapore's most popular night haunts.

In fact, your jaw is likely to drop, either in horror or admiration, the first time you see the eccentric design of the new Clarke Quay waterfront. The wooden decks are OK, the gumdrop railings done out in kids' paintbox colours you might forgive, but the giant Dr Seuss–like lilypad umbrellas are just plain offensive, obscuring what was once a handsome strip of colourful shophouses, now painted in equally revolting hues. Opinions vary, but in our opinion it looks like Jellybean Town.

Aside from marvelling at one of the world's most grievous design follies, or contemplating a ride on the **G-Max Reverse Bungy** (☎ 6338 1146; rides $30), there are a couple of interesting places of worship near the quay

CHETTIAR HINDU TEMPLE Map p230

☎ 6737 9393; 15 Tank Rd; 8am-noon & 5.30-8.30pm; Clarke Quay or Dhoby Ghaut MRT

The Chettiar Hindu Temple was completed in 1984 and replaces a much earlier temple built by Indian *chettiars* (moneylenders). This Shaivite temple, dedicated to the six-headed Lord Subramaniam and properly known as the Sri Thandayuthapani Temple, is at its most active during the festival of Thaipusam (see p9), when the procession ends here.

TAN SI CHONG SU TEMPLE Map p230

15 Magazine Rd; Clarke Quay MRT

On the south side of the river is the ornate Tan Si Chong Su Temple, dating from 1876. With its decorative roof, guardian dragons and lions, and painted wooden doors, this is a particularly fine example of temple design, sadly now overshadowed by the Central Expressway.

ROBERTSON QUAY

At the furthest reach of the river, Robertson Quay was once used for storage of goods. Now some of the old *gowdowns* (warehouses) have been tarted up into flash places to party, such as the mega-club Zouk (p133). You'll also find several good hotels and restaurants clustered around here.

SINGAPORE TYLER PRINT INSTITUTE

Map pp224-5

☎ 6336 3663; www.stpi.com.sg; 41 Robertson Quay; admission free; ⏲ 1-5pm Sun & Mon, 9.30am-6pm Tue-Sat; bus 54 from Clarke Quay MRT

The Tyler Print Institute, established by the American printmaker Kenneth E Tyler, features a gallery that holds exhibitions on various aspects of printmaking four times a year, as well as a paper mill and educational facility.

CHINATOWN & THE CBD

Eating p107; Shopping p144; Sleeping p169

Strange as it might seem to have a Chinatown in a city dominated by Chinese, this colourful district provides a glimpse into the ways of the Chinese immigrants that shaped and built modern Singapore.

That glimpse is not nearly as clear as it used to be, thanks largely to a concerted gentrification effort that has seen a lot of the area's distinctive seediness make way for more tourist-friendly businesses. The area has changed incredibly since the early 1990s. Many old shopfronts have been restored, or rather ripped down and rebuilt in the same style, under the direction of the Urban Redevelopment Authority. While the redevelopments are faithful to the originals, these now desirable properties command high rents, which means some of the traditional businesses have had to move out and, in a few streets at least, make way for the New Chinatown of boutique hotels, antique shops, fashionable restaurants, expensive retailers and tourist markets.

Tourist strips like Pagoda St can be a little much, packed with cheap *cheongsam* (Chinese dresses), calligraphers, henna tattooists and overpriced antique shops. Having said that, Chinatown is still an excellent area to stay, and to wander around (see the walking tour, p90). It contains some of Singapore's most notable temples and, once you negotiate the tacky tourist market stalls, there are plenty of bargains to be found, plus excellent food and some of the best nightlife in Singapore.

Chinese lanterns for sale in Chinatown (left)

Between Chinatown and the Singapore River is the central business district (CBD), the financial pulse of the city. Once the city's vibrant heart, Raffles Pl is now a rare patch of grass above the MRT station surrounded by the gleaming towers of commerce. There are some interesting sculptures here and along the nearby Singapore River (see The Sculpture Trail, p23), including the latest incarnation of the island's much-hyped *Merlion*, which is in Merlion Park.

While the area is unlikely to captivate the visitor, amid all the modern architecture are a few preserved relics of days past. The somewhat insalubrious Clifford Pier is the place to hire a boat or catch a harbour cruise (see p48), while the Fullerton Building, once the general post office, now houses one of Singapore's swankiest hotels.

Further south along the waterfront you'll find Lau Pa Sat (p109), a hawker centre occupying the old Telok Ayer Market building, a fine piece of cast-iron Victoriana.

Splitting the CBD from the colonial district is the Singapore River, the site of the

TRANSPORT

The centre of any trip to Chinatown will be Chinatown MRT on the North East Line, two stops from Dhoby Ghaut MRT at the end of Orchard Rd. Exit A from the station lands you right on Pagoda St. Coming from the Colonial District, hop on bus 61, 145 or 166, which takes you from North Bridge Rd to South Bridge Rd. From Hill St, bus 2, 12 or 147 runs you down New Bridge Rd. It's possible to walk from the CBD to Chinatown, but from Raffles Quay bus 608 goes to South Bridge Rd, or take bus C2 from Clifford Pier.

CHINATOWN & THE CBD TOP FIVE

- Exploring the interactive displays at the **Chinatown Heritage Centre** (below)
- Drinking at **Bar Sá Vanh** (p125) on Club St
- Taking tea the traditional way at the **Tea Chapter** (p110)
- Perusing the natural remedies in the **Eu Yan Sang Medical Hall** (right)
- Peeking inside the **Sri Mariamman Hindu temple** (p58)

first British arrivals and for over a century the main artery of trade.

Orientation

Chinatown is roughly bounded by the Singapore River to the north, New Bridge Rd to the west, Maxwell and Kreta Ayer Rds to the south and Cecil St to the east. The main centres of visitor attention are clustered between New Bridge Rd and South Bridge Rd, where you'll find the Chinatown Complex, the Pagoda and Trengganu St pedestrian strips (or tourist traps) and the temples, while the Club St bar area lies just to the east of South Bridge Rd.

The central business district, south of the river, is centred on Raffles Pl, a short walk across the Cavenagh Bridge from the Colonial District.

CHINATOWN HERITAGE CENTRE

Map pp234-5

☎ 6325 2878; www.chinatownheritage.com.sg; 48 Pagoda St; adult/child $8.80/5.30; 🕑 9am-8pm Mon-Thu, 9am-9pm Fri-Sun; Chinatown MRT

It may not look like much from the outside, but this enthralling place is one of Singapore's best museums. A reflection of the oft-frenetic atmosphere of Chinatown itself, it is crammed to the rafters with interactive, imaginative displays on the area's history. Three restored shophouses have been combined to make the three-storey centre, part of which recreates very evocatively and accurately the cramped and miserable living quarters that many Chinese immigrants once endured. There are absorbing recreations of the labourer's depressing quarters, a prostitute's bedroom and an old style hawker's kit (basically a burner that was lugged around the streets along with a few ingredients).

The oral and video histories of local people, describing what life was like in the days when Singapore was less than immaculate, are fascinating, from the old woman who survived through unspeakable suffering, to the stories of the Triad-style secret societies that patrolled and terrorised the neighbourhoods.

There's a lot to take in here in one go, so keep your ticket stub and the attendants will let you return the same day, if you fancy a break.

EU YAN SANG MEDICAL HALL

Map pp234-5

☎ 6223 6333; 269 South Bridge Rd; 🕑 8.30am-6pm Mon-Sat; Chinatown MRT

First opened in the early 20th century and now very tastefully refurbished, this is Singapore's most famous Chinese medicine centre, which has spawned branches across the country. Founded in Malaysia in 1879, the business spread to Singapore in 1910 and onward to Hong Kong and China. It can be an intimidating place, if only because of the smell, but a few of the staff are approachable and, if you have a genuine ailment, will talk you through the remedies on offer. Beware, besides an offer of free ginseng tea and countless other ginseng products, you might be prescribed anything from deer antlers or tails, crushed centipedes or scorpions, gall bladders and penises.

SENG WONG BEO TEMPLE Map pp234-5

113 Peck Seah St; Tanjong Pagar MRT

Tucked behind red gates next to the Tanjong Pagar MRT, this temple, seldom visited by tourists, is dedicated to the Chinese City God who is not only responsible for the wellbeing of the city but also for guiding the souls of the dead to the underworld. It's also notable as the only temple in Singapore that still performs ghost marriages.

When an unmarried girl dies, so that her soul isn't condemned to wander the afterlife alone, it behoves her relations to find a suitable partner. The family may know of another family that has lost a son who is suitable and may in that case make a direct approach. If not, a matchmaker is called in to find a prospective spouse.

The marriage ceremony is performed in the temple and officiated by the temple medium. The bride and groom are represented by paper effigies, as are all the wedding presents, which may include paper cars and houses. At the end of the ceremony the effigies and presents are burnt and the two families share a celebratory feast.

SRI MARIAMMAN TEMPLE Map pp234-5

☎ 6223 4064; 244 South Bridge Rd; 7.30-11.30am & 5.30-8.30pm; Chinatown MRT

This popular South Indian Dravidian-style Hindu temple, right in the heart of Chinatown, is Singapore's oldest. It was originally built in 1827 as a wood and *atap* (thatched-roof) hut by Nariana Pillay, who arrived in Singapore on the same ship as Sir Stamford Raffles. It was built in its present form in 1843 in a style similar to the enormous Sri Meenakshi temple in Madurai, South India.

Its distinctive, colourful *gopuram* (tower), crowded with deities, soldiers and floral decoration over the entrance gate, dominates the street. Inside are a series of shrines. The main one, straight ahead after you walk through the gate, belongs to the healing goddess Mariamman. Another shrine is devoted to Periyachi Amman, who is supposed to protect children.

At the end of October each year the temple is the scene for the Thimithi festival, during which devotees walk barefoot over burning coals – supposedly feeling no pain, although spectators report that quite a few hot-foot it for the final few steps!

THIAN HOCK KENG TEMPLE Map pp234-5

☎ 6423 4626; 158 Telok Ayer St; Raffles Place or Chinatown MRT

Its name translates as Temple of Heavenly Bliss, which is entirely apt given the gorgeous decoration of this, the oldest and most important Hokkien temple in Singapore. It was built between 1839 and 1842 on the site of the shrine to Ma-Chu-Po, the goddess of the sea, which was once the favourite landing point of Chinese sailors (believe it or not, Telok Ayer St used to run along the shoreline). All the materials came from China except, interestingly, the gates (which came all the way from Scotland) and the tiles (from Holland). The temple was magnificently restored in 2000.

As you wander through the courtyards of the temple, look for the rooftop dragons, the intricately decorated beams, the gold-leafed panels and, best of all, the beautifully painted doors. During the restoration, a calligraphic panel from 1907 and from the Emperor of China, Guang Xu of the Qing dynasty, was discovered above the central altar.

TIONG BAHRU BIRD AREA Map pp224-5

cnr Tiong Bahru & Seng Poh Rds; Tiong Bahru MRT

This famous gathering spot for bird owners is particularly lively on Sunday mornings, from about 6.30am onwards, when the place is packed with singing birds, though in fact it takes place every day. Each bird is housed in an attractive lacquered bamboo cage, decorated with china feeding and water bowls and other trinkets. Similar

MARINA SOUTH

For years, the large reclaimed thumb of land that is Marina South has been a shining example of what happens when big plans fall flat. Built in the '80s, Marina South's wide, palm-lined boulevards sit unused, unkempt and overgrown. The large, U-shaped entertainment complex of bars, bowling alleys and countless barbecue steamboat restaurants has the desolate air of an off-season seaside town.

That looks likely to change. The construction of the Marina Barrage, a tidal barrier to control flooding, will create a large reservoir in the city that the government plans to turn into a marine playground, ringed with high-class condominiums, bars and restaurants. The Barrage should be ready by 2008.

Marina South (to be renamed Marina Bay for branding purposes) will house one of the two fluffily named integrated resorts, the casino-driven cash cows Singapore is banking on to fuel a tourism boom.

Until these developments are in place, the only thing likely to draw you to Marina South, apart from a barbecue steamboat of course, is the very pleasant Marina City Park (Map pp224–5). Wrapped around an ornamental lake, this quiet, undulating patch of manicured greenery features eight large statues of Chinese luminaries like Confucius and Qu Yuan, a seaside promenade and, unusually for Singapore, a large number of gum trees.

Bus 400 from Marina Bay MRT takes you to the park and the entertainment strip.

CHINESE TEMPLE DESIGN

Many Chinese temples, whether Buddhist, Taoist or Confucian, share similar design elements. There's usually a furnace in front of the main altar where prayers, incense and ghost money (symbolic tender for use in the afterlife) are burnt to appease the ancestors. A screen will often separate the entrance from the main hall, where an image of the deity to whom the temple is dedicated is fronted by an altar. Funerary tablets dedicated to deceased members of the community are displayed, often in a separate room.

species of birds are hung near each other from numbered hooks.

It's as much a social gathering as anything else. The **Bird Area Coffee Shop** nearby supplies *kopi* (coffee with milk), *kaya* toast (toast topped with coconut and egg) and cold drinks while the birds chirp away.

Across the road is a little shop selling various birds, including parrots, a range of cages (from around $100 apiece), and the various little bowls and baubles that go with them. Also nearby is the excellent **Tiong Bahru Cooked Food Centre** (p110) and wet market. The Tiong Bahru estate was Singapore's first public housing estate, built in the 1930s along the lines of an English suburb, and is nowadays largely populated by elderly residents.

From Tiong Bahru MRT, walk around 500m southeast to get here.

URA GALLERY Map pp234-5

☎ 6321 8321; www.ura.gov.sg; 45 Maxwell Rd; admission free; 🕑 9am-4.30pm Mon-Fri, 9am-12.30pm Sat; Tanjong Pagar MRT

To understand how Singapore's urban environment has changed over recent decades and how it will change further in the future, pop into the URA Gallery. This showcase of the Urban Redevelopment Authority (URA) includes video shows, interactive exhibits and a huge scale model of the island state with its own six-minute sound-and-light show.

WAK HAI CHENG BIO TEMPLE

Map pp234-5

cnr Phillip & Church Sts; Raffles Place MRT

On the CBD edge of Chinatown, this Taoist temple is also known as the Yueh Hai Ching Temple, which translates as Calm Sea Temple. Dating from 1826, it's an atmospheric place, with giant incense coils smoking over its empty courtyard, and a whole village of tiny plaster figures populating its roof.

LITTLE INDIA & THE ARAB QUARTER

Eating p110; Shopping p146; Sleeping p171

If you've been spending your time on Orchard Rd and in the Colonial District, Little India will look like another world. Abandon all thoughts of sterile Singapore here; this colourful enclave of the Indian community is anything but organised and clean. Fruit and vegetable shops crowd the grubby five-foot ways with their boxes of eggplants, okra and tomatoes, jostling for space with the goldsmiths and raucous stores selling electronics and cheap CDs from India. And everywhere is the smell of incense and spices, wafting from the merchants' shops and countless eateries, offering some of Singapore's best food.

It's a fascinating area to wander around, shopping, browsing, eating and, in traditional Indian style, being stared at by groups of men. The Tekka Centre, with its pungent, bustling wet market, hawker centre and clothes stalls is a must-see, and for shopping there probably isn't anywhere in Singapore to match the 24-hour Mustafa Centre for sheer chaotic variety.

Little India is also home to many of Singapore's most important Hindu temples (see the walking tour, p92).

TRANSPORT

Little India MRT station is the starting point for most visits, which lands you at the end of the bustling Buffalo Rd food market. Bus 65 runs from Orchard Rd to Serangoon Rd. From the Colonial District, catch bus 131 or 147 on Stamford Rd to Serangoon Rd.

For the Arab Quarter, get off at Bugis MRT station – it's a 10-minute walk to Arab and Bussorah Sts. If the walk from Little India is too much, there are no direct bus services, but a cab will cost about $4. From Orchard Rd, catch bus 7 to Victoria St and get off at the Stamford School, just past Arab St. From the Colonial District, buses 130, 133, 145 and 197 head up Victoria St and buses 100 and 107 run along Beach Rd from the Raffles Hotel to the end of Bussorah St.

LITTLE INDIA & THE ARAB QUARTER TOP FIVE

- Shopping on **Bussorah St** (p146)
- Enjoying mint tea and *sheesha* pipes at **Café Le Caire** (p111) on Arab St
- Indulging in a bargain vegetarian pig-out at **Ananda Bhavan** (p110)
- Browsing the grimy, bustling food and clothing stalls at the **Tekka Centre** (p113)
- Wandering the side streets of **Serangoon Rd** (Map p232)

A 15-minute walk southeast brings you to the Arab Quarter of Kampong Glam, the Muslim centre of the city. Its name derives from kampong, the Malay for village, and *gelam*, a type of tree used for boat-building that once grew here when Beach Rd was actually on the seafront.

The area of Kampong Glam was once a thriving area, filled with merchants and famous for its printing houses. Not too long ago however, it was a virtual ghost town, particularly after dark. But the area immediately surrounding the Sultan Mosque has seen a resurgence recently, and now after dark has become a focal point for a strange social mix of the Middle Eastern community and the city's trendy, alternative youth, who come here to indulge in *sheesha* smoking, the latest hip pastime. After years of neglect, Bussorah St has burst into life again and been tranformed into one of the most attractive streets in the city. The old shophouses have been beautifully restored and are now occupied by cafés, shops, galleries, an excellent hostel and even a spa. Behind Arab St, the narrow backstreet of Haji Lane has developed a scene of its own, with alternative record shops, offbeat boutiques and some more superb Middle Eastern cafés.

Around the rest of the area, among the mouldering buildings, the occasional trendy renovated shophouse architect or design company office gives off a clear signal that Kampong Glam is undergoing a slow transformation.

It's still small scale; quieter, much less touristed and, dare we say, more pleasant than Little India or Chinatown. It's worth visiting now, before it really takes off.

See p94 for a further description of Kampong Glam.

Orientation

Teeming Serangoon Rd forms the spine of Little India, but many of the more interesting parts of the neighbourhood are the narrow streets branching off this central artery. Little India's borders are roughly marked by Lavender St to the north, Bukit Timah and Sungei Rds to the south, Race Course Rd to the east and Jalan Besar to the west. Following Serangoon Rd south, you will eventually hit the eastern end of Orchard Rd.

Head southeast from Serangoon Rd along Upper Weld Rd and you'll enter Kampong Glam. This quarter is roughly bounded by Victoria St, Jalan Sultan and Beach Rd, all immediately northeast of Bugis MRT. The areas around Arab St are the centres of attraction. Heading south from Arab St along Beach or North Bridge Rds will bring you to Raffles Hotel and the Colonial District.

HAJJAH FATIMAH MOSQUE Map p232

☎ 6297 2774; 4001 Beach Rd; Lavender or Bugis MRT

The architecturally interesting Hajjah Fatimah Mosque was constructed in 1846 and is named after a Malakan-born Malay woman named Hajjah Fatimah; the site was once her home. It has two unusual features. First is its architecture, which is British influenced, rather than traditional

Tekka Centre market (p113)

Middle Eastern. The second is its leaning minaret, which leans about six degrees off-centre.

KUAN IM THONG HOOD CHO TEMPLE Map p232

178 Waterloo St

Bugis may have lost a lot of its atmosphere over the decades, but one part of the area that is always lively is the precinct just in front of this colourful Chinese temple. Dedicated to Kuan Yin (Guan Yin), one of the most popular deities, the temple attracts a daily crowd of devotees seeking divine intervention. Flower sellers can always be found outside the temple and it's particularly busy on the eve of Chinese New Year when it stays open all night. Just up from the temple, near the South-East Asia Hotel is a large money god, with a polished belly where the faithful rub their hands for good luck.

Next door is the recently renovated and even more polychromatic **Sri Krishnan Temple**, which also attracts worshippers from the Kuan Yin Temple, who show a great deal of religious pragmatism by also burning joss sticks and offering prayers at this Hindu temple.

LEONG SAN SEE TEMPLE Map p232

☎ 6298 9371; 371 Race Course Rd; 🕑 6am-6pm; Farrer Park MRT

Across the road from the Temple of 1000 Lights is this less gaudy Taoist place of worship (dating from 1917 and dedicated to Kuan Yin, goddess of mercy). The name translates as Dragon Mountain Temple and it's beautifully decorated with timber beams carved with chimera, dragons, flowers and human figures.

MALABAR MUSLIM JAMA-ATH MOSQUE Map p232

☎ 6294 3862; 471 Victoria St; Lavender MRT

The blue-tiled Malabar Muslim Jama-Ath Mosque, the only one on the island dedicated to Malabar Muslims from the South Indian state of Kerala, is one of the most distinctive in Singapore, but it didn't always look this way. Work on the building started in 1956, but it wasn't officially opened until 1963 due to cash-flow problems. The magnificent tiling on the mosque was only finished in 1995!

PILGRIM'S PROGRESS

In the late 19th and much of the 20th century, Kampong Glam was the centre of activity for the long-dead business of pilgrimage agents. These men, who occupied ramshackle little offices around Arab St and Bussorah St, specialised in arranging passages to Mecca for Muslims from all over East Asia during the annual hajj.

Once a year, the area would descend into chaos, as pilgrims piled into the area to make their final preparations and say their final goodbyes before boarding vessels bound for the Arabian Gulf on Beach Rd (back in the days when Beach Rd was by the sea).

None of the shops remain, but a few of the agents' artefacts have been preserved in the Malay Heritage Centre, along with some evocative photographs of the pre-hajj melee.

MALAY HERITAGE CENTRE Map p232

☎ 6391 0450; www.malayheritage.org.sg; 85 Sultan Gate; adult/child $3/2; 🕑 10am-6pm Tue-Sun, 1-6pm Mon; Bugis MRT

The Kampong Glam area is the historic seat of the Malay royalty, resident here before the arrival of Raffles, and the *istana* (palace) was built for the last Sultan of Singapore, Ali Iskander Shah, between 1836 and 1843. An agreement allowed the palace to belong to the Sultan's family as long as they continued to live there. Even though this was repealed in 1897, the family stayed on for more than another century and the palace gradually slid into ruin.

In 1999 the family moved out and a long period of renovation ended in 2004 with the opening of the Malay Heritage Centre. The building and grounds are a delight and the museum itself is a sparse but interesting account of Singapore's Malay people, featuring a reconstructed kampong house upstairs.

There are daily performances of Malay dance and music at 11.30am, 3pm and 5pm, costing $8/4 for adults/children (though there are plans to double these prices).

SAKAYA MUNI BUDDHA GAYA TEMPLE Map p232

Temple of 1000 Lights; ☎ 6294 0714; 366 Race Course Rd; 🕑 8am-4.45pm; Farrer Park MRT

In 1927 a Thai monk founded this Buddhist temple, popularly known as the Temple of

A MAID'S LIFE

Around 150,000 maids, or 'foreign domestic workers' as the government calls them, work in Singapore. They mostly come from Indonesia, the Philippines, India and Sri Lanka in the proverbial search for a better life and money to send home. At around $280 per month, their wages are low, but in some cases this is better than an entry-level degree-holder could get in their home country, even after they spend months paying off their maid agency's fees. For many of the maids, it's a tolerable life of domestic duty and some who stay with their employers for years become part of the family. But you only have to scan the local newspapers for a few days to see that, for a disturbing number of them, life is hell. The following are just a few of the examples picked up from a two-month period in 2005:

- Two Indonesian maids, aged 20 and 17, on trial for murdering an employer who they said physically and mentally abused them solidly for months. (The pair was spared the gallows.)
- Fifty-nine-year-old woman arrested and jailed for punching her maid nine times over one five-day period.
- Elderly woman fined for punching maid and repeatedly burning her with an iron.
- Married couple both jailed for physically abusing their maid.
- Man arrested and sent for psychiatric treatment after sexually abusing maid.
- Maid throws employers' baby from balcony, then jumps to her own death, after apparent breakdown brought on by ill-treatment.
- Man jailed for 18 years for abusing and starving maid to death.

And that's not counting the reportedly high number of employers who withhold their maid's pay, sometimes for years.

Happily, the government is finally taking stronger action and has introduced stiffer jail terms and fines for employers who abuse maids, or fail to pay them. They have also raised the age limit and introduced compulsory language competence tests and safety courses for new maids. Police report that there were 'only' 59 'substantiated' cases of maid abuse in 2004, compared with 157 in 1997.

1000 Lights. It's dominated by a brightly painted 15m-high, 300-tonne Buddha that sits alongside an eclectic range of deities including Kuan Yin, the Chinese goddess of mercy, as well as Brahma and Ganesh (both Hindu deities).

Flanking the entrance to the temple are yellow tigers, symbolising protection and vitality. On your left as you enter the temple is a huge mother-of-pearl footprint, complete with the 108 auspicious marks that distinguish a Buddha foot from any other 2m-long foot. It's said to be a replica of the footprint on top of Adam's Peak in Sri Lanka.

You can walk round the back of the giant Buddha and go inside it through a low door. Here you'll see a smaller image of the reclining Buddha, Maitreya. Around the base of the statue, models tell the story of the Buddha's life, and, of course, there are the electric lights that give the temple its name.

For 50¢ you can also have a spin on the wheel of fortune (men spin to the right, women to the left). An attendant will match your wheel of fortune result with a typed forecast that you may take away.

SRI SRINIVASA PERUMAL TEMPLE

Map p232

☎ 6298 5771; 397 Serangoon Rd; 🕑 6.30am-noon & 6-9pm; Farrer Park MRT

This large complex, dedicated to Vishnu, dates from 1855 but the 20m-tall *gopuram* is a relatively recent addition, built in 1966 at a cost of $300,000. Inside the temple you will find a statue of Perumal, or Vishnu, his consorts Lakshmi and Andal, and his bird-mount, Garuda.

This temple is the starting point for devotees who make the walk to the Chettiar Hindu Temple during the Thaipusam festival.

SRI VEERAMAKALIAMMAN TEMPLE

Map p232

☎ 6293 4634; 141 Serangoon Rd; 🕑 8am-12.30pm & 4-8.30pm; Little India MRT

This Shaivite temple, dedicated to Kali, is one of the most colourful and bustling in Little India. Kali, bloodthirsty consort of Shiva, has always been popular in Bengal, the birthplace of the labourers who built this temple in 1881. Images of Kali within the temple show her wearing a garland of skulls and ripping out the insides of her victims, and sharing more peaceful family moments with her sons Ganesh and Murugan.

SULTAN MOSQUE Map p232

☎ 6293 4405; 3 Muscat St; ⏲ 5am-8.30pm; Bugis MRT

Singapore's biggest mosque is the golden-domed focal point of Kampong Glam. It was originally built in 1825 with the aid of a grant from Raffles and the East India Company, as a result of Raffles' treaty with the Sultan of Johor that allowed him to retain sovereignty over the area. A hundred years later in 1928, the original mosque was replaced by the present magnificent building which, interestingly, was designed by an architect from Ireland – who worked for the same company that designed the Raffles Hotel.

The building follows classic Turkish, Persian and Moorish style. Inside the huge prayer hall, which can accommodate around 5000 people, the mosaic tiled walls bear inscriptions from the Koran calling the faithful to prayer. The luscious rug on the floor was donated to the mosque by a Saudi Prince, whose emblem is woven into it. You might also notice a number of incongruous looking digital clocks, which were installed so that prayer times could be accurately observed.

Bear in mind that this is a functioning mosque and only go inside if there isn't a prayer session going on. Pointing cameras at people during prayer time (as we saw on our visit) is not particularly appropriate.

ORCHARD ROAD

Eating p114; Shopping p156; Sleeping p173

Singapore's wall-to-wall consumerist nirvana is an assault on your senses – and your wallet. Faced with this immense stretch of towering malls, some will scream with delight, others will run screaming. From quirky, rundown Lucky Plaza to the imposing chocolate-coloured marble edifice of Ngee Ann City and the chic, exclusive grey of Paragon, it's possible to spend days here and never visit the same mall twice. It can be almost intimidating. Each mall is like a little town unto itself (see Shopping, p140), with speciality food stores, countless designer labels, Japanese teen fashion and antiques.

If the variety is endless, then so are the crowds. Except for a blissful window of peace between around 10am and 11am, when you can have the shops almost to yourself, Orchard Rd teems with people day and night. On Saturday nights, the huge bookshops are more crowded than many pubs.

It wasn't always this way though. The trees that shade the ever-present crowds are almost the only reminder that this area was, in the 19th century, an orchard lined with nutmeg and pepper plantations. However, between the five-star hotels and hulking shrines to materialism, a few architectural relics from this time remain. When you've had your fill of the shops and chilly air-conditioning, escape is close to hand with the serene Botanic Gardens a short bus ride from the west end of the road.

Believe it or not, there are plans afoot to make Orchard Rd even bigger and brasher. The rare patch of greenery surrounding the Orchard MRT station, a respite from the onslaught of glass and concrete, and favourite meeting spot of Filipina maids, will soon have a huge mall on top of it; likewise the empty spot in front of Somerset MRT station.

Orchard Rd, like time, never stands still.

Orientation

From the colonial district, Bras Basah Rd heads northwest to become Orchard Rd, which then winds through the leafy glades of Nassim Rd to the Botanic Gardens, or along Tanglin Rd and Napier Rd towards the expat enclave of Holland Rd. Heading north from the western end of Orchard Rd along Prinsep St and Selegie Rd brings you to Little India.

TRANSPORT

Orchard Rd is important enough to have three MRT stations: Orchard MRT at the eastern end, Somerset in the centre and Dhoby Ghaut at the west end. (Believe it or not, some Singaporeans do take the train between them rather than walk.) Dhoby Ghaut is an important MRT junction, from which trains fan off to City Hall and Raffles Pl (Colonial District), Little India, Clarke Quay and Chinatown. Buses from Orchard Rd and Scotts Rd also fan out across the island.

CUPPAGE TERRACE & EMERALD HILL Map pp226-7

Cuppage Rd; Somerset MRT

Named after William Cuppage, who was the 19th-century owner of the nutmeg estate here, Cuppage Tce, a renovated terrace of Peranakan-style shophouses dating from the 1920s, is overwhelmed by the surrounding shopping malls and hotels. Most of the terrace is given over to bars and restaurants, as is the Orchard Rd end of Emerald Hill. Take some time out, though, to wander up from pedestrianised Peranakan Pl to Emerald Hill Rd, where some fine terrace houses remain; the quiet atmosphere feels a million miles from bustling Orchard Rd. Check out Nos 39 to 45, built in 1903 with an unusually wide frontage and grand Chinese-style entrance gate, and the Art Deco–style Nos 121 to 129, dating from 1925.

ISTANA Map pp226-7

☎ 6737 5522; www.istana.gov.sg; Dhoby Ghaut MRT

Home of Singapore's president, the Istana was built between 1867 and 1869 as Government House, a neoclassical monument to British rule. Public works were never a high priority in laissez-faire colonial Singapore, but the need to impress the visiting Duke of Edinburgh convinced the island's Legislative Council to approve the building's huge budget. The actual construction was done by Indian convicts transported from Bencoolen on Sumatra.

The Istana is set about 750m back from the road in beautifully maintained grounds including a nine-hole golf course and terraced garden. Most of the time the closest you are likely to get to it are the well-guarded gates on Orchard Rd, but the Istana is open to the public on selected public holidays, such as New Year's Day – call or check the website for details. If you are lucky enough to be in Singapore on one of these occasions, take your passport and join the queues to get in.

THE KING & 'EYESORE'

It's a question many visitors to the blissfully quiet and efficient Royal Thai Embassy on Orchard Rd quietly ask themselves. What on earth is it doing here? An ageing house that some consider an eyesore (we love it), surrounded by a lush compound on a prime spot on one of the most expensive real estate strips in Singapore? And why hasn't the Thai government sold the plot for the fortune it's undoubtedly worth?

The answer lies in history. The plot was bought for Thailand in 1893 for $9000 by the revered King Chulalongkorn (King Rama V), whose picture, as most visitors to Thailand will know, is hung in virtually every house and building in the country.

There has been talk of developing it for decades. The Thai government was reportedly offered $139 million for the plot in the late '90s, but turned it down. Thai Prime Minister Thaksin Shinawatra revived the idea of developing the site in 2003, but nothing has happened as yet and, since selling the plot would be seen as an affront to the great monarch's memory, it's likely to remain a delightful peculiarity for some time to come.

SINGAPORE BOTANIC GARDENS

Map pp226-7

☎ 6471 7361; www.sbg.org.sg; 1 Cluny Park Rd; admission free; 5am-midnight; Orchard MRT, then bus 7, 77, 123 or 174 from Orchard Blvd

You can't beat the Botanic Gardens as a spot to recover from your jet lag, have a picnic or just lie around forgetting you're in a large metropolis. Established around 1860 and covering 52 hectares, the gardens originally acted as a test ground for potential cash crops – such as rubber – and botanical research. Today they still host a herbarium housing more than 600,000 botanical specimens and a library with archival materials dating back to the 16th century.

Visitors can enjoy manicured garden beds or explore a four-hectare patch of 'original Singaporean jungle', a sample of the kind of forest that once covered the entire island – though **Bukit Timah Nature Reserve** (p77) and **MacRitchie Reservoir** (p78) give a more accurate picture of that. Still, it's worth taking one of the rainforest tours. They usually cost $15 for a group of up to 15 people, but call ahead because there are free tours at certain times.

Also don't miss the extraordinary **National Orchid Garden** (adult/child $5/free; 8.30am-7pm), one of the world's largest orchid displays featuring over 60,000 of these delicate-looking but incredibly hardy plants, including the vanda Miss Joaquim. This hybrid orchid, Singapore's national flower, was discovered in 1893 by Agnes Joaquim in her garden.

Singapore Botanic Gardens contain a couple of decent restaurants, **Au Jardin** (p114) and **Halia** (p115), and there are often open-air concerts at the impossibly genteel Symphony Lake, where a new shell-like stage in the centre of the water has been opened recently (if you want the ultimate posh night out combine one of these concerts with a meal at Au Jardin). Give the visitor centre a call for details of forthcoming events.

Walking is possible, but a little unpleasant in the heat, but buses are available.

TAN YEOK NEE HOUSE Map pp226-7

207 Clemenceau Ave; Dhoby Ghaut MRT

Near Orchard Rd, on the corner of Penang Rd, Tan Yeok Nee House was built in 1885 as the townhouse of a prosperous merchant, and is the sole surviving example in Singapore of a traditional Chinese mansion. Today it's part of the Asian campus of the University of Chicago Graduate School of Business, but you can still admire its fine roof decoration from outside.

EASTERN SINGAPORE

Eating p117; Shopping p161; Sleeping p176

A short distance east of the city centre are some of the city's oldest neighbourhoods. Geylang and Katong are both largely Malay districts rarely frequented by foreign visitors, partly because of their lack of obvious attractions. Geylang is as close to a 'Little Malaysia' as you'll find, a grubby, bustling district that has been the focal point of Malay culture since the 19th century when plantation labourers made it their home.

Camera shop, Lucky Plaza (p159)

It's not so obviously Malay these days, but is best known as the centre of Singapore's red-light activities.

Katong, centred around busy East Coast and Joo Chiat Rds, has strong Peranakan influences and offers some tasty dining and excellent shopping possibilities.

Stretching for several kilometres along the seafront, from the city right up to Tanah Merah, is East Coast Park, a popular recreational haunt and another good feeding and watering spot.

TRANSPORT

The East Coast is poorly served by the MRT network, which runs too far north of the seafront to be convenient. Aljunied and Paya Lebar are the closest MRT stations for Geylang Rd, the main shopping area in the district.

Bus 14 goes from Orchard Rd to East Coast Rd. To and from the Colonial District, buses 12 and 32 head into the city along North Bridge Rd.

To get to East Coast Park, you can get bus 401 from Bedok MRT, but only on weekends. At other times, you'll be forced to take a taxi ($10 to $12 from the city), or walk from East Coast Rd.

GEYLANG

Geylang is a Malay residential area, but you are not going to see traditional *atap* (thatched-roof) houses or any sarong-clad cottage industry workers here. The area consists of Singaporean high-rise, though there are some older shophouse buildings around, especially in the *lorongs* (alleys) that run off Geylang Rd, now home to one of Singapore's most notorious red-light districts.

Orientation

Geylang Rd runs from east to west, with small numbered side streets called *lorong* running off either side. The lower-numbered *lorong* are closer to the city, while the higher-numbered *lorong* are nearer to Katong. The even-numbered *lorong* are home to the red-light areas. At the eastern end of Geylang Rd is Geylang Serai, home to the dismal

Malay Cultural Village and the much more appealing hawker centre.

GEYLANG SERAI WET MARKET
Map p236

Geylang Serai; Paya Lebar MRT

For more atmosphere than the Malay village can ever hope to muster, duck into the nearby Geylang Serai Wet Market, hidden behind some older-style housing blocks on Geylang Rd. Its entrance is through a small lane that leads to a crowded, traditional Asian market, crammed with stalls selling food, fabrics and other wares. It reaches its peak of activity during Ramadan, when the whole area is alive with evening market stalls. Of course, as with many things in Singapore that attain a certain ageing charm, it's going to be torn down and replaced with a new multimillion-dollar market complex, complete with 'authentic' Malay designs.

MALAY CULTURAL VILLAGE Map p236

☎ 6748 4700; 39 Geylang Rd; adult/child $5/3; 🕐 10am-10pm; Paya Lebar MRT

While in the area you could check out the Malay Cultural Village, an attempt to recreate the kampong life that once dominated the area, but which has now almost completely disappeared from Singapore. This complex of traditional Malay-style houses was built as a showpiece of native culture, but to be frank it's a depressing failure. Hardly anybody visits and the fake kampong houses that were supposed to accommodate tourist shops stand largely unused. Entry is free, but there is a charge to visit the village attractions, like the small museum displaying a forgettable series of cultural artefacts. The Kampong Days display, a recreation of a traditional Malay house, is equally missable.

On weekends there are free dance displays near the food centre, which serves up Malay specialities that can easily be found elsewhere. Avoid.

KATONG

From the Geylang Serai Market you can head down Joo Chiat Rd to East Coast Rd and explore the Katong district. Joo Chiat Rd has a host of local daytime businesses, and at night the restaurants and music lounges are popular. Many Peranakan-style terraces remain intact, providing some atmosphere of old Singapore.

Joo Chiat Rd runs into the busy, traffic-plagued East Coast Rd, also noted for its Peranakan influence, mostly because of the opportunity to sample Peranakan food, also known as Nonya cuisine.

Heading west back to the city, just off East Coast Rd is the Hindu **Sri Senpaga Vinayagar Temple** (Map p236; Ceylon Rd), and about a kilometre away the **Sri Guru Nanak Sat Sangh Sabha Sikh temple** (Map p236; Wilkinson Rd). East Coast Rd changes its name to Mountbatten Rd where it crosses Tanjong Katong Rd, which leads back to Geylang and Paya Lebar MRT station. Around here and Mountbatten Rd you'll see a number of grand bungalows dating from the early 20th century.

AMOY TEA Map p236

331 Joo Chiat Rd; Paya Lebar MRT

Stop in at Amoy Tea, a traditional shop selling a variety of Chinese teas and superbly crafted tea sets.

KATONG ANTIQUE HOUSE Map p236

☎ 6345 1220; 208 East Coast Rd; 🕐 11am-6pm; bus 12, 14 or 32

Combining Peranakan food and culture is the Katong Antique House, where you can view a large collection of antiques including beautifully beaded slippers, wedding costumes and traditional ceramics and furniture. Call in advance and you can arrange to have tea ($10) or a meal (from $23) including Peranakan delicacies.

PERANAKAN TERRACE HOUSES
Map p236

Koon Seng Rd; Paya Lebar MRT

Just off Joo Chiat Rd you'll find some of the finest Peranakan terrace houses in Singapore. Exhibiting the typical Peranakan love of ornate design, they are decorated with stucco dragons, birds, crabs and brilliantly glazed tiles. *Pintu pagar* (saloon doors) at the front of the houses are another typical feature, allowing in breezes while retaining privacy. (For background information on the Peranakan people, see p14).

(Continued on page 75)

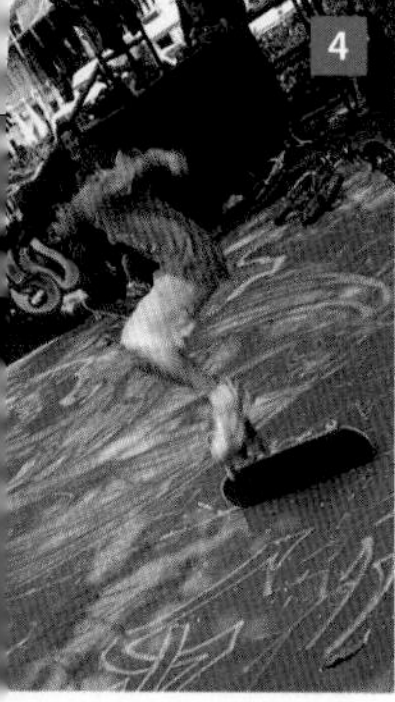

1 *Tekka Centre (p113), Little India* **2** *Hawker stalls, Chinatown (p56)* **3** *Peak hour at City Hall MRT (p49), Colonial District* **4** *National Youth Centre Skate Park (p50), near Orchard Rd*

1 Dalhousie Obelisk (p96), Colonial District **2** *Chinese opera performance, Chinese Theatre Circle (p131), Chinatown*
3 *Esplanade – Theatres on the Bay (p51), Colonial District*
4 *Shophouse architecture (p25), Kampong Glam*

1 *Sculpture detail, Sri Srinivasa Perumal Temple (p62), Little India* **2** *Jamae Mosque (p92), Chinatown* **3** *Thian Hock Keng Temple (p58), Chinatown* **4** *Wak Hai Cheng Bio Temple (p59), Chinatown*

1 *Bumboat on the Singapore River (p48)* **2** *Wax soldier at the entrance to the Battle Box (p52) in Fort Canning Park, Colonial District* **3** *Chijmes (p50), Colonial District* **4** *Raffles Hotel (p52), Colonial District*

1 *Traditional shop fronts and dwellings along Ann Siang Rd, Chinatown (p91)* **2** *Clifford Pier (p96), Marina Bay* **3** *Fullerton Hotel (p166), Colonial District* **4** *Hindu figures in the* gopuram *of Sri Mariamman Temple (p58), Chinatown*

1 *Shophouses on Kandahar St, Kampong Glam (p60)* **2** *A Jaffar Spices Centre (p146), Little India* **3** *Tekka Centre (p113), Little India* **4** *Sultan Mosque (p63), Kampong Glam*

1 National Orchid Garden (p64), Singapore Botanic Gardens **2** *Women's fashion display at Robinsons (p157) at Centrepoint, Orchard Rd* **3** *Hilton International (p174), Orchard Rd* **4** *Lucky Plaza (p159), Orchard Rd*

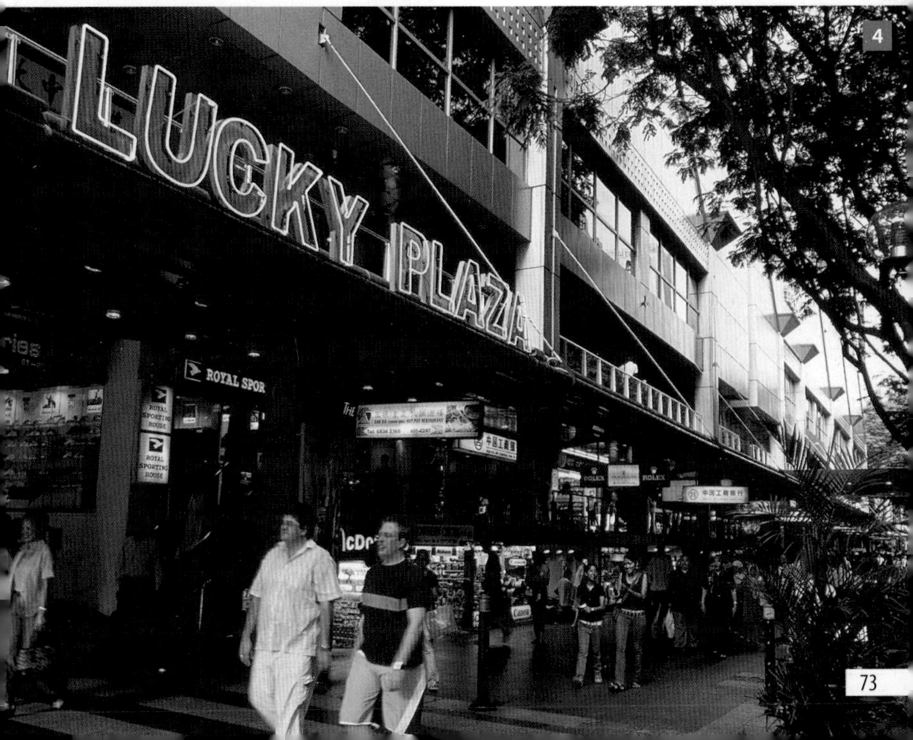

1 *Changi prison chapel (p75), Changi* **2** *East Coast Park (p75), eastern Singapore* **3** *Message board at Changi prison chapel* **4** *East Coast Park*

(Continued from page 66)

EAST COAST PARK

A thoroughly commendable use of reclaimed land, this 11km stretch of seafront park is one of Singapore's most pleasant urban escapes, where Singaporeans come in their thousands to swim, windsurf, kayak, picnic on the sand, bicycle, rollerblade and, of course, eat. The whole park has been superbly designed so that the surroundings constantly shift and change and the many leisure facilities don't crowd the green space. In this single, narrow strip, there are several bird sanctuaries, patches of unmanaged bushland, golf driving ranges, tennis courts, a resort, the Big Splash water park, several ponds and a lagoon, sea sports clubs, hawker centres and some excellent bars and restaurants.

Renting a bicycle (or rollerblades) and gently pedalling from one end to the other, enjoying the sea breezes, watching the veritable city of container ships out in the Strait and capping it off with a meal and a few beachfront beers is one of the most pleasant ways to spend a Singapore afternoon.

On weekends the park is packed and you can spend more time dodging other cycle track users than enjoying your surroundings, so try to visit on a weekday when it's much more sedate and enjoyable.

Bicycle/rollerblade rental stations are located at four points along the park. Rentals cost about $6 to $8.

Orientation

The East Coast Park starts at the end of Tanjong Katong Rd in Katong and ends at the National Sailing Centre in Bedok, which is actually nearer to Tanah Merah MRT. At the western end of the park, the bicycle track continues right through to Geylang, ending at the Kallang River.

MARINE COVE RECREATION CENTRE Map p236

East Coast Park Service Rd; bus 401 from Bedok MRT station (weekends only), taxi from Bedok MRT ($4-5) or the city ($8) on weekdays

Midway along the park, near the end of Still Rd South, this outdoor leisure complex has tenpin bowling, squash, crazy golf and a large selection of restaurants, food stalls and bars, plus a McDonald's. On the beach side of the complex there are a couple of bicycle/rollerblade rental stations and a kayak/sailboat rental place on the beach itself. The Big Splash water fun park, with swimming pools and a huge waterslide, is a short walk to the west. For details of where to rent sailboards and laser-class boats, see p137.

CHANGI & PASIR RIS

These 'remote' neighbourhoods at the extreme east of the island are classic modern heartlands Singapore. Once, these areas were dominated by Malay kampong (villages). The stilted houses are long gone, replaced by modern housing estates and reclamation projects, but the area, particularly Pasir Ris, still has a pleasant atmosphere, with manicured lawns, ma-and-pa stores and attractive seafront parks. Here's where you'll find the moving Changi Prison Museum & Chapel site, a few resorts and theme parks for the kids, a sprinkling of malls and the giant space-age Expo centre.

At Changi Village you'll also find the ferry terminal for bumboats to Pulau Ubin (p181) and Johor in Malaysia.

CHANGI PRISON MUSEUM & CHAPEL Map pp222-3

☎ 6214 2451; www.changimuseum.com; 1000 Upper Changi Rd North; admission free; 9.30am-5pm; bus 2

A steady stream of visitors make their way to this quietly moving museum commemorating the Allied POWs who were captured, imprisoned and suffered horrific treatment at the hands of the invading Japanese forces during WWII. It was shifted from the original Changi prison site in 2001 when Singapore Prisons reclaimed the land to expand its operations.

TRANSPORT

Pasir Ris is easily reachable by MRT – it's at the end of the East West Line. From the station, all the attractions are within easy walking distance. To get to Changi, get off the train at Tanah Merah MRT and hop on bus 2, which will take you to both the Changi Chapel and Changi Village, which is the end of the line.

A taxi from the city to either area costs about $15.

Former POWs, veterans and historians will feel the loss of the actual site most keenly, but to the architects' credit the understated design of the new building is well suited to its dual role as a shrine and history museum. The square white façade is reminiscent of a concrete bunker, yet the greenery hints at healing and renewal. The gaping entrance and open plan suggest accessibility. The museum's centrepiece is a replica of the original Changi Chapel built by inmates as a focus for worship and presumably as a sign of solidarity. Tucked into the walls beside the altar, with its cross made of ammunitions casings, are little mementos left by visitors – white crosses, red poppies, fresh flowers and handwritten notes. Services are held on Sundays (9.30am and 5.30pm), but the shadeless courtyard heats up like an oven.

In keeping with the memorial theme the exhibits are strictly low-key and the story of Changi and wartime suffering in Singapore is told poignantly through photographs, artefacts and survivors' testimonials. You can also view full-sized replicas of the famous **Changi murals** painted by POW Stanley Warren in the old POW hospital. The originals are off-limits in what is now Block 151 of the nearby Changi army camp. Reading James Clavell's *King Rat* (Clavell was a POW at Changi) before you visit will lend an added poignancy to your trip. Guided tours cost $6.

The original walls and clocktower of the Changi prison camp were finally torn down in 2004, a wrenching experience for some, though a section has been preserved as a memorial. Happily, parts of the clocktower, cell doors, windows and sections of the wall have been claimed and retained by various interested parties and are now displayed in Australia, New Zealand and the UK. The British High Commission in Singapore has a piece on its lawn.

Bus 2 from Victoria St or Tanah Merah MRT will take you past the entrance. Get off at bus stop B09, just after the Changi Heights condominium. The bus terminates at Changi Village.

Changi Village

On the far northeast coast of Singapore, Changi Village is an escape from the hubbub of central Singapore. The buildings are modern (although there are some interesting old 'black-and-white' bungalows along Loyang Ave), but there's still a village atmosphere with the lively and quite renowned hawker centre next to the bus terminus being a focal point. There's a small, attractive beachfront camp site across the Changi Creek from the bus terminal, where you can watch the planes gliding into Changi airport while relaxing on the imported sand. It's popular on weekends but almost deserted during the week. You might want to avoid swimming here though.

Changi's beach is where thousands of Singaporean civilians were executed by the Japanese during WWII. A memorial marks the site.

Next to the bus terminal is the Changi Point Ferry Terminal, where you can catch bumboats to Pulau Ubin (p181) or Johor.

In the evenings, Changi Village is a notorious cruising spot for transvestites.

ESCAPE THEME PARK Map pp222-3

☎ 6581 9112; www.escapethemepark.com.sg; adult/child $16.50/8.30; 🕑 10am-10pm Sat, Sun & school holidays; bus 354 from Pasir Ris MRT

Next to NTUC Lifestyle World, the fairground attractions and thrill rides here are showing their age (when we went, several rides were shut for repair), but unless your kids are very theme park–savvy they won't be complaining. Highlights are the large, rusty and slightly terrifying Wet & Wild flume, the pitch-dark Alpha 8 rollercoaster, the stomach-churning Revolution and the winding Daytona Go-Kart track. On hot days the place can be a furnace, so bring protection.

PASIR RIS PARK Map pp222-3

Pasir Ris Dr 3; Pasir Ris MRT

Stretching along a couple of kilometres of the northeast coast, a short walk from Pasir Ris MRT station, this peaceful place is the third-largest park in Singapore and certainly among the best. There's a surprising variety of attractions here, including a maze garden, adventure playground and sea fishing for kids; fish ponds; bicycle, rollerblade and kayak rentals; and a pristine five-hectare mangrove swamp, complete with boardwalks and signboards describing the ecology of the area, and large observatory tower for bird-watchers.

Another attraction is the popular **Fisherman's Village** (☎ 6585 1211) collection of seafood restaurants, where you can catch your own fish for dinner. It's a bit overpriced, but the beachfront location is superb.

WILD WILD WET Map pp222-3

☎ 6581 9135; www.wildwildwet.com; adult/child $12.90/8.80; ⌚ 1-7pm Mon & Wed-Fri, 10am-8pm Sat, Sun & school holidays; bus 354 from Pasir Ris MRT

Part of the same Downtown East complex occupied by Escape Theme Park, this water fun park is a great day out for families, with waterslides, a wave pool, a raft ride (lots of fun) and various activity areas for kids, encircled by a 350m river. Best of all is the fearsome Slide-Up, which involves packing two people face-to-face into a rubber dinghy and pushing them down a near-vertical three-storey-high half pipe (try not to be the one going backwards). The park uses a handy cashless system in which you carry a pre-paid card around your wrist.

NORTHERN & CENTRAL SINGAPORE

Eating p119; Shopping p161

Even the shortest drive through the central and northern areas of the island is enough to dispel any notion of Singapore as a purely urban city. Yes, there is never-ending construction and land reclamation, but Singapore also has an astonishing variety of green spaces, from the many delightful city parks to large nature reserves and forests. Apart from Rio de Janeiro, it is the only city in the world that retains an area of primary rainforest, in the form of Bukit Timah Nature Reserve. Just 15 minutes from Orchard Rd, you could be standing next to a centuries-old tree surrounded by macaque monkeys and monitor lizards, with not a mall or high-rise apartment building in sight.

There is no shortage of options up here and some of the highlights are the Singapore Zoological Gardens and wonderful night safari; Bukit Timah Nature Reserve and the MacRitchie Reservoir (see p97); and for the more hardcore nature lover, the Sungei Buloh Wetland Reserve.

The area is also home to Singapore's largest Buddhist temple complex: the Kong Meng San Phor Kark See Monastery.

BUKIT TIMAH NATURE RESERVE Map pp222-3

☎ information desk 1800 468 5736; www.nparks.gov.sg; ⌚ 8.30am-6pm; bus 65, 170, 75 or 171

The only area of primary forest remaining in Singapore, this 164-hectare nature reserve offers a range of nature walks, testing jungle treks and even mountain-bike trails. It's a haven for plants (one naturalist estimated there are more species here than in the whole of North America) and 160 species of animals. It also boasts the highest point on the island, Bukit Timah (163m), though the dense foliage doesn't afford much of a view.

The most popular and easiest walk in the park is along a paved road to the top of Bukit Timah. Even during the week it attracts a number of walkers, but few venture off the pavement to explore the side trails, which are more interesting. For a distinctly out-of-Singapore experience, try the North View, South View or Fern Valley paths. These involve some scrambling over rocks and tree roots and can be quite testing in parts.

Pick up a map of the park's trails from the **Visitor Centre** (⌚ 8.30-6pm), where an exhibition details the various flora and fauna that can be found in the reserve. A small shop here sells drinks, snacks, guidebooks and the all-important mosquito repellent.

Bukit Timah has two challenging mountain-bike trails, 6km in all, running around the edge of the nature reserve between Chestnut Ave and Rifle Range Rd. The trails cut though jungle and abandoned quarry sites and are hilly in parts. There's also a bike trail running through the neighbouring Central Catchment Nature Reserve to the MacRitchie Reservoir, 6km east.

Several buses run close to the park, including buses 65 and 170 from Newton MRT, bus 75 from the CBD and Chinatown, and bus 171 from the YMCA on Orchard Rd or from Scotts Rd. Get off at the Bukit

TRANSPORT

Central Singapore is encircled by the North South Line of the MRT network and while none of the stops are particularly close to any of the nature reserves, they'll get you close enough to limit your taxi costs. The area is also threaded with expressways, which means getting there by taxi from the city is only a matter of minutes.

Timah Shopping Centre; the entrance to the park is about 1km north along Hindhede Dr.

CENTRAL CATCHMENT NATURE RESERVE Map pp222-3

bus 162

Encompassing the MacRitchie and Lower and Upper Peirce Reservoir parks, this 2000-hectare area is Singapore's largest nature reserve. The area is crisscrossed by a series of trails, ranging from short boardwalks around the reservoirs to long treks through the forest. The most popular entry point to this precious wilderness is the MacRitchie Reservoir, a delightful, partly manicured park wrapped around the water's edge, where you can rent a kayak (see p135), and get a bite to eat at the small hilltop food centre overlooking the water and a bizarre zigzagging pontoon bridge. It's also the starting point for some fairly arduous forest walks (see p97). To get here, take bus 162 from Orchard Blvd or Scotts Rd and get off at the reservoir entrance at the top of Thompson Rd.

KONG MENG SAN PHOR KARK SEE MONASTERY Map pp222-3

☎ 6453 4046; http://kmspks.org; 88 Bright Hill Dr; 🕑 7am-6pm; bus 410

A fascinating couple of hours can be had exploring this monastery and temple complex, Singapore's largest. Founded in 1921, the monastery's main function is as a crematorium (see The Buddhist Way of Death, p80), which is huge. There are also several monumental halls housing various guises of the Buddha. A highlight is the Pagoda of 10,000 Buddhas, with its golden cone-shaped stupa lined on the inside with 9999 Buddha images – the 10,000th Buddha is the giant one inside the pagoda.

For a few weeks every year during April's Qing Ming festival, the monastery swarms with Chinese families paying respect to their ancestors and cleaning their tombs.

Call in advance if you want to arrange a guided tour of the complex.

Free vegetarian meals are served in the refectory, but they are supposed to be for the needy, not tourists. On the 27th of each month an informal flea market is held in the monastery's grounds.

Opposite the monastery is Singapore's largest park, **Bishan Park**, the northern section of which is a beautiful, quiet spot with a series of linked ponds spanned by small wooden Japanese-style bridges, immaculately kept gardens and a delightful ornamental lily pond. An outdoor café called **Explorer Zone** is next to the park entrance north of the temple and is a perfect spot for a pond-side lunch or dinner.

Bus 410 runs here from behind the Junction 8 shopping centre above Bishan MRT station.

KRANJI WAR MEMORIAL Map pp222-3

☎ 6269 6158; 9 Woodlands Rd; admission free; 🕑 24hr; Kranji MRT or bus 170

Near the Causeway off Woodlands Rd, the Kranji War Memorial includes the graves of thousands of Allied troops who died in the region during WWII. The walls are inscribed with the names of 24,346 men and women, and registers, stored inside unlocked, weatherproof stands, are available for inspection. The memorial can be reached by bus 170 from Rochor Rd, or it's about 10 minutes' walk from Kranji MRT station.

MANDAI ORCHID GARDENS Map pp222-3

☎ 6269 1036; Mandai Lake Rd; adult/child \$2/50¢; 🕑 8.30am-5.30pm; bus 138 from Ang Mo Kio MRT

Singapore has a major business in cultivating orchids, and the Mandai Orchid Gardens, a short walk from the zoo (or one stop on bus 138), is one of the best places to see them (with four solid hectares of orchids) though nonenthusiasts might find there's little to hold their attention. You can arrange to have a gift box of fresh orchids flown to just about anywhere in the world. To get here see the Singapore Zoo section, following.

SINGAPORE ZOOLOGICAL GARDENS & NIGHT SAFARI Map pp222-3

☎ 6269 3411; www.zoo.com.sg; 80 Mandai Lake Rd; adult/child \$14/7; 🕑 8.30am-6pm; bus 138 from Ang Mo Kio MRT

In the far north of the island, Singapore's world-class zoo has 3600 animals, representing 410 species including endangered white rhino, Bengal white tigers and even polar bears. Wherever possible, moats replace bars, and the zoo is beautifully spread out over 28 hectares of lush greenery beside the Upper Seletar Reservoir. As far as zoos go, this is one of the best. Some of the animal shows might be a little circus-like, like the elephant rides and the sea lion performance, but most are magnificent – particularly the white tiger, elephant, crocodile and, best of all, baboon enclosures. Feeding times are well staggered to allow you to catch most of them as you walk around.

It's also possible to get up close to a number of animals, including an otter, a reticulated python and one of the zoo's famous orang-utans at the Jungle Breakfast or Tea (breakfast per adult/child $15.45/11.33, tea $13/10.30) at 9am and 4pm respectively.

There are trams (adult/child $4/2) that shuttle you around if it's too hot, or you're too lazy.

Next door, but completely separate from the zoo, is the acclaimed **Night Safari** (☎ 7269 3412; www.nightsafari.com.sg; adult/child $18/9; 7.30pm-midnight), which many people count as the highlight of their trip to Singapore. This 40-hectare forested park allows you to view 120 different species of animals, including tigers, lions and leopards. In the darkness the moats and other barriers seem to melt away and it actually looks like these creatures could walk over and take a bite out of you. The atmosphere is heightened even further by the herds of strolling antelope, which often pass within inches of the electric trams that are available to take you around. For an even creepier experience, walk through the enclosed Mangrove Walk, where bats flap around your head and dangle from trees a few feet above your head.

You are asked not to use a flash on your camera since they disturb the animals and annoy fellow visitors.

Singapore Zoological Gardens (opposite)

As well as exploring the park on foot, it is worth taking the night safari tram tour (adult/child $6/3), which lasts about 45 minutes and also has a live commentary. Expect queues since it's very popular.

You can save a bit of money with a combined zoo and night safari ticket (adult/child $25/12.50) – but specify when you buy this whether you want to view both parks on the same day or different days. Both parks have plenty of decent food outlets (plus the usual junk) and the zoo boasts award-winning, clean and creatively designed 'outdoor' toilets!

When returning from the night safari you should catch a bus at around 10.45pm to ensure you make the last train leaving Ang Mo Kio at 11.28pm. A taxi to or from the city centre costs around $15; there is a taxi stand at the zoo entrance, though queues are often long and taxis can be maddeningly infrequent.

SIONG LIM TEMPLE Map pp222-3

☎ 6259 6924; 184E Jalan Toa Payoh; 7am-5pm; Toa Payoh MRT or bus 238

Nestled in a corner of the Toa Payoh HDB estate is Siong Lim Temple, also known as Lian Shan Shuang Lin Monastery (Twin Groves of the Lotus Mountain). The original buildings date from 1912 and the main hall is wonderfully atmospheric – a towering space stained by decades of incense smoke and perpetually buzzing with visitors. The adjoining complex of newer temples is also beautifully decorated and surrounded by neatly clipped bonsai. Sadly the ambience is ruined somewhat by traffic thundering by on the expressway.

You can walk to the temple – it's about 1km east of Toa Payoh MRT station – or take one of several buses for three stops from Toa Payoh bus interchange.

SUN YAT SEN NANYANG MEMORIAL HALL Map pp222-3

☎ 6256 7377; www.wanqingyuan.com.sg/english; 12 Tai Gin Rd; admission $3; 9am-5pm Tue-Sun, closes 6pm Sat; Toa Payoh MRT or bus 145

This national monument, built in the 1880s, was the headquarters of Dr Sun Yat Sen's Chinese Revolutionary Alliance in Southeast Asia, which led to the overthrow of the Qing dynasty and the creation of the first Chinese republic. Dr Sun Yat Sen briefly stayed in

THE BUDDHIST WAY OF DEATH

Sago St in Chinatown used to be full of death houses – places where the sick and old would go to end their days, as to die at home was regarded as inauspicious. Coffin makers and funeral parlours occupied premises on the street level, along with places selling paper effigies and wreaths made of frangipani flowers.

Now, of course, these places have disappeared and Sago St is better known for its cake and confectionery shops.

The last resting place for tens of thousands of Singaporeans is a niche in the columbarium (a repository for cremation urns) of Kong Meng San Phor Kark See Monastery in Bishan. Here is one of Singapore's main crematoriums, where you can see the full rights of a Buddhist funeral ceremony any day of the week.

In the crematorium five ovens stand side by side and it's not uncommon for several funeral ceremonies to be conducted at the same time, with nothing separating the grieving families and the chanting monks of each party but a few metres' space between the stainless-steel biers. Once the body has passed into the furnace it will take 1½ hours for it to be reduced to ashes, during which time the family usually retires home or to a separate hall for the wake.

In the past, the wakes went on for 49 days; now they are restricted by legislation to seven.

When ready, the steaming ashes are brought out for the family's inspection and the largest pieces of bone are picked out and placed in yellow earthenware caskets. The caskets are sealed, signed with the deceased's name and embossed with their black-and-white photograph before being placed in one of the halls of the adjoining columbarium.

The caskets lie in neat towering ranks, just like the rows of HDB flats that the dead more than likely occupied during their lives. For those associated with the monastery and with more cash to spare (the average funeral costs well into five figures), fancier niches are available; these are the gold labelled ones, closest to the shrine of Bodhisattvas.

the house, which was donated to the Alliance by a wealthy Chinese businessman, while touring Asia to whip up support for the cause. It's a fine example of a colonial Victorian villa and houses a museum with items pertaining to Dr Sun's life and work. A magnificent 60m-long bronze relief depicting the defining moments in Singapore's history runs the length of one wall in the garden.

Next door is the **Sasanaramsi Burmese Buddhist Temple** (14 Tai Gin Rd; 6.30am-9pm), a towering building guarded by two *chinthes* (half-lion, half-griffin figures).

Bus 145 from Toa Payoh bus interchange stops on Balestier Rd near the villa and temple.

SUNGEI BULOH WETLAND RESERVE Map pp222-3

☎ 6794 1401; www.sbwr.org.sg; 301 Neo Tiew Cres; adult/child $1/50¢; 7.30am-7pm Mon-Fri, 7am-7pm Sat & Sun; bus 925 TIBS from Kranji MRT

This 87-hectare wetland nature reserve, situated in the far northwest of the island overlooking the Strait of Johor, is home to 140 species of birds, most of which are migratory. It has been formally declared a nature reserve by the government and recognised as a migratory bird sanctuary of international importance. From the visitors centre, with its well-presented displays, trails lead around ponds and mangrove swamps to small hides, where you can observe the birds and, sometimes, massive monitor lizards. The birdlife, rather than the walks, is the main reason to visit (the best time for viewing them is before 10am).

Free guided tours begin at 9am, 10am, 3pm and 4pm on Saturdays. On other days, tours have to be pre-booked and cost $50 per group, though they claim you need to book a month in advance. Audiovisual shows on the park's flora and fauna are held at 9am, 11am, 1pm, 3pm and 5pm (hourly between 9am and 5pm on Sunday). Allow yourself three hours to do the park justice.

On weekdays, the bus stops at the carpark a 15-minute walk from the park. On weekends, the bus goes right to the park entrance.

SOUTHERN & WESTERN SINGAPORE

Eating p119; Shopping p162

Western Singapore is a mass of contradictions. It's the engine room of the country's economic success and home to the huge, if slowly declining, manufacturing industry. At the same time, it's also full of greenery.

It boasts an entire island devoted to heavy industry, yet another island nearby, Sentosa, is Singapore's centrepiece tourist attraction. And though the area bristles with Housing Board tower blocks and industrial estates, it has the largest number of specialised attractions for kids of any district in Singapore.

Hence, not far from the unnerving spires of the Jurong Island chemical plants and oil refineries, you have the magnificent Jurong BirdPark, Singapore Science Centre, Snow City and Singapore Discovery Centre and the outlandishly tasteless Haw Par Villa, plus a few interesting WWII sites. Not far from these is the phenomenon of Sentosa, the ever-changing and ever-developing resort and leisure island that attracts millions of visitors every year, which is connected to the mainland by a bridge and a memorable cable car; see p85 for more on Sentosa.

CHINESE & JAPANESE GARDENS Map pp222-3

☎ 6261 3632; 1 Chinese Garden Rd; admission free; ⌚ 6am-10pm Mon-Fri, 6am-11pm Sat & Sun; Chinese Garden MRT

These spacious gardens, which occupy 13½ hectares in the vicinity of Jurong Lake, are a very pleasant place for an afternoon stroll, though by themselves they are not worth the trek from the city.

The Chinese Garden is actually an island containing a number of Chinese-style pavilions and a seven-storey pagoda providing a great view. Apart from the pavilions, there is an extensive and impressive *penjing* (Chinese bonsai) display, as well as some more of those spectacularly clean 'outdoor' public toilets that seem to be catching on all over Singapore.

Inside the large compound near the bonsai display is an unusual **Live Turtle & Tortoise Museum** (adult/child $5/3; ⌚ 10am-7pm), where, among other things, you can see a live two-headed, six-legged turtle – one of the few in the world ever to have survived – and a large pond literally teeming with the little, one-headed fellows.

Don't bother with the Japanese Gardens, which have fallen into abject disrepair, though vague promises of restoration have been made.

The gardens are a five-minute walk on a pedestrian path from Chinese Garden MRT station.

TRANSPORT

Most of the attractions in western Singapore are within easy reach of Jurong East MRT station, which lies near the western end of the East West Line. A cab ride out here from the city will cost around $12. Alternatively, take bus 502 from Orchard Blvd (behind Orchard MRT). Sentosa is easily reached via the Harbour Front MRT station, from where you can get the Sentosa bus, or the cable car.

HAW PAR VILLA Map pp222-3

☎ 6872 2780; 262 Pasir Panjang Rd; admission free; ⌚ 9am-7pm; bus 200 from Buona Vista MRT, bus 10, 30 or 188 from HarbourFront MRT

'What I have in mind will be unique, like nothing anybody has seen,' said Aw Boon Haw, one of the brothers behind the Tiger Balm miracle-ointment fortune, who stumped up over $1 million in the 1930s to build this tacky, unbelievably kitsch Chinese mythology theme park. It certainly is unique. You've never seen anything like it (and may never want to again), but though it's depressingly rundown, the '10 courts of hell' alone make it thoroughly worthwhile. This cave-like enclosure sits inside the body of a giant dragon and displays a series of graphic, bloody tableau depicting the hideous tortures awaiting a multitude of sinners in Buddhist Hell, before they are carted off to have their memories erased and are sent back to earth to try again. Spooky tours are run here on Friday and Saturday evenings; call ☎ 6872 2003 for details.

HOLLAND VILLAGE Map pp222-3

Buona Vista MRT, bus 7, 105 or 106 from Penang Rd or Orchard Blvd

This popular expat enclave, a short bus ride from the Botanical Gardens, is best known for its host of fashionable restaurants and cafés concentrated on Lorong Mambong just back from the main road. Also popular are the arts and craft shops inside the **Holland Road Shopping Centre** (p162), which are home to some genuinely excellent, though very pricey, antiques and art, as well as some New Age wares that promise to help you throw off the shackles of materialism for twice the going rate. Opposite the Lorong Mambong restaurant strip is a surprisingly (and appealingly) unkempt market selling fruit and veg, meat and fish. No doubt it'll be torn down and renovated soon. On the other side of Holland Ave, Jalan Merah Saga looks like a Sydney suburb; a strip of classy cafés, galleries, restaurants, suburban homes and condos populated largely by expat families.

Buona Vista MRT station is about a 15-minute walk along Buona Vista Rd from Holland Village.

JURONG BIRDPARK Map pp222-3

☎ 6265 0022; www.birdpark.com.sg; 2 Jurong Hill; adult/child $14/7; 🕑 8am-6pm; bus 194 or 251 from Boon Lay MRT

Over 8000 birds representing around 600 species can be seen at this beautifully landscaped 20-hectare park, which is fun to visit even if you're only mildly interested in our feathered friends. Highlights include the walk-through Waterfall Aviary (with its 30m-high custom-made waterfall, the highest in Southeast Asia); the Penguin Parade, which simulates a slice of Antarctica; a lake with pink flamingos; the fascinating Pelican Cove enclosure featuring some massive specimens; and an underwater viewing gallery where you can watch the birds catch fish. There's also the World of Darkness, in which day and night have been reversed to allow visitors a look at nocturnal birds doing something other than sleeping. A monorail (adult/child $4/2) will transport you around it all.

As with the zoo (which is run by the same management) there are bird shows at various times during the day, kicking off with the 'breakfast with the birds' show (adult/child $18/12, from 9am to 10.30am) and including the birds of prey show, starting at 10am.

If you're planning to visit the Singapore Zoo and Night Safari as well (and you should be), you can buy an all-inclusive ticket that gets you entrance to all three (adult/child $30/15), though it doesn't include the Night Safari tram ride.

JURONG REPTILE PARK Map pp222-3

☎ 6261 8866; 241 Jalan Ahmad Ibrahim; adult/child $8/7.50; 🕑 9am-6pm; bus 194 or 251 from Boon Lay MRT

Across the car park from the BirdPark, this recently upgraded reptilian theme park makes an entertaining add-on to the BirdPark. Crocodiles are the star attraction here, although there's also a scaly collection of other reptiles and amphibians, including giant tortoises, arapaima fish and large snakes, which are available for the inevitable 'snake around the neck' photo opportunities. The reptile show (held 11.45am and 2pm daily) showcases the skills of croc handlers, and afterwards you can have your photo taken ($5) with a tiny croc. Croc feeding takes place at 10.30am and 5pm daily.

MING VILLAGE & PEWTER MUSEUM Map pp222-3

☎ 6265 7711; 32 Pandan Rd; admission free; 🕑 9am-5.30pm; shuttle service

Reproduction Ming and Qing dynasty pottery is made in this workshop, where you can watch the craftspeople at work. The complete production process is done on the premises and guided tours are available.

Ming Village is owned by Royal Selangor Pewter, whose products are on sale on Orchard Rd's Centrepoint and Takashimaya department stores. There's also a small pewter museum here with some interesting pieces. The pewter is made in Malaysia, but the polishing and hand-beaten designs are demonstrated at the village. The showroom sells an extensive selection of pewter as well as porcelain.

The company runs a free shuttle service from Orchard, Mandarin, Raffles and Pan Pacific Hotels daily from 9.20am; enquire with the hotel concierges.

MT FABER PARK Map pp224-5

cable car from HarbourFront MRT

Off Kampong Bahru Rd, 116m-high Mt Faber forms the centre point of Mt Faber Park, one of the oldest parks in Singapore. The hillside slopes, covered with secondary rainforest, offer some fine views over the harbour and central Singapore, and on the hike up here you'll catch glimpses of colonial-era black-and-white bungalows and the strikingly stripy **Danish Seaman's Mission** built in 1909. It's a steep, sweaty walk to the top, so if this sounds unappealing the **cable car** (☎ 6270 8855; adult/child $8.90/3.90; 🕑 8.30am-9pm) might be a better option. It connects the World Trade Centre, next to HarbourFront MRT, with the summit and Sentosa Island.

At and around the summit are a number of red-brick paths through manicured gardens, pavilions, look-out points and, beside the distinctly tacky souvenir shop, a cafeteria with fantastic views over the Singapore Strait and onward to the Indonesian Riau Islands.

At the time of writing, a massive $8-million revamp of the Mt Faber hilltop was in progress. The cable car station was set to be transformed into a glass-fronted dining and entertainment centre called the Jewel Box, boasting a ballroom, look-out points, chairlifts and even harbour-view toilets!

NUS MUSEUMS Map pp222-3

☎ 6874 4616; www.nus.edu.sg/museums; 50 Kent Ridge Cres; admission free; 🕑 9am-5pm Mon-Sat; bus 95 from Buona Vista MRT

On the campus of the National University of Singapore (NUS), these three small but exquisite art museums all hold fine collections. On the ground floor is the **Lee Kong Chian Art Museum** with works spanning 7000 years of Chinese culture, from ancient ceramics to modern paintings done in traditional style.

The concourse level houses the **South & Southeast Asian Gallery**, showing a mixture of art from across the region, including textiles and sculptures. On the top level is the **Ng Eng Teng Gallery**, which displays the paintings, drawings and sculptures of Ng Eng Teng (1934–2001), one of Singapore's foremost artists specialising in imaginative, sometimes surreal, depictions of the body.

While you're in the area, be sure to make the time to pop into the **Raffles Museum of Biodiversity Research** (right) too.

OMNI-THEATRE Map pp222-3

☎ 6425 2500; adult/child $10/5; Jurong East MRT

An essential part of any trip to the Science Centre, this vast domed cinema is an unforgettable experience, showing short 15- to 20-minute movies on anything from African wildlife to space exploration and simulated thrill rides, on a huge screen that envelopes you on your reclining seat. The sound quality is magnificent. It's also worth taking a moment to examine the bizarrely complex Sputnik-like device that projects the images onto the screen.

RAFFLES MUSEUM OF BIODIVERSITY RESEARCH Map pp222-3

☎ 6874 5082; http://rmbr.nus.edu.sg; Block 56, Level 3, NUS Faculty of Science, Science Dr 2, Lower Kent Ridge Rd; admission free; 🕑 9am-5pm Mon-Fri, 9am-1pm Sat; bus 95 from Buona Vista MRT

One of the oddities you often find tucked away in unexpected corners, this small but fascinating museum in the National University of Singapore campus honours Sir Stamford Raffles' less recognised work as a naturalist. The collection of zoological specimens was proposed by Raffles in 1823 and completed in 1849 as part of the Raffles Museum. There are stuffed and preserved examples of some rare and locally extinct creatures, including a tiger, a leopard, a huge elephant's leg bone, a slightly creepy preserved banded leaf monkey, a huge king cobra killed recently at the Singapore Country Club, a crocodile skull and a massive, frankly terrifying, Japanese spider crab.

The museum is not exactly on the tourist trail, but it's well worth the extra effort to get here, especially if you combine it with the **NUS Museums** (left) nearby. Kids will be happily spooked by some of the exhibits and if you still subscribe to the sterile Singapore myth, take a look at some of the snakes that still slither around the island.

REFLECTIONS AT BUKIT CHANDU Map pp222-3

☎ 6375 2510; www.s1942.org.sg; 31K Pepys Rd; admission $2; 🕑 9am-5pm Tue-Sun; bus 10, 30, 51 or 143

Atop Bukit Chandu (Opium Hill) in Kent Ridge Park, this 'WWII interpretive centre' based in an old renovated villa is a worthwhile and moving memorial. Its focus is the brave sacrifice made by the 1st and 2nd Battalions of the Malay Regiment defending the hill in the Battle of Pasir Panjang when the Japanese invaded in 1942. The battalion was all but wiped out when, facing 13,000 Japanese soldiers, they decided to make a stand. Hi-tech displays, using films from the period and audio effects to transport you to the scene of the battle, are all quite evocative. It's also possible to hold the kind of rifles and wear the heavy iron helmets those soldiers wore in the 'Hands-On' room.

DOWN ON THE FARM

Believe it or not, there are about a dozen farms in Singapore, rearing and growing hydroponic vegetables, frogs, birds, goats, bees, eggs, fish and orchids. They are mostly concentrated around the Choa Chu Kang area and all of them are open to visits from the public. Kids in particular might find them fascinating and, what's more, they're nearly all free.

The following lists some of the most interesting:

Avifauna Bird Farm (Map pp222-3; ☎ 6794 0197; 2 Lim Chu Kang Lane; admission $2; 🕑 10am-4.30pm Sat & Sun) One of the largest exotic bird breeding and research farms in Southeast Asia. Take bus 175 from Choa Chu Kang MRT.

Farmart Centre (Map pp222-3; ☎ 6767 0070; 67 Sungei Tangah Rd; 🕑 10am-7pm) A one-stop showcase of small farms, including bees, goats, quails, ornamental fish, herbs and frogs. Take the free shuttle bus from Choa Chu Kang MRT. You pay according to what you want to see.

Qian Hu Fish Farm (Map pp222-3; ☎ 6766 7087; 71 Jalan Lekar; admission free; 🕑 9am-6pm Mon-Thu, 9am-7pm Fri-Sun) A very modern farm breeding more than 200 species of exotic ornamental fish for sale, with an attached café. Take bus 172 or 175 from Choa Chu Kang and walk from the junction of Old Choa Chu Kang Rd and Jalan Lekar.

Jurong Frog Farm (Map pp222-3; ☎ 6791 7229; 56 Lim Chu Kang Lane 6; 🕑 7am-6pm) Breeding station for bullfrogs, sold for their meat and medicinal value. A taxi from Choa Chu Kang MRT should cost around $4.

Hay Dairies Goat Farm (Map pp222-3; ☎ 6792 0931; 3 Lim Chu Kang Lane 4; 🕑 9am-4pm) Goats bred for milking. Demonstrations and tours take place in the morning and cost $3, including a free bottle of goat's milk. Take bus 175 from Choa Chu Kang MRT and get off at Lim Chu Kang Lane 4. It's a three-minute walk from there.

Orchidville (Map pp222-3; ☎ 6552 5246; Lot MD1A Lorong Lada Hitam; 🕑 8am-8.30pm) Massive orchid farm with more than two million specimens for sale. Education programmes also available. Take bus 138 from Ang Mo Kio MRT and get off at Stop B13 on Mandai Rd.

It's worth staying on to explore **Kent Ridge Park**, which enjoys refreshing sea breezes and some great views over the Singapore Strait. There is also a memorial to the Battle for Pasir Panjang, a tank and a pair of artillery guns on display, a nature trail and a couple of ponds filled with fish and terrapins.

The nearest bus stops are on Pasir Panjang Rd, from where it's a steep hike up the hill. A taxi from the nearest MRT station at Queenstown should not cost more than $6.

SINGAPORE DISCOVERY CENTRE Map pp222-3

☎ 6792 6188; www.sdc.com.sg; 510 Upper Jurong Rd; adult/child $9/5; 🕑 9am-7pm Tue-Sun; bus 192 or 193 from Boon Lay MRT

This family-oriented centre is a thinly veiled promo for Singapore's defence programme (see Do Mention the War, p42), peppered up with interactive robots, a motion simulator ride and **iWERKS** (adult/child $8/5), a five-storey-high movie theatre that occasionally shows 3-D films.

Because it's well off the beaten track in west Jurong, unless you have particularly restless kids, it can safely be skipped.

SINGAPORE SCIENCE CENTRE Map pp222-3

☎ 6425 2500; www.sci-ctr.edu.sg; 15 Science Centre Rd; adult/child $6/3; 🕑 10am-6pm Tue-Sun; Jurong East MRT

It's quite easy to spend all day in here, especially if you have kids and combine it with the **Omni-Theatre** (p83) and **Snow City** (opposite) in one visit. The centre is showing its age a little, but the multiple levels of interactive displays (nearly 900 of them in all) covering subjects like the human body, aviation, optical illusions, ecosystems, the universe and robotics are thoroughly absorbing.

Regular special exhibitions and displays keep the interest factor ticking over, but permanent highlights include the **Millennium Simulator** (adult/child $3/2) ride that takes you through the heart of an active volcano.

The Science Centre is a very popular item on the school trip calendar and you can often find yourself overwhelmed by hordes of jostling, wild, uniformed scamps eager to prevent you from trying out the exhibits.

Singapore Science Centre (opposite)

SNOW CITY Map pp222-3

☎ 6560 1511; www.snowcity.com.sg; 21 Jurong Town Hall Rd; adult/child $12/8; ⏲ Tue-Sun, snow sessions at 11.15am, 12.45pm, 2.15pm, 3.45pm & 5.15pm; Jurong East MRT

A hangar-size deep freeze chilled to a numbing -5°, the centrepiece of Snow City features a slope three storeys high and 70m long, accessed via a silvery Star Trek–style airlock. Each session gives you half an hour to throw yourself at high speed down the slope on a black inner tube, throw snowballs and generally lark around until the blood drains from your extremities. This is obviously a huge novelty if you live in the tropics, but new arrivals from the northern hemisphere winter might find it less invigorating. There are extra sessions at 9.45am and 6.45pm during school holidays. Ski and snowboarding lessons are available from the **Ski Venture school** (☎ 6569 6948).

To reach the centre from Jurong East MRT, take the left-hand exit and walk through the shopping centre and across Jurong Town Hall Rd (Jurong East's main road).

SENTOSA & THE SOUTHERN ISLES

Eating p120; Sleeping p177

SENTOSA ISLAND

Five hundred metres off the south coast of Singapore is **Sentosa Island** (Map p237; ☎ 1800 736 8672; www.sentosa.com.sg; basic admission $2; ⏲ 24hr), the city's favourite resort getaway. Like its beaches of imported sand, Sentosa is almost entirely a synthetic attraction, but who's complaining? Thanks in part to its energetic policy of nonstop renovation and upgrading, it sets new visitor records for itself every year, drawing locals and tourists alike. Children in particular will love it, and adults won't be disappointed by the

TRANSPORT

The easiest way to get to Sentosa Island is to take the MRT to HarbourFront station and then hop on the shuttle bus, which runs every 15 minutes or so from 7am to 11pm Sunday to Thursday, and until 12.30am on Friday and Saturday. You pay $3 ($2 admission and $1 for the bus) when you get to the Visitor Arrival Centre.

For a more memorable trip with some spectacular views, there is the cable car, which runs from the top of Mt Faber or from the Cable Car Towers adjacent to the World Trade Centre. Standard cabins cost $8.90/3.90 for adults/children. For $15/8, you can take the distinctly unsettling glass-bottom cabins, which afford a relaxing view of the sea 60m below your feet. It operates between 8.30am and 9pm daily. The cable-car ride is one of the best parts of a visit to Sentosa. If the weather is fine, take it at least one way.

A Sentosa Express rail link running from the mammoth new VivoCity shopping/entertainment complex next to HarbourFront MRT should be up and functional by 2007.

All the transport on the island is covered in the admission price. The monorail that once took visitors on a slow loop around the island's attractions has been shut down, but it's easy to get around using the four colour-coded bus routes linking the island's attractions. There is also the Siloso Line, which links with the HarbourFront shuttle to the Merlion, Palawan Beach and Siloso Beach. A Beach Train (which is not a train, but an electric float) runs from 9am to 7pm between Siloso, Palawan and Tanjong Beaches.

The *Sentosa Island Guide*, a free pamphlet available all over the island, has good maps and transport guides.

You can also hire bicycles and roller blades for between $5 and $10 per hour at Siloso and Palawan Beaches or at the Ferry Terminal, which on weekends in particular is a tempting way to avoid the long queues at some of the bus stops.

decent museums, fine aquarium and outdoor activities including cycling and golf. There's easily enough to do to fill a day and night, and if that's not enough time you could stop over at one of Sentosa's four resorts.

Entry to the island is cheap, but bear in mind that most of the attractions cost extra and the charges can really add up if you want to see them all. If that's your plan, it's a good idea to invest in one of the ticket packages, starting at $19.90/13.90 per adult/child – check the website for details. There's also quite a bit that's free including transport around the island and the entertaining nightly musical fountain and laser show. Aquabikes, canoes, kayaks and sailboards are available for hire.

Along Sentosa's southern coast are three beaches: Siloso at the western end, Palawan in the middle and Tanjong Beach at the eastern end. As a beach paradise, Sentosa has a long way to go to match the islands of Malaysia or Indonesia, but the imported sand and planted coconut palms do lend it a tropical ambience even if the muddy Singapore Strait and the towering industrial chimneys of Jurong Island in the distance might make you think twice about swimming. The beaches are also the best place to eat and a number of decent restaurants and bars have sprung up in recent years.

Sentosa, like most of Singapore, is in constant flux and is in the middle of a particularly massive makeover that will see four new resorts, new and upgraded attractions, a new marina and huge housing development built on the island's eastern side, so expect to encounter a few construction sites along the way.

BUTTERFLY PARK & INSECT KINGDOM Map p237

adult/child $10/6; 9am-6.30pm; shuttle bus from HarbourFront MRT

Just next to the cable-car station, more than 50 species of butterflies flutter around you inside the conservatory of the Butterfly Park. In the Insect Kingdom museum there are thousands of mounted butterflies, rhino beetles, Dynasties hercules (the world's largest beetles) and scorpions, among other, thankfully dead, creepy-crawlies. Kids, at least, will be entranced. Don't miss the impressive firefly enclosure.

CINEMANIA Map p237

adult/child $12.50/8; 11am-8pm; shuttle bus from HarbourFront MRT

Cinemania offers two 3-D virtual reality–style thrill rides.

FORT SILOSO Map p237

adult/child $5/3; 9am-6.30pm; shuttle bus from HarbourFront MRT

This fascinating slice of history has been improved even further by an expensive upgrade and reorganisation, which presents the island's history dating from the time it was called Pulau Blakang Mati (Malay for 'island behind which lies death', thought to be a reference to a deadly malaria outbreak that killed hundreds of villagers).

Fort Siloso itself was built in the 1880s as a military base to protect Britain's valuable colonial port with a series of gun emplacements linked by underground tunnels. Designed to repel a maritime assault, the guns had to be turned around when the Japanese invaded from Malaya in WWII. The fort was later used by the Japanese as a POW camp.

The path around the fort leads to the gun emplacements, tunnels and buildings, with jolly waxwork re-creations and voice-overs about life in a colonial barracks. There's also a small obstacle course to try your army skills out on.

The tunnel networks have been upgraded with trendily designed information posters and a short historical documentary film about the defence of Singapore.

The two surrender chambers, featuring more waxwork figures that re-create the British surrender to the Japanese, and the Japanese surrender to the Allies, completes the journey.

From 1989 until 1993, Fort Siloso housed Sentosa's most unusual 'attraction' – political prisoner Chia Thye Poh. Arrested in 1966 for allegedly being a communist, Chia served 23 years in jail before being banished to complete his sentence among the holiday delights of Sentosa.

IMAGES OF SINGAPORE Map p237

adult/child $8/5; 9am-9pm; shuttle bus from HarbourFront MRT

This diverting historical and cultural museum starts with Singapore as a Malay sultanate and takes you through its establishment as a busy port and trading centre, its trials during WWII, and the subsequent Japanese surrender. Scenes are re-created using lifelike wax dummies, film footage and dramatic light and sound effects. The 'festivals of Singapore' section is particularly colourful.

Next door is the **Stories of the Sea** exhibition, an interactive 'all-sensory' journey that takes you through Singapore's maritime heritage.

MERLION Map p237

adult/child $8/5; 10am-8pm; shuttle bus from HarbourFront MRT

Among the trashier of Sentosa's attractions, which are frankly best avoided, is the *Merlion*, the 37m-tall hybrid lion-mermaid statue towering over the island; it does offer a good view but you'll see the same view from the cable car.

MUSICAL FOUNTAIN & MAGICAL SENTOSA Map p237

shuttle bus from HarbourFront MRT

The Musical Fountain (5pm and 5.30pm daily) and, in particular, the Magical Sentosa (7.40pm, 8.40pm Monday to Friday, extra 9.30pm show Saturday, Sunday and public holidays) shows, combining the musical fountain with a spectacular $4-million sound, light and laser extravaganza, are both well worth hanging around for.

NATURE WALK Map p237

shuttle bus from HarbourFront MRT

Of the free attractions, there's a Nature Walk, livened up – in typical Sentosa style – with plaster dragons and fossils. Long-tailed macaques are common, but they can be aggressive so hide your food. You can also wander around the florid ferry terminal, Fountain Gardens and Flower Terrace.

SENTOSA GOLF CLUB & SIJORI WONDERGOLF Map p237

Sentosa Golf 6275 0022; Sijori Wondergolf adult $8-10, child $4-7; 9am-7pm; shuttle bus from HarbourFront MRT

There are two 18-hole golf courses at the Sentosa Golf Club, but nonmembers will have to pay $200 for a round, or $280 on weekends. On a mini scale, Sijori Wondergolf offers 54 putting greens in three fun courses, two of international tournament standard.

SKY TOWER Map p237

adult/child $10/6; 9am-9pm; shuttle bus from HarbourFront MRT

Next to the cable-car station (strangely, for an attraction promoting its height) is the Sky Tower, a revolving air-conditioned cabin that lifts you up a 110m pole for panoramic views over the city and the Southern Islands.

TRAPEZE SCHOOL Map p237

Siloso Beach; per swing $10; 9am-6pm Mon-Fri, 9am-7pm Sat & Sun; shuttle bus from HarbourFront MRT

Kids might also like a go on the trapeze at Siloso Beach, where they can try out this old circus favourite with the help of instructors.

UNDERWATER WORLD Map p237

6275 0030; www.underwaterworld.com.sg; adult/child $19.50/12.50; 9am-9pm; shuttle bus from HarbourFront MRT

This spectacular aquarium is deservedly one of Sentosa's most popular attractions. The star attraction is the 'travellator', an acrylic tunnel with moving walkway that takes spectators through the main tanks. There is nothing quite like the sight of 60kg giant gropers, brown stingrays and sharks swimming overhead. You can watch divers feeding the fish at various times of the day, and even get in the tank yourself on the 90-minute 'dive with the sharks or dugongs' experience, which costs $70 for certified divers and $95 for non-certified divers (call 6275 0030 or email ayu@uws.hawpar.com). After 7pm, when the lights are turned off and torches handed out to visitors, the aquarium takes on a whole new atmosphere.

Your ticket to the aquarium also includes entry to the specially constructed **Dolphin Lagoon** (10.30am-5.30pm) at Palawan Beach. Here you can see the Indo-Pacific humpback dolphins, commonly known as pink dolphins, perform in shows at 1.30pm, 3.30pm and 5.30pm daily with an extra 11am session on the weekends, when you can find yourself fighting for seats. It's possible to get in the water to feed and touch the dolphins, too.

For $120, kids can go on a one-hour Swim with the Dolphins session, which takes place at 9.45am every day.

VOLCANOLAND Map p237
adult/child $10/6; 1-6pm; shuttle bus from HarbourFront MRT
Quite naff is VolcanoLand, an ageing fantasy journey dominated by a concrete volcano, which you can see 'erupting' every half-hour with a bang and a puff of smoke; spend your money elsewhere.

ST JOHN'S & KUSU ISLANDS

The Sentosa Development Corporation is also in charge of two other tiny islands, popular with locals as city escapes: St John's (Pulau Sakijang Bendera) and Kusu (Pulau Tembakul). On weekends they can both become rather crowded but during the week you'll find them fairly quiet and good places for a peaceful swim, though the water can be a bit on the polluted side – hardly surprising given all the ships that pass through. Both islands have changing rooms, toilet facilities, grassy picnic spots and swimming areas.

TRANSPORT

The ferry from the World Trade Centre (round trip adult/child $9/6) runs to both islands at 10am and 1.30pm Monday to Saturday, more frequently on Sunday and public holidays (call ☎ 6321 2802 for details), stopping first at Kusu and then St John's.

The only way to see both islands without hanging around for hours is on Sunday when you can hop off the ferry at Kusu, then get on again when the next one passes through to St John's.

During the annual Kusu pilgrimage, ferries leave every 30 minutes from Clifford Pier (round trip $10 Monday to Saturday, $11.50 Sunday). Also most harbour tours pass St John's Island and stop at Kusu for 20 minutes or so (see p48).

St John's Island is much bigger than Kusu. It was once a quarantine station for immigrants, drug rehabilitation centre and prison. There's not much to do here other than walk along its uninspiring concrete pathways and relax in its shady picnic areas. Bring your own picnic, as the culinary offerings are limited. You can stay overnight in colonial-style bungalows or camp; contact the **Sentosa Development Corporation** (☎ 6275 0388) for details.

Kusu is more interesting, famous for its Taoist temple and Malay *kramat* (shrine), where people come to pray for health, wealth and fertility. Tua Pek Kong temple and turtle sanctuary is next to the ferry jetty; it's a yellow-painted shrine atop a small wooded hill, reached by a steep flight of steps – both can be visited in less than an hour, leaving you the rest of the day to laze around on the quiet beaches. Again, bring your own food and water.

The liveliest time to visit Kusu is during the annual pilgrimage of Taoists in the ninth lunar month (around October) when there are constant daily ferries from Clifford Pier. Try to avoid weekends in this period, though, as the island is swamped with visitors.

OTHER ISLANDS

Many of the islands on Singapore's southern shore have refineries that provide much of Singapore's export income, but among the relatively unspoilt islands are the very appealing **Sisters' Islands** (Pulau Subar Darat and Pulau Subar Laut). The sea is certainly much better for swimming and snorkelling here and the nearby coral reefs make it a good spot for divers, too (you'll need to bring your own equipment). Bring your own food and water since there are no amenities here.

Even less frequently visited is **Pulau Seking**, one of the last enclaves of traditional Malay stilted houses and far less developed than Pulau Ubin.

Further south of Singapore's southern islands are many more islands, including the scattered Indonesian islands of the Riau Archipelago (see Excursions, p181).

TRANSPORT

To reach these islands you must rent a bumboat with an operator from Clifford Pier at Marina Bay. Expect to pay around $100 per hour per boat, which takes six to 12 people. You can approach individual boat owners or contact the **Singapore Motor Launch Owners' Association** (Map pp234-5; ☎ 6532 5652) at Clifford Pier.

Walking Tours

Walking Tours

To really get a feel for the ethnic areas of Chinatown, Little India and Kampong Glam (the Malay quarter) it's best to explore them on foot. A stroll around the colonial core of the city will take you past many impressive historical and modern buildings and monuments. And if you're in search of greenery and wildlife, head for MacRitchie Reservoir in the centre of the island. More information on the places of interest detailed along these walks can be found in the Sights chapter.

CHINATOWN

Take a moment as you emerge at Raffles Pl to consider how much the surrounding CBD has changed over the last century. A graceful note amid the gleaming towers is the Mass Rapid Transport (MRT) entrances, scaled-down copies of the façade of the long-gone John Little department store that once stood here. Head west along Chulia St and turn south down Phillip St to the **Wak Hai Cheng Bio Temple** 1 (p59), which vies with the Thian Hock Keng Temple for the title of Singapore's oldest Chinese temple. Admire the many tiny figures on its roof.

Cross over Church St to Telok Ayer St – the name means 'bay water', for this street once ran alongside the bay. On your right, practically swallowed up into the Far East Sq dining precinct, is the small **Fuk Tak Ch'i Museum** 2. Further along is **Ying Fo Fui Kun** 3, a two-storey building established in 1822 for the Ying Fo Clan Association, which services Hakka Chinese.

At the junction with Boon Tat St is the **Nagore Durgha Shrine** 4, a mosque built between 1828 and 1830 by Chulia Muslims from South India's Coromandel Coast. A little further down is the beautifully restored **Thian Hock Keng Temple** 5 (p58), Singapore's most impressive Chinese temple. Continue along Telok Ayer St to the **Al-Abrar Mosque** 6, built between 1850 and 1855 on the site of a simple thatched hut, hence its Tamil name Kuchu Palli (mosque hut). By the Amoy St hawker centre turn right into Amoy St, where at No 66 you'll see the **Siang Cho Keong Temple** 7, built between 1867 and 1869. Left of the entrance is a small 'dragon well' into which you can drop a coin and make a wish.

At the junction of Amoy and McCallum Sts you'll see a small brown archway next to the temple marked Ann Siang Hill Park. Go through here, then follow the walkways and wooden steps upwards to what is Chinatown's highest point. Climb up past the historical site of the old **Anglo-Chinese School** 8, up a spiral wrought iron staircase, then follow the charming backstreet downhill, emerging on Club St, where you can reward yourself with a drink or lunch at the friendly hotel restaurant, **Damenlou (Swee Kee)** 9 (p108).

After a rest, head up Club St. The highly decorated terraces here once housed Chinese guilds and clubs, but now it's almost all trendy bars and restaurants. At the foot of Club St across the car park, the **Mohamed Ali Lane Market** 10 (p145) is held most afternoons, and on Mohamed Ali Lane, just behind busy South Bridge Rd, you can see a **traditional barber shop 11**, which is open 10am to 6pm Wednesday to Monday. Clients sit outside in an antique barber chair and haircuts costs $6.

Head back down Club St and along Ann Siang Rd and emerge beside the Maxwell Food Court, across the road from which is the **Urban Redevelopment Authority (URA) Gallery 12** (p59), where you can view what the URA has planned for the city. Also here, on the corner of Neil and Tanjong Pagar Rds, is the triangular **Jinriksha station 13**, once the depot for the hand-pulled rickshaws, but now a restaurant.

Walk southwest along Neil Rd to Keong Saik Rd, a curving street of old terraces with coffee shops, clan houses, clubs and small hotels. At the junction with Kreta Ayer Rd is the small Indian **Layar Sithi Vinygar Temple 14**. Heading into the heart of Chinatown along Keong Siak Rd, you'll hit the back of the **Chinatown Complex 15** (p108). If you're hungry, stop for a cheap bite here; there's a fascinating wet market and bustling food centre. Outside, facing the corner of Sago and Trengganu Sts, is a square that's a popular meeting place for the old folks in the cool of the evening. At the back of **Fong Moon Kee 16** (16 Sago St), an elderly gentleman still makes and mends traditional rattan matting using an antique sewing machine. The mats, once widely used for sleeping on, are durable and absorbent.

The next three streets – Smith, Temple and Pagoda – all run off Trengganu St and are the heart of tourist Chinatown. Consequently they are packed with shops, restaurants and outdoor stalls. On the corner of Smith and Trengganu Sts is a former Cantonese opera house, **Lai Chun Yuen 17**, designed

WALK FACTS

Start Raffles Place MRT

End Chinatown MRT

Distance 2km

Duration 2½hr

Fuel stops Damenlou (Swee Kee)/ Chinatown Complex

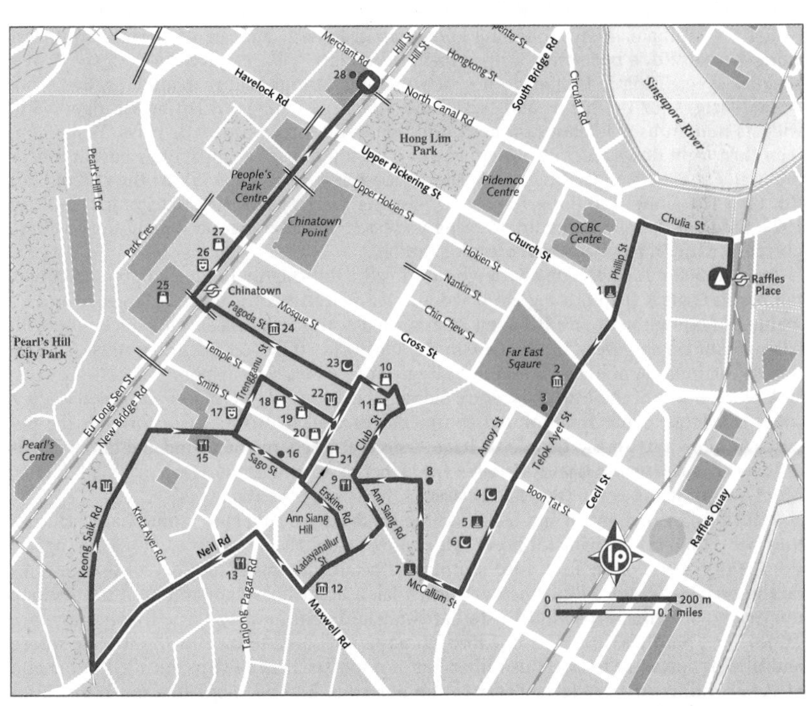

by the same architect responsible for Raffles and the Victoria Theatre. In days gone by, Temple St used to have tin smiths down one side and ceramics shops on the other. Today the tradition lingers in places such as **Bao Yuan Trading** 18 (p144) at No 15 and **Sia Huat** 19 (p145) at Nos 9–11; along nearby South Bridge Rd there are also the traditional Chinese medicine shops **Thye On Gingseng Medical Hall** 20 (p146) and **Eu Yan Sang** 21 (p145).

Also worth stopping by on South Bridge Rd are the **Sri Mariamman Temple** 22 (p58), Singapore's oldest Hindu temple; and the nearby **Jamae Mosque** 23 (also known as Chulia), built by Indian Muslims from the Coromandel Coast of Tamil Nadu between 1830 and 1855. You could spend a long time pottering around this part of Chinatown, particularly if you also visit the **Chinatown Heritage Centre** 24 (p57), which is highly recommended. It's the only place that will give you an insight into what the quarter looked like before all the tarting up for tourism happened.

You can finish at the MRT at the west end of Pagoda St, but if you fancy exploring more, take the pedestrian bridge across busy, parallel New Bridge Rd and Eu Tong Sen St. The huge **People's Park Complex** 25 (p145) on Eu Tong Sen St was the first large-scale shopping centre when built in 1970. Next to it are a couple of old beauties: the fancy Art-Deco **Majestic Theatre** 26, a former cinema and Cantonese opera hall, built in 1927; and the stately **Yue Hwa Department Store** 27 (p146), once the Great Southern Hotel and in the 1930s the area's tallest building.

Further northeast along Eu Tong Sen St towards the river is the former **Thong Chai Medical Institution** 28. Built in 1892 to provide free medical care, it was designed to look like a Chinese palace, with two large inner courtyards and a glazed tile roof.

LITTLE INDIA

From Little India MRT, walk to the bustling **Tekka Centre** 1 (p113), home to a good food centre and one of the liveliest wet markets in Singapore. Upstairs, stalls stock a variety of clothes, brassware and Indian textiles. Emerge from the Tekka Centre on to Buffalo Rd and then take a shortcut to Kerbau Rd (*kerbau* means 'buffalo' in Malay). Note the fine, two-storey, Peranakan-style building known as **Tan House** 2, built in 1905. Head southeast along Kerbau Rd, a pedestrian strip designated an 'arts village', given over to shops and galleries specialising in Indian clothes, artwork and various beauty treatments, including henna designs for the hands and feet – and a beer garden. Turn left at Serangoon Rd, with its numerous gold shops on both sides with glittering window displays. Walk 50m, then turn right down Cuff Rd, where you can get a glimpse of Singapore's past at one of the island's last spice-grinding shops, **Khan Mohamed Bhoy & Sons** 3 (p155). At the end of Cuff Rd, turn left along Kampong Kapor Rd past the **Kampong Kapor Methodist Church** 4, built in 1929, then left up Veerasamy Rd, to bring you back up to Serangoon Rd and the bustling, polychromatic **Sri Veeramakaliamman Temple** 5 (p62).

Around 500m further along Serangoon Rd is the thoroughly Indian shopping complex the **Mustafa Centre** 6 (p155) – a great place for well-priced electrical goods, luggage and all manner of household items. It's open 24 hours a day and always seems to be seething with bargain-hungry shoppers. In this area, in the alleyways off Desker Rd, are brothels, successors to the long-demolished ones in old Bugis St (see Sleazy Singapore, p122).

A block north of the Mustafa Centre along Serangoon Rd, the **Sri Srinivasa Perumal Temple** 7 (p62) is a large, ornately decorated complex dedicated to Vishnu. Cut through the pedestrian alley next to the temple to Race Course Rd, where you'll find the glitzy, Thai-influenced **Sakaya Muni Buddha Gaya Temple** 8 (p61), better known as the Temple of 1000 Lights. More beautiful still is the **Leong San See Temple** 9 (p61) over the road.

Return to Serangoon Rd and retreat to the **French Stall** 10 (p111) for some Gallic specialities (we'd hold off the wine for now) before moving on. Head southwest down Serangoon Rd, then turn left on to Petain Rd, noting the beautifully restored block of **shophouses** 11 on the corner of Surdee Rd. When you reach Jalan Besar turn right and head south along this grimy, busy main road lined with hardware and lighting shops. The Indian influence wanes here, but there are still some fine old pastel-coloured terraces with intricate stucco and tiles. If you want to skip this rather hot, not too fascinating strip, turn left at the end of Petain Rd, cross over Jalan Besar to the bus stop, hop on a bus (64, 65, 130, 139 or

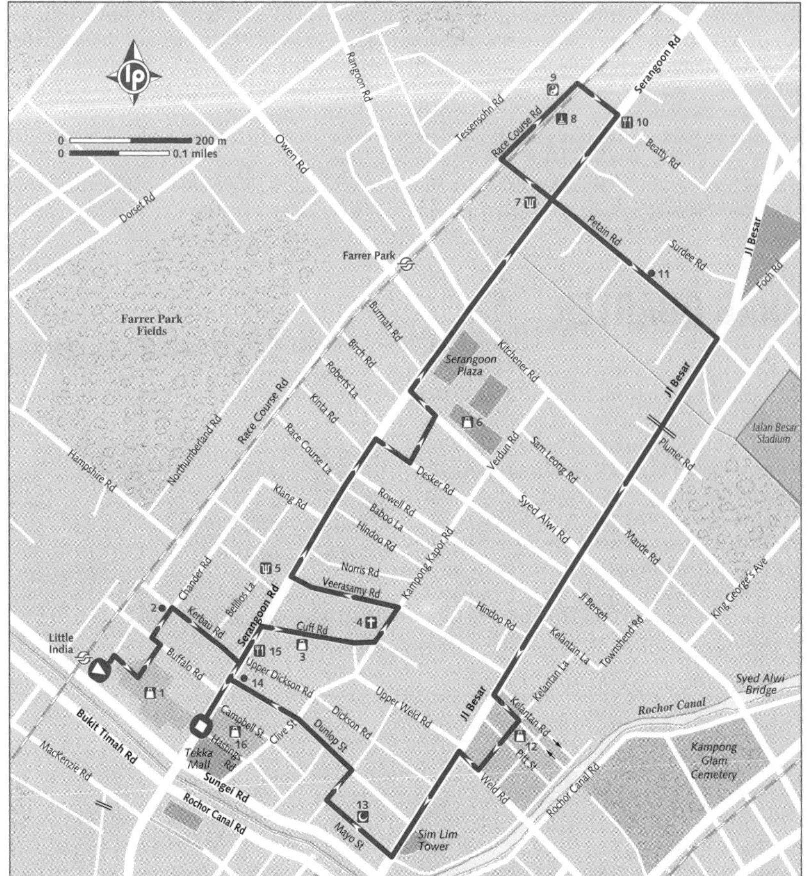

147) and get off at the third stop, before Sim Lim Tower.

Near the end of Jalan Besar, be sure to take a detour into the **Sungei Rd Thieves Market** 12 (p156) next to Sim Lim Tower, an arresting jumble of wares sold by anybody from fashionable students, gnarled old Hokkien 'uncles' and some of Singapore's homeless.

WALK FACTS

Start/end Little India MRT

Distance 2.5km

Duration 2hr

Fuel stops French Stall/Ganges

Back on Jalan Besar, turn right on to Mayo St to view the **Abdul Gaffoor Mosque** 13. An intriguing blend of Arab and Victorian architecture, it was declared a national monument in 1979.

From here, take some time to explore the atmospheric backstreets bearing the names of imperial India, such as Clive, Hastings and Campbell. This is the heart of Little India, with a whole manner of colourful shops and street life. Dunlop St, named for Major Samuel Dunlop, inspector-general of police for the Straits Settlements in the 1870s, in particular maintains much of its old-fashioned charm – at the Serangoon Rd end you'll find **fortune tellers** 14 who use birds to pick your fortune (though bear in mind that some people say these birds are not treated well). Campbell St was named after Sir Colin Campbell, an administrator who can't have been too pleased that his road was primarily the home of small abattoirs. Now, it's becoming something of a tourist strip, lined with shops selling souvenirs, crafts and 'antiques'. You'll also find a few garland makers scenting the air with their jasmine flowers.

If you're peckish – and it's lunchtime – pop into **Ganges 15** (p111) on Upper Dickson Rd for its excellent lunchtime buffet.

Finish up at the **Little India Arcade 16**, a block of renovated shophouses containing various shops selling spices, Ayurvedic remedies, textiles, tapes, brassware, homeware, and souvenirs.

ARAB QUARTER

From Bugis MRT station, head southwest down Victoria St, turn right into the markets of New Bugis St and keep going until you hit Waterloo St. Along this street you'll find the busy and colourful Chinese **Kuan Im Thong Hood Cho Temple 1** (p61) and Indian **Sri Krishnan Temple 2** (p61). Just across the junction with Middle Rd, you might also want to visit **Sculpture Square 3** to check out the art exhibits in the old church. Retrace your steps to Victoria St and walk north until you reach the **Kampong Glam cemetery 4** on the left-hand side, the last resting place of Malay royalty. Many of the graves have fallen into ruin and are overgrown but it's an atmospheric spot to explore. On the corner with Jalan Sultan

WALK FACTS

Start/end Bugis MRT

Distance 2.5km

Duration 2hr

Fuel stops Tepak Sireh/Café Le Caire

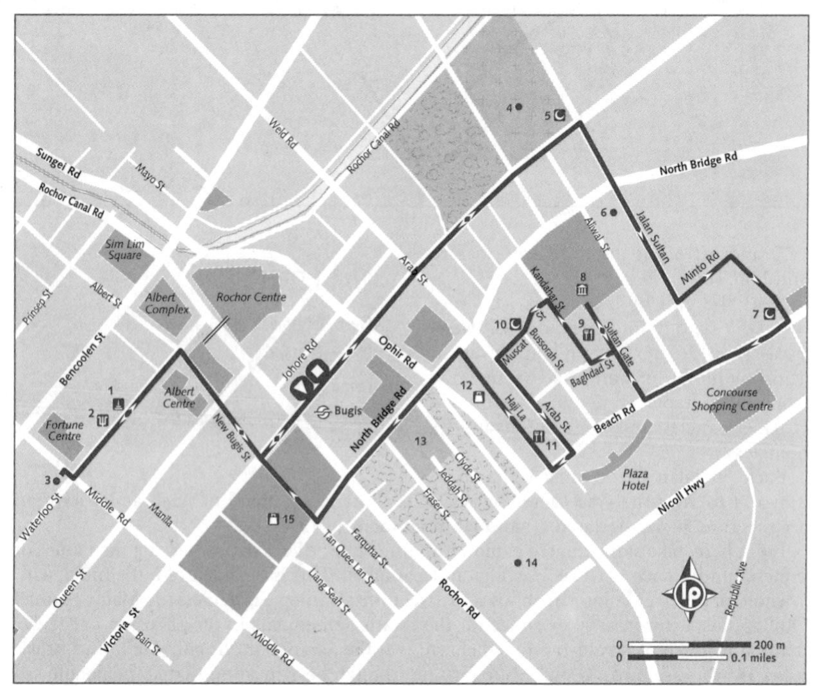

Inside a fabric shop on Arab St (below)

is the blue-tiled **Malabar Mosque 5** (p54), at its fairy-tale best when lit up in the evenings during Ramadan. Head southeast along Jalan Sultan and pass the **Alsagoff Arab School 6**, founded by the Alsagoff family in 1912 and one of the few Islamic religious schools in Singapore. Turn left into Minto Rd and continue until you reach the **Hajjah Fatimah Mosque 7** (p60) with its distinctive, slightly leaning minaret.

Walk southwest along Beach Rd until you reach Sultan Gate. At the end of this street are the historic gates that lead to the Istana Kampong Glam, the modest palace of the last Sultan of Singapore. This building now houses the **Malay Heritage Centre 8** (p61), which is a mildly interesting museum that is set in some pleasant grounds. Also restored is Gedong Kuning (Yellow Villa), a 1920s house built for the *bendehara*, the Sultan's highest official, which now houses the grand **Tepak Sireh 9** (p113), where you can stop for a spanking Malay buffet lunch.

Adjacent Kandahar St sports an ornate row of decorative shophouses, and some decent restaurants. At the junction with Muscat St is the **Sultan Mosque 10** (p63), the largest in Singapore. The view of the mosque's golden dome is most striking from along pedestrianised Bussorah St, which has blossomed recently into an 'artists village' housing various shops and galleries, a few cafés and an excellent hostel.

Busier, older and more unkempt is Arab St, the traditional textile district, where you'll find several caneware shops near the junction with Baghdad St. Stop here for a well-deserved rest and some bread, dips and grilled lamb at the area's best Muslim restaurant, **Café Le Caire 11** (p111), also known as Al Majlis. Swing around into Haji Lane, a picturesque, narrow lane running parallel to Arab St. There are some fascinating shops along here, including three places selling non-mainstream CDs, books and DVDs. There's also a shop selling *sheesha* pipes. **Kazura 12** (☎ 6293 1757; 51 Haji Lane; 🕑 10am-5pm Mon-Sat) is a traditional perfume business with rows of decanters containing perfumes, such as Ramadan, for the faithful.

Turn left out of Haji Lane and walk along North Bridge Rd towards the Art Deco **Parkview Square 13** (p26), noting the contrast with the clean lines of the twin towers of the **Gateway 14** (p26) on Beach Rd. Then continue down North Bridge Rd to the **Parco Bugis Junction shopping mall 15** (p155) and finish up where you started at the Bugis MRT.

COLONIAL LOOP

From Raffles Pl, cut through the **Clifford Centre** 1 and then go across the Change Alley arcade bridge on the 2nd level to the historical **Clifford Pier** 2. Walk north up the promenade to **One Fullerton** 3, the modern office and dining complex that fronts the bay. From here you can admire the **Fullerton Hotel** 4 (p166), once the city's post office. Head north to Merlion Park, where you'll also find the **Merlion statue** 5, and across the bay you'll see the spiky domes of **Esplanade – Theatres on the Bay** 6 (p51).

If the footway under the Esplanade Bridge is closed, walk up and over the bridge and cross the adjacent Anderson Bridge. The **Dalhousie Obelisk** 7, dedicated to free trade, is to your left. Turn right along the pedestrian Queen Elizabeth Walk, passing the **Lim Bo Seng Memorial** 8, built in honour of a WWII hero, followed by the **Indian National Army Monument** 9. Continue to the British war memorial, the **Cenotaph** 10, and on to the Victorian-style **Tan Kim Seng Fountain** 11. Across Stamford Rd is the **Civilian War Memorial** 12, locally known as the chopsticks – it's not difficult to see why.

At the **Singapore Recreation Club** 13, turn left on to St Andrew's Rd, pausing by **St Andrew's Cathedral** 14 (p54), which is off Coleman St. Continue walking south – on one side you will see the green expanse of the Padang, and on the other the handsome colonial duo of **City Hall** 15 (p52) and the **old Supreme Court** 16 (p52); located right next to the old court is the brand new Foster Partners–designed Supreme Court (see Singapore's Top Five Modern Buildings, p26), with its unmistakable spaceship design. As St Andrew's Rd swings left past the **Singapore Cricket Club** 17 you will reach **Old Parliament House** 18 (p52).

Cut through Old Parliament Lane to **Raffles Landing** 19, where you'll find the quintessential Raffles statue (which is actually a replica), arms folded, looking resolute against the incongruous backdrop of the CBD's towering skyscrapers. This is a charming place to stop for a rest, a drink and some lunch by the river at **Café Society** 20 (p103). The original Raffles statue, which once stood at the Padang, is now in front of the nearby **Victoria Theatre & Concert Hall** 21.

If you have time, explore the extremely impressive branch of the **Asian Civilisations Museum** 22 (p50) at Empress Pl. Otherwise, take the cute, pedestrian Cavenagh Bridge, built in 1869, over to the Boat Quay side of the river, noting several modern sculptures clustered along the bank (see The Sculpture Trail, p23). Nip into the Fullerton Hotel for refreshments, or head down to Boat Quay.

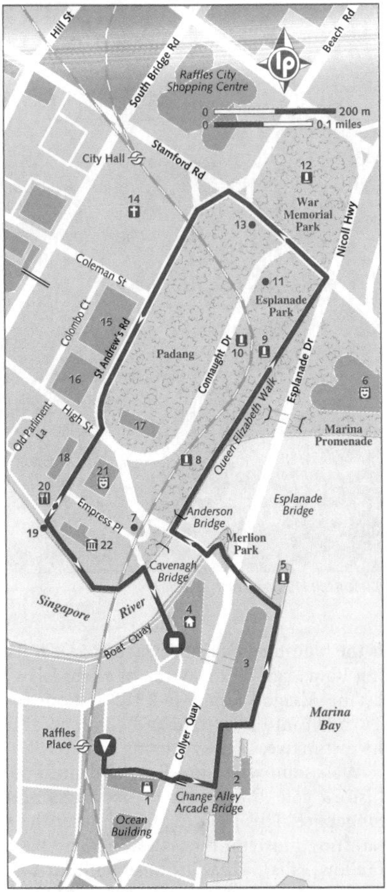

WALK FACTS

Start/end Raffles Place MRT
Distance 2.5km
Duration 2hr
Fuel stop Café Society

MACRITCHIE RESERVOIR NATURE WALK

Start at the bus stop on Lornie Rd and walk up to the edge of the reservoir. Head right (anticlockwise) around the reservoir, past the kayak rental station until you reach a boardwalk going off to your left and a track heading straight ahead. Take the track, which leads you on to the MacRitchie Nature Trail, or follow the boardwalk along the water's edge – looking out for terrapins or, if you're very lucky, a massive monitor lizard zipping through the water at remarkable speed. At various points along the boardwalk, you'll come across signs pointing you towards the Nature Trail; take one of these.

If you haven't encountered them already, you'll see plenty of long-tailed macaques as you follow the 3km-long stretch along the northeast side of the reservoir. (Watch out; if you have food they can sometimes be aggressive but generally they just ignore you. Don't look them in the eye!)

After about 3km of uninterrupted jungle you will emerge at the **Singapore Island Country Club** 1. Turn left and follow the signs to the Treetop Walk, which takes you alongside the gargantuan, heavily protected tanks of the Kallang Service Reservoir. After some twists and turns you'll eventually come to the **Ranger Station** 2 and interpretation centre, from where it's a short walk to the wooden steps leading down to the **Treetop Walk** 3, a narrow 250m suspension bridge through the upper levels of the jungle canopy, affording excellent views (and apparently the odd snake encounter).

On the other side, a boardwalk and a long series of steps up and down through some dense forest – known as the Petaling

WALK FACTS

Start/end MacRitchie Reservoir Park (bus 157 from Toa Payoh MRT, or bus 162 from Scotts Rd)

Distance 12km

Duration 4hr

Fuel stops Le P'tit Breton/MacRitchie Food Centre

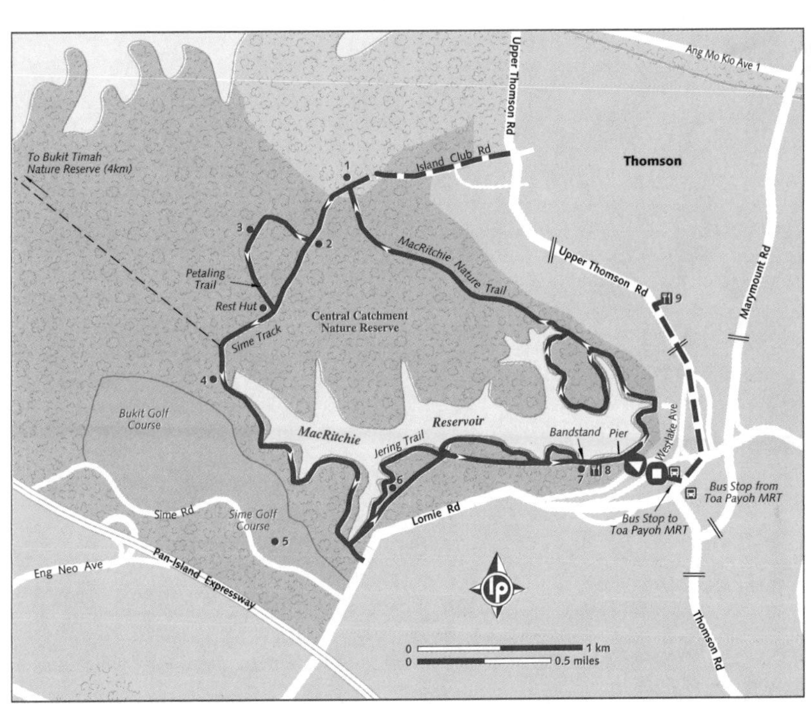

Trail – brings you out to a rest hut. (To shorten your walk to about 7km, turning left from here will take you back to the Country Club, from where it's a 25-minute walk along Island Club Rd to Upper Thompson Rd.)

Turn right and follow the Sime Track, then Golf Link to the **Jelutong Tower 4**, an observation deck providing a good view over the trees to the reservoir. After this you hit another boardwalk running downhill through jungle and alongside the **Sime Golf Course 5**, coming to a slightly unnerving, slightly surreal sign describing the differences between crocodiles and monitor lizards. (In the event of a crocodile confrontation, we don't think there would be much doubt, but in any case be wary of any swishing in the water just beneath the boards!)

After diverting away from the golf course and hugging the edge of the reservoir for about 1km, you'll hit the fairways again for another 1km before hitting a junction. Follow the Jering Trail boardwalk left along the water's edge, looking out for a lone Chinese **tombstone 6** near the water's edge. It dates from 1876, but apparently no record exists of who is buried there. Not surprisingly, there are rumours of a 'water ghost' that haunts this area, dragging unsuspecting walkers to their doom.

Winding along the boardwalk, you'll emerge, finally, back into civilisation. Cross the bizarre **zigzag bridge 7** that adjoins the bandstand, where concerts are sometimes held at the weekend, and reward yourself with a drink and something to eat at the hilltop **food centre 8**. Or, if you still have energy, catch bus 162 one stop to Upper Thompson Rd and head to **Le P'tit Breton 9** (p119) for a French crepe feast.

Eating

Eating

You don't diet in Singapore. Singaporeans live to eat and while you're here you might as well join them.

For Singaporeans, what's on the plate is far more important than the quality of the china (or plastic, come to that). The smartest-dressed businessman is as comfortable sitting down on a cheap plastic chair at a plastic table wading into a $3 plastic plate of *char kway teow* as he is eating $50 crabs in an air-conditioned restaurant. Combine this unpretentiousness with infinite variety, strict standards of hygiene and the prevalence of the English language and you have the best eating opportunities in Southeast Asia, if not the whole of Asia.

The city has every imaginable cuisine, for every imaginable budget. Not surprisingly, Chinese food in its many varieties dominates, but there are significant pockets of North and South Indian food, particularly in the area of Serangoon Rd, which along with Kampong Glam is also home to a large number of Muslim eateries.

For uniquely Singaporean food you have to try Peranakan, or Nonya, food, a blend of Chinese and Malay cuisines that is hugely popular and widely available (see p33 for more details on local cuisine).

In the Colonial District and the Quays, expensive restaurants hold sway and here you'll find the greatest concentration of international food. Eastern Singapore is well known for its seafood and its Peranakan cuisine.

Everywhere, from the city to the heartlands, you will find countless hawker centres, food courts and coffee shops, where the majority of ordinary Singaporeans spend an extraordinary amount of their time.

It's not all superlatives, though. If your taste buds have been surgically removed, you'll have no trouble locating one of the many junk food chain outlets dotted around the island.

Opening Hours

Generally, the fancier the restaurant, the shorter the opening hours. Top restaurants generally open from noon to 2.30pm, then from around 6pm to 11pm (we've listed the hours where they differ). Food courts, coffee shops and hawker centres operate throughout the

GOURMET GUIDES

Of the two annual restaurant guides available from good bookstores, *Wine & Dine* magazine's *Singapore's Top Restaurants* and *Singapore Tatler* magazine's *Best Restaurants* both focus on the best top-end establishments in town. *Makansutra*, meanwhile, is the bible of hawker-centre food, whose founder KF Seetoh has attained guru status.

The reviews in the monthly *Where Singapore* and biweekly *I-S Magazine*, available at hotels, cafés and Singapore Tourism Bureau (STB) offices, are more wide-ranging and a good source of news on Singapore's ever-changing restaurant scene. Also look out for reviews in the *Sunday Times* newspaper and the glossy monthly magazine *Wine & Dine*.

On the Web, check out the following:

Islamic Religious Council of Singapore (www.muis.gov.sg) The website has a list of halal (food prepared according to Muslim dietary laws) restaurants and cafés.

Makan Time (www.makantime.com) Covering hawker centres, budget eateries and restaurants, this website has lots of local feedback, but is dated.

Makansutra (www.makansutra.com) The website of the TV food show *Makansutra* is lively and up-to-date.

Singapore's Best Food Online Directory (www.sbestfood.com) An excellent site for hunting down hawker food, with listings arranged by type of food and by location. Reviews, though, are scant.

Vegetarian Society Singapore (www.vegetarian-society.org) Home to vast listings of vegetarian restaurants in Singapore, including late-night eateries, organic cafés, caterers and retailers.

BRUNCH, TIFFIN & HIGH TEA

Singaporeans have a mania for elaborate buffet brunches, high teas and tiffin (the traditional midday light meal of colonials). The five-star hotels all do a good job in laying out Eastern and Western savouries, cakes, puddings, fruits and even champagne for the hungry hordes. Prices range from $45 to $80 per head; young kids sometimes eat for less (or even free) and child-minding facilities may be available.

For the latest deals it's best to check the local papers and magazines (see Gourmet Guides, opposite). To be assured of a seat, book several days ahead.

Mezza9 (p116; ☎ 6416 7189; Grand Hyatt Hotel) Renowned for its free-flow champagne Sunday brunch.

Sheraton Towers (p176; ☎ 6737 6888) Inside a charming waterfall room.

Bar & Billiard Room (p53; ☎ 6331 1612; Raffles Hotel) High tea colonial style; try for the veranda.

Tiffin Room (p106; ☎ 6331 1612; Raffles Hotel) As pukka as it comes, North Indian tiffin for the genteel.

Courtyard (Map p230; ☎ 6877 8129; Fullerton Hotel) Try the 1m-high chocolate fountain on Friday or Saturday evenings.

Town (Map p230; ☎ 6877 8128; Fullerton Hotel) Superb riverside location for a Sunday champagne brunch.

Marmalade Pantry (p116; ☎ 6734 2700) For stylish Western-style brunches in more intimate surroundings, consider this place on Orchard Rd.

day – sometimes 24 hours a day – and usually close down sometime between 10pm and 1am. Chain cafés like Coffee Bean also stay open as late as 1am.

How Much?

You can spend as much or as little as you like on food in Singapore and still be almost guaranteed top quality – the mark of a great eating city. At a hawker centre or coffee shop, a meal with coffee, tea or juice will set you back as little as $4, while a food court might cost you an extra $2. For a midrange restaurant, expect to pay at least $50 per person, including alcohol. Top-of-the-range restaurants will set you back at least $100 and if you're drinking wine a decent bottle will cost a minimum of $40. Bear in mind that all menu prices will have 16% added to them at the end, for service charge, government tax and GST.

Tipping

It is not necessary to tip in Singapore, unless you feel the service has been particularly remarkable. A 10% service charge is added to all bills.

Self-Catering

If you have your own cooking facilities, or want to pick up a few munchies, there are plenty of quality supermarkets and markets in Singapore. The two biggest chains are **FairPrice** (www.fairprice.com.sg), which is a reasonably cheap but inconsistent heartlands stalwart stocking quite a decent range of basics and luxuries; and **Cold Storage** (Map pp222-3; www.coldstorage.com.sg), which is slightly pricier. Both of these can be found all over Singapore. More luxurious is the French chain **Carrefour** (www.carrefour.com.sg), which has outlets at Plaza Singapura

Drink containers (p36)

MOST MEMORABLE BREAKFASTS

Forget plain old tea and toast at your hotel; Singapore has a few early morning options that'll liven up the sleepiest head:

Jungle Breakfast Eat a splendid buffet breakfast in the company of orang-utans, pythons and otters at the Singapore Zoological Gardens (p78), or pelicans and parrots at Jurong BirdPark (p82).

Botanic Gardens After those tai chi exercises, sample both Western and traditional Asian breakfast dishes in lush surrounds at Au Jardin (p114) or Halia (p115).

Killiney Kopitiam (p115) Munch *kaya* toast and drink *kopi* (coffee) amid the din.

Bird Area Coffee Shop (p59) If you can get up as early as 6.30am, especially at weekends, have a Chinese breakfast surrounded by hundreds of twittering caged birds.

on Orchard Rd and at Suntec City, where you can find a huge range of cheeses, meats, wines and other Gallic favourites alongside the usual well-priced staples.

For wet markets, try the overwhelming sights and smells of the **Tekka Centre** (p113) or the equally gory **Chinatown Complex** (p108), both of which have excellent hawker centres too. **Geylang Serai Market** (p66) also has good seafood stalls.

Once a week on Saturdays, from 8am to 2pm, there is an **organic fruit and vegetable market** (🕒 6836 1091; Block 18, Dempsey Rd) in the decidedly offbeat Dempsey Rd area, selling produce freshly flown from Australia and New Zealand. Prices are high.

COLONIAL DISTRICT & THE QUAYS

The Colonial District and the three quays are the home of the fancy eatery and the range of expensive international restaurants is quite overwhelming. Traditional coffee shops have slowly disappeared from the area to make way for development, but a few remain – and all the major shopping malls have the obligatory food courts.

AH TENG'S BAKERY Map p230 Café

☎ 6337 1886; Raffles Complex, 1 Beach Rd; snacks from $4.50; 🕒 7.30am-11pm; City Hall MRT

This is a great place for breakfast and possibly the only part of Raffles Hotel that you can enter without your wallet trying to make a run for it. With its genteel wooden chairs and marble-top tables, it has the same colonial air, but its sandwiches, pastries and coffees are very reasonably priced. Chinese dim sum and *choi pau* also available.

★ ANNALAKSHMI Map p230 Indian Vegetarian

☎ 6339 9993; 02-10 Excelsior Hotel & Shopping Centre, 5 Coleman St; 🕒 11.30am-3pm & 6-9.30pm Mon-Sat, 11.30am-2.30pm Sun; City Hall MRT

Far and away one of the best Indian eateries in Singapore, vegetarian and otherwise, this is actually a charity institution, where the home-style food and superb range of Indian drinks is served up by volunteers. When you've had your fill, you just pay whatever you feel it's worth, with all the proceeds going towards various charities. Giving $10 is fair. Any less than that is not doing the food – and the institution – justice.

ARMENIAN KOPITAIM

Map p230 Coffee Shop

☎ 6339 6575; 34 Armenian St; dishes $3; 🕒 7am-9pm; City Hall MRT

An old stalwart serving up the breakfast staples of *kaya* toast and coffee that could melt your teeth, in a no-fuss old-Singapore environment of grimy walls, plastic tables and loud chatter. Its location opposite the Asian Civilisations Museum means they are used to tourists wandering in and staring blankly around. Noodle and rice lunches are also available.

A-ROY THAI Map p230 Thai

☎ 6338 3880; 04-06 Funan The IT Mall, 109 North Bridge Rd; mains $7-20; City Hall MRT

Widely considered among the best Thai restaurants in the country, this is apparently the favourite refuelling stop for visiting Thai dignitaries, which means the food should be appropriately hot. A-roy (which means delicious in Thai) certainly lives up to its name. The *tom yum* is properly fiery and tangy, the curries thick and rich, while the whole steamed fish is worthy of a group effort.

BOOK CAFÉ Map pp224-5 Café

☎ 6887 5430; 01-02 Seng Kee Bldg, 20 Martin Rd; mains $10-15; 🕒 8.30am-10.30pm Sun-Thu, 8.30am-1.30pm Fri & Sat; bus 54 from Clarke Quay MRT

At the river end of Mohamed Sultan, Book Café is a convivial place with large, comfy sofas, and a reasonable selection of old books (including a few Lonely Planet guides), magazines and foreign newspapers to browse through while you lounge around enjoying breakfast or a coffee. There are two terminals with free Internet access. Occasional Quarterly Literary Review Singapore events are held here (check www.qlrs.com for details).

CHRISTA & NAOMI CAFÉ (CAN)
Map p230 Café

☎ 6337 3732; 01-12/14, 1 Liang Seah St; snacks & mains from $5.50; 🕒 3pm-1am; Bugis MRT

Perpetually packed with lounging youths prodding at their electronic devices, Christa & Naomi Café is a delightful snub to Singaporean order, decked out in mismatched furniture, quirky what-nots and old movie posters. Grab a coffee, beer, snack or a trademark strawberry soda ice-cream floater; over-30s might feel a little past it in here though.

CORIANDER LEAF Map p230 Asian Fusion

☎ 6732 3354; www.corianderleaf.com; 3A Merchant Ct, River Valley Rd, Clarke Quay; mains $21-33; Clarke Quay MRT

A fusion of Middle Eastern and Southeast Asian menus, Coriander Leaf offers a wide selection of dishes, all of them superb. Try mixing and matching Thai and Indian, for example, for a meal of naan bread with mint chutney, followed by rack of lamb and Thai barramundi curry. Coriander Leaf also has a small deli and cooking studio (see Cookery Courses, p33).

CAFÉ SOCIETY Map p230 International

☎ 6338 8151; 1 Old Parliament Lane; mains $14-25; 🕒 11am-1am; Raffles Place MRT

Set in the old Parliament building now belonging to the Arts House, this tastefully renovated bar/café features a breezy al fresco dining area facing the Singapore River, a dreadfully fashionable upstairs bar in what used to be the Magistrate's Courts and, best of all, a veranda overlooking one of Singapore's most attractive urban vistas. The café-style menu is predictably pricey (the sandwiches are excellent), but the fantastic location makes it worth the money.

COLOURS BY THE BAY
Map p230 International

☎ 6835 7988; 01-13A/G, Esplanades Mall, 8 Raffles Ave; mains $10-20; 🕒 11.30am-11pm; City Hall MRT

Seven entirely different restaurants housed under one roof, all in a fabulous setting looking out across Marina Bay. The choices range from Chinese to Thai, Japanese, Italian and Asian fusion. The best part is that irrespective of where you're seated you can order from any of the seven restaurants' menus, though like many large set-ups the service can be a bit below par. Pick of the bunch is **Al Dente** (☎ 6341 9188), where you can slurp down some lobster spaghetti in a rooftop setting.

CRYSTAL JADE KITCHEN
Map p230 Chinese

☎ 6338 3511; B1-013/014 Suntec City, 3 Temasek Blvd; mains $10-20; 🕒 11am-10.30pm; Bugis MRT

The reliable Crystal Jade group of restaurants, with outlets across the city, has the Crystal Jade Kitchen downstairs at Suntec City. It's a busy Cantonese place with a vast à la carte menu and several set menus. It offers a good selection of fish, chicken and pork as well as vegetables cooked to perfection.

DOC CHENG'S Map p230 International

☎ 6412 1264; Level 2, Raffles Hotel Arcade, 1 Beach Rd; mains from $20; City Hall MRT

Voted as the restaurant with the best dining experience by the Singapore Tourism Board in 2000, Doc Cheng's lives up to its accolade. Decked out with curtained booths, high ceilings, soft lighting and chequered tiles, the atmosphere is discreetly colonial, but the food is decidedly modern. The miso butterfish is unbelievable, while the wasabi-crusted veal is a surprisingly good fusion creation. The $39 weekday set lunch is good value.

Equinox (below)

EQUINOX Map p230 International

☎ **6431 5669; Level 70, Swissôtel, 2 Stamford Rd; mains from $30; City Hall MRT**

Seventy floors up, with the city sprawled below, you'll wonder what brought you – the view or the food. Fortunately, the answer is both. Tastefully decorated with plush red carpets, hanging Chinese screens and subdued lighting, Equinox is a must-visit. The food is not extraordinary – though the grilled beef tenderloin ($45) and poached chicken with herbs ($34) are recommended – but the friendly staff and the view definitely make it a must-see. Retire for a drink at the **New Asia Bar** (p129) afterwards.

FOOD JUNCTION Map p230 Food Court

Basement, Parco Bugis Junction, 200 Victoria St; 11am-10pm; Bugis MRT

One of the new and very popular breeds of upmarket food court, more like a boutique hawker centre, in the comfortable air-conditioned surrounds of the Seiyu department store basement in Bugis Junction mall. Best are the teppanyaki stall, Thai stall and a wonderfully smoky claypot rice.

GARIBALDI Map p230 Italian

☎ **6837 1468; 36 Purvis St; mains from $22; City Hall or Bugis MRT**

One of the most accomplished Italian restaurants in Singapore – and there is no shortage of competition – this is the perfect spot for a romantic occasion, offering rich, hearty country food in an intimate, friendly environment. As well as a splendid range of pastas, the Atlantic cod with truffle sauce is delicate and juicy beyond belief, while the more adventurous might try a baked snail with asparagus sauce. Expect to come out at least $150 lighter if you have wine.

HAI TIEN LO Map p230 Chinese

☎ **6826 8338; 37th fl, Pan Pacific Hotel, 7 Raffles Blvd; mains from $20; City Hall MRT**

Provides great views of the city and Marina Bay and fine Cantonese food. Chicken marinated with five-spice powder and fried so that it's crisp on the outside and moist on the inside is a speciality. Seafood such as fried lobster with chilli sauce, sautéed prawns and baked cod are also highly recommended.

IMPERIAL HERBAL RESTAURANT Map p230 Chinese

☎ **6337 0491; 3rd fl, Metropole Hotel, 41 Seah St; mains from $20; City Hall MRT**

A Chinese physician will check you over, then prescribe something on the menu to rebalance your *yin* and *yang*. Some of the concoctions will sound much more appetising than others – double-boiled crocodile soup with dried worms, anyone? This place is worth going to with a group, since individual dishes can be pricey. A qi-balancing with your *yin* and *yang* dinner for two can cost up to $150.

INDOCHINE WATERFRONT

Map p230 Southeast Asian

☎ 6339 1720; 1 Empress Pl; mains from $18; Raffles Place MRT

This is boutique dining at its peak, surrounded by Buddha statues and with a superb view across the Singapore River to the CBD and the Fullerton Hotel. It's often packed inside, but the food is excellent (if you can forget that you're paying top dollar for what are essentially Lao, Khmer or Vietnamese street dishes). The Cambodian Tiger Prawns are particularly good. Next door is the equally trendy **Bar Opiume** (p125). The original wine bar and restaurant, **Indochine** (Map pp234-5; ☎ 6323 0503; 49 Club St), in the rapidly spreading chain, is situated in Chinatown and is also worth checking out.

JADE Map p230 Chinese

☎ 6877 8188; The Fullerton, 1 Fullerton Sq; mains from $20; Raffles Place MRT

Run by the reliable Tung Lok group, Jade has some very fancy Chinese dishes (Peking duck with five-spiced pate de foie gras for example) to match its fancy surrounds in the swanky Fullerton Hotel. You'll find dishes here that are unique to this restaurant, including a magnificent South African abalone in truffle sauce with spinach tofu. Dress smart and don't forget to make reservations.

KEYAKI Map p230 Japanese

☎ 6434 8335; 4th fl, Pan Pacific Hotel, 7 Raffles Blvd; mains from $20; City Hall MRT

A real treat, set in a delightful garden with koi ponds and done out like an ancient Japanese inn, this hushed and slightly rarefied restaurant has a large, comprehensive menu, from superb sashimi to some hearty Japanese hotpots (the duck is particularly good). A large range of sake and *soju* completes the experience.

KOPITIAM Map p230 Coffee Shop

cnr Bencoolen St & Bras Basah Rd; 🕑 24hr; dishes $6; Dhoby Ghaut MRT

One of the top spots in the district for a late-night feed, this branch of the Kopitiam chain is brisk and blindingly bright. The food, from Chinese to Malay to Korean, is uniformly good and uniformly cheap. You won't pay much more than $6 maximum for a meal.

MAX BRENNER'S CHOCOLATE BAR

Map p230 Chocolate

☎ 6235 9556; 01-06 Esplanade Mall, 8 Raffles Ave; 11am-11pm Mon-Thu, 11am-midnight Fri-Sun; City Hall MRT

Unashamedly indulgent, this branch of the Israeli chain serves up everything chocolate: chocolate nuggets, chocolate soufflés and chocolate fondue are among the favourites. Understandably, it's popular with women. While the sweets are irreproachable, we found the service pretty poor. Even addicts need to see a smile now and then.

MIRCHI Map p230 Indian

☎ 6334 5590; Esplanade Mall, 8 Raffles Ave; mains from $20; City Hall MRT

The excellent North Indian food here is a cut above the norm, and the warm, wood-panelled room is particularly inviting. All the standards are here, but it's worth trying more unusual items like the rich lamb leg tandoori and, for starters, the amazing green chilli stuffed with potato. The place is run by the owners of **Harry's** (p128), on Boat Quay.

MY HUMBLE HOUSE

Map p230 Chinese

☎ 6423 1881; 02-27/29 Esplanade Mall; mains $15-20; City Hall MRT

Anything but humble – the décor is sort of Alice in Wonderland meets Philippe Starck, designed by Chinese artist Zhang Jin Jie – and the food is hip Chinese dishes with poetic names such as 'Memories of Spring Rain' and the more predictable 'Land of the Rising Sun' (crab claws with prawns and wasabi mayonnaise). There are also some slightly less melodramatic Chinese staples. Service is patchy, but you come here for the outlandish theatricality as much as the food.

SAINT PIERRE Map p230 French

☎ 6438 0887; 01-01 Central Mall, 3 Magazine Rd; mains from $30; 🕑 closed Sun; Clarke Quay MRT

Actually run by a Belgian chef, this low-key place serves very modern French cuisine (with an unusual Japanese undertone) in a stylishly minimalist setting, with plain white walls and pale wooden floors. Try one of the five types of pate de fois gras for starters, and the grilled rack of lamb is a must for mains. Friendly and attentive service complements the top-notch food. Easily one of the best French restaurants in town.

SEAH STREET DELI Map p230 American

☎ 6337 1886; 01-22 Raffles Hotel Arcade, 1 Beach Rd; mains $10-15; 11am-10pm Sun-Thu, 11am-11pm Fri & Sat; City Hall MRT

Swing back to 1950s New York at the Seah Street Deli, an open, airy joint that does a pretty decent job of imitating the look of a Big Apple deli, with a jukebox and some rather weird outsized crayons. The menu comprises eastern seaboard classics like bagels, huge pastrami sandwiches, pumpkin pie, pretzels, a variety of salads and a 'traditional' Philly cheesecake. Just sit back and soak up the cholesterol.

SUMMER PAVILION Map p230 Chinese

☎ 6434 5288; Level 3, Ritz-Carlton, 7 Raffles Ave; mains from $20; City Hall MRT

As classy as the hotel in which it's based, Summer Pavilion overlooks tranquil gardens and serves up some of the finest, most delicate nouveau Chinese cuisine in Singapore. Specialities include the zucchini flowers, an excellent Peking duck and a melting beef with black pepper sauce.

TIFFIN ROOM Map p230 Indian

☎ 6431 6156; Lobby, Raffles Hotel, 1 Beach Rd; lunch/dinner buffet $38/40; City Hall MRT

A Raffles institution to rank with the Long Bar and Bar & Billiard Room, this priceless dining room, complete with lazy ceiling fans, is a little over-touristed, but nonetheless a memorable event. The largely North Indian buffet is renowned for its mulligatawny soup, though pretty much everything is excellent. The low chilli quotient will please some and outrage others.

VICTORIA STREET FOOD CENTRE
Map p230 Food Centre

143 Victoria St; 24hr; Bugis MRT

Next to Allson Hotel, with a distinctive small shrine outside, this is a great place for a late-night feed. The dim yellow lights make it a much better bet for post-drinking food than many of the glaring fluorescent-lit joints around town. You can have anything from the richly sweet duck rice to fish

TOP 10 HAWKER CENTRES/FOOD COURTS

Hawker centres are one Singaporean institution you simply should not miss. Traditionally, hawkers wandered the streets, carrying their stoves, ingredients and a stool or two, setting up on the pavement wherever there were customers. Now, dozens, if not hundreds, of them are gathered in open-air spots around the city. Be prepared for a noisy, crowded, hot and wonderful time. Food courts are often air-conditioned, or at least covered, but are slightly more expensive. The best hawker centres in Singapore include the following:

- **Tekka Centre** (p113) The grimy, bustling heart of Little India, where you'll find dozens of Indian and Muslim stalls, wrapped in the noise and smells from the wet market.
- **Golden Mile Complex** (p112) Popular with Thai and Malay workers, this is the spot to get a *tom yum* and a *som tam* just like they make in the Land of Smiles.
- **Newton Circus Hawker Centre** (p116) OK, it's a well-worn stop on the tourist trail, but the food is still excellent and unlike most hawker centres it's open well beyond midnight.
- **Tiong Bahru Cooked Food Centre** (p110) Reputedly where the mistresses of high-flying Singaporeans used to get their food.
- **Kopitiam** (p105) A 24-hour food court perfect for post-drinking munchies, if you can stand the blazing lights.
- **Maxwell Road Hawker Centre** (p109) A throwback to the old days in the heart of Chinatown; noisy and chaotic.
- **SoulFood Hawker Bistro** (Map pp222–3; 30 Biopolis St, Western Singapore; Buona Vista MRT) Possibly the fanciest food centre in Singapore, drawing together the most acclaimed stalls featured in the popular *Makansutra* street food guide. It's off Buona Vista Rd.
- **Chinatown Complex** (p108) A large, bewildering centre where the food, some of the best in the neighbourhood, is much more appealing than the building.
- **Lau Pa Sat Food Court** (p109) Dating back to 1822, it's been substantially modernised, but good food and some 24-hour stalls pull in the crowds.
- **Food Junction** (p104) The best of a chain of modern, air-conditioned shopping mall food centres. Don't be put off by the bright, clinical appearance.

TOP FIVE CHICKEN RICE STALLS

Chicken rice, even though it hails from the Chinese island of Hainan, is widely cited as Singapore's national dish. When it comes to picking the best, there are as many opinions as there are stalls, but here are five places where you're sure to get a great one:

- **Tian Tian** (p109) Famously rude, but famously good.
- **Hai Huang Foong** (Map pp234-5; 02-87 Chinatown Complex, Smith St, Chinatown) Served with pickled vegetables, as opposed to the usual fresh cucumber slices.
- **Hai Kee Sauce Chicken Rice Noodle** (Map p236; 131 East Coast Rd, East Coast) Variations on the theme, with rich, dark sauce.
- **Ross Hailam Nasi Ayam** (Map pp234-5; 01-64 Lau Pa Sat Food Centre, Raffles Quay, CBD) Halal version, with wonderful roast chicken.
- **Chicken Rice** (Map pp222-3; SoulFood Hawker Bistro, 30 Biopolis St, western Singapore) Chicken rice purveyor selected by popular *Makansutra* food guide. It's off Buona Vista Rd.

porridge or, if alcohol has blinded your better judgment, that Southeast Asian speciality, the Western mixed grill.

WAH LOK Map p230 — Chinese

☎ 6311 8188; 2nd Level, Carlton Hotel, 76 Bras Basah Rd; mains over $20; City Hall MRT

Its rotunda hall with the high dome ceiling, floor-to-ceiling glass windows, bright interior and warm ambience creates an atmosphere of elegance in this upmarket Cantonese restaurant. The restaurant's wide choices of dim sums are favourites prepared by a team of Hong Kong chefs. Cantonese-style roast pigeon, roast chicken and baked fish is a must for meat lovers. The meat is well complemented with homemade tofu and spinach.

CHINATOWN & THE CBD

Chinatown brims with character and offers visitors one of the liveliest and most diverse eating scenes, from the chaotic old-Singapore atmosphere of the Maxwell Rd hawker centre to the genteel teahouses, the chic renovated shophouses along Club St to the hawker-stall gems among the grime of the Chinatown Complex.

BELACHAN Map pp234-5 — Peranakan

☎ 6221 9810; 10 Smith St; mains $15-25; Chinatown MRT

Free of the kitsch mannequins in dusty Nonya costumes present in some other Peranakan restaurants, this place is worth trying for the prawn and papaya soup or Grandma's *itek manis* (duck simmered in ginger and black-bean sauce). The food here has won awards for excellence.

BENG HIANG RESTAURANT Map pp234-5 — Chinese

☎ 6221 6695; 112 Amoy St; mains from $12; 🕑 11am-9.30pm; Chinatown MRT

An old-style cacophonous Hokkien restaurant that invites adventurous diners who don't have sensitive ears. As a foreigner, you might get a few looks walking in here (and be treated like a zoo creature as you eat), so impress and surprise them by ordering your fish maw soup and duck with sea cucumber. Don't come for a special night out; the service is as bad as the food is good.

BLUE GINGER Map pp234-5 — Peranakan

☎ 6222 3928; 97 Tanjong Pagar Rd; mains $15-25; Tanjong Pagar MRT

The colonial atmosphere of the old shophouse is enlivened by the striking contemporary paintings of local artist Martin Loh. There is an extensive Peranakan menu, but the pan-fried halibut, deep-fried eggplant with chilli paste and classic beef *rendang* all come highly recommended.

BOON TAT ST Map pp234-5 — Hawker Centre

🕑 7pm-3am Mon-Fri, 3pm-3am Sat & Sun; Raffles Place MRT

A great spot for cheap late-night munchies after a night's drinking on Club St has left you with a couple of mangled $5 notes in your pocket. Settle into a table under the mildly cool sky and tuck into some spicy chicken satay, or whatever takes your fancy.

BROTH Map pp234-5 International

☎ 6323 3353; 21 Duxton Hill; mains $15-25; Tanjong Pagar MRT

Based in a lovingly converted shophouse; the short menu zips from the daily broth ($6.90) to pies and veal *saltimbocca* (Roman speciality of sliced veal with sage and prosciutto) for $22.90. Staff members are friendly and the modern-meets-colonial interior gives this place a welcoming, informal feel.

CHINATOWN COMPLEX

Map pp234-5 Hawker Centre

cnr Sago & Trengganu Sts; Chinatown MRT

As you'd expect, the large, eternally busy Chinatown Complex has some great Chinese food stalls on the 2nd floor. The choice is vast. Some of the vendors from here and other renowned hawker stalls and restaurants across the city have set up along Smith St, where you can sit on the street under red lanterns that bob in the breeze – it's very touristy but fun, and popular with locals too.

CHUAN JIANG HAO ZI

Map pp234-5 Steamboat

☎ 6225 1518; 12 Smith St; steamboat per person $19.80; 🕑 11am-midnight; Chinatown MRT

A departure from the standard Singaporean chuck-it-all-in steamboat, Chuan Jiang serves up the delicious traditional Sichuan variety, which has a strict etiquette (helpfully described in signs on the walls). The special octagonal pots, imported from China, have two chambers so that two stocks can be used simultaneously, and some of the ingredients are unique to Sichuan steamboat, such as duck gizzard, sweet potato and pork trotters. You can also blend your own dip. Beware: the stock can be very fiery.

CI YAN ORGANIC VEGETARIAN HEALTH FOOD Map pp234-5 Chinese

☎ 6225 9026; 2 Smith St; mains $10; 🕑 noon-10pm; Chinatown MRT

Detox at Ci Yan Organic Vegetarian Health Food, where the food is organic, 100% vegetarian and contains no garlic or onions. The tiny wooden tables and chairs and the spiritual book selection give this place a schoolhouse atmosphere to complement your rising sense of worthiness.

DAMENLOU (SWEE KEE)

Map pp234-5 Chinese

☎ 6221 1900; 12 Ann Siang Rd; mains $10-15; Chinatown MRT

A long-running family restaurant. The décor might not be a match for most Club St eateries, but the friendliness, the food (and the prices) are magnificent. Try the prawn-paste chicken, the black-pepper beef or, if you're feeling adventurous, the *ka shou* fish-head noodles for which the founder was famous. The Peranakan-style ground-floor room is pleasant enough, or alternatively get a table on the newly renovated rooftop for a postcard view across Chinatown.

FATTY OX HONG KONG ROAST DUCK

Map pp234-5 Chinese

☎ 6222 0923; 10 Murray St; mains around $10; 🕑 10am-10pm; Tanjong Pagar MRT

How can you refuse a place with a name like this? Apart from roast duck and goose, Fatty Ox Hong Kong Roast Duck dishes up fried cuttlefish, hot-pan beancurd, bubbling claypot dishes and tasty soups that change daily.

HOCK LAM STREET Map pp234-5 Chinese

☎ 6220 9290; 22 China St, 01-01 Far East Sq; noodles $4; 🕑 11am-11pm; Raffles Place MRT

The *beef kway teow* at this place is legendary among Singaporeans, both for the quality of the meat and for the 'secret' sauce that is slathered over it. You can choose from *kway teow*, yellow noodles or *bee hoon*, or if you're not in the mood for anything soupy, try the *gan lau mian* (dry beef noodles). At $4 a bowl, this is noodle heaven.

L'AIGLE D'OR Map pp234-5 French

☎ 6227 7678; 83 Duxton Rd; mains from $30; Tanjong Pagar MRT

About as fancy as you can get, the plush surrounds of L'Aigle d'Or set the scene for some lavish, hearty food. Skip the starters (if only to leave room for the cheeses at the end) and try the rack of lamb or perhaps the house speciality pigeon. The cheeses are a wonder to behold – especially if you've come to Singapore from elsewhere in Asia – and the sorbets are a must.

LAU PA SAT Map pp234-5 Hawker Centre

18 Raffles Quay; 11am-3am; Raffles Place MRT

Lau Pa Sat means 'old market' in Hokkien, appropriate as this food court occupies a handsome iron lacework structure, shipped out from Glasgow in 1894, and once used as a market. A few souvenir stalls hug its perimeter, but the emphasis is on eating.

MAXWELL ROAD HAWKER CENTRE

Map pp234-5 Hawker Centre

cnr South Bridge & Maxwell Rds; Chinatown MRT

This open-sided shed-like structure is an interesting place to watch the hawkers at work. Don't miss the *ham chin pang* (long pieces of deep-fried dough) or the fine chicken rice at **Tian Tian** (stall 10), the dim sum at stall 79/80, the pork porridge at stall 54 or the juicy banana fritters at stall 61.

MOZZAIC Map pp234-5 International

☎ 6325 3360; 36 Club St; mains from $14; Chinatown MRT

Very probably the only Japanese-European-Brazilian restaurant in the world, Mozzaic is a good choice for those who can never make up their minds. All three cuisines are handled by specialist chefs, serving up meaty Brazilian (or fishy; try the salmon *churrasco* for $16), delicate Japanese (the roast *kamo* duck is excellent) or an eclectic range of European classics from paella to pasta.

MY DINING ROOM

Map pp234-5 European

☎ 6327 4990; 81 Club St; mains from $21; Chinatown MRT

The interior of this modern restaurant, with rough finishes and intimate atmosphere, does justice to the rather uninspiring name. The food is excellent, though we would steer away from the fruit-and-meat combinations and stick with the hearty basics like egg and Portobello mushrooms, steaks, pork shoulder and baked cod, and wash it all down with one of the Australian wines.

OSO RISTORANTE

Map pp234-5 Italian

☎ 6327 8378; 27 Tanjong Pagar Rd; mains from $18; Tanjong Pagar MRT

One of the newer Italian restaurants in town and gradually gaining a loyal following, thanks to its fresh ingredients flown in weekly from Italy, fine Italian cheeses and wines, and superb meals. Our pick was the pumpkin soup with scallops and roasted cod with rosemary potato puree. Magnificent.

SENSO Map pp234-5 Italian

☎ 6224 3534; 21 Club St; mains from $20; Chinatown MRT

One of the best, and best-regarded, Italian restaurants in Singapore; Senso's courtyard is especially pleasant on balmy evenings when the well-heeled chow down over pan-fried duck's liver, fluffy, filling gnocchi and a cooling *gelato*. Other highlights include a giant octopus salad (the octopus is giant, not the salad) and a baby lobster pasta. Perfect for a special evening – to be rounded off with a drink in one of Club St's bars.

SPIZZA Map pp234-5 Italian

☎ 6224 2525; 29 Club St; pizzas $14-17; Chinatown MRT

These are easily among the finest pizzas in Singapore; wood-fired, thin but filling crust and not overzealous on the toppings, all turned out by the toiling pizza chef in front of you. This is a deservedly popular place on the busy Club St entertainment strip, with a casual, jovial atmosphere.

TEOCHEW RESTAURANT HUAT KEE

Map pp234-5 Teochew

☎ 6423 4747; 74 Amoy St; mains from $10; Raffles Place or Chinatown MRT

A fairly recent entry on the scene; the reputation of this place has been growing and it's well worth a visit. Teochew classics like paper-baked chicken and steamed goose are definite crowd pleasers (judging by the loud chatter that accompanies their arrival); the more adventurous might want to have a stab at the claypot eels, a heavily fishy dish best shared between a group.

THANYING Map pp234-5 Thai

☎ 6222 4688; 2nd fl, Amara Hotel, 165 Tanjong Pagar Rd; mains $15-20; Tanjong Pagar MRT

Looking a bit dated in the contemporary surrounds of Amara Hotel, Thanying has long been considered one of Singapore's best Thai restaurants, known for its grilled chicken, roast-duck red curry and other royal Thai dishes. The *tom yum* here is particularly good, sharp and fiery, unlike many of the thick, oily versions served up around town.

THE ART OF TEA APPRECIATION

Taking time out in a teahouse is a pleasant way to relax and learn about the finer points of many kinds of tea and how to appreciate them. The best place to start is **Yixing Yuan Teahouse** (Map pp234-5; ☎ 6224 6961; 30/32 Tanjong Pagar Rd; 11am-11pm), where former banker Vincent Low explains all you need to know about sampling different types of tea. The demonstration with tastings lasts around an hour ($15).

Once you know your green tea from your oolong, nip around the corner to **Tea Chapter** (Map pp234-5; ☎ 6226 1175; www.tea-chapter.com.sg; 9-11 Neil Rd; 10am-11pm), where Queen Elizabeth and Prince Philip dropped by for a cuppa in 1989. There are several different areas in which to sit, but choose carefully: the more private incur a higher surcharge. If you don't know the drill, the waiter will give you a brief demonstration of how to make tea.

Teajoy (Map p230; ☎ 6339 3739; 420 North Bridge Rd; 11am-10pm) has a wide selection of teas, teapots and implements. The cover charge for the short demonstration and tea here is $12.

TIONG BAHRU COOKED FOOD CENTRE Map pp224-5 — Food Centre

cnr Seng Poh & Lim Liak Sts; Tiong Bahru or Outram Park MRT

Around 1.5km along Outram Rd, northwest of Outram Park MRT, is the truly excellent and authentic Tiong Bahru Cooked Food Centre. Come here for the *char kway teow* (fried flat noodles; stall 11A), oyster omelette (stall 19C), the *shui kueh* (steamed radish cakes; stall 15E) or the Koh brothers' famed pig's organ soup.

XIN MIN VEGETARIAN FOOD COURT Map pp234-5 — Chinese

☎ 6324 2481; 29 Kreta Ayer Rd; mains $5-10; closed Mon; Chinatown or Outram Park MRT

Located just a few doors down from the Chinese Buddhist Association, this cheap vegetarian place is notable for its fine, silky beancurd, as well as its noodles and rice. The traditional shophouse location epitomises the pleasures of Asian vegetarian eating, without the attendant baggage of preachiness or sanctimony that sometimes accompanies similar places in the West.

LITTLE INDIA & THE ARAB QUARTER

It goes without saying that these two adjacent neighbourhoods are prime spots for Indian and Muslim food, in all its wonderful variety, from Yemeni and Egyptian to North and South Indian. Exploring the side streets off Serangoon Rd and Arab St is one of the culinary highlights of any trip to Singapore.

AL-TAZZAG Map p232 — Egyptian

☎ 6295 5024; 24 Haji Lane, Kampong Glam; mains from $12; 11.30am-4am Mon-Sat, 4pm-4am Sun; Bugis MRT

One of the pioneers of the new Haji Lane scene, this small Egyptian café is richly painted, with leather cushions on the bench seats and a backlit display of *sheesha* pipes. At night it spreads out, putting up tables and laying out rugs under the five-foot ways of the crumbling old shophouses. It's quieter, more relaxed and far more atmospheric than Café Le Caire on Arab St and the food is just as good. A plate of dips costs $7.50, magnificent kebabs cost from $12, while *sheesha* costs $12.

AMBROSIA CAFÉ Map p232 — Mediterranean

☎ 6292 7313; 19 Baghdad St, Kampong Glam; mains $8-20; noon-4am; Bugis MRT

All low lighting and dark wood, with low tables and floor cushions for diners upstairs, the Ambrosia promises much. As a place to relax with a *sheesha* (from $14) and a pot of mint tea or a cardamom coffee, it's splendid, particularly late at night when the music is soft and it attracts a diverse range of Singaporean night denizens. However, the food, sadly, is decidedly average.

ANANDA BHAVAN Map p232 — Indian Vegetarian

☎ 6297 9522; 58 Serangoon Rd, Little India; 7.30am-10pm; Little India MRT

Far better than the Komala Vilas chain (and far less like a fast-food restaurant). You can fill yourself up here with outstanding *idli* (steamed semolina patties) and *masala thosai* ($2.30), or the enormous 'mini' set meal

($4), all washed down with sublime ginger tea. You can also get takeaway snacks and a tempting range of Indian sweets. There are two other branches: just outside the **Tekka Centre** (☎ 6294 0684) and at **221 Selegie Rd** (☎ 6336 3891; ⏰ from 5.30am).

BANANA LEAF APOLO

Map p232 — Indian

☎ 6293 8682; www.bananaleafapolo.com; 54-58 Race Course Rd, Little India; dishes from $6; ⏰ 10am-10pm; Little India MRT

Outstanding South Indian food and the novelty of eating off banana leaves has made this a popular stop on the tourist route, but nevertheless the Apolo attracts a wide mixture of people and has never compromised on the quality or spiciness of its curries. It's most famous for its blistering fish-head curry ($18 to $26). Its North Indian sister restaurant **Spice Mela** (☎ 6299 0078; 66-68 Race Course Rd; ⏰ 11am-11pm) is a few doors away.

BLUE OASIS Map p232 — International

☎ 6396 5905; 60 Bussorah St, Kampong Glam; snacks & mains from $3; ⏰ 10am-9pm Mon-Thu, 10am-11pm Fri & Sat, 10am-7pm Sun; Bugis MRT

A friendly ma-and-pa café with a modern twist. Airily decorated in, not surprisingly, blue, this is a pleasant place to sip excellent coffee, snack on spring rolls, sandwiches and samosas, and watch the gentle Bussorah St activity. On Fridays and Saturdays there is live jazz and $5 beers. Upstairs are yoga and pilates classes.

BUMBU Map p232 — Thai/Indonesian

☎ 6392 8628; 44 Kandahar St, Kampong Glam; mains $10-15; Bugis MRT

Fairly well known among Singapore's opinionated foodies for its toothsome Thai dishes, this unassuming shophouse is one of the mid-priced stalwarts on an emerging Kandahar St food strip. Thai staples are excellent – the crispy fish is particularly memorable.

CAFÉ LE CAIRE (AL MAJLIS)

Map p232 — Middle Eastern

☎ 6292 0979; 39 Arab St, Kampong Glam; dishes under $10; ⏰ 10am-2am; Bugis MRT

This highly informal, Egyptian hole-in-the-wall street café attracts a multinational crowd and is run by a former accountant who went on a quest to preserve Arab culture in Singapore. It's a particularly popular spot for relaxing with tea and a *sheesha* pipe ($8), so popular that on busy nights they even lay out rugs on the pavement across the street for *sheesha* smokers. The plastic tables might not be inspiring, but the food is magnificent. Dips, breads and a melting spring chicken are highlights.

CLE AFRICAN RESTAURANT

Map p232 — African

Kim Leng Eating House, Verdun Rd, Little India; dishes under $4; ⏰ 11.30am-11pm; Farrer Park MRT

A definite curiosity, right next to the Mustafa Centre, CLE is run by three Nigerians, including a former professional football player. Specialities include beef and mutton soups with *suji* (flour and potato) and wild mango seeds. They say all the important ingredients come from Nigeria, but even so it's very cheaply priced.

EL-SHIEKH CAFÉ Map p232 — Lebanese

☎ 6296 9116; 18 Pahang St, Kampong Glam; mezze platter $17.95; ⏰ 6pm-midnight; Bugis or Lavender MRT

Each of the many rooms of this new Lebanese restaurant is a delight. Regular restaurant downstairs, lounge with floor cushions upstairs, a roof garden with potted palms for *sheesha*-smoking under the stars – the décor is more than matched by the excellent food. A large *mezze* platter includes humus, *baba ganoush*, grape leaves, *kibbeh* and *labeh*.

FRENCH STALL Map p232 — French

☎ 6299 3544; 544 Serangoon Rd, Little India; mains $10-20; ⏰ 6-10pm Tue-Sun; Farrer Park MRT

It's cash-only at the French Stall, a charming Gallic hawker stall owned and run by a two-star Michelin chef all the way from Brittany. Enjoy scrumptious set French meals (from $11.80) and wine at a bargain $6.80 per glass amid a Euro-savvy crowd.

GANGES Map p232 — Indian

☎ 6294 3547; 3A-9A Upper Dickson Rd, Little India; lunch/dinner $9.50/11.50; ⏰ closed Sun; Little India MRT

Up a narrow staircase, this air-conditioned oasis of quiet is best visited early lunchtime

VEGETARIAN OPTIONS

Singapore is a meat- and seafood-eaters' paradise, but thanks to the role of vegetarianism in both Indian and Chinese religions, there are plenty of options for non-meat eaters too. For a complete list, see www.vegetarian-restaurants.net/Asia/Singapore. Here's our top 10, grouped by cuisine:

Indian

Ananda Bhavan (p110) Top notch informal eatery, with three branches.
Annalakshmi (p102) Magnificent pay-what-you-like buffet lunches.
Bombay Woodlands (p114) Superb, affordable North Indian food just off Orchard Rd.
Madras New Woodlands (opposite) Excellent thalis and *dosai*, away from the Komala Vilas tourist crowd.

Chinese

Ci Yan Organic Vegetarian Health Food (p108) One-hundred percent organic, onion and garlic-free, surrounded by spiritual books.
Lingzhi Vegetarian (p115) Excellent traditional and modern Chinese food on Orchard Rd.
Xin Min Vegetarian Food Court (p110) Old shophouse eatery with superb Chinese beancurd.

Other

Original Sin (p120) Stylish Mediterranean fare in the Holland Village expat enclave.
Sunflower Vegetarian (p116) Tucked away in Far East Plaza, a perfect rest stop for vegetarians on shopping trips.
Yogi Hub (opposite) Cheap and wonderful international veggie dishes in an unpretentious atmosphere.

(and preferably on a very empty stomach), when the North and South Indian buffet is fresh and steaming. Be sure to leave room for at least two serves of *payasam* – a concoction of condensed milk, raisins, cardamom, cashews and jaggery. It's unbelievable.

GOLDEN MILE COMPLEX

Map p232 Food Court
5001 Beach Rd; Lavender MRT
The Golden Mile Complex, across the road from the Golden Mile Food Centre, near Kampong Glam, is like a mini Thailand. It's particularly packed at weekends, when Thai migrant workers pile down there to get a taste of home and get blind drunk. Try **Diandin Leluk** (01/67-69; dishes under $10; 9am-10pm), known for its tasty *tom yum* soup, *som tam* (green papaya salad) and beef noodles.

GOLDEN MILE FOOD CENTRE

Map p232 Food Court
505 Beach Rd; Lavender MRT
The vast Golden Mile Food Centre, situated near Kampong Glam, is one of the best spots in Singapore to sample soup *tulang* (check out stalls 14, 15 and 17 in the basement – open from 2pm till late). Soup *tulang* ($4) consists of meaty bones stewed in a rich, spicy, blood-red tomato gravy. Gnaw off the flesh, suck out the marrow (a straw comes in handy), and sop up the tomato sauce with bread. It's very messy and filling.

KAKI GALLERY & CAFE Map p232 Café

9820 1261; 9 Haji Lane; Bugis MRT
This tiny artists' café, which is sumptuously designed in deep reds, doubles as a gallery space for young painters and sculptors. Like its Haji Lane neighbours, its tables occupy the laneway after nightfall, where coolly subdued patrons sip lychee cocktails. They don't do *sheesha* here, but you are allowed to bring one from a neighbouring café.

KERALA CUISINE Map p232 Indian Seafood

6297 1011; B1-09 Tekka Mall, Sungei Rd, Little India; mains from $12; noon-10pm; Little India MRT
Tucked away in the basement of the unremarkable Tekka Mall, Kerala Cuisine is one of the most exceptional exponents of Indian seafood in Singapore and is well worth seeking out. If the speciality Malabar fish-head curry doesn't appeal, the crab *masala* and *chemen* (prawn) *masala* certainly will. Being from Kerala, the meals are heavy on the coconut milk.

KOMALA VILAS

Map p232 Indian Vegetarian

☎ 6293 6990; 76-78 Serangoon Rd, Little India; dishes under $10; 🕑 7am-10.30pm; Little India MRT

Komala Vilas has become like the McDonald's of Indian vegetarian food in Singapore. With outlets everywhere, it's often the place vegetarians head to without realising that there are plenty of other options. Still, the food is very reliable, cheap and healthy, with some excellent *dosa*, *idli* and a decent biryani. The restaurant has an **outlet** (82 Serangoon Rd) selling a tempting range of Indian sweets.

MADRAS NEW WOODLANDS

Map p232 Indian Vegetarian

☎ 6297 1594; 12-14 Upper Dickson Rd, Little India; mains $5-10; 🕑 7.30am-11.30pm; Little India MRT

Another reputable vegetarian joint dishing up some huge portions (if you ever wondered how vegetarians get fat, this is the reason) on banana leaves. The thalis are magnificent and need at least an hour to finish and the service is friendlier and more accommodating towards confused foreigners than many of the Little India eateries.

SAMAR Map p232 Middle Eastern

☎ 6398 0530; 60 Kandahar St, Kampong Glam; mains $10-22; 🕑 24hr; Bugis MRT

In terms of atmosphere, this is just about the best Middle Eastern restaurant in the area, though in terms of food **Café Le Caire** (p111) leaves it in the shade. With deep leather armchairs outside, white mosaic tile walls and black-and-white portraits of various Arab heroes, you could easily be in Amman (well, maybe not). Avoid the dips – the portions are way too small – and try the Yemeni lamb or quail ($22) or the Palestinian *mansaf* ($18). A perfect spot to end a walk around the area with a refreshing mint tea.

TEKKA CENTRE Map p232 Hawker Centre

cnr Serangoon & Buffalo Rds, Little India; dishes $3-5; Little India MRT

Like most of Little India, the perfect antidote to any notions of 'sterile Singapore'. Wrapped around the hacked bones, sloshed guts and pungent odours of the wet market, the Tekka hawker centre serves up excellent Indian and Muslim food. Particularly recommended among the non-

Tekka Centre (left)

Indian stalls is **Heng Gi Roasted Goose and Duck Rice** (stall 01-406; 🕑 closed Mon & Tue).

TEPAK SIREH Map p232 Malay

☎ 6396 4373; 73 Sultan Gate, Kampong Glam; buffet $14.90; Bugis MRT

Rightly viewed as one of the best Malay restaurants in the city – and with a great location right next to the former Sultan's palace (now Malay Heritage Centre, p61) – this large heritage house, once the 'Prime Minister's' residence, is a treat. The buffet spread is a virtual encyclopaedia of Malay specialties. It often caters for functions, so call ahead.

YOGI HUB Map p232 Vegetarian

☎ 6298 8198; 16 Madras St, Little India; mains from $6; 🕑 11.30am-10pm Tue-Sat, 11.30am-5pm Sun; Little India MRT

Clean and sparkling white, this ultra-modern organic vegetarian place is warm, welcoming and free of any aura of beatific exclusivity. The food – from the Western salads and pastas to the Asian noodles and the juices – is exceptional and inexpensive. Try the spinach pine nut pasta or the superb anise-flavoured fried rice. There's also another branch in **Chinatown** (☎ 6220 4344; 1 Boon Tat St; ⌚ 11.30am-8.30pm Mon-Fri, 11.30am-4pm Sat).

ZAM ZAM Map p232 Muslim

☎ 6298 7011; 699 North Bridge Rd, Kampong Glam; dishes under $10; ⌚ 7am-11pm; Bugis MRT

Fluorescent-lit and bang on the busy corner of North Bridge Rd and Arab St, this place is not exactly relaxing or peaceful, but it's a great spot to watch the skilful *murtabak* (*roti prata* filled with mutton, chicken or vegetables) makers at work. It's been going since the early 1900s, so they know what they're doing.

ORCHARD ROAD

Like the Colonial District, fancy dominates the scene around Orchard Rd, which houses literally thousands of places for shoppers to fill their stomachs. The dominance of malls does not mean absence of character, however. Being Singapore, all budgets and tastes are catered for and many shopping centres house food courts (where you can sample local specialities in a noisy, chaotic environment for a few dollars), reliable chain outlets and sophisticated restaurants offering the best in design and food.

AU JARDIN Map pp226-7 French

☎ 6466 8812; EHJ Corner House, Singapore Botanic Gardens, Cluny Rd; mains from $30; Orchard MRT, then bus 7, 77, 123 or 174 from Orchard Blvd

Set in a refurbished colonial mansion and surrounded by the extravagant lushness of the Botanic Gardens; there can hardly be a more charming restaurant in Singapore. Of course, the classic French food (fish and lobster are particularly recommended) comes at a price – at least $100 each – but it's worth it. Dress up, forget the bill and have a romantic promenade through the gardens afterwards. Memorable.

BLU Map pp226-7 Modern American

☎ 6213 4598; 24th fl, Shangri-La Hotel, 22 Orange Grove Rd; mains from $30; ⌚ 7-10.30pm Mon-Sat; Orchard MRT

Top-notch sophisticated Californian cuisine against a backdrop of posh residential suburbs, all bathed in a seductive low blue light and serenaded by some accomplished jazz acts make this a good option for the fashionably minded. Signature dishes include a wonderful crab bisque, an excellent beef tenderloin and a Baileys cappuccinos *crème brûlée* that'll make you weak at the knees.

BLOOD CAFÉ Map pp226-7 Café

☎ 6735 6765; 02-20/21 The Paragon, 290 Orchard Rd; dishes $10-15; ⌚ 10am-8.30pm; Orchard MRT

Tucked away at the back of the trendy Project Shop Blood Brothers' boutique, Blood Café looks like it was transported direct from Sydney, complete with racks of style magazines. It serves excellent modern café-style food and drinks, but reserve most of your stomach space for the desserts. The mango-and-banana crumble and key lime pie deserve some sort of award.

BOMBAY WOODLANDS RESTAURANT

Map pp226-7 Indian Vegetarian

☎ 6235 2712; B1-01/02 Tanglin Shopping Centre, 19 Tanglin Rd; mains $5-7; ⌚ 9.30am-10pm; Orchard MRT

Tucked away below street level in the Tanglin Shopping Centre, Bombay Woodlands is the sort of place you could easily pass by without a glance. Don't. The food here is magnificent and cheap; *idli* with terrific mint chutney, excellent *dosai* (try the Mysore Masala) and a very rich *bhindi* (okra), all washed down with lassi. The $14 thalis could easily be shared between two. With its attentive old white-shirted waiters and ramshackle '70s décor, this place has a charm not easily found in the Orchard Rd vicinity.

CLUB CHINOIS Map pp226-7 Chinese

☎ 6834 0660; 02-18 Orchard Parade Hotel, 1 Tanglin Rd; brunch buffet from $38; ⌚ 6.30-10.15am, 11.30am-2.30pm & 6.30-11.30pm; Orchard MRT

In old-world Shanghai style, Club Chinois remains one of Singapore's pioneer Chinese restaurants. However, it has kept up with changing times and has created fantastic Asian fusion cuisine. The service here is friendly and helpful and the weekend brunch buffet of 'free flow' oysters, sashimi and dim sum is good value for money. Try the famous crispy Peking roast duck skin.

DIN TAI FUNG Map pp226-7 Chinese

☎ 6836 8336; B1-03 Paragon Shopping Centre, 290 Orchard Rd; dishes from $7; 🕑 11am-10pm Mon-Fri, 10am-10pm Sat & Sun; Orchard MRT

One of the best restaurants in the country, this is the first Singapore branch of Taiwan's oldest dumpling and noodle chain. The food here, carefully prepared by the large team of chefs visible through the full-length glass of the kitchen, is simply unbelievable. A simple pork-and-shrimp dumpling soup, in a delicate broth, deserves savouring, while the fried rice, delicately flavoured with spring onion, is superb. A must visit.

GORDON GRILL Map pp226-7 International

☎ 6730 1744; Goodwood Park Hotel, 22 Scotts Rd; mains $25-35; 🕑 noon-2.30pm & 7-10.30pm; Orchard MRT

With its old Scottish military club atmosphere, complete with 'family' portraits, and its emphasis on robust beef dishes, the Gordon Grill is an old-world oasis in the middle of ultra-modern Orchard. As you might expect, there are hearty British Isles favourites like roast beef with Yorkshire pudding and sherry trifle, but in fact the menu is thoroughly international and caters to all tastes and appetites. If you don't fancy beef, try the seafood bouillabaisse.

HACHI Map pp226-7 Japanese

☎ 6734 9622; 03-06 Orchard Plaza, 150 Orchard Rd; dishes from $7; 🕑 7pm-midnight; Somerset MRT

One of the hidden gems of Orchard Rd, Hachi is a rough-and-tumble rural inn-style place that dispenses with the minimalist gentility of the usual Japanese restaurant (they won't even promise you a place if you call ahead). It's usually heaving with Japanese diners, but if there's a free space at the counter, just sit down and wait. There's no ordering; you simply eat whatever the chef's cooking until you've had enough, but you won't be disappointed. Count on spending $50, with a beer or two.

HALIA Map pp226-7 Modern Asian

☎ 6476 6711; Singapore Botanic Gardens, 1 Cluny Rd; mains $10-20; 🕑 11am-5.30pm & 6.30-10.30pm daily, plus 8-10am Sat & Sun; Orchard MRT, then bus 7, 77, 123 or 174 from Orchard Blvd

The outdoor deck at Halia, surrounded by the verdant fronds of the ginger plants in the Botanic Gardens, is a lovely place for a buffet breakfast ($15), lunch or, best of all, a romantic candlelit dinner. To be frank, the lunch menu is not particularly enticing, but in the evening things improve dramatically. Its speciality, a seafood stew filled with mussels, squid, lobster tails and fish, is superb and you shouldn't miss its signature ginger-honey drink.

IZAKAYA NIRUMARU

Map pp226-7 Japanese

☎ 6235 4857; 02-10 Cuppage Plaza; 5 Koek Rd; mains from $12; 🕑 closed lunch Sun; Somerset MRT

Modelled on the Japanese *izakaya* (drinking restaurant), the emphasis here is as much on boozing as it is eating. Sit down, order some sake and endless rounds of skewered meat and kiss the evening goodbye. Cuppage Plaza is extremely popular with expatriate Japanese, so don't be surprised to find yourself in a minority of one.

KILLINEY KOPITIAM Map pp226-7 Café

☎ 6734 3910; 67 Killiney Rd; 🕑 6am-11pm Mon & Wed-Sat, 6am-6pm Tue & Sun; Somerset MRT

A Singaporean institution. You come here more for the experience than the *kaya* toast, which is far better at **Ya Kun** (p116). But you can't beat the chaos and the cacophony – and the dubious pleasure of having a waiter yell your order so loud you'd think the cook was in Indonesia.

LINGZHI VEGETARIAN

Map pp226-7 Chinese

☎ 6734 3788; 05-01/02 Liat Towers, 541 Orchard Rd; mains $12-20; Orchard MRT

Offers traditional and imaginative modern Chinese vegetarian dishes. Unlike most vegetarian outlets, Lingzhi capitalises on fresh vegetables and this is reflected in its imaginative menu. At the entrance is a takeaway outlet selling dumplings, cakes and spring rolls. There's also a branch situated in **Chinatown** (Map pp234-5; Far East Sq).

MAGIC OF CHONGQING HOT POT

Map pp226-7 Chinese

☎ 6734 8135; 04-06/07 Tanglin Shopping Centre, 19 Tanglin Rd; buffet lunch/dinner from $15.90/24.90; Orchard MRT

Done out like an old Chongqing fisherman's café, with stone floors and a no-nonsense approach to food, this enormous eatery is the best place in the area for traditional cook-it-yourself spicy Sichuan-style steamboat. You can choose from an extensive MSG-free menu that includes a range of seafood, meat, eggs and vegetables. It gets very popular at weekends when the quality of service takes a dip and as a foreigner you may find yourself ignored, so go during the week.

MARMALADE PANTRY

Map pp226-7 Café

☎ **6734 2700; www.marmaladegroup.com; B1-08 Palais Renaissance, 390 Orchard Rd; mains $15-20; 11.30am-9pm; Orchard MRT**

Something of a hang-out for beautiful people (hence, presumably, the seating arranged in a circle) and the Carrie Bradshaws of Singapore (hence the location under Prada), the food is excellent, with the miso-baked tofu and sea bass both standouts. Of course, with a crowd like this, the desserts have to be exquisite – and you'll find lots of freshly manicured hands prodding at double chocolate pudding. Sunday brunch (10.30am to 4pm) is a particular event, but bookings are essential.

MEZZA9 Map pp226-7 International

☎ **6416 7189; Grand Hyatt Singapore, 10-12 Scotts Rd; mains $25; noon-11pm; Orchard MRT**

Flash Mezza9, on the mezzanine floor of the Hyatt's expansive lobby, wows with six display kitchens offering everything from sushi to elaborate desserts; sit where you like and order from any one of them. High tea is served 3pm to 5pm daily and the champagne Sunday brunch is popular.

NEWTON CIRCUS HAWKER CENTRE

Map pp226-7 Hawker Centre

Scotts Rd; 24hr; Newtown MRT

Near Newton MRT and best visited late in the evening when the atmosphere is liveliest, this is one of Singapore's iconic hawker centres and a long-time favourite with tourists. This popularity has of course led to some unSingaporean practices by the stall owners, like accosting you as you arrive and trying to direct you to a particular stall, but shrug them off and head in search of some excellent barbecued seafood at stall 47, duck rice at stall 85 or fried oyster at stall 65. Be sure to check the prices before you order.

SOUP RESTAURANT

Map pp226-7 Chinese

☎ **6333 8033; 25 Scotts Rd, 02-01 DFS Scottswalk; mains $4-15; Orchard MRT**

Serves dishes feasted on by Samsui women, who made up an important part of the construction industry in the pre-war era. It's good value for money, with an unpretentious menu consisting mostly of healthy soups and rice. A must-try is the restaurant's signature Samsui ginger chicken. A good meal with drinks will cost less than $30 per person. Among several other outlets are ones in **Chinatown** (Map pp234-5; ☎ 6222 9923; 25 Smith St) and **Suntec City** (Map p230; ☎ 6333 9886; B1-059 Suntec City).

SUNFLOWER VEGETARIAN

Map pp226-7 Vegetarian

☎ **6737 2854; 05-27 Far East Plaza, Scotts Rd; mains from $3; 11am-8pm Mon-Thu, 11am-8.30pm Fri & Sat; Orchard MRT**

Top-notch vegetarian food nestling in a far corner of Far East Plaza; deservedly popular for its $3 'Green Lunch' special (so called because the rice or *bee hoon* is cooked in a homemade spinach oil), which offers a choice of up to 14 dishes, starting from 11am until everything's sold out. After that it's à la carte – the wonton laksa ($5.80) and sesame beancurd ($3) are particularly tasty.

TOP OF THE M Map pp226-7 International

☎ **6831 6258; 39th fl, Mandarin Singapore, 333 Orchard Rd; mains from $25; Somerset MRT**

This revolving restaurant provides a 360° view of Singapore and is a perfect spot for a not-too-serious romantic evening (it's hard to be earnestly lovey-dovey when you're being serenaded by a wandering quartet of musicians). The French and Italian menu is as large as the portions, but you won't be disappointed by the lobster or the pepper steak, both of which are house specialities. Come before 7.30pm to catch the sunset.

YA KUN KAYA TOAST

Map pp226-7 Breakfast

☎ **6738 4815; Basement, Takashimaya, Ngee Ann City, 391A Orchard Rd; 10am-9.30pm; Orchard MRT**

Started by a Hainanese immigrant in Telok Ayer in the 1920s, before moving to Cross St, the classic coffee, *kaya* toast and eggs

THE INVENTION OF CHILLI CRAB

In 1956 Mr and Mrs Lim opened a seafood restaurant called the Palm Beach. It was here that Mrs Lim first concocted the now-famous tomato, chilli and egg sauce that makes the quintessential Singapore chilli crab. At least that's the story according to her son Roland, who is the proprietor of the eponymous Roland Restaurant (p118). (Singaporean food outlets love their rags-to-riches tales.)

The Lims emigrated to New Zealand in the 1960s but Roland returned to Singapore to find his Mum's dish a huge hit. He opened his own restaurant in 1985, and since moving to its present location along Marine Pde in 2000, the 1300-seater place has built up a solid reputation – so much so that former prime minister Goh Chok Tong always dines here on National Day.

Apart from the chilli crab, Roland has also won an award for his USA duck – meat roasted in a palm sugar sauce. Mrs Lim's original sauce is available in jars to take away ($3.50).

breakfast here is the best in the city. Thanks to the wonders of modern chain-store thinking, you can now sample the stuff in 15 locations around Singapore, including **Raffles Hospital** (Map p232), **Far East Sq** (Map pp234–5) and **Tanjong Pagar Rd** (Map pp234–5).

EASTERN SINGAPORE

Few visitors spend a great deal of time in eastern Singapore, except perhaps to visit East Coast Park, but there are several exceptional eating options in the area, from the Peranakan delights around Katong to the superb seafood along the East Coast.

328 KATONG LAKSA

Map p236 Peranakan

216 East Coast Rd; laksa $5; bus 12, 14 or 32

As controversial food subjects go, the source of the original, authentic Katong laksa is one of the most emotive. Apparently this one is the original, though it is no longer in the original location, which has been taken over by a rival who claims his is the authentic laksa (starting to get the picture?). Anyway, the laksa here, sprinkled with fresh cockles, is magnificent, so who really cares?

CHARLIE'S CORNER

Map pp222-3 American

☎ 6542 0867; 01-08 Changi Village Hawker Centre; dishes $10; bus 2 from Tanah Merah MRT

This Western food outlet, unlike most hawker-centre Western food, is something of an institution, serving up fish and chips, barbecue chicken wings and chilli dogs with a choice of more than 50 types of beer (which, more than the food, might account for its legendary status). Pop in if you're heading to the ferry terminal for Pulau Ubin.

EAST COAST LAGOON FOOD VILLAGE Map p236 Hawker Centre

East Coast Park Service Rd; bus 12, 14 or 32

Perfect for a cheap outdoor lunch and a beer or two after a stroll, cycle or rollerblade through East Coast Park, this popular hawker centre gets packed at weekends, but there's usually enough space to bag yourself a table. Options are limited compared with other hawker centres, but try the Leng Heng BBQ Seafood at stall 6 (which stays open until 2am), or the very tasty beef *kway teow* at stall 33.

EAST COAST SEAFOOD CENTRE

Map p236 Seafood

☎ 6442 3435; www.jumboseafood.com.sg; East Coast Parkway; dishes $25-30; 🕒 5pm-midnight; bus 12, 14 or 32

This hugely popular hall of marine indulgence was undergoing extensive renovation at the time of writing, but its reopening will no doubt be a cause for celebration, as the original was always packed. The breezy waterside location makes this a prime spot to enjoy some of the best seafood in Singapore.

GUAN HOE SOON Map p236 Peranakan

☎ 6344 2761; 214 Joo Chiat Rd; mains under $20; 🕒 closed Tue; Payar Lebar MRT

Lee Kuan Yew gets his takeaway from this place, which has been turning out fine Nonya cuisine for around 50 years, but it caters to everyone from the father of modern Singapore to the vest-and-flip-flops HDB

TOP FIVE MEALS WITH A VIEW

Singapore is not short of restaurants that offer sweeping views of the city. Here's our pick of the best five, in order of height:

- **Equinox** (p104) Seventy floors up; the most staggering views of the city from Southeast Asia's highest restaurant.
- **Top of the M** (p116) Thirty-nine floors up; Filipino wandering minstrels in a revolving dining room.
- **Hai Tien Lo** (p104) Thirty-seven floors up; superb modern Chinese cuisine, accessed by a dizzying bubble lift.
- **Sky Dining** (p120) Sixty metres up; riding in your private cable car cabin, you can forgive the mediocre meal.
- **Blu** (p114) Twenty-four floors up; bathed in blue, with extremely low lighting and jazz, an ideal spot for romantics.

heartlanders. This is the place to sample *ayam buah keluak* (chicken and ground-nut curry).

LONG BEACH SEAFOOD RESTAURANT Map p236 — Seafood

☎ 6445 8833; 1018 East Coast Parkway; dishes $25-30; bus 12, 14 or 32

The casual and huge Long Beach Seafood Restaurant, which has been around since the 1950s, is famous for its black-pepper crabs and 'live drunken prawns', which are soaked in brandy. It's the only place you can get crab all year round. Try the Alaskan King crab with white pepper sauce which, even at $88 a kilo, is memorable.

MANGO TREE Map p236 — Indian

☎ 6442 8655; 1000 East Coast Parkway; mains $10-25; 🕐 6.30-10.30pm Sun-Thu, 11.30am-11pm Fri & Sat; bus 12, 14 or 32

One of the classiest restaurants at East Coast Park's Marina Cove, this small, stylish beachfront eatery specialises in coastal Indian food, mainly from Goa and Kerala in the southwest, where the flavours and spices are gentler. The prawn and coconut curry is excellent and try the superlative creamy black *dahl* as a filling side dish. Prices are a little steep, but the breezy beachfront location is excellent.

NO SIGNBOARD SEAFOOD Map pp224-5 — Seafood

☎ 6344 9959; 50 Stadium Blvd, Kallang; mains from $20; 🕐 noon-midnight; Kallang MRT

In one of the three pods hovering over the water is a branch of the famous No Signboard Seafood where you can have their renowned white pepper crab, cereal prawns, *sambal kangkong* or Sri Lankan crabs ($30 a kilo) cooked to order. The restaurant, originally a hawker-centre stall in the 1970s, is hugely successful; other branches can be found at its original location at **414 Geylang Rd** (Map p236; ☎ 6842 3415) and at the **Esplanade** (Map p230; ☎ 6336 9959).

ROLAND RESTAURANT Map p236 — Seafood

☎ 6440 8205; Block 89, 06-750 Marine Parade Central; crabs from $14; bus 12, 14 or 32

On top of a car park, but don't let that put you off. If its chilli crab and USA duck (see The Invention of Chilli Crab, p117) are good enough for the prime minister, they're good enough for us.

VILLAGE WOK RESTAURANT Map pp224-5 — Chinese

☎ 6743 9743; 10, Lorong 3, Geylang; mains from $12; Kallang MRT

A no-nonsense eatery serving up hearty Cantonese rural fare; locals come here for specialities like village smoked chicken and steamed live pa-ting fish and fried eggplants with squid. The owner is quite a celebrity and counts several well-known Singaporeans among his devoted customers.

WERNER'S OVEN BAKERY & RESTAURANT Map p236 — German

☎ 6442 3897; 6 Upper East Coast Rd; mains $7.50-21.50; 🕐 8.30am-10pm Tue-Sun; bus 12, 14 or 32

It lacks the ostentatiously Teutonic décor of other German restaurants in town (in fact it's downright plain looking), but the food here is robust and tasty. Ignore the spaghetti and burgers and plunge into a rich oxtail stew, a bratwurst, *bockwurst* or splendid wild garlic sausage (all served with a fine sauerkraut and mashed potatoes), some crispy pork knuckle or German meatloaf, washed down with some Erdinger or Paulaner beer. There are some superb breads in the bakery, too.

NORTHERN & CENTRAL SINGAPORE

BORSHCH Map pp222-3 European
6280 4351; 58 Serangoon Garden Way; dishes $15; Ang Mo Kio MRT

Among Serangoon Gardens' oodles of other restaurants and cafés is Borshch, specialising in Western food – mainly steaks – with a few Russian favourites, such as the beetroot soup, thrown in for variety. It's good value and the portions are hearty.

CHOMP CHOMP Map pp222-3 Food Court
Kensington Park Rd; 6pm-1am; Ang Mo Kio MRT

The focus of the former British military married quarters in Serangoon Gardens is the massively popular Chomp Chomp food court, bang opposite the roundabout, and going strong since 1972. Wander the smoky aisles to see what takes your fancy – we took a serious shine to the *sambal stingray* at stall 8 and the *wantan mee* at stall 12.

LE P'TIT BRETON Map pp222-3 French Crepes
6259 4300; 200 Upper Thompson Rd; crepes from $4; noon-2.30pm Wed-Sat, 6.30-9.30pm Tue-Sun, 10am-3pm Sun; bus 410 from Bishan MRT

Well worth a detour if you're heading to or from **MacRitchie Reservoir** (p78), or the **Kong Meng San Phor Kark See Monastery** (p78). This tiny Breton-style café with its quaint little net curtains makes the most unbelievably delicious crepes (or *galettes*, as they are known in Brittany) in the most unlikely location. Try the pork sausage, *forestiere* (mushroom), or goat's cheese for savoury, or the orgasmic banana rum, chocolate strawberry and apple caramel for dessert. The real French cider is easily worth a trip on its own.

SOUTHERN & WESTERN SINGAPORE

The main dining hub in this part of Singapore is Holland Village. Don't be surprised to find yourself surrounded by other foreigners here – this is Expat Central after all and one of the only places outside the quays where locals are outnumbered. Prices are high and the atmosphere can be a shade cliquey, but there are a few outstanding restaurants that make this little ghetto worth a visit. Most of the cafés and eateries are clustered along Lorong Mambong, many of them reliable chain outlets like Coffee Bean, Thai Express, Crystal Jade, NYDC, Haagen Dazs and Al Dente. For a less crowded and mall-like atmosphere, head for the classier stretch along Jalan Merah Saga, where you can find the area's more exclusive restaurants.

AL HAMRA Map pp222-3 Middle Eastern
6464 8488; 23 Lorong Mambong; mains $15-24; Buona Vista MRT

A worthy range of dips (try the *mezze* platter for $10 or huge mixed grill) and juicy kebabs and friendly service make this a popular spot. The outdoor tables are frequently packed, but even on a busy night the softly-lit interior has a cosy feel. Unlike many Arabic restaurants, this one serves alcohol.

BADEN-BADEN Map pp222-3 German
6468 5585; 42 Lorong Mambong; dishes from $12; 11.30am-midnight Mon-Fri, 11.30am-1am Sat, 12.30pm-midnight Sun; Buona Vista MRT

A Teutonic-themed bar popular with the expat crowd, which offers some very hearty, meaty German food, from the usual range of sausages to an excellent pork knuckle. Of course, there's a range of German beers on tap to wash down all the grease.

FOSTERS Map pp222-3 English
6466 8939; 277 Holland Ave; dishes from $15; 11am-11pm Sun-Thu, 11am-1am Fri & Sat; Buona Vista MRT

The words 'English' and 'cuisine' might not get your stomach rumbling, but this is actually an appealing place, with scones-and-cream afternoon teas, a pub-style menu and a surprisingly rustic outdoor terrace. Not surprisingly, the crowd is mostly expats, which means prices are high ($18 for fish and chips and $28 for a steak).

GEEZ BARBECUE FISH
Map pp222-3 Seafood
Block 40, Holland Dr 01-39; dishes $5-10; 5-10.30pm Tue-Sun; Buona Vista MRT

You could be moved to tears – literally – by the *sambal stingray* ($8 to $10, or $5 set meal) here, with its impossibly delicious, and impossibly hot, homemade chilli sauce. The succulent prawns are also magnificent.

Even though it's in Holland Village, expats don't usually find their way here.

MICHELANGELO'S Map pp222-3 Italian

☎ 6475 9069; 44 Jalan Merah Saga 01-60; mains from $20; ⌚ closed lunch Sat; Buona Vista MRT

Along peaceful, upmarket Jalan Merah Saga, Michelangelo's is definitely a place for the hungry. Ignore the cheesy reproduction artwork and dive into the epic portions of mussels, lamb shanks and pastas. There's also an impressive wine list.

ORIGINAL SIN Map pp222-3 Vegetarian

☎ 6475 5605; 43 Jalan Merah Saga 01-62; mains $20-30; Buona Vista MRT

Friendly and relaxed; the food is exceptional, accompanied by one of the best wine lists in the city. Try the stuffed portobello mushrooms ($15), ricotta cake ($20) or Moroccan eggplant ($22), washed down with a Portuguese port and try to forget that it looks like you're in a fancy Australian suburb. Fantastic.

SAMY'S CURRY RESTAURANT

Map pp226-7 Indian

☎ 6472 2080; Civil Service Club, Block 25, Dempsey Rd; mains from $3; bus 7 or 174 from Orchard MRT

A Singaporean institution; not strictly in Holland Village, but worth the effort to get here for the magnificent food served up on banana leaves, and also the colonial throwback ambience. Set in an old hall with wooden shutters, ceiling fans and a veranda surrounded by greenery – you'll hardly know you're in Singapore. Go in, sit down and pick from the array of curries brought round in silver buckets by the waiters. Someone else will come and take your beer order ($17 for a jug of Tiger from the Civil Service Club next door; you pay on the spot). A vegetarian meal of rice, *dahl*, raita and pappadam costs less than $3. Add a couple of meat dishes and you'll pay around $10. Priceless.

SENTOSA ISLAND

Sentosa eating has come on in leaps and bounds recently, once the management realised it wasn't against the law to provide something other than junk food at a tourist attraction. Siloso Beach is the centre of the island's culinary renaissance, but there are also a couple of reasonable options on Palawan and Tanjong Beaches. Many of the eateries double as bars in the evenings, catering mainly to the bikini-clad club crowd (see Entertainment, p125).

COASTES map p237 International

☎ 6338 8832; Siloso Beach; snacks & mains $5-16; ⌚ 10am-10pm Mon-Thu, 9am-1am Fri & Sat, 9am-10pm Sun; shuttle bus from HarbourFront MRT

One of Sentosa's newest and trendiest eateries, with an attractive, open wooden deck; serves up tasty thin-crust pizzas, burgers and enormous curries to an acid jazz soundtrack. Sit at the wooden tables or get your food served to you on one of the loungers.

SAKAE SUSHI map p237 Japanese

☎ 6276 5516; Siloso Beach; sushi/sashimi from $2; ⌚ 11am-9.30pm Mon-Thu, 11am-11pm Fri, 10am-11pm Sat, 10am-9.30pm Sun; shuttle bus from HarbourFront MRT

The latest in a chain of Sakae restaurants, considered among the best in Singapore, this one boasts a huge conveyor belt and a bewilderingly large menu. You can sit at one of the wooden picnic benches outside, but somehow sashimi and sand doesn't quite fit, so we prefer the air-conditioned interior.

SKY DINING Map p237 European

☎ 6377 9633; www.mountfaber.com.sg; 4-course meals $68-138; ⌚ 6.30-8.30pm Tue-Sun; shuttle bus from HarbourFront MRT

Mt Faber Leisure Group's dining cabins are not quite the mile-high dining club, but as close as you're going to get. The novelty might wear thin by dessert, but gliding from Mt Faber to Sentosa taking in the sunset cityscape is a stunning way to spend an evening. The four-course meal with glass of wine costs $68/138 midweek/weekend. The food is frankly forgettable, but the experience isn't. Booking at least 24 hours in advance (48 hours for weekends) is essential.

TRAPIZZA Map p237 Italian

☎ 6376 2622; Siloso Beach; pizzas from $10; ⌚ 11am-9pm Sun-Thu, 11am-midnight Fri, 11am-11pm Sat; shuttle bus from HarbourFront MRT

Open wooden-deck affair next to the trapeze school (hence the name); the emphasis is on families rather than posing. The Italian pizzas here are top-notch. Great spot for dinner at the end of a long hot day on the sand.

Entertainment

Entertainment

Boring Singapore? Forget it. For a tiny island, the country packs in a remarkable number of things to do. It's not just drinking either – though the nightlife is among the best in Asia. There's a thriving theatre scene, music from indie to jazz and classical, and plenty of cinemas showing Hollywood, Bollywood, Hong Kong and everything in between.

Thanks to the Singapore government's tight control over development zoning, there are numerous areas given over almost entirely to bars, clubs and restaurants. The most popular strips, where a bar crawl means you won't have to walk more than 300m all night, are Mohamed Sultan (drop the 'Rd' if you don't want to sound like a tourist), Chijmes in the Colonial District, Clarke Quay, Robertson Quay and Boat Quay (including Circular Rd), Club St in Chinatown, Emerald Hill and, to a lesser extent, the expat ghetto Holland Village.

The once ascendant Boat Quay has fallen out of favour in the ever-fickle world of drinking fashion, though it still heaves with people. Despite its ludicrous gumdrop makeover, Clarke Quay is the place to go (though how cool you can look sitting on a giant lilypad is debatable). Robertson Quay is also popular. Mohamed Sultan is perennially packed, though for our money the road is too wide to give the area much atmosphere.

Emerald Hill, a strip of former Peranakan shophouses off Orchard Rd, houses a number of very tastefully renovated bars with a great atmosphere. Similarly, Club St is full of mostly excellent bars inside old shophouses and clan headquarters.

Sentosa's nightlife scene has become much more lively in recent years as part of a seemingly successful attempt to make this once unfashionable island popular with the club crowd, for whom the prospect of partying on a beach, artificial or not, has proven too good to resist.

Activity junkies won't be disappointed either. Singaporeans are very keen on sport and, without a winter to keep them indoors, there's a whole range of opportunities throughout the year to jump around, skim across, run about and hit back and forth.

Tickets & Reservations

SISTIC (☎ 6348 5555; www.sistic.com.sg) has a virtual monopoly on event ticket sales in Singapore and its outlets can be found all over the city, including the DBS Arts Centre (Map pp224–5), Parco Bugis Junction (Map p232), Suntec City (Map p230), Victoria Theatre & Concert Hall (Map p230) and Wisma Atria (Map pp226–7) on Orchard Rd. The website provides a convenient rundown of all the major events coming up in Singapore.

SLEAZY SINGAPORE

It comes as quite a surprise to many, but Singapore has a seedy underbelly of some repute. Prostitution is legal, but there are still large numbers of illegal sex workers, particularly from China. Meanwhile, an unintended offshoot of the budget airline boom has been the number of prostitutes flying down from Thailand, earning money they only dreamed of back home, then flying back before their visas run out.

The sleaze centre of the city is undoubtedly Geylang, where it is officially restricted to the even-numbered Lorong. There is also a significant pocket of activity along Joo Chiat Rd. Both of these areas are popular mainly among ethnic Chinese.

The Indian sleaze hotspot is Desker Rd, the successor to the famous Bugis St, where prostitutes and transvestites ply their trade.

Orchard Towers – the famous 'four floors of whores' – is the venue of choice for Europeans, though it has recently become a fashionably ironic hangout for trendy Singaporeans as well. The escalators of the towers are usually patrolled by transvestites trying to pick up men before they reach the bars.

For a fascinating insider's look into the high-class sex industry, read *Invisible Trade* by Gerrie Lim, available in most bookshops.

THEATRE

The **Singapore Arts Festival** (www.singaporeartsfest.com), which features many drama performances, is held in June. Music, art and dance are also represented at the festival, which includes a Fringe Festival featuring plenty of street performances.

The opening of the **Esplanade – Theatres on the Bay** (Map p230; ☎ 6828 8222; www.esplanade.com; 1 Esplanade Dr) has thrown the spotlight on Singapore's vibrant theatre and dance scene. Other performance venues include the following:

Black Box (Map p230; ☎ 6338 4077; Fort Canning Centre)

DBS Arts Centre (Map pp224-5; ☎ 6733 8166; 20 Merbau Rd)

Drama Centre (Map p230; ☎ 6336 0005; Canning Rise)

Guinness Theatre (Map p230; The Substation, 45 Armenian St)

Jubilee Hall (Map p230; ☎ 6331 1732; 3rd fl, Raffles Hotel Arcade, 328 North Bridge Rd)

Kallang Theatre (Map pp224-5; ☎ 6345 8488; Stadium Rd)

Substation (Map p230; ☎ 6337 7800; www.substation.org; 45 Armenian St; box office 4-8.30pm Mon-Fri)

Victoria Theatre & Concert Hall (Map p230; ☎ 6345 8488; 11 Empress Pl)

ACTION THEATRE Map p230

☎ 6837 0842; www.action.org.sg; 42 Waterloo St; Dhoby Ghaut MRT

Set in a two-storey heritage house, this established theatre group shows local and international plays with contemporary themes in its small, 100-seat upstairs theatre and in the two open-air venues.

NECESSARY STAGE Map p236

☎ 6440 8115; www.necessary.org; B1-02 Marine Parade Community Bldg, 278 Marine Parade Rd; bus 12, 14 or 32

One of Singapore's best-known experimental theatre groups; does some great interactive and collaborative works with schools.

NRITYALAYA AESTHETICS SOCIETY

Map p230

☎ 6336 6537; www.nas.org.sg; 01-01 Stamford Arts Centre, 155 Waterloo St; Dhoby Ghaut MRT

Singapore's only full-time Indian dance and music troop. The society also holds an annual drama festival.

SINGAPORE DANCE THEATRE Map p230

☎ 6338 0611; www.singaporedancetheatre.com; 2nd storey, Fort Canning Centre, Cox Tce; Dhoby Ghaut MRT

This top dance company performs traditional ballets and contemporary works. The group's Ballet under the Stars season at Fort Canning Park is very popular. There are regular classes in ballet, jazz ballet and pilates.

SINGAPORE REPERTORY THEATRE

Map pp224-5

☎ 6221 5585; www.srt.com.sg; DBS Arts Centre, 20 Merbau Rd; bus 54 from Clarke Quay MRT

Based at the DBS Arts Centre but also performing at other venues, this theatre group offers up repertory standards such as works by Shakespeare, Tennessee Williams and Arthur Miller, as well as some modern Singaporean plays.

THEATREWORKS Map p230

☎ 6338 4007; www.theatreworks.org.sg; The Black Box, Fort Canning Centre, Cox Tce; Dhoby Ghaut MRT

One of the more experimental and interesting theatre companies in Singapore. Often performs at the Black Box theatre.

TOY FACTORY THEATRE ENSEMBLE

Map pp234-5

☎ 6222 1526; www.toyfactory.org.sg; 15A Smith St; Chinatown MRT

The cutting-edge bilingual Toy Factory Theatre Ensemble gives foreign works a local spin and brings plays such as *Shopping and F***ing* to Singaporean audiences. It also stages traditional Chinese performances.

WILD!RICE

☎ 6223 9081; www.wildrice.com.sg

Possibly Singapore's most accomplished theatre group, due in no small part to the talents of artistic director Ivan Heng. Wild Rice's productions range from farce to serious politics and fearlessly wade into issues not commonly on the agenda in Singapore.

CINEMAS

Movie-going is hugely popular in Singapore, and, at around $8.50 per ticket, it's great value. Multiplex cinemas abound, and you can find city centre ones at Parco Bugis

Junction (Map p230), Shaw Towers on Beach Rd (Map p230), Suntec City (Map p230), Marina Square Complex (Map p230), Cathay Cineleisure Orchard (Map pp226–7), Plaza Singapura (Map pp226–7) and Shaw House (Map pp226–7), all on or near Orchard Rd, among other places. For screening times, check the *Straits Times*.

The roster of movies consists mainly of Hollywood blockbusters and Chinese, Korean and Japanese crowd pleasers, plus a few art-house hits from around the world. The **Singapore International Film Festival** (www.filmfest.org.sg) held each April brings an enormous collection of independent films to the country.

Singapore's cinemas are notoriously chilly places, so bring something warm to wear.

Latest screenings usually start around midnight, but Level 4 at the Cathay Cineleisure Orchard has three 24-hour cinemas on Fridays and Saturdays.

Outdoor mini-festivals are occasionally held in Fort Canning Park.

ALLIANCE FRANÇAISE Map pp226-7

☎ 6737 8422; www.alliancefrancaise.org.sg; 1 Sarkies Rd; Newton MRT

Screens classic and contemporary French films Tuesdays at 8pm. Tickets are $8 for nonmembers. Check the website for times.

A movie poster in Little India (p59)

BRITISH COUNCIL Map pp226-7

☎ 6473 1111; 30 Napier Rd; Orchard MRT

The British Council has occasional screenings of British movies.

GOLDEN VILLAGE Map pp226-7

☎ 6735 8484; www.gv.com.sg; 1 Kim Seng Promenade; Somerset MRT

For the ultimate pampered cinematic experience, $25 gets you a ticket to this 'gold class' cinema on the 3rd floor of the Great World City mall. There are seats that can be reclined and adjusted with little levers, little tables for your food and drinks, and waiters who take your order.

CABARET & COMEDY

Singapore has two regular comedy clubs, both of which charge around $50 a ticket for top acts from the UK, US and Australia. **1nitestand Comedy Club** (tickets from CalendarOne TicketCharge) has a regular gig at **Milieu** (Map pp226–7; ☎ 6732 7012; 2nd fl, Peranakan Pl, 180 Orchard Rd), while **Punchline Comedy Club** (Map pp226–7; ☎ 6831 4656; Bar None, Singapore Marriott, 320 Orchard Rd) has shows on the last Tuesday and Wednesday of the month (tickets from SISTIC). The Crazy Horse nude cabaret from France was set to open at Clarke Quay late in 2005, to the delight and surprise of many.

IGOR'S MAIN EVENT Map pp224-5

☎ 6440 2725; 50 Stadium Blvd; Kallang MRT

On Thursday, Friday and Saturday nights from 7.30pm, near the Indoor Stadium in Kallang, you can go all Rocky Horror at Igor's Main Event, which bills itself as (perhaps thankfully) Southeast Asia's only horror-theme theatre restaurant. The $60 ticket includes the comedy and music show, and a three-course meal that no-one raves about.

NEPTUNE Map pp234-5

☎ 6224 3922; 7th fl, Overseas Union House, 50 Collyer Quay; Raffles Place MRT

Neptune is a Chinese cabaret serving Cantonese food that is rarely patronised by Westerners. Its status as Singapore's only topless cabaret has been undermined by the arrival of the Crazy Horse at Clarke Quay.

DRINKING

Despite relatively high prices for alcohol, Singapore's bar scene is incredibly lively and, since the licensing laws were substantially relaxed, some even say it's overtaken Bangkok as Southeast Asia's nightlife capital.

It's not all $15 beers either. Hit the bars early to take advantage of the happy hours, which typically stretch from around 5pm to 9pm (unless stated otherwise). At these times you'll generally get two of most drinks for the price of one and cheaper 'house-pours', which are the bar's selections of spirits or wine. On Wednesday or Thursday night, some bars offer cheaper, and sometimes free, drinks to women, presumably on the assumption that drunk women attract paying men.

Singapore's newly liberal licensing laws mean many bars and clubs stay open until the early hours, some right through to breakfast. Round Midnight, Insomnia and Bed Room Bar are all popular with boozers who don't like to go home until the birds are twittering.

This all comes at a price, though. If you don't want to end the evening broke and don't mind plastic tables and fluorescent lights, you can drink bottles of Tiger for as little as $5 at hawker centres and coffee shops. In fact, sitting outdoors on a balmy night with a few large bottles and a few plates of food may just be one of the abiding memories you take away from Singapore, rather than blowing $200 in a club.

GAY & LESBIAN NIGHTLIFE

For a while, Singapore was threatening to become the gay party capital of Asia, with the Nation event on Sentosa and the SnowBall party at Christmas seemingly established annual events. But in 2005 the government decided enough was enough and shut them down, saying such events contributed to an alarming rise in HIV infections in the country. There was an enraged reaction, but the Prime Minister remained adamant that Singapore was not ready for the 'promotion' of 'alternative lifestyles'.

That said, the day-to-day gay night scene continues to thrive. The centre of the action is Chinatown, where there is a concentration of pubs and clubs around Tanjong Pagar Rd and beyond. See the website **Utopia** (www.utopia-asia.com) for detailed listings.

ACTORS' BAR Map p230

☎ 6533 2436; 13/15 South Bridge Rd; 5pm-2am Mon-Thu, 5pm-3am Fri & Sat; Clarke Quay MRT

The Backstage Bar's lesbian-friendly sibling is the Actors' Bar, a classy two-storey place over the 7-Eleven. There are different theme nights, and pool ($2) is a popular pastime.

ALLEY BAR Map pp226-7

☎ 6732 6966; 2 Emerald Hill Rd, 180 Orchard Rd; 5pm-2am Sun-Thu, 5pm-3am Fri & Sat; Somerset MRT

Emerald Hill Rd has a collection of bars in the renovated terraces just up from Orchard Rd that formerly housed many Peranakan families. The focal point of Alley Bar has to be the large gilded mirror hanging at the far end of the room, while the décor reflects the name of the bar, which has been done up to look like a street, with fake shop-fronts, parking meters and street signs.

BACKSTAGE BAR Map pp234-5

☎ 6227 1712; 13A Trengganu St; 7pm-2am Sun-Thu, 7pm-3am Fri & Sat; Chinatown MRT

One of the best bars in Singapore – gay or straight – is the Backstage Bar, which is friendly and relaxed with a roomy balcony on which to hang out if the cosy interior gets too packed. Most people drop by here first before heading on to the clubs later. The entrance is up the stairs on Temple St.

BAR OPIUME Map p230

☎ 6339 1720; 1 Empress Pl; 5pm-2am Mon-Thu, 5pm-3am Fri & Sat, 5pm-1am Sun; Raffles Place MRT

Very posey, Bar Opiume is next to its sibling restaurant **Indochine Waterfront** (p105) facing Boat Quay. The expensive, slightly mismatched décor features a huge chandelier and large standing Buddhas. Not surprisingly for a location like this, the drink prices might have you sipping slowly, but the quiet spot next to the river is priceless.

BAR SÁ VANH Map pp234-5

☎ 6323 0145; 49 Club St; 5pm-2am Mon-Thu, 5pm-3am Fri & Sat; Chinatown MRT

If you're after more than just a drink, this is one of those 'do you remember…' places. The main attraction is a large waterfall cascading into a tranquil koi pond, surrounded by large Buddha statues, wafting incense and teak furniture. The music is mostly alternative, fusion style, which does not drown out conversation. Drinks are expensive, but it's worth having at least one.

BARRIO CHINO Map pp234-5
☎ 6324 3245; 60 Club St; 🕒 4pm-midnight Mon-Thu, 4pm-2am Fri, 4pm-1am Sat; Chinatown MRT
This cosy Spanish bar boasts great frozen margaritas, a large wine selection and some tasty tapas. Either sit out on the five-foot way or enjoy the intimate set-up inside. Good Latin music sets the mood.

BEAUJOLAIS WINE BAR Map pp234-5
☎ 6224 2227; 1 Ann Siang Hill; 🕒 11am-midnight Mon-Thu, 11am-2am Fri, 6pm-2am Sat; Chinatown MRT
A cute, cosy, welcoming shophouse bar that has the occasional cheese-and-wine night for around $30. Space is very limited inside, but there is seating upstairs and a few tables outside in the five-foot way. The placid ambience is enhanced by soft lighting and low-level jazz.

BED ROOM BAR Map p230
☎ 9009 7424; 68 Circular Rd; 🕒 5pm-7am; Raffles Place MRT
Yes, you read right: this narrow Canadian-owned hole-in-the-wall bar stays open until 7am – and as such is a magnet for the city's hardcore drinkers. Gloomy, decorated with Chinese lanterns, ice-hockey jerseys and a decent pool table, it has a certain dingy charm and is one of the few places in the city to get Canadian beer. Happy hour runs from 5pm to 9pm.

BISOUS BAR Map pp234-5
☎ 6226 5505; 25 Church St, Capital Square Three; 🕒 11am-1am Mon-Thu, 11am-2am Fri, 5pm-2am Sat; Raffles Place MRT
Bisous occupies three Chinese shophouses with lovely architectural designs and is popular with business types and sports fans, thanks to its large TV screens. Regular promotions – like the Wednesday night $5 Heineken Hour (7pm to 8pm) – draws in the crowds. There's also some decent Mexican, Mediterranean and other international cuisine for both lunch and dinner.

BLUE COW Map pp234-5
☎ 6227 9527; 87 Club St; 🕒 3pm-midnight Mon-Wed, 1pm-2am Thu & Fri, 4pm-2am Sat, 4pm-midnight Sun; Chinatown MRT
The Blue Cow is a funky café and bar that was recently relocated to burgeoning Club St. It's a great place to chill over some beers, play pool and listen to some pumping US rock and Britpop.

BORA BORA BEACH BAR Map p237
☎ 9005 4238; Palawan Beach; 🕒 11am-9pm Sun-Thu, 11am-11pm Fri & Sat; shuttle bus from HarbourFront MRT
Bora Bora is one of the more established beach bars on Sentosa, but it attracts a crowd during the weekends and holidays, drawn to its relaxed atmosphere and jazzy music. The food is nothing to write home about though.

BREWERKZ Map p230
☎ 6438 7438; 01-05 Riverside Point Centre, 30 Merchant Rd; 🕒 noon-midnight Sun-Thu, noon-1am Fri & Sat; Clarke Quay MRT
One of Singapore's gems, this sprawling microbrewery and restaurant offers eight beers brewed on site, all of which are superb, varying in strength from 4.5% to 6%. The India Pale Ale is apparently the most popular, but the dark beer and the Golden Ale are excellent. Even the Strawberry Beer isn't nearly as bad as it sounds. A seven-set sampler is a good way to discover which is your favourite and get mildly tipsy in the process. Best of all is the lunchtime happy hour, when between noon and 3pm you can down mugs for an incredible $3. The food is superb too.

BRIX Map pp226-7
☎ 6416 7107; Basement, Grand Hyatt Singapore, 10 Scotts Rd; 🕒 7pm-3am Sun-Wed, 7pm-4am Thu-Sat; Orchard MRT
A popular place divided into three distinct sections, each with its own atmosphere. The music bar is the spot for dancing. The band, which changes every few months, features many international and local artists, while DJs fill in the slots with the latest R&B, disco and soul. The funky brickwork wine bar has an impressive wine list, while a nice range of single malts await you at the whiskey bar.

CAFÉ IGUANA Map p230

☎ 6236 1275; 01-03 Riverside Point, 30 Merchant Rd; 6pm-1am Mon-Thu, 6pm-3am Fri & Sat, noon-1am Sun; Clarke Quay MRT

Iguana claims to have the largest range of tequila in Southeast Asia, and with more than 100 varieties on offer, who's arguing? A friendly Mexican-themed café with bright colours and some decidedly eccentric décor, serving up some excellent Mexican finger-food staples on long, communal tables. Score an outside table for more privacy.

CHIHULY LOUNGE Map p230

☎ 6434 5288; 3rd fl, Ritz-Carlton Millenia Singapore, 7 Raffles Ave; 8am-1am; City Hall MRT

With its distinctive blue arched roof and amazing Daly Chihuly glass sculpture on the wall (his work is also on display at the Singapore Art Museum), this refined hotel lounge deserves a bit of sartorial effort and is worth a visit for an early evening loosener or a late-night wind-down cocktail.

CLUB BY APHRODISIAC Map pp234-5

☎ 6325 8529; 47 Club St; 5pm-2am Mon-Thu, 5pm-3am Fri & Sat; Chinatown MRT

Sports classical Greek statues, chrome and leather furniture – all apparently designed to set the mood for lovin'. With jasmine incense in the background and lots of dark corners with just the right blue luminous lighting, it does a pretty good job. It has recently transformed into a club and gives you access to the adjoining **Bar Sá Vanh** (p125). Drinks are pricey.

CLUB ISLANDER Map p237

☎ 6376 2950; Palawan Beach; 11am-7pm Mon-Fri, 11am-9pm Sat & Sun; shuttle bus from HarbourFront MRT

The early closing times are not going to make it a huge party spot, but with a live band playing most weekend nights it's a great place to start your evening before heading off to one of the late-night bars.

COOL DECK Map p237

☎ 6274 3425; Siloso Beach; 11am-9pm Mon-Fri, 11am-11pm Sat & Sun; shuttle bus from HarbourFront MRT

On the beach just below the Underwater World bus stop, this square-shaped open-air bar has a classic beach-bar feel to it and probably the most extensive alcohol selection on Sentosa. Great for a boozy get-together.

CRAZY ELEPHANT Map p230

☎ 6337 1990; www.crazyelephant.com; 01-07 Clarke Quay, 3E River Valley Rd; 5pm-1am Sun-Thu, 3pm-2am Fri & Sat; Clarke Quay MRT

The Crazy Elephant is very popular with tourists and locals alike because of its live heavy blues and rock. The noise alone means you can't miss this Clarke Quay stalwart, which pre-dates the area's trendy reincarnation. If the live music gets too loud after a few pints, and believe us it can, there is outdoor seating available under the grotesque lilypads.

CU Map pp224-5

☎ 6836 2529; 15 Mohamed Sultan Rd; 6pm-3am Fri & Sun, 6pm-4am Sat; bus 54 from Clarke Quay MRT

Formerly known as Coyote Ugly (before the owners of the American original took umbrage), CU is famous for Singapore's recently legalised bar-top dancing. Barmaids dancing on the narrow wooden bar have become an ogling attraction.

DEMPSEY'S HUT Map pp226-7

☎ 6473 9609; 130E Minden Rd; bus 7 from Orchard Blvd

This jovial open-air bar is deep in the thickly forested former British army barracks around Dempsey Rd. Like its nearby wine bar rivals, it's worth a visit as one of the few places near the city where you can enjoy a spot of unbridled nature – at a reasonable price too. The tables are laid out under the trees (bring repellent) and the beer costs a meagre $5 per mug, or $20 a jug. Bar food available.

DUBLINERS Map pp226-7

☎ 6735 2220; 165 Penang Rd; 11.30am-1am Sun-Thu, 11.30am-2am Fri & Sat; Somerset MRT

Located off the quieter part of Orchard Rd, Dubliners is one of the friendliest Irish pubs in Singapore, with the usual range of Irish beers at reasonable prices and an outstanding menu (go in hungry; the portions are huge). The front veranda is a great spot for balmy nights and the service is excellent.

ESKI Map pp234-5

☎ 6327 3662; 124 Tanjong Pagar Rd; ⌚ 2pm-1am Sun-Thu, 2pm-3am Fri & Sat; Tanjong Pagar MRT
Singapore's first sub-zero bar is cool blues and whites. The temperatures here plummet to a shocking -10°. You can risk frostbite in the freezer bar – which has a counter carved out of ice – or in the 'igloo', which is slightly less cold. There's an outdoor area. Winter clothing is handed out at the door.

FABULOUS FIZZ Map p230

☎ 6336 9918; 8 Raffles Ave, Esplanade Mall; ⌚ 11am-11pm Sun-Thu, 11am-1am Fri & Sat; City Hall MRT
On the ground floor of the Esplanade Mall, this is a place for champagne lovers. The bar stocks more than 200 labels of bubbly and, by Singapore standards at least, the prices aren't half bad. The restaurant is also an excellent spot for a romantic, jazzy dinner.

FATHER FLANAGAN'S Map p230

☎ 6333 1418; 01-06 Fountain Court, Chijmes, 30 Victoria St; City Hall MRT
Legend has it that Father Flanagan was Singapore's favourite Irish priest at the Chijmes convent, where he brewed his own ale to keep the sisters happy. All this is open to rather scandalous debate; what's not in question is that this is one of the best of Singapore's sometimes tiring range of Irish pubs – and the only one with its own brand of beer, an Irish red ale called Monk's Brew. Pints of Guinness aren't cheap, but there's a jovial atmosphere and the food isn't bad.

FEZ LOUNGE BAR Map p230

☎ 6535 5606; 57B Boat Quay; ⌚ 6pm-midnight Sun-Thu, 6pm-1am Fri & Sat; Raffles Place MRT
A relaxed, unpretentious upstairs bar with a Moroccan-theme – lots of cushions, lamps, *sheesha* pipes and candles. Located above the Kinara Indian Restaurant (look for a camel on a yellow pillar), Fez feels like one of those exclusive gentleman's clubs no-one knows about, except for the music, which is dominated by house and R&B.

FRONT PAGE/NEXT PAGE Map pp224-5

☎ 6238 7826; 17/18 Mohamed Sultan Rd; ⌚ 4pm-2am Mon-Thu, 4pm-3am Fri & Sat; bus 54 from Clarke Quay MRT
On a strip where bars regularly change names and concepts, the Front Page and adjoining Next Page have remained consistently popular with locals and visitors alike. Dimly lit Front Page was one of the first bars to open on Mohamed Sultan and still attracts punters seeking post-work de-stress tipples. Next Page has old-world Chinese décor (those ubiquitous red lanterns), a frequently retro soundtrack and is popular with over-30s expats looking for younger companions.

GLASSY JUNCTION ENGLISH PUB Map p232

☎ 6297 1036; 45 Haji Lane; Bugis MRT
Looking a little out of place in a largely Muslim-Arabic area, this is one of the first watering holes to test the traditional unspoken restrictions on alcohol. Nestling in quiet Haji Lane, it's small, cosy and friendly, with a pleasantly furtive backstreet feel about it. Beer is only $20 a jug all night.

HARRY'S Map pp234-5

☎ 6538 3029; www.harrys-bar.com.sg; 28 Boat Quay; ⌚ 11am-1am Sun-Thu, 11am-2am Fri & Sat; Raffles Place MRT
The one-time hang-out of Barings' bank breaker Nick Leeson, Harry's is still a city-slickers' favourite, with the suits flocking here for happy hour until 8pm. Later it turns into a good jazz venue (9.30pm to 12.30am from Tuesday to Saturday). The upstairs bar is quieter and a comfortable place for Sunday brunch.

HIDEOUT Map p230

☎ 6536 9445; 31B Circular Rd; ⌚ 7pm-midnight Wed & Thu, 7pm-3am Fri & Sat; Clarke Quay or Raffles Place MRT
The walk up three floors might put you off, but this tiny, ultra-trendy place is worth a little legwork, with its deep red walls, hotch-potch furniture and indie/hip-hop playlist. A little cliquey, so dress your coolest.

HOME BEACH BAR Map pp224-5

☎ 6835 2413; 15 Merbau Rd, Robertson Quay; ⌚ 3pm-1am Sun-Thu, 3pm-2am Fri & Sat; Clarke Quay MRT
An odd name and an odd setting by the river – the beach loungers are a bit silly - but it's a popular and surprisingly unpretentious spot to chill out with the locals. An outdoor screen shows movies and sports events, or you can play pool on the 'outdoor' table.

ICE COLD BEER Map pp226-7

☎ 6735 9929; 9 Emerald Hill; 🕒 6pm-2am Sun-Thu, 6pm-3am Fri & Sat; Somerset MRT

Raucous, boozy establishment at the top of the Emerald Hill bar strip, offering a huge range of chilled beers from around the world to a rock soundtrack. Like most bars in Emerald Hill, it's housed in a 1900s Peranakan shophouse, though the frontage is pretty much all that remains. A definite bonus is the late-night 1am to 3am happy hour.

INSOMNIA Map p230

☎ 6338 6883; 01-21/23 Fountain Ct, Chijmes, Bras Basah Rd; 🕒 11am-3am Sun-Tue, 11am-5am Wed-Sat; City Hall MRT

As the name suggests, this place stays open pretty late. Though it often seems to function primarily as a pick-up joint, it's by no means sleazy. This large set-up boasts lots of space and a continually rotated blend of live bands, DJs and recorded music, plus a quiet courtyard overlooking the old chapel.

KM8 Map p237

☎ 6274 2288; Tanjong Beach; 🕒 11am-midnight Sun-Thu, 11am-3am Fri & Sat; shuttle bus from HarbourFront MRT

If you are in the mood for sea, sand, thumping music and oily tanned bodies punching the air, this is the place. It's successfully staked a claim as Sentosa's top party spot – with its late closing time, free-for-all Jacuzzi, shamelessly Ibizan design and expensive alcohol.

LOT, STOCK & BARREL Map p230

☎ 6338 5340; 29 Seah St; 🕒 11.30am-3pm Mon-Fri, 5pm-1am Sun-Thu, 5pm-2am Fri, 6pm-2am Sat; City Hall or Bugis MRT

A no-frills pub, with pool table, darts, cable TV sports channel and decent range of beers. More recently frequented by backpackers staying nearby but also has a nice mix of after-work office drinkers.

MOLLY MALONE'S Map p230

☎ 6536 2029; 53-56 Circular Rd; Raffles Place MRT

Just behind Boat Quay on burgeoning Circular Rd, Molly Malone's has moved from its old location to larger premises just down the road. Well-travelled drinkers will have seen the mock Irish interior and the Genuine Irish Stew/fish-and-chip menu a hundred times before, but that doesn't make it any less cosy or welcoming.

MOX BAR Map pp234-5

☎ 6323 9438; 21 Tanjong Pagar Rd; 🕒 7.30pm-2am Tue-Sun, 7.30pm-3am Fri & Sat; Tanjong Pagar MRT

Located above the wildly popular Happy, this retro gay bar is used as a pre-dance warm-up joint, though plenty of people stay on even after the club is raging downstairs.

MUDDY MURPHY'S Map pp226-7

☎ 6735 0400; Orchard Hotel Shopping Arcade, 442 Orchard Rd; 🕒 11.30am-1am Mon-Thu, 11.30am-2am Fri & Sat, 11.30am-midnight Sun; Orchard MRT

Located below street level in a courtyard, Muddy's is more appealing than the standard fake Irish pub. The quieter Ballymoon top bar is narrow and smoky and only opens in the evening. Happy hour ends at a rather stingy 7.30pm.

NEW ASIA BAR Map p230

☎ 6431 5672; Swissôtel, The Stamford, 2 Stamford Rd; 3pm-1am Sun-Thu, 3pm-3am Fri & Sat; City Hall MRT

Zip up 70 floors from the reception-style Introbar on the ground floor for far and away the most spectacular view of any bar in Southeast Asia. A trendy, lounge-style place; drinks are pricey (there's a $25 cover charge on Fridays and Saturdays), but for views like this any price is worth it. Strict dress codes apply.

PAULANER BRAUHAUS Map p230

☎ 6883 2572; 01-01 Times Square@Millenia Walk, 9 Raffles Blvd; 🕒 11.30am-1am Sun-Thu, 11.30am-2am Fri & Sat; City Hall MRT

A three-storey wood-and-brass German microbrewery bar and restaurant serving up its excellent signature Munich lager and Munich dark brews. There are also special seasonal brews like Salvator Beer (March), Mailbock Beer (May) and Oktoberfest Beer (October). Beers are served in either 0.3L, 0.5L or 1L mugs! Tours of the brewery are available for $40, but you have to book well in advance.

PENNY BLACK Map pp234-5

☎ 6538 2300; 26/27 Boat Quay; 11am-1am Mon-Thu, 11am-2am Fri & Sat, 11am-midnight Sun; Raffles Place MRT

Fitted out like a 'Victorian' London pub (without the tuberculosis and dodgy gin), the Penny Black's interior was actually built in London and shipped to Singapore, so it has some claim to authenticity. Specialises in hard-to-find English ales for the swathes of expat Brits that work in the area. The upstairs bar is particularly inviting.

POST BAR Map pp234-5

☎ 6733 8388; Fullerton Hotel; noon-2am; Raffles Place MRT

Named the Post Bar as it retains the original ceiling of the General Post Office, this classy lounge bar within the glorious Fullerton Hotel lobby is way upmarket, without being snobbish. It also serves the best *mojitos* this side of Havana.

PROVIGNAGE – THE WINE CAVE

Map pp224-5

☎ 6834 1490; 30 Robertson Quay; 6pm-midnight Mon-Thu, 6pm-2am Fri & Sat; bus 54 from Clarke Quay MRT

Who would have thought bare breeze blocks could look as good as this? This cosy, dimly lit wine bar has a couple of very comfortable sofas and only really gets busy towards the weekend. The wines are reasonably priced for the area (expect to pay at the very least $40 for a decent bottle) and there is a small but excellent tapas menu (the cheese platter recommended).

QUE PASA Map pp226-7

☎ 6235 6626; 7 Emerald Hill Rd; 6pm-2am Sun-Thu, 6pm-3am Fri & Sat; Somerset MRT

An extremely pleasant wine and tapas bar with a convincingly run-down interior reminiscent of a real Spanish bar – except for the icy air-con. The wine list is impressive and in keeping with the rest of Emerald Hill, extravagantly expensive. Tapas are uniformly excellent – try the mushrooms and the ubiquitous spicy sausage.

RAFFLES HOTEL Map p230

1 Beach Rd; City Hall MRT

We know it's a cliché, but a visit to Singapore is practically incomplete without having a drink at Raffles Hotel. Of the several options, our favourite is the **Bar & Billiard Room**, underneath which a tiger was shot in 1904. This bar has live jazz nightly and a nice veranda on which to sip your drink. The **Gazebo Bar**, in the courtyard of the attached Raffles Hotel Arcade, is also a top spot for a tipple and has live music in the evening. The plantation-style **Long Bar**, located on the Arcade's 2nd level, is a little touristy these days. If you must, order a Singapore Sling ($16, or $25 with a souvenir glass). We think it tastes like cough medicine, but others find it fruity and invigorating.

RED LANTERN BEER GARDEN

Map pp234-5

50 Collyer Quay; Raffles Place MRT

For a taste of old Singapore, head to the seedy, bayside Red Lantern Beer Garden where bands often play, cheap meals are served, and you can get a reasonably priced beer. It can get pretty rowdy late at night. There are so many bars, most with outdoor tables, that you can just wander along until one takes your fancy.

SUNSET BAY Map p237

☎ 6275 0668; www.sunsetbay.com.sg; 60 Siloso Beach Walk; shuttle bus from HarbourFront MRT

A bona fide beach bar where it's perfectly OK to wear very little – most of the young customers seem to. For groups of at least 20, they'll throw a mini beach games tournament and for $750 you can have your own DJ Dance Party on weekdays.

TANTRIC BAR Map pp234-5

☎ 6423 9232; 78 Neil Rd; 8pm-3am; Outram Park MRT

A peaceful spot to relax among the fountains, palm trees and Arabian chic in the courtyard, this gay bar is a pleasant antidote, or warm up, to the queues and pounding music elsewhere.

VINCENT'S Map pp234-5

☎ 6736 1360; 15 Duxton Rd; closes 2am; Outram Park MRT

Singapore's first gay bar spent years in Lucky Plaza on Orchard Rd before moving to bigger, better premises to take advantage of the developing gay ghetto around Tanjong Pagar. It's a popular starting-out point and offers a free gay guide to Singapore.

WATER BAR Map pp234-5

☎ 6221 5739; 38/39 Craig Rd; 🕒 9pm-2am Mon-Sat; Outram Park MRT

A hedonistic atmosphere pervades the Water Bar, sister establishment of **Taboo** (p133), in a dazzlingly whitewashed shophouse hung with luxurious velvet drapes.

WINE NETWORK Map pp226-7

☎ 6479 2280; Block 13, Dempsey Rd; 🕒 11am-midnight Sun-Thu, 11am-1am Fri & Sat; bus 7 from Orchard Blvd

Tucked away in the Dempsey Rd furniture and antiques ghetto, this is a real find. A small, intimate bar with rough wooden floors and crumbling brick walls lined with wine bottles, where the wine is as cheap or expensive as you like (bottles start at $18, or it's $7 a glass). Sit inside, or enjoy the sight of the semi-derelict colonial barracks and the sound of twittering birds on the deck. Pizzas, German sausages and cheese platters fight off hunger. Get off the bus at stop B03 on Holland Rd; from here it's a 10-minute walk.

XPOSÉ Map pp234-5

☎ 6323 2466; 208 South Bridge Rd; 🕒 6pm-midnight Mon-Wed, 6pm-1am Thu & Sun, 6pm-2am Fri & Sat; Chinatown MRT

Another more relaxed gay bar, which also serves up some excellent Thai and Vietnamese food, though karaoke-phobes might want to stay away until after midnight, when the mike is turned off.

CHINESE OPERA

CHINESE THEATRE CIRCLE Map pp234-5

☎ 6323 4862; www.ctcopera.com.sg; 5 Smith St; Chinatown MRT

A low-key introduction to Chinese opera can be had at one of the teahouse evenings organised by the nonprofit opera company, the Chinese Theatre Circle. Every Friday and Saturday evening at 8pm there is a brief talk (in English) on Chinese opera, followed by a short excerpt from a Cantonese opera classic, performed by professional actors in full costume. Delicious lychee tea and little tea cakes are included in the price ($20). The whole thing lasts about 45 minutes and you are able to take photos. Bookings are recommended. For $35, turn up at 7pm and you can enjoy a full Chinese meal beforehand.

CLUBBING

All clubs have cover charges which vary from $10 to $30, with women usually paying less. The price will almost always include at least one drink. Venues change names and concepts frequently so check the local press before venturing out. Check magazines like *8 Days* or the freebie *I-S* for the latest on venues. Also look out for outdoor rave parties, usually held on Sentosa.

ATTICA Map p230

☎ 6333 9973; www.attica.com.sg; 3A River Valley Rd, 01-02 Clarke Quay; Clarke Quay MRT

One of the most popular of Singapore's new crop of nightspots, Attica is nestled down a side alley and models itself on New York's hippest clubs, with a relaxed atmosphere early and feverish dancing at the upstairs Attica Too from midnight until it closes around 3am or 4am. The outdoor courtyard overlooking the river is perfect for early evening drinks. Be prepared to queue at weekends.

BAR NONE Map pp226-7

☎ 6222 8117; www.barnoneasia.com; Basement, Marriott Hotel, 320 Orchard Rd; 🕒 7pm-3am Sun-Thu, 7pm-4am Fri & Sat; Orchard MRT

One of the more popular spots along Orchard Rd, Bar None offers live music and DJs playing mainstream music, from R&B and pop classics to salsa and rock. It's the home of monthly performances by the Punchline Comedy Club and draws in a crowd of mostly expats and young executives

CENTRO Map pp234-5

☎ 6220 2288; www.centro360.com; One Fullerton, 1 Fullerton Rd; 🕒 10pm-3am Tue-Sun; Raffles Place MRT

Nominated top club in 2002 by the Singapore Tourism Board, Centro is a dreamy, roomy venue that really gets going at weekends, with a gorgeous view across Marina Bay to the Esplanade. Raised platforms provide a showcase for exhibitionists, while downstairs from the club is a 160-seater tapas café/bar if you need some munchies.

CHINABLACK Map pp226-7

☎ 6734 7677; 12th fl, Pacific Plaza Penthouse, 9 Scotts Rd; 🕒 8pm-3am Wed-Sat; Orchard MRT

Spinning everything from '70s hits to house, this dimly-lit, fancy club with its sofas and

East-West décor tries to please everyone. The crowd is mostly young (and often very drunk), but it's unpretentious and lots of fun.

COCCO LATTE Map pp224-5

☎ 6735 0402; 01-09, Gallery Hotel, 76 Robertson Quay; 🕑 5pm-1am Mon & Tue, 5pm-3am Wed-Fri, 5pm-4am Sat; bus 54 from Clarke Quay MRT

The unpredictable, slightly bizarre Cocco Latte has theme nights from Tuesday to Sunday. Not only does the theme change but the art and décor tries to keep up. Start off the evening at the lounge downstairs with a few drinks and finger food before moving upstairs to the trendy club and try to blend in with the theme of the night. Good beer deals are offered on Monday and Tuesday nights at the lounge with all beers one-for-one (buy one, get one free) all night. Tuesday night is 'beer bellies are sexy' night!

DBL O Map pp224-5

☎ 6735 2008; 01-24, 11 Unity St, Robertson Walk; 🕑 8pm-3am Wed-Sun, 8pm-4am Sat; bus 54 from Clarke Quay MRT

Shamelessly outrageous three-bar dance club, popular with trendy young clubbers wearing very little – and a sprinkling of older people who like to look at them. Top attractions are the mesmerising, 10m-high Light Wall and cheap jugs of beer. Music ranges from Top 40 on Thursdays to house Fridays and retro Saturdays. Cover charge ranges from $10 to $25 for men. Women only pay cover charge on Fridays and Saturdays ($10).

EN LOUNGE Map pp224-5

☎ 6732 6863; 01-59/60 UE Sq, 207 River Valley Rd; 🕑 7pm-3am; bus 54 from Clarke Quay MRT

Slightly older and more sophisticated than the usual young-and-wasted Mohamed Sultan crowd, En Lounge is wisely divided into dancing and sitting areas, where you can get some decent food; there's also an outdoor seating area if it all gets too much. Happy hour runs from midnight to 1am on Saturdays. On Sundays you get two drinks for the price of one all night. No cover charge.

HAPPY Map pp234-5

☎ 6227 7400; 21 Tanjong Pagar Rd; 🕑 7pm-3am Sun-Fri, 7pm-4am Sat; Tanjong Pagar MRT

Currently one of the most popular gay dance spots, there is often a long queue outside and a rowdy, packed dance floor inside.

LIQUID ROOM Map pp224-5

☎ 6333 8117; www.liquidroom.com.sg; Gallery Hotel, 76 Robertson Quay; bus 54 from Clarke Quay MRT

In comparison to its trendsetting rivals, Liquid is positively tiny. But don't let size put you off – this is one of Singapore's most progressive dance spaces, hosting some of the island's best DJs including satirical cultural observer Chris Ho. Its candlelit outdoor riverside area, called soundbar, is a great chill-out spot, featuring 'downtempo' DJs.

MUSIC UNDERGROUND Map pp226-7

☎ 6235 3301; B1-00, International Bldg, 360 Orchard Rd; 🕑 7pm-3am Mon-Fri, 8pm-4am Sat; Orchard MRT

Hidden away in a basement, this is, as the name suggests, not the place for a quiet chat. The house band thumps out danceable tunes every night except Monday and one of the best features here is the 'love seats', deep couches hugging the wall. It attracts a mostly local crowd and a few foreigners, and happy hours run until 10pm, except Fridays. Women get in free on Thursdays.

PLANET PARADIGM Map pp226-7

☎ 6338 3805; Level 6, Singapore Shopping Centre, 190 Clemenceau Ave; 🕑 noon-1am Mon-Thu, noon-3am Fri & Sat; Dhoby Ghaut MRT

A slightly weird all-in-one concept, comprising techno dance club, pool hall, noodle shop and surprisingly sophisticated wine bar complete with wine library. The dance club and American-style pool hall draws a young, mostly local crowd. No cover charge.

RAV Map p230

☎ 6327 4900; 69 Circular Rd; 🕑 6pm-3am Sun-Fri, 6pm-4am Sat; Raffles Place MRT

Decked out in overwhelming red, RAV is the stand-out club on blossoming Circular Rd, pumping out everything from acid jazz to Motown to a largely under-30s crowd. Also hosts renowned local DJ Illusion. Women get a free flow of 'housepours' after 8pm on Thursdays.

ROUGE Map pp226-7

☎ 6732 6966; www.rougeclub.com; 2F Peranakan Pl, 180 Orchard Rd; 🕑 6pm-3am; Somerset MRT

On a stretch of restored shophouses trying to maintain their Peranakan themes, Rouge

Velvet Underground, part of Zouk (below)

features a host of little snuggly nooks and crannies with an emphasis on deep red and velvet. Very sexy. Wednesday is the funk and groove–themed Love Hotel night, Thursday and Saturday are hip-hop, and Friday can be anything in between.

TABOO Map pp234-5
☎ 6225 4172; 01-04, 21 Tanjong Pagar Rd; 🕑 9pm-2am Mon-Sat; Outram Park MRT
Still the biggest gay club in Singapore, Taboo is a pumping spot where patrons are not afraid to rip off their shirts and strut on the podiums and bar tops.

UNION SQUARE Map pp234-5
☎ 6224 6116; 02-05, The Amara, 165 Tanjong Pagar Rd; 🕑 11am-1am Mon-Thu, 11am-2am Fri, 11am-3am Sat; Tanjong Pagar MRT
Another red-themed club, this is *the* place if you love a bit of Latin groove – there are even special Latin dance nights on Tuesdays and Thursdays. Don't be put off by the run-down shopping centre location; this is a classy joint for dancing or to relax over a few wines or sherries. Women get free champagne all night on Tuesdays. There is no cover charge.

ZOUK Map pp224-5
☎ 6738 2988; www.zoukclub.com; 17 Jiak Kim St; 🕑 9pm-3am Tue-Sat; Tiong Bahru MRT
One of Asia's legendary clubs and perhaps the only one in Singapore with an international reputation, Zouk attracts big-name DJs from around the world, like Paul Oakenfold and John Digweed. It's actually three clubs and a wine bar in one, and $35 (men) or $25 (women) gets you into all of them. The main event, Zouk, is an Ibiza-inspired party space on several levels throbbing to techno and house beats. The Wednesday Mambo Jambo retro night is also hugely popular with students – and people who remember when Duran Duran was new and exciting. For the same cover charge you'll gain access to the edgier, more experimental **Phuture** (Wednesday, Friday and Saturday), which attracts the wannabe gangsta crowd with its hip-hop and drum 'n' bass – though being in Singapore you won't feel out of place even if you don't wear chunky jewellery. Far more exclusive is the **Velvet Underground** dance club, a favourite haunt of the dahlings and beautiful people, with its plush sofas, red velvet and Andy Warhol/Keith Haring artworks. Happy hours at all three run from 11pm to midnight. If you need a breather, head for the outdoor **Zouk Wine Bar.**

MUSIC

ALTERNATIVE/INDIE/ROCK

ANYWHERE MUSIC PUB Map pp226-7
04-08 Tanglin Shopping Centre, 19 Tanglin Rd; Orchard MRT
This place has been around forever, and so has its house band, Tania, who pull a loyal crowd of locals and expats – often 35-plus. No need to get dressed up here. The walls of the pub are adorned with posters of rock bands, mainly from the '80s – enough said. There's no happy hour on Saturdays.

CRAZY ELEPHANT Map p230

☎ 6337 1990; www.crazyelephant.com; 01-07 Clarke Quay, 3E River Valley Rd; 6pm-late; Clarke Quay MRT

This raucous pub has been blasting Clarke Quay for years with its heavy blues/rock live acts. A Sunday night blues jam might appeal to those who like to bend a string now and then, or sing about the women who left them.

PRINCE OF WALES Map p232

☎ 6299 0130; 101 Dunlop St, Little India; 9am-1am; Little India MRT

Australian-style corner pub, with rough wooden floors, minimal furnishings and that unmistakeable knocked-about feel. The line-up features mostly alternative/indie acts, with unplugged nights during the week and definitely-plugged-in gigs on Fridays and Saturdays. Liquid attractions include the rare Beamish Irish stout. It's also a hostel (see p173).

CLASSICAL

Keep an eye out for concerts at either venue and also check out the SSO's free concerts in the Botanic Gardens. The SSO plays most Friday and Saturday nights throughout the year (except June).

ESPLANADE – THEATRES ON THE BAY Map p230

☎ 6828 8222; www.esplanade.com; 1 Esplanade Dr; City Hall MRT

The 1800-seater state-of-the-art concert hall at the Esplanade – Theatres on the Bay is now the home of the highly respected Singapore Symphony Orchestra (SSO).

SINGAPORE CHINESE ORCHESTRA

☎ 6557 4034; www.sco.com.sg

Definitely worth catching is Southeast Asia's only such professional group, playing Indian and Malay music as well as Chinese orchestral pieces.

JAZZ

For the price of a drink you can listen to reasonable jazz bands at both Baladava (Map p230; ☎ 6339 1600; 01-01B Suntec City, 1 Raffles Blvd; 3pm-1am; City Hall MRT) and the Bar & Billiard Room at Raffles Hotel.

BLUJAZ CAFE Map p232

☎ 6292 3800; 1 Bali Lane, Kampong Glam; City Hall MRT

Another recent arrival in the Arab Quarter's blossoming night scene, laying on some decent jazz in an intimate bistro atmosphere. The food, from burgers and fries to Nonya laksa and *agedashi* (deep-fried) tofu, is not bad.

JAZZ@SOUTH BRIDGE Map p230

☎ 6327 4671; www.southbridgejazz.com.sg; 82B Boat Quay; 5.30pm-1am Tue-Thu, 5.30pm-2am Fri & Sat, 6pm-1am Sun; Clarke Quay MRT

Upstairs overlooking Boat Quay is this intimate jazz bar, which has plush sofas and chairs in front of the small stage and a more informal bar area behind, where you can watch the live acts on a TV if the crowd is too large. With the exception of a rather indulgent pianist, the house band is excellent and this place often hosts well-known international musicians. The sets kick off around 9.15pm, and sometimes there's a cover charge of $20.

LIVE JAZZ@THE GREEN ROOM

Map p230

☎ 6334 1032; 01-05/07 Esplanade Mall; City Hall MRT

Like its sister venue Harry's (p128) over on Boat Quay, this place offers good live jazz along with a mixture of Eastern and Western food.

SOMERSET'S Map p230

Level 3, Raffles, The Plaza, 2 Stamford Rd; 5pm-midnight Sun-Thu, 5pm-2am Fri & Sat; City Hall MRT

Somerset's boasts one of the longest bars in Singapore and sometimes attracts top performers, though for a more authentic smoky jazz bar atmosphere you might prefer to go elsewhere. Music starts at around 8pm.

ROUND MIDNIGHT Map pp226-7

☎ 6737 1507; 43-45 Cuppage Tce; 10pm-6am; Somerset MRT

Formerly known as Swing and, before licensing laws were relaxed, one of the few late-night drinking holes in the city, this reborn upstairs jazz bar still has the peeling walls and slightly insalubrious feel to it, but is a little less rowdy these days. There's a decent line-up of local live jazz artists and a 10pm to midnight happy hour, but it doesn't really fill up until the early hours.

BALLROOM

UPPER CLUB Map p230

☎ 6338 1313; 02-01A Chijmes; ⏰ 7pm-1am Tue-Thu & Sun, 7pm-2am Fri & Sat; City Hall MRT

A dinner-and-dance club as fancy as you can get. Dancers will love the 1200-sq-ft air-cushioned parquet dance floor and the 11-piece band, while the white-gloved waiters add a special touch. Dinner costs $68 for a four-course set menu; if you don't want to eat, the cover charge is $38.

ACTIVITIES

HEALTH & FITNESS

Massage & Spas

There are so many spas in Singapore these days that you can hardly turn your head without bumping into Balinese furniture and Sounds of the Forest music. 'Wellness' is the latest big thing – covering spas, massage and foot reflexology – but as with many big things, quality gets harder to find the more popular it becomes. Many of the top hotels now boast decent quality spas and generally the older institutions, with the most loyal following, are the best. Rates vary from around $25 for a foot massage to more than $200 for a full-day package.

Dodgy massage parlours do still exist, though the authorities have embarked on a pretty rigorous covert mission to weed them out (we're sure there are plenty of officers volunteering to go undercover for that operation).

AMRITA SPA Map p230

☎ 6336 4477; www.amritaspas.com; Level 6, Raffles, The Plaza, 2 Stamford Rd; City Hall MRT

Amrita boasts of being Asia's most extensive spa with 35 treatment rooms, a fitness centre, a variety of plunge and bubble pools and a long menu of spa treatments; the day-spa escape package with back massage and express facial is $150. There are branches at Swissôtel, Merchant Court Singapore and Raffles Hotel.

KENKO

www.kenkofootreflexology.com

Kenko is the McDonald's of reflexology, with outlets all over the city centre, including two on **Tanglin Rd** (Map pp226-7; No 19; 01-17, B1-08). Its **'wellness boutique'** (Map pp234-5; ☎ 6223 0303; 211 South Bridge Rd; Chinatown MRT), loctated in Chinatown, is the most upmarket of its operations.

NGEE ANN FOOT REFLEXOLOGY

Map pp226-7

☎ 6235 5538; 4th fl, Midpoint Orchard, 220 Orchard Rd; Somerset MRT

Offers foot and body massage by visually impaired masseuses in friendly and refreshingly unpretentious surroundings.

SPA BOTANICA Map p237

☎ 6820 6788; www.spabotanica.com; The Sentosa Resort & Spa; ⏰ 10am-10pm; shuttle bus from Orchard Rd Paragon Shopping Centre

Singapore's original indoor and outdoor spa. The signature treatment here is the galaxy steam bath, a 45-minute wallow in medicinal chakra muds in a specially designed steam room. There's also a mud pool outside as well as landscaped grounds and pools.

ST GREGORY JAVANA SPA Map p232

☎ 6290 8028; www.stgregoryspa.com; Level 3, The Plaza, 7500A Beach Rd; Bugis MRT

Set in Balinese-style gardens, St Gregory Javana Spa also has an operation at the **Grand Plaza Parkroyal Hotel** (Map p230; ☎ 6432 5588; 10 Coleman St; City Hall MRT) specialising in hydrotherapy treatments.

WAYAN RETREAT Map p232

☎ 6392 0035; 61 Bussorah St; Bugis MRT

This is another Balinese outfit, offering massage and body wraps, all in luxury surroundings.

OUTDOOR ACTIVITIES

While it may not be the best city in the world for spectator sports, Singapore has a wealth of options for those who want to take part. Aside from the S.League football, the only regular sporting event is the horse racing at the Singapore Turf Club. Everything from pop concerts and soccer games to celebrity wrestling take place at the **Singapore Indoor Stadium** (Map pp224-5; ☎ 6344 2660; www.singaporeindoorstadium.com; 2 Stadium Walk; Kallang MRT).

Bowling

Tenpin bowling is extremely popular and very cheap in Singapore. The cost per game is between $2.40 and $3.90 per person per game, depending on the time of day you play. Shoe hire is around $1 and they'll even sell you a pair of fetching white ankle socks for 50¢.

Cathay Bowl (Map p236; ☎ 6444 0118; 1018 East Coast Parkway; noon-2am; bus 12, 14 or 32)

Orchard Bowl (Map pp226-7; ☎ 6238 2088; Level 9, Cathay Cineleisure Orchard; closes 3am; Somerset MRT)

Victor Superbowl (Map pp224-5; ☎ 6223 7998; 7 Marina Grove, Marina South; 9am-3am Sun-Thu, 24hr Fri & Sat; Marina Bay MRT)

Cricket

SINGAPORE CRICKET CLUB Map p230

☎ 6338 9271; Connaught Dr; City Hall MRT

The Singapore Cricket Club holds matches every weekend on the Padang from March to October. The club is for members only but spectators are welcome.

Go-karting

KART WORLD Map pp222-3

☎ 6266 2555; Yung Ho Rd; 11am-10pm; Jurong East MRT

Out in Jurong, Kart World features a challenging 700m track. Sessions of 10 minutes cost $35 for single-engine karts, $40 for the worryingly zippy two-engine models.

Golf

Singapore has plenty of golf courses; most are members-only so they charge visitors a premium and usually don't allow you to play on weekends. A game of golf costs around $90 on weekdays and from $100 to $220 on weekends. Club hire ranges from $15 at Sentosa to $42 at Jurong. Try the following:

Jurong Country Club (Map pp222-3; ☎ 6560 5655; www.jcc.org.sg; 9 Science Centre Rd; Jurong East MRT)

Laguna National Golf & Country Club (Map pp222-3; ☎ 6541 0289; www.lagunagolf.com.sg; 11 Laguna Golf Green; Tanah Merah MRT)

Raffles Country Club (Map pp222-3; ☎ 6861 7655; www.rcc.org.sg; 450 Jalan Ahmad Ibrahim; SBS bus 182 from Boon Lay MRT)

Sentosa Golf Club (Map p237; ☎ 6275 0022; www.beaufort.com.sg/resort_golf.html; 27 Bukit Manis Rd, Sentosa Island; shuttle bus from HarbourFront MRT)

Horse Racing

SINGAPORE TURF CLUB Map pp222-3

☎ 6879 1000; www.turfclub.com.sg; 1 Turf Club Ave; Kranji MRT

This is a hugely popular day out – not nearly as manic as Hong Kong, but a rousing experience nonetheless. There is a four-level grandstand with a seating capacity of up to 35,000 and foreigners must bring their passports to get in. Admission to the non-air-conditioned seating is $3, or $7 for the upper air-conditioned level. For $15 tourists can access the air-conditioned Gold Card Room, or for $20 the exclusive @Hibiscus lounge.

A strict dress code applies here: men must wear a collar, plus a jacket or tie for the exclusive lounges (no shorts or jeans) and both men and women must wear closed shoes. All betting is government controlled and the minimum bet is $5. The odds are a little deceptive and not what you might be used to. Each unit is worth $5, so that 4-1 odds, for example, means that you win $4 for every $5 unit you bet, not $4 for every dollar.

Races take place on Fridays, Saturdays or Sundays during racing months (check the *New Paper* for details and coverage), starting at 6.30pm, 2pm and 2.30pm respectively.

Enormous sums pass through the windows on race days (the Esplanade complex was mainly funded by profits from the operation).

Paintball

TAG PAINTBALL Map pp222-3

☎ 6324 0038; www.paintballasia.com; 1 Orchid Club Rd; Khatib MRT

Tag Paintball runs the perennially popular battle game for groups (maximum five people per group). It costs $15 per person during the day and $20 at night. Paintballs cost an additional $25 for 50.

Racket Sports

Tennis, squash and badminton are popular in Singapore. Court hire is between $7 and $10; bookings essential. Racket hire is available.

Kallang Squash & Tennis Centre (Map pp224-5; ☎ 6440 6839; Stadium Rd; Kallang MRT)

Singapore Badminton Hall (Map p236; ☎ 6345 7554; 102 Guillemard Rd; 🕑 7am-10pm; Aljunied MRT)

Singapore Tennis Centre (Map p236; ☎ 6442 5966; 1020 East Coast Parkway; 🕑 7am-11pm; bus 12, 14 or 32)

Rock Climbing

DAIRY FARM QUARRY Map pp222-3

bus 65, 170, 75, 171

Near Bukit Timah, Dairy Farm Quarry, with some 20 routes, is the only legal place to rock climb in Singapore. Most routes are bolted and can be done with a 50m rope; you'll need to bring your own gear. To find out about joining up with climbers who come here regularly on weekends, contact an outdoor equipment shop such as **Campers' Corner** (Map p230; ☎ 6337 4743; www.camperscorner.com.sg; 01-13 Capitol Bldg, 11 Stamford Rd; 🕑 11am-8pm Mon-Sat, noon-7pm Sun).

Cricket game in front of City Hall (p52)

Swimming

Given the polluted waters, none of Singapore's beaches are particularly great for swimming, although there are safe swimming areas at East Coast Park, Sentosa and the other islands.

A better option, if you're not staying at a hotel with its own pool, is the excellent public swimming complexes at **Farrer Park** (Map p232; ☎ 6299 1002; 2 Rutland Ave; 🕑 8am-9.30pm; Little India MRT) or **River Valley Swimming Complex** (Map p230; ☎ 6337 6275; 1 River Valley Rd; 🕑 8am-9.30pm; Clarke Quay MRT) at the foot of Fort Canning Park. Admission to both is $1/0.50 per adult/child ($1.30/0.60 on weekends).

Water Sports

Singapore has just begun to allow water sports on its reservoirs, the first being MacRitchie Reservoir's **Paddle Lodge** (Map pp222-3; ☎ 6258 0057; kayak rental per 1/2hr $10/15; 🕑 9am-6pm Tue-Sun). Paddle boating is possible in the Upper Seletar Reservoir park near the zoo. Take bus 138 from Ang Mo Kio MRT station. Further east of Upper Seletar is the Lower Seletar Reservoir, where you can go fishing. To get here, take the MRT to Yishun, then bus 851, 852, 853, 854 or 855.

For more details, see the website of the **National Parks Board** (www.nparks.gov.sg).

CHANGI SAILING CENTRE Map pp222-3

☎ 6545 2876; www.csc.org.sg; 32 Netheravon Rd; bus 2 from Tanah Merah MRT

This centre rents out j-24s (24ft keel boats) on one-day charters for $180 a day, including petrol. You will need to show a sailing proficiency certificate.

PASTA FRESCA SEASPORT CENTRE

Map p236

☎ 6449 5118; sailing@singaporesport.com.sg; 1212 East Coast Parkway; bus 12, 14 or 32

This is the place to go for windsurfing and sailing. Sailboards cost $30 for two hours' hire; lessons are also available. The centre rents laser-class boats for $30 per hour and organises sailing courses as well. Sailboards and aquabikes are also available for hire on Sentosa.

SCUBA CORNER Map p232
☎ 6338 6563; www.scubacorner.com.sg; 04-162 Kitchener Complex, Block 809 French Rd; Lavender MRT
Diving trips and courses can be arranged through the outfit Scuba Corner; it's office is located conveniently close to Lavender MRT station.

SINGAPORE WATERSKI FEDERATION
Map pp224-5
☎ 6440 9763; 10 Stadium Lane; Kallang MRT
Here you can arrange water-skiing and wakeboarding lessons and equipment from $90 per hour on weekdays and $120 on weekends, including boat, driver and equipment; bookings are required.

Shopping

Shopping

Indifference is not an option. Shopping is the second national obsession in Singapore – after food – and the retail onslaught will either seduce you instantly into maxing out your credit cards and emptying your wallet or send you screaming back to your hotel room to shiver under the blankets.

Though its reputation as a bargain hunters' paradise has lingered, Singapore is no longer a match for neighbouring countries like Malaysia or Thailand. However, what does lure many visitors is the sheer simplicity. There's no urban chaos to negotiate, it's easy to get around (even laden with shopping bags), you rarely have to haggle or worry about rip-offs and the choice and quality are generally excellent.

And there are bargains to be had. If you are thinking of buying something specific, check out the price before you leave and then compare it with what's on offer in Singapore.

The best items to pick up are electronics (which *can* be cheaper here, but you need to shop carefully and arm yourself with the standard retail price before looking for bargains), art and antiques (unless you're travelling on to other Southeast Asian countries) and clothes. Books and CDs are also cheaper than in most Western countries.

One of the greatest pleasures, though, is simply browsing, whether you are gawping at the $1000 handbags in an Orchard Rd boutique, picking your way through the small neighbourhood shops of Little India or the Arab Quarter, or venturing out to one of the towering suburban malls (now affectionately known as 'Orchard in the heartlands').

The best time of year to shop, if you can cope with the crowds, is during the **Great Singapore Sale** (www.greatsingaporesale.com.sg), held every year from the end of May to the beginning of July – and sometimes extended for a week or two if retailers are feeling the pinch that year. Many stores offer discounts at this time but, again, it pays to shop around. For details on this and other shopping possibilities see the *Singapore Shopping Guide*, free from STB offices. Also check out the free monthly magazine *Where Singapore*, which has the latest on the shopping scene.

Shopping Areas

Everybody's heard of Orchard Rd, Singapore's overwhelming shopping mecca that bursts with every purchasable item you could ever imagine.

If you're after art or antiques, it pays to know your original piece from your cheap copy. While there are many dedicated art galleries and antique shops throughout Singapore, there is a fair degree of overlap between them and craft shops. For Chinese/Japanese/Korean crafts and antiques the best place to head is Chinatown, and for Indian crafts, Little India. Arab St is known for Southeast Asian crafts, such as cane ware, batik and leather goods, while Bussorah St in Kampong Glam has several galleries, craft shops and antiques offering stuff from Indonesia, Thailand and Vietnam.

For electronics, the latest hi-tech audiovisual equipment is available all over Singapore, much of it at very competitive prices. It pays to do a little research into makes and models before you arrive. When you buy, make sure your guarantees are worldwide, your receipts are properly dated and stamped, and your goods are compatible with electricity supplies and systems in your country of origin (see Buyer Beware, opposite).

Lucky Plaza (p159), Sim Lim Square (p156), Sim Lim Tower (p156) and the Mustafa Centre (p155) are all good places to start looking, but you'll have to be prepared to hunt around. For computers and peripherals, the Funan – The IT Mall (p143) is a good place to start looking for brand name items. Sim Lim Square is much cheaper, but recommended only for people who know their IT.

If bargaining isn't your bag, decent discount prices can still be had for all kinds of electronic goods at **Best Denki** (Map pp226-7; ☎ 6835 2855; 05-01/05 Ngee Ann City, 391 Orchard Rd) and **Harvey Norman** (Map p230; ☎ 6332 3461; 02-001 Suntec City Mall).

Sony (www.sony.com.sg) has dedicated shops at Parco Bugis Junction (p155) and in Isetan (p161).

Fashion stores abound and although clothes and shoes are not as cheap as in some other Asian countries, the range of styles and quality is hard to beat. The annual Singapore Fashion Festival in March showcases international and local designers.

For clubbing fashions the best places to scope are the Heeren (p158), Far East Plaza (p157) and Parco Bugis Junction (p155), all of which have sections packed with fun boutiques and stalls. Also check out the top floor of the Golden Mile Food Centre (p112), which, apart from stalls selling army gear, has several trendy clothes and shoe dealers.

You can buy saris and sari material, as well as Punjabi suits, at numerous shops along Serangoon Rd in Little India, as well as at **Nalli** (Map p232; ☎ 6334 0341; 27 Campbell Lane) where a deluxe gold-threaded silk sari can cost anything from $200 to $1000. The 1st floor of the Tekka Centre (p113) is filled with sari and *salwar kameez* stalls – with very low prices.

For books and CDs, you should head to Orchard Rd, which houses huge chain shops as well as small speciality music centres.

It's worth remembering that most of Singapore's 'heartlands' areas now have their very own malls and shopping strips, where the same big names you find on Orchard Rd sell the same stuff at lower prices. Causeway Point (p161), Junction 8 (p161) and Tampines Mall (p161) are all worth checking out.

Buyer Beware

Singapore has stringent consumer laws and promotes itself as a safe place to shop. However, you should still be wary when buying. This is particularly true in smaller shops where a salesperson may match your low price but short-change you by not giving you an international guarantee or the usual accessories. Guarantees are an important consideration if you're buying electronic gear, watches or cameras. Make sure it's international and that it is filled out correctly, with the shop's name and the serial number of the item written down. When buying antiques, ask for a certificate of antiquity, which is required in many countries to avoid paying customs duty.

Singapore enforces international copyright laws, so being palmed off with pirated goods is not really a problem. If you do run into trouble, take your purchases back to the shop. If you fail to get satisfaction, contact the **Small Claims Tribunal** (Map p230; ☎ 6435 5994; www.smallclaims.gov.sg; 1st level, Subordinate Courts, 1 Havelock Sq; 8.30am-1pm Mon-Sat, 2-5pm Mon-Fri) or any of the visitors centres (see p205). Tourist complaints are usually heard within two or three days.

Service

In Singapore you buy on one basis – price. Hi-tech goods are just the same as you'd get back home, so quality doesn't enter into it. You're not coming back for after-sales service, so service doesn't come into it either.

Consequently, shop staff members are not always that helpful or friendly. They may be a long way behind Hong Kong shop assistants when it comes to out-and-out rudeness, but many assistants leave a lot to be desired.

Things are improving though, due partly to the endless courtesy campaigns the government runs and generous awards for good service handed out by the STB. Service in many of the larger stores can be wonderfully professional, particularly from some older assistants who sometimes take you under their wing and won't let you leave until completely satisfied.

Opening Hours

Wet markets aside, Singapore is not an early bird's shopping destination. Most big shopping centres will be quiet until around 11am, so take your time and have a leisurely breakfast. Most shops are open from 10am or 11am through until 9pm and 10pm daily and the quietest and most enjoyable time to look around can be that small window of calm between 10am and 11am, when you can even sometimes hear the birds twittering along Orchard Rd.

Consumer Taxes

Singapore has a 5% Goods and Services Tax (GST) applied to all goods. Visitors purchasing goods worth $300 or more through a shop participating in the GST Tourist Refund Scheme can apply for a GST refund. These shops display a 'tax-free shopping' logo, and when you purchase an item you must fill in a claim form and show your passport. You will receive a global refund cheque – these are issued only for purchases of $100 and above.

Present this cheque (or cheques), your passport and goods at the Customs GST Inspection counter in the departure hall at Changi airport, before you check your bags (and the goods) in. Customs then stamps your cheque(s), which you can then cash at the cash refund counters inside the airport, or have credited to your credit card or bank account. Refer to the STB brochure *Singapore Shopping Guide* for more details.

Bargaining

Prices are usually fixed in shops, except at markets and in some shops in touristy areas. If you do have to haggle, stay good humoured and don't get petty – this causes everyone to lose face. Name a realistic price, smile a lot and, if you don't get what you want from the shop owner, make a polite move towards the door (this can often spark a sudden change of heart).

COLONIAL DISTRICT & THE QUAYS

Not quite the consumerist blitzkrieg you'll find on Orchard Rd, the Colonial District has more than its fair share of fancy malls. Among the best known are Suntec City, CityLink Mall, Bugis Junction and Marina Square, which are all a match for their Orchard rivals. For computers, Funan is IT heaven, while for down-and-dirty flea market shopping head to Bugis or, at weekends, to Clarke Quay.

ASEANA Map p230 Department Store

☎ 6338 1090; 01-73/75 Millenia Walk, 9 Raffles Blvd; City Hall MRT

A stylish Malaysian boutique with some original local clothing in silks and batik prints and ready-to-wear fashion from designers like Paul Ropp and Milo. It also has a decent range of homewares and gifts.

CHIJMES COMPLEX Map p230 Art & Antiques

30 Victoria St; City Hall MRT

A good place to browse for crafts among the bars and restaurants. Here you'll find **Peter Hoe Evolution** (☎ 6339 6880; 01-05), which does a nice line in modern batik clothing as well as the usual craft items.

CITYLINK MALL Map p230 Mall

☎ 6238 1121; 1 Raffles Link; City Hall MRT

The first underground mall in Singapore, designed by Kohn Pederson Fox from New York, this tunnel of retail links City Hall MRT with Suntec City and features a **Links of London**, a **Lee Hwa Jewellery** store, a **Dymocks** bookshop, **HMV** and a speciality cigar shop called **Acanta**.

CLARKE QUAY FLEA MARKET

Map p230 Market

Clarke Quay MRT

Held every Sunday between 10am and 6pm, this jolly flea market attracts a mix of browsers as broad as its range of wares,

TOP FIVE FLEA MARKETS

- **Sungei Rd Thieves' Market** (p156) The oldest and most distinctive in Singapore, where gems hide among the junk.
- **Clarke Quay** (opposite) Usual flea-market array of handicrafts, clothes and music.
- **Tanglin Mall** (p160) Aimed at the expat set, full of homemade crafts, jewellery etc.
- **Far East Square** (p145) Old records and general knick-knacks.
- **Mohamed Ali Lane Market** (p145) Wide array of old and often bizarre wares.

thought it's not as popular as it used to be. Stalls often change weekly, but you can usually find homewares, homemade jewellery, clothes and even antiques.

ESPLANADE MALL Map p230 — Mall

☎ 6828 8399; 8 Raffles Ave; City Hall MRT

With more than 8000 sq metres to cover, it's not hard to spend several hours browsing the speciality shops here. Start perhaps with the widest selection of tea leaves from China and Taiwan at the **Chinese Tea House** on Level 2, or indulge in luxurious ethnic wear ranging from Straits-Chinese sarong, kebayas and cheongsams at **Amor Meus** (☎ 6336 6930; 02-06). Also check out **Chocz** (☎ 6238 0803; 02-15), renowned for its fresh pralines and truffles that use only the finest Swiss and Belgian chocolate.

FUNAN – THE IT MALL

Map p230 — Computers & Electronics

☎ 6337 4235; 109 North Bridge Rd; City Hall MRT

The principal computer centre, Funan is the place for brand-name goods, a better bet than Sim Lim Square if you don't know exactly what you're doing. There are dozens of computer shops on the top floors, as well as a large **Challenger Superstore** (☎ 6336 8327).

MARINA SQUARE Map p230 — Mall

☎ 6339 8787; www.marinasquare.com.sg; 6 Raffles Blvd; City Hall MRT

It looks dowdy, but packs in 225 outlets in a massive shopping space, including big brand names like **Calvin Klein, Levis** and **Esprit**. It is centrally located in the Marina Centre area with easy access to and from CityLink Mall, Suntec City, Millenia Walk and the Esplanade.

MITA BUILDING Map p230 — Art

140 Hill St; Clarke Quay MRT

Among the several galleries in the brightly coloured colonial MITA Building is **Art-2 Gallery** (☎ 6338 8713), which specialises in contemporary art from Myanmar, as well as Singaporean and Malaysian artists. Another contemporary art dealer in the building is **Gajah Gallery** (☎ 6737 4202), with pieces from as far afield as Indonesia and India. And there's also **Soobin Art Gallery** (☎ 6837 2777), a terrific gallery representing the best of China's vibrant avant-garde scene.

PAGODA HOUSE Map p230 — Art & Antiques

☎ 6883 0501; www.pagodahouse.com; 02-34 Raffles Hotel Arcade, 328 North Bridge Rd; City Hall MRT

Sells antiques and gifts, while its branches at **Tanglin Rd** (139 & 143/145 Tanglin Rd) in the English-style Tudor Court strip specialise in chic, contemporary (and extremely expensive) Chinese furniture as well as Buddhas, architectural artefacts and the like.

ALL THAT GLITTERS…

Gold shops are all over town, but you'll find a concentration in Little India along Serangoon Rd, where the shops teem with Indians from all over the diaspora stocking up on jewellery, often for weddings and other special events. Gold is also popular in the People's Park Complex (p145) in Chinatown, where 22- and 24-carat gold is sold by weight.

The concentration of gold shops in these areas reflects its importance to Chinese and Indians, for whom it is not only an overt symbol of prosperity but also, for the Chinese particularly, a good luck symbol usually given at births, weddings and at Chinese New Year.

Singapore is also a good place to buy pearls and gemstones but you really need to know the market. Jade is a Chinese favourite and usually the lighter the colour, the more expensive it is. There's plenty of imitation jade around waiting for a mug to buy it. If it's dark coloured, chances are it's not real. Examine jade pieces for flaws, as these could become cracks.

RAFFLES CITY Map p230 Mall

☎ 6338 7766; www.rafflescity.com; 252 North Bridge Rd; City Hall MRT

Raffles City has a soaring atrium and wide range of shops, including a branch of the excellent **Robinsons** department store dominating three levels, and some decent gift shops like **Hó'glund Art Glass** (☎ 6338 4062; 03-26) and the **Metropolitan Museum of Art** (☎ 6336 1870; 01-37).

RAFFLES HOTEL ARCADE Map p230 Mall

328 North Bridge Rd; City Hall MRT

Attached to the hotel is the stylish Raffles Hotel Arcade which, as you would expect, is firmly upmarket, with designer clothes, galleries (including one selling ancient fossils) plus the excellent **Raffles Hotel gift shop** and the **Thossb SB Raffles** (☎ 6412 1148; 01-30/31) food shop, which is a great place for gourmet gifts, including handmade chocolates and nicely packaged teas, coffees and biscuits. There is also a good range of wine.

RED SEA GALLERY Map p230 Art

☎ 6732 6711; www.redseagallery.com; 232 River Valley Rd; bus 54 from Clarke Quay MRT

Exceptional modern Asian art gallery that will captivate even the non-art lover. It features often-stunning works by painters from around Asia – as well as some from the West. The works are so beautifully presented you could spend hours in here.

SUNTEC CITY Map p230 Mall

☎ 6821 3668; www.sunteccity.com.sg; 3 Temasek Blvd; City Hall MRT

Singapore's largest mall with endless shops selling clothes, books, furniture, electronics, sports equipment and music, and a staggering 60 restaurants, cafés and a food court. One of the biggest crowd pullers is the Fountain of Wealth, once accorded the status of 'World's Largest Fountain' (though not, you'll observe, world's most attractive fountain) in the *Guinness Book of Records*.

TOWER RECORDS Map p230 Music Store

☎ 6338 0758; Suntec City, 3 Temasek Blvd; City Hall MRT

The global music chain has a predictably wide selection, plus a decent number of listening stations with pre-selected CDs of the moment.

CHINATOWN & THE CBD

If you're looking out for an Asian antique statuette, a magnificent antique wardrobe or just a cheap souvenir, Chinatown is the place to come. Pagoda St has become the centre for tourist tack, but behind and beyond the stalls crammed with 'Fine City' T-shirts and two-minute calligraphers, are located countless small shops selling everything from modern Asian homewares to old furniture, but it pays to know your Khmer antique from your Javanese sweatshop knock-off. The area is also famous for its Chinese medicine centres if you're feeling a little heaty, and no-one should miss the wet market in the Chinatown Complex.

AIK TUAN SCULPTURE SHOP Map pp234-5 Art

26 Mohamed Ali Lane; 9am-5pm Mon-Sat; Chinatown MRT

This shop, specialising in Chinese effigies, is notable for its repair as well as its retail services. Bring your worn-out temple guardian, or your Lord Guan Gong with his arm lopped off by the dog and they'll fix it up as good as new.

ART SEASONS Map pp234-5 Art

☎ 6221 1800; The Box, 5 Gemmill Lane; Chinatown MRT

Just off Club St, this excellent gallery specialises in contemporary art from China and Myanmar, as well as Korea and Japan. Gentle bargaining is possible.

BAO YUAN TRADING Map pp234-5 Art

☎ 6227 1189; 15 Temple St; 9am-6pm; Chinatown MRT

Stocks a reasonable range of ceramics and a familiar selection of Singaporean souvenirs. Its speciality is replica Han dynasty ceramics, the kind you see in Chinese restaurants.

CHINATOWN COMPLEX Map pp234-5 Market

11 New Bridge Rd; Chinatown MRT

The wet market here is an experience in itself – and not for the sensitive. Brimming with seafood, fruit and vegetables, it's a fun place to explore, though if you're buying you may find communication a bit tricky. Alongside one of Singapore's best hawker centres, there are several good-quality antique shops.

CHINATOWN POINT Map pp234-5 Mall

133 New Bridge Rd; Chinatown MRT

Another bargain-hunter's paradise. Apart from tonnes of souvenir handicraft stalls, you'll find anything from shoes, cosmetics, clothes and travelling bags to Chinese products including lacquer-ware and those painted umbrellas.

EU YAN SANG Map pp234-5 Chinese Medicine

☎ 6223 6333; 269A South Bridge Rd; Chinatown MRT

Venerable Eu Yan Sang has been revamped into looking like a modern chemist – until you get a load of the traditional remedies on the shelves. A consultation with the resident herbalist is $8 and most stock comes with English instructions.

FAR EAST LEGEND Map pp234-5 Antiques

☎ 6323 5365; 233 South Bridge Rd; Chinatown MRT

A small warren-like shop selling an excellent collection of furniture, lamps, handicrafts, statues and screens from Korea, Thailand, Myanmar and China.

FAR EAST SQUARE FLEA MARKET

Map pp234-5 Market

76 Telok Ayer St; noon-10pm Sat & Sun; Raffles Place MRT

Held every weekend; stallholders set up displays or spread blankets on the ground, selling pictures, old vinyl LPs, watches, pots and pans – anything. A bit on the small side, but a half-hour browse may turn up something special.

MOHAMED ALI LANE MARKET

Map pp234-5 Market

Mohamed Ali Lane; ☎ 1-7pm; Chinatown MRT

A lot smaller than the Sungei Rd Thieves Market, located in the car park at the corner of Club St and Cross St. You'll find a wide array of old and often bizarre wares here, though the atmosphere is more subdued. Some of the hawkers here (and at Sungei Rd) are homeless and depend on what they sell to live.

ORIGINASIA Map pp234-5 Homeware

☎ 6226 2680; 225 South Bridge Rd; Chinatown MRT

This is a beautiful shop selling sumptuously designed furniture, lamps, statues and accessories, adding a distinctly modern flavour to what are essentially traditional Asian designs. There is another **branch** (Map p230; 372 River Valley Rd), which has an art gallery.

PEOPLE'S PARK CENTRE

Map pp234-5 Mall

110 Upper Cross St; Chinatown MRT

A good place to browse around if you're in the area (though we wouldn't go out of our way to get here). There's a decent range of electronics, clothing and department stores here.

PEOPLE'S PARK COMPLEX

Map pp234-5 Mall

1 Park Rd; Chinatown MRT

This is an interesting mall to wander around if you are after some good-quality Chinese souvenirs and don't feel like bargaining too hard for them. There are Chinese instruments, lacquer-ware and jade (only for the knowledgeable), as well as cheongsams and some excellent woodworking.

RED PEACH GALLERY Map pp234-5 Crafts

☎ 6222 2215; 68 Pagoda St; Chinatown MRT

An upmarket decorative homeware shop selling large, expensive couches, silk cushions and jewellery. It also houses a 'boutique spa' done out Ming dynasty–style with lanterns, wooden floors and fancy furniture.

SHING'S ANTIQUE GALLERY

Map pp234-5 Antiques

☎ 6224 4332; 24A-26 Pagoda St; Chinatown MRT

One of the better options along this often tacky tourist strip, this large shop retains some of its crumbling shophouse charm, with beautiful wooden screens and antique window grills, huge temple guardians and antique statues small enough to take home.

SIA HUAT Map pp234-5 Kitchenware

☎ 6223 1732; 9-11 Temple St; 🕑 8.30am-6.30pm Mon-Fri, 8.30am-5pm Sat; Chinatown MRT

Singaporean chefs flock here; it stocks all manner of top-of-the-range pots, pans and utensils. A place for the serious foodie.

THYE ON GINGSENG MEDICAL HALL
Map pp234-5 Chinese Medicine
264 South Bridge Rd; Chinatown MRT
Dusty and authentic; you can buy everything from Dettol to restorative homemade herbal drinks to packets of *po chai* pills ($3.30; traditional remedy for travellers' diarrhoea and minor stomach problems).

TONG HENG PASTRIES Map pp234-5 Food
☎ 6223 3649; 285 South Bridge Rd; 🕑 10am-10pm Tue-Sun; Chinatown MRT
Going strong for more than 70 years; arguably Singapore's most popular place for egg tarts and other tempting cakes and cookies.

UTTERLY ART Map pp234-5 Art
☎ 6226 2605; 208 South Bridge Rd; Chinatown MRT
One of the more interesting pure art galleries is Utterly Art, a small, welcoming exhibition space with pieces ranging from classical to avant-garde; check out the wire sculptures made by visually impaired artist Vicker Tan. The gallery also has live performances and installations occasionally.

YONG GALLERY Map pp234-5 Antiques
☎ 6226 1718; 260 South Bridge Rd; Chinatown MRT
Specialises in Chinese antiques, old jade, calligraphy and wood carvings. If you're after jade, which is so often a lottery in Asia, you can be assured of the real stuff here.

YUE HWA CHINESE PRODUCTS
Map pp234-5 Department Store
☎ 6538 4222; 70 Eu Tong Sen St; Chinatown MRT
This department store, in an old six-storey building with echoes of Shanghai, specialises in products from the motherland. Downstairs you'll find Chinese medicine and herbs, as well as clothes and cushions. Moving up to Level 5, you'll pass through silks, food and Chinese tea, arts and crafts, and household goods, before ending up at the large (though unattractively lit) furniture section.

ZHEN LACQUER GALLERY
Map pp234-5 Crafts
☎ 6222 2718; 1 Trengganu St; Chinatown MRT
This attractive shop houses a reliable range of Vietnamese lacquer-ware (the eggshell lacquer-work is particularly appealing), fine Chinese porcelain and embroidery as well as some decent baskets.

LITTLE INDIA & THE ARAB QUARTER

A wander around Little India and the Arab Quarter (Kampong Glam) is a browser's delight – and a thoroughly different experience from the air-conditioned order of Orchard Rd and the Colonial District. The ramshackle streets are a treasure-trove of art, antiques, textiles, food, music and the infamous cut-price palace of Mustafa Centre. Keen bargainers might find the discounted electronics that were once abundant in Singapore, while computer enthusiasts will make a beeline for Sim Lim Square. Heading down to Bussorah St, you'll find a newly resurgent pedestrian strip filled with arts, crafts, antiques and cafés.

A JAFFAR SPICES CENTRE
Map p232 Food
☎ 6294 4833; 01-69 Campbell Block, Little India Arcade, 48 Serangoon Rd; Little India MRT
You'll find big red buckets of spices – everything you need for a decent curry.

ANSA STORE Map p232 Art
☎ 6295 6605; 29 Kerbau Rd; Little India MRT
This is the place to come if you want a frame for that painting you bought in Indonesia, freshly carved to your specifications. This gaudy shop also sells wildly coloured posters and extravagant pictures of religious icons.

BHASKAR'S ART ACADEMY
Map p232 Art
☎ 6396 4523; 19 Kerbau Rd; Little India MRT
Established to promote the work of Indian artists from Singapore, India and Malaysia, there are some eye-catching pieces at this place; much of the work is uninspiring, however.

BUGIS VILLAGE Map p232 Night Market
cnr Victoria St & Rochor Rd; Bugis MRT
Now carefully restored and polished to remove most signs of its ignoble past as a den of sin, just like Bugis St nearby. The main attraction here is the night market, where you can pick up cheap clothes, CDs (some of them even pirated) and watches.

(Continued on page 155)

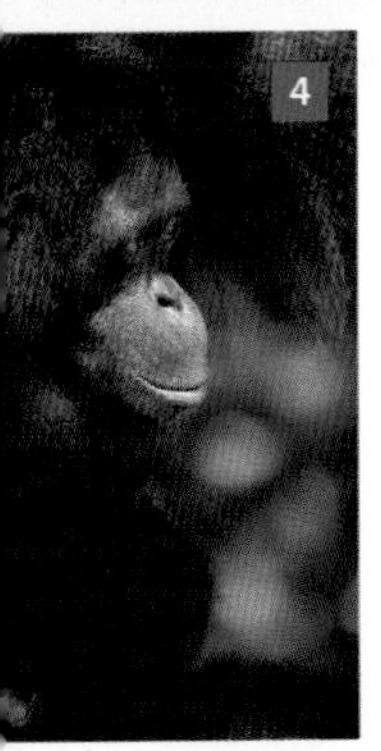

1 *The summit at Bukit Timah Nature Reserve (p77)* **2** *Singapore Zoological Gardens (p78), northern Singapore* **3** *Road to the summit, Bukit Timah Nature Reserve* **4** *Singapore Zoological Gardens*

1 *Singapore Science Centre (p84), western Singapore* 2 *Pagoda in the Chinese Garden (p81), western Singapore* 3 *Haw Par Villa (p81), southern Singapore*
4 *Penguin Parade at Jurong BirdPark (p82), western Singapore*

1 *Images of Singapore (p86), Sentosa Island* **2** *Underwater World (p87), Sentosa Island* **3** *Sentosa Island (p85) beach* **4** *The* Merlion *(p87), Sentosa Island*

1 Raffles Hotel (p130) bar, Colonial District **2** *Raffles Hotel's (in)famous Singapore Sling*
3 *Velvet Underground (p133) dance club, central Singapore*
4 *Penny Black (p130), Boat Quay*

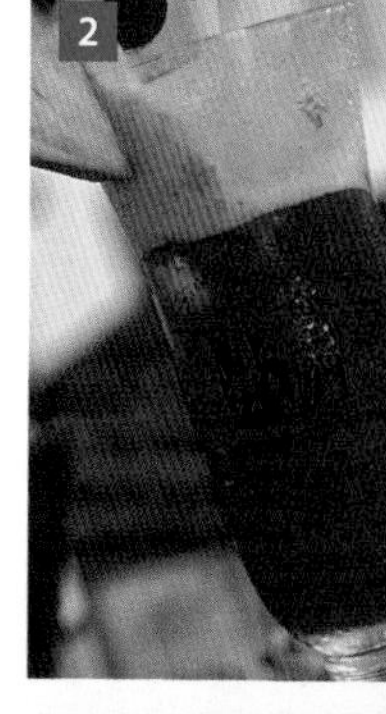

1 *Street café, Orchard Rd (p114)* **2** *Tekka Centre (p113), Little India* **3** *Satay (p32) cooked in the traditional wood-fired way* **4** *Hawker stall in the Chinatown Complex (p108)*

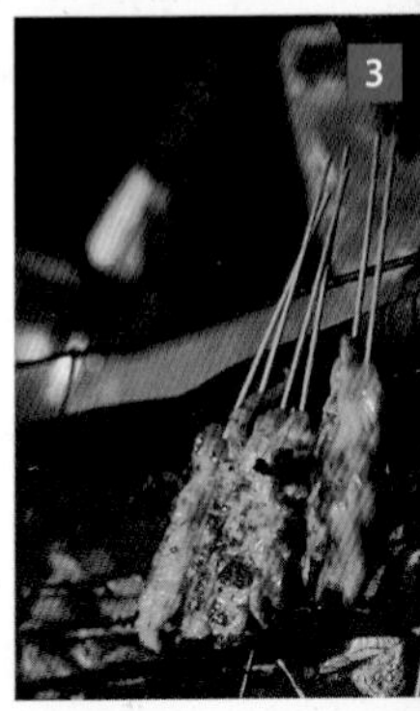

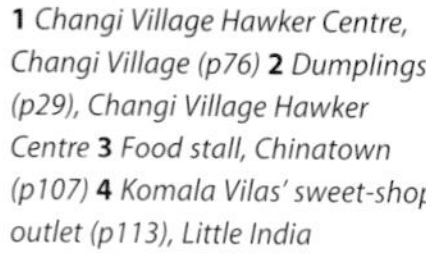

1 *Changi Village Hawker Centre, Changi Village (p76)* **2** *Dumplings (p29), Changi Village Hawker Centre* **3** *Food stall, Chinatown (p107)* **4** *Komala Vilas' sweet-shop outlet (p113), Little India*

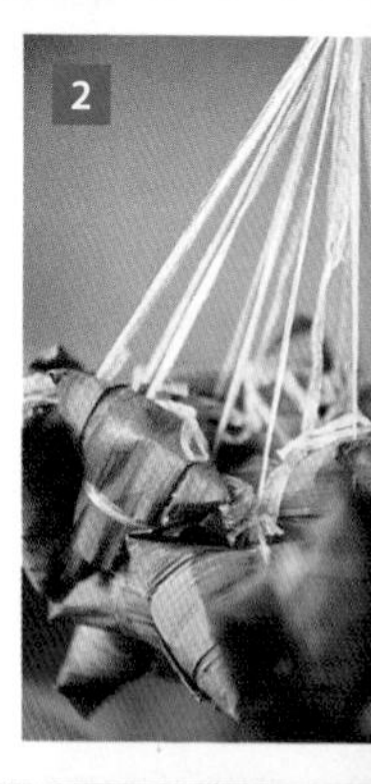

1 *Zouk (p133) dance club, central Singapore* **2** *Movie poster, Little India (p59)* **3** *I-S magazine (p100), a what's-on guide to Singapore* **4** *Giant video screen on Orchard Rd (p63)*

1 *Berjaya Tioman Beach Resort (p188), Pulau Tioman* **2** *Main street of Pulau Ubin'* *village (p181)* **3** *Bicycle rent* *shops (p182), Pulau Ubin*

(Continued from page 146)

COMME DES GARCONS GUERRILLA STORE Map p232 Fashion

☎ 6224 3236; 47 Haji Lane; Bugis MRT

Not quite in keeping with the cheap and trendy tone along this little backstreet, the clothes from the well-known Japanese label are, of course, extremely hip and extremely expensive.

GRANDFATHER'S COLLECTIONS

Map p232 Curios

☎ 6299 4530; 42 Bussorah St, Arab Quarter; Little India MRT

A wonderful, dusty bric-a-brac shop that does indeed look like your grandfather's attic, with pre-war radios, clocks, typewriters, old Coke bottles, Ovaltine and Horlicks tins, vinyl records...In fact, there's not much that isn't here. A true oddity.

HOUSE OF JAPAN Map p232 Fashion

☎ 6396 6657; 55 Haji Lane; Bugis MRT

Like a hip Salvation Army store, this rather dank shop sells very cheap, ultra-fashionable secondhand clothes straight from Japan. Hopefully it'll help sharpen up Singaporean teenagers somewhat.

INDIAN CLASSICAL MUSIC CENTRE

Map p232 Music

☎ 6291 0187; 01-29 Hastings Block, Little India Arcade, 48 Serangoon Rd; Little India MRT

As well as Indian music CDs, also sells sitars, tabla, bells – everything you need to create your own Bollywood soundtrack.

KHAN MOHAMED BHOY & SONS

Map p232 Food

☎ 6293 8783; 20 Cuff Rd; Little India MRT

You can't miss this bright yellow building off Serangoon Rd, which houses one of Singapore's last spice grinding (and flour milling) shops – perhaps the last of a dying breed. Inside, workers, often chewing betelnut to keep themselves going, pound away all day. They might not appreciate gawpers, so buy a little bag of something while you're there.

KHIM'S COLLECTIONS

Map p232 Arts & Crafts

☎ 6299 1192; 23 Bussorah St; Bugis MRT

Khim's Collections boasts a beautiful assortment of Vietnamese lacquer-ware, modern paintings and eggshell mosaic.

MELOR'S CURIOS Map p232 Arts & Crafts

☎ 6292 3934; 39 Bussorah St; Bugis MRT

Pre-dating the restoration of Bussorah St, this is a reasonably priced place (by Singapore standards) to pick up Javanese furniture, antiques, lamps and other crafts.

MUSTAFA CENTRE

Map p232 Department Store

☎ 6298 2967; 145 Syed Alwi Rd; Farrer Park MRT

The bustling 24-hour Mustafa Centre in Little India is a magnet for budget shoppers, most of them from the subcontinent. This place has just about everything – electronics, jewellery, household items, shoes, bags, CDs – all at bargain rates. Forget about presentation or service; price is king here. There's also a large supermarket. Avoid the evenings at weekends, when it seems the entire subcontinental male migrant worker population descends on the area.

PARCO BUGIS JUNCTION

Map p232 Mall

200 Victoria St; Bugis MRT

One of the more distinctive of Singapore's malls, featuring two streets of re-created shophouses, covered with a glass ceiling and air-conditioned. Along these surreally cool strips are big names like Converse, as well as market stalls selling curios. Make sure you stop off for a wonderful gelato at **Studio cKono** (01-60). As well as the large **Seiyu department store** (☎ 6223 2222; 230 Victoria St) and the Hotel Inter-Continental, Bugis Junction is one of the top fashion malls, with a 3rd-floor section devoted to hip clothes shops like **Solid Fuel** (03-30m), **Strawberry** (03-30w), **77th Street** (03-30a) and accessory stores. The ground floor has some notable local fashions, like **M)phosis** (01-02) and **LVER** (01-20/36).

PLASTIQUE KINETIC WORMS

Map p232 Art

☎ 6292 7783; www.pkworms.org.sg; 61 Kerbau Rd; Little India MRT

Singapore's only artist-run, non-profit gallery promoting the works of young and contemporary visual artists. The somewhat

Entrance to Robinsons, Centrepoint (opposite)

pretentious name is not necessarily a reflection of the work inside, some of which is excellent.

SAMRA Map p232 Dance

☎ 6296 2624; 36A Arab St; Bugis MRT

An irresistible little shop selling seductive belly-dancing outfits and accessories, and a few Middle Eastern knick-knacks. You can also take lessons in belly-dancing and Bollywood/Bangra dance here.

SHOMA STUDIO Map p232 Art

☎ 6296 2285; 34 Petain Rd; 🕒 11am-6pm Thu-Sun or by appointment; Farrer Park MRT

A striking, modern gallery in a renovated shophouse, with several floors of beautiful art, craft and furniture from all over Southeast Asia. Shipment can be arranged.

SIM LIM TOWER Map p232 Electronics

☎ 6295 4361; 10 Jalan Besar; Bugis MRT

A big electronic centre with everything from capacitors to audio and video gear – and not far removed from Sim Lim Square. Again, arm yourself with knowledge and be prepared to bargain hard.

SIM LIM SQUARE

Map p232 Computers & Electronics

☎ 6332 5839; 1 Rochor Canal Rd; Bugis MRT

Six floors packed with computers, components, DVDs, mobile phones and software, Sim Lim is a geek's paradise and not for the faint-hearted or uninformed. Most of the stuff is not brand name, but it's cheap. Take your time and shop around. There's stiff competition in here, so it often pays to play vendors off against each other.

STRAITS RECORDS Map p232 Music

☎ 9341 1572; 43 Haji Lane; 🕒 noon-11pm Mon-Fri, noon-midnight Sat & Sun; Bugis MRT

Startlingly painted in red-and-white stripes and adorned with clenched fists, Straits is positioning itself as a focal point for the subculture developing on Haji Lane, stocking alternative, hip-hip, hardcore and reggae CDs, as well as some old vinyl LPs, T-shirts and books.

SUNGEI RD THIEVES MARKET

Map p232 Market

Jalan Besar Rd; 🕒 1-7pm; Bugis MRT

More than 30 years old and a fascinating glimpse into Singapore's underbelly (it's amazing the authorities still allow it to exist). A huge jumble of goods, often sold by grizzled old Chinese 'uncles' trying to make the odd 10 bucks from their old record players, battered woks and shirts they wore to a wedding in 1971. There's the occasional amazing find lurking in there somewhere, but even if you don't buy anything, it's an absorbing way to spend an hour or two.

ORCHARD ROAD

Orchard Rd is absolutely mind-boggling. Although some Singaporeans maintain that they can visit every mall in a day, human beings without supernatural shopping powers might spend three days here and not even see a quarter of it. Prices aren't necessarily the best, but the range is almost infinite. The following is an overview of the main malls found on Orchard Rd, and reviews of some of the notable shops within them.

APPLE CENTRE Map pp226-7 Computer

☎ 6238 9378; www.applecentreorchard.com; 02-07/08 Wheelock Pl, 501 Orchard Rd; Orchard MRT

Apple's flagship Singapore store is surprisingly small, given the number of people usually inside gazing lustfully at the iPods and Cinema Displays. Shuffle in and join the faithful – prices are often a little better than in Europe or Australia (don't forget your GST rebate), but check before you leave home.

BORDERS Map pp226-7 Bookshop

☎ 6235 7146; 01-00 Wheelock Pl; Orchard MRT

Though Borders stocks a vast range of books, periodicals and CDs, it's not as user-friendly since all the comfy sofas were removed – apparently there were too many families bunkering down here for weekend picnics. Nevertheless, it's still one of the few places in the world where you can see a bookshop as crowded as a nightclub on a Friday night.

CENTREPOINT Map pp226-7 Mall

☎ 6737 9000; 176 Orchard Rd; Somerset MRT

This spacious, practical, no-nonsense shopping centre has long been a favourite with Singaporeans and draws a fair number of visitors too. The biggest draw is **Robinsons** department store, established in 1858. Robinsons is well known for some of the best service in Singapore (how long since you had someone in a department store measure you for a shirt?). Children's retail, home furnishings, jewellery, electronics and bookshops are other attractions at Centrepoint. It is one of the liveliest malls you'll find on Orchard Rd, especially during the Christmas holidays.

DFS GALLERIA SCOTTSWALK

Map pp226-7 Mall

☎ 6229 8100; 25 Scotts Rd; Orchard MRT

DFS Galleria, with its distinctive bright red exterior, is an alluring place – and the interior is no less attractive. The ground floor is done out surprisingly tastefully with replica shophouse and Asian architecture and here you'll find good quality souvenirs, though it's a little pricey. Everything from SIA stewardess dresses, to nicely packaged chopsticks to pre-packaged local food like chicken rice. At the top of a massive escalator, you begin a three-storey descent through exclusive boutiques featuring the usual array of expensive brand names.

CLOTHING SIZES

Measurements approximate only, try before you buy

Women's Clothing						
Aus/UK	8	10	12	14	16	18
Europe	36	38	40	42	44	46
Japan	5	7	9	11	13	15
USA	6	8	10	12	14	16
Women's Shoes						
Aus/USA	5	6	7	8	9	10
Europe	35	36	37	38	39	40
France only	35	36	38	39	40	42
Japan	22	23	24	25	26	27
UK	3½	4½	5½	6½	7½	8½
Men's Clothing						
Aus	92	96	100	104	108	112
Europe	46	48	50	52	54	56
Japan	S		M	M		L
UK/USA	35	36	37	38	39	40
Men's Shirts (Collar Sizes)						
Aus/Japan	38	39	40	41	42	43
Europe	38	39	40	41	42	43
UK/USA	15	15½	16	16½	17	17½
Men's Shoes						
Aus/UK	7	8	9	10	11	12
Europe	41	42	43	44½	46	47
Japan	26	27	27½	28	29	30
USA	7½	8½	9½	10½	11½	12½

EM TRADE & DESIGN

Map pp226-7 Crafts

☎ 6475 6941; www.emtradedesign.com; 1 Chatsworth Rd, 14-25 Chatsworth Ct; Orchard MRT

A visit-by-appointment gallery in a residential block on Chatsworth Rd, a short walk from Orchard Rd. The collection of silk weaves, pottery and lacquer-ware from Cambodia, Laos, Vietnam and Japan is exquisite.

FAR EAST PLAZA Map pp226-7 Mall

☎ 6732 6266; 14 Scotts Rd; Orchard MRT

A favourite hang-out spot for teenagers, with its startling array of funky stalls selling Japanese-style street fashions and accessories, it's also good for tailored suits, electronics, **Sunny Books** (p160), shoe shops, hair and beauty salons and even tattoo parlours. Far East is a must-stop for bargain hunters and an antidote to the sparkle and splash on much of Orchard. Retailers here are definitely much easier to haggle with and the chances of scoring a good price for jewellery and electronic goods are high. There's a popular food court in the basement.

FORUM – THE SHOPPING MALL

Map pp226-7 Mall

☎ **6732 2479; 583 Orchard Rd; Orchard MRT**

This is one for the kids. Dominated by kids' fashion and toy retail outlets, Forum has a branch of the world's largest toy store, **Toys 'R' Us**, which occupies most of the top floor. Other levels are taken over by designer wear, namely **Guess Kids, DKNY Kids, Ralph Lauren Children, Benetton, Gap** and **Hush Puppies**. If Toys 'R' Us is not sufficient, you can always check out some bookshops like **Twinkle Thinkers** for the little ones.

HEEREN Map pp226-7 Mall

☎ **6733 4725; www.heeren.com.sg; 260 Orchard Rd; Somerset MRT**

Another magnet for the young and hip; Levels 4 and 5 house about 50 retailers selling everything from surf and street vintage to beads and piercings. Check out the **ButtCheeks** Brazilian bikinis, or the innovative **iTX Concept Store**, which has food, clothes and electronics. There's also a huge **HMV** (below).

HMV Map pp226-7 Music

☎ **6733 1822; 01-11 The Heeren, 260 Orchard Rd; Somerset MRT**

Arguably the most extensive selection of CDs can be found here, where there are separate floors dedicated to Western pop, Asian pop, and classical and jazz. Look out for the bargain VCD movie section, where among the dross you can find classic films – both old and modern – for as little as $5 each. There is a smaller branch in the **Citylink Mall** (p142).

JAZMIN ASIAN ARTS

Map pp226-7 Art & Antiques

☎ **6737 1552; 125 Tanglin Rd, B1-01; Orchard MRT**

Another Asian and Indian antiques shop in the exclusive and pricey Tudor Court strip near Tanglin Mall, this one is particularly worth visiting for its collection of extremely artistic Chinese advertisement posters dating back to the 1920s and '30s. They're advertising anything from batteries to cigarettes, though from the quality of the paintings you'd never guess it.

KINOKUNIYA Map pp226-7 Bookshop

03-10/15 Ngee Ann City, 391 Orchard Rd; Orchard MRT

Claims to be Southeast Asia's biggest bookshop, and who are we to argue?

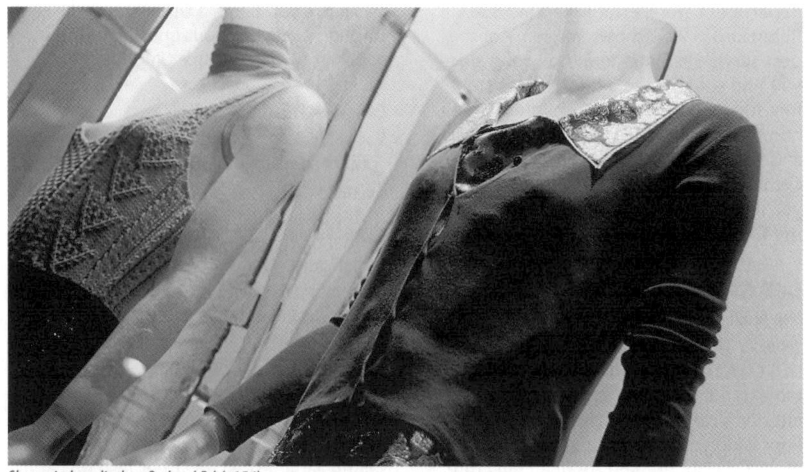

Shop window display, Orchard Rd (p156)

Occupying a massive 43,000 sq ft, and providing an extensive collection of over 500,000 quality titles from all over the world, including English, Japanese, Chinese, French and German publications. You could spend hours browsing the options here, or use the irresistible electronic book locater inside the entrance, which finds the title of your choice and prints out a map telling you exactly where you can find it. In a shop this size, you probably need it.

LUCKY PLAZA Map pp226-7 Mall

☎ **6235 3294; 304 Orchard Rd; Orchard MRT**

Like Far East Plaza, this is one of the older, dingier and for many people more interesting malls on Orchard. Lucky Plaza is probably one of the best places to pick up gifts and souvenirs. You can get anything from clothes, bags and shoes to electronic goods; discounts are possible if your bargaining skills are good. Annoying tailors promising the best suits can make the experience a bit frustrating but it's a fascinating place to browse around. Fill your stomach in the hawker-style food court in the basement.

NGEE ANN CITY Map pp226-7 Mall

☎ **6739 9323; 391 Orchard Rd; Orchard MRT**

You could easily spend an entire day in the monolithic, chocolate-coloured behemoth dominating the western end of Orchard. Home to many department and smaller retail stores, Ngee Ann City can be overwhelming even for a seasoned shopper. **Takashimaya** (a Japanese department store) is a famously exclusive place to get anything from kitchenware to designer outfits. Other international chains at Ngee Ann include **Guess?**, **Hugo Boss Woman**, **U2**, **Country Road**, **Louis Vuitton**, **Chanel** and **Burberry**. In the basement, look for locally designed clothes at **M)Phosis**. For jewellery iconoclasts, there's a **Tiffany & Co** on the 4th floor. Or make a beeline for Southeast Asia's largest bookstore, **Kinokuniya** (opposite).

ONE PRICE STORE

Map pp226-7 Art & Crafts

☎ **6734 1680; 3 Emerald Hill Rd; Somerset MRT**

This Chinese craft shop has plenty of decent stuff, including wooden carvings, pottery and embroidered silk, at reasonable prices.

OPERA GALLERY Map pp226-7 Art

☎ **6735 2618; www.operagallery.com; 02-12H Ngee Ann City, 391 Orchard Rd; Somerset MRT**

A large, sumptuous space featuring magnificent fine art and sculpture from contemporary Vietnamese to 19th-century French. Staff are friendly and knowledgeable – though if you're wearing thongs (flip-flops) they might be less inclined to help.

PACIFIC PLAZA Map pp226-7 Mall

☎ **6733 5655; 9 Scotts Rd; Orchard MRT**

Another mall popular with teenagers (aren't they all, you might ask?), Pacific is targeted at the more mainstream adolescent with outlets for Stussy, Mambo, Quicksilver and Billabong. A unique find is the Vintage Place on the 2nd level, which sells secondhand designer outfits. Look out for a vintage Fendi, Gucci or Donna Karan number in the racks here.

PALAIS RENAISSANCE Map pp226-7 Mall

☎ **6737 6933; 390 Orchard Rd; Orchard MRT**

Houses both international and local designer label boutiques, such as DKNY, Prada and Jim Thompson Thai silks. Another must if you're aiming for the exclusive shopping scene. Very popular with the very wealthy locals, of whom there are many, and the expatriate community. The **Marmalade Pantry** (p116), located in Basement 1, is a favourite lounging spot for ladies who shop.

PARAGON Map pp226-7 Mall

☎ **6738 5535; 290 Orchard Rd; MRT Orchard**

There is no shortage of upmarket malls in Singapore, but Paragon (which screams exclusivity) is yet another addition to the list. If you're up for more designer shopping this is your stop. **Marks & Spencer**, and trendy fashion shops such as **Diesel**, **Ermenegildo Zegna** and **Salvatore Ferragamo**. Streetwear favourite **Project Shop Blood Brothers** can be found here; it also has the **Blood Café** (p114) serving some of the best desserts you'll ever taste. The basement houses a supermarket, cafés and wine shops, with a wide variety of choices.

PLAZA SINGAPURA

Map pp226-7 Mall

☎ **6332 9298; 68 Orchard Rd; Dhoby Ghaut MRT**

Conveniently located on top of the Dhoby Ghaut MRT station and the North East

ANTIQUES ON PARADE

Along Dempsey Rd, southwest of Singapore Botanic Gardens off Holland Rd, the former British Army barracks have been turned into warehouse shops specialising in antiques. In this delightful, pleasantly disorganised rural setting, you'll find anything from Kashmiri carpets and teak furniture to landscaping ornaments and antiques. It's a fascinating place to wander around and attracts crowds of expats and well-to-do Singaporeans at weekends. Try **Jehan Gallery** (Map pp226-7; ☎ 6475 0003; No 26) for excellent and well-priced rugs and carpets, **Shang Antiques** (Map pp226-7; ☎ 6388 8838; No 16) for huge stone and wooden Buddha images, **Linda Gallery** (Map pp226-7; ☎ 6476 7000; No 15) for interesting contemporary artwork, the enormous **Pasardina Fine Living** (Map pp226-7; ☎ 6472 0228; No 13) for just about everything, or **Asiatique** (Map pp226-7; ☎ 6471 0786; No 14-8) for Indonesian furniture made from recycled wood. **Eastern Discoveries** (Map pp226-7; ☎ 6475 1814; Block 26, 01-04) has a superb range of antique opium pipes, Buddha statuettes and old signboards in Chinese from around Southeast Asia.

Afterwards, head to Samy's (p120) for a curry, or to the Wine Network (p131) for a bottle or two.

MRT line interchange, Plaza Singapura was Singapore's first multistorey mall, and is as popular as it is vast. This massive place features a 10-screen **Golden Village cineplex**, fashion and music. Check out the **French Carrefour** supermarket in the basement for a wide selection of imported cheeses, wines and an impressive range of gourmet treats.

SHANGHAI TANG
Map pp226-7 Clothing

☎ 6735 3537; HPL House, 50 Cuscaden Rd; Orchard MRT

Top Hong Kong fashion design store with beautiful but pricey silk cheongsams, Mandarin collared shirts and kitsch Mao Zedong watches and mugs.

SELECT BOOKS Map pp226-7 Bookshop

☎ 6732 1515; www.selectbooks.com.sg; 03-15 Tanglin Shopping Centre; 19 Tanglin Rd; Orchard MRT

For nearly 30 years, Select has been Singapore's Asian book specialist, carrying an astonishing number of titles on anything from Tibetan furniture and Japanese history to Singaporean fiction.

SEMBAWANG MUSIC CENTRE
Map pp226-7 Music

☎ 6738 7727; 03-01 Cineleisure Orchard, 8 Grange Rd; Somerset MRT

Found at nearly every heartland shopping centre – and many city ones – these days. You won't find any rarities, but some surprises often reward dedicated browsers and it's one of the cheapest places to pick up a CD. And if by some chance you love Chinese pop, this is the place for you.

SHOPPING GALLERY AT HILTON
Map pp226-7 Mall

☎ 6737 2233; 581 Orchard Rd; Orchard MRT

One of the most exclusive shopping spots in Singapore, housing a series of elegant boutiques like **Gucci, Donna Karan, Missoni, Giorgio Armani, Paul Smith** and **Louis Vuitton**, to name just a few. The mall is linked to the **Four Seasons Hotel** (p173) shopping gallery, where you can find some fine art pieces.

SUNNY BOOKS Map pp226-7 Bookshop

☎ 6733 1583; 03-58/59 Far East Plaza, 14 Scotts Rd; ⏲ 10am-8pm Mon-Sat, 11am-6pm alternate Sun; Orchard MRT

One of the few secondhand bookshops in Singapore, Sunny stocks a good range, including the latest hit novels and travel guides, most in excellent condition.

TANGLIN MALL Map pp226-7 Mall

☎ 6736 4922; 163 Tanglin Rd; Orchard MRT

A favourite of the expatriate community, Tanglin offers a range of expensive ethnic homeware and gift shops all aimed at the many *tai-tais* (local term for European ladies of leisure) who gather on the red sofas of its central café to discuss their maid woes. Prices are generally high and you'll find a large branch of fashion chain **British India**, home furniture stores like the excellent **Barang Barang**, facilities for kids and a gourmet supermarket in the basement. One of Tanglin's gems is **That CD Shop**, an ultra-cool, minimalist place specialising in jazz, world and New Age music, with a larger-than-usual number of listening stations (HMV, take note). Look out for local pottery at **Boon's Pottery**.

TANGLIN SHOPPING CENTRE
Map pp226-7 Art & Antiques
☎ 6732 8751; 19 Tanglin Rd; Orchard MRT
This rather dim, gloomy place houses the largest number of antique, art and craft shops in Singapore. Within the building, **HaKaren Art Gallery** (☎ 6733 3382; www.hakaren.com), **Kwan Hua Art Gallery** (☎ 6733 8368) and **Akemi Gallery** (☎ 6735 6315) are all good places to start your treasure hunt. Also try **Antiques of the Orient** (☎ 6734 9351) for a superb collection of historical books and reproduction historical maps from all over Asia and beyond. Gentle bargaining in all places is quite acceptable. The excellent **Select Books** (opposite) can also be found here.

TANGS Map pp226-7 Department Store
☎ 6737 5500; 320 Orchard Rd; Orchard MRT
Since opening its doors more than 70 years ago, Tangs has kept up with changing trends and become a Singaporean institution. This five-floor department store with a sloping green-tiled roof is popular with all generations, selling business suits, formal evening attire and street wear in the huge clothes section, electronics, shoes and some of the best homeware in town. Luxurious silk and batik prints are quite popular with tourists.

WISMA ATRIA Map pp226-7 Mall
☎ 6235 2103; 435 Orchard Rd; Orchard MRT
You can't miss Wisma – dominated by a huge, boastful sign and a flashy glass exterior, its central circular aquarium is a popular meeting spot. Its crowded basement level, which doubles as a throughway to Orchard MRT, has a number of fashion and shoe shops, while the levels above house high-street fashion boutiques like **Topshop**, **Warehouse** and **People of Asia**. The **Isetan** (☎ 6733 7777) department store is equal in quality to rivals Tangs and Takashimaya.

EASTERN SINGAPORE

CHANGI VILLAGE Map pp222-3
☎ 6788 8370; 4 Tampines Central 5; bus 2 from Tanah Merah MRT
A wander around Changi Village offers a window into a more relaxed side of Singapore, where singlets, bermudas and thongs (flip-flops) – the quintessential heartlander uniform – is the look and people are slightly less accustomed to seeing *ang mor* in their midst. The atmosphere is almost village-like and a browse around the area will turn up cheap clothes, batik, Indian textiles and electronics. For a different kind of Singapore day, combine a few hours here with a trip to Pulau Ubin and round the day off with a meal at the famous hawker centre, then a few beers at **Charlie's** (p117).

TAMPINES MALL Map pp222-3 Mall
☎ 6788 8370; 4 Tampines Central 5; Tampines MRT
One of Singapore's largest suburban shopping centres, conveniently located right at the Tampines MRT station. Aimed at the middle-class heartlanders, you'll find a branch of the **Isetan** department store, a **Golden Village** cinema and several bookshops inside this bottle-green monster.

NORTHERN & CENTRAL SINGAPORE

CAUSEWAY POINT Map pp222-3 Mall
☎ 6894 2237; 1 Woodlands Sq; Woodlands MRT
Named Singapore's best mall by the *Straits Times*, this is located in the heart of Woodlands, next to the Woodlands MRT station and bus interchange. Causeway Point has become quite popular with many Singaporeans who opt to shop in the suburbs. It has about 250 shops, including fashion, book and food outlets. It caters mainly to the locals, but features international brands like **Marks & Spencer** and **Esprit** at lower prices than the city centre malls.

JUNCTION 8 Map pp222-3 Mall
☎ 6354 2955; 9 Bishan Pl; Bishan MRT
Junction 8 is another suburban mall that is extremely popular with Singaporeans and with an increasingly fashionable reputation, though not so much that you'll feel out of place in shorts and thongs (flip-flops). It gets packed well into the night with shoppers and diners, and houses a **Golden Village cinema**, a variety of clothes and shoe shops, **Best Denki**, **Seiyu** department store, an excellent **Food Junction** and also a branch of the fabulous **Din Tai Fung** (p115).

SOUTHERN & WESTERN SINGAPORE

CHO LON Map pp222-3 Art

☎ 6473 7922; 43 Jalan Merah Saga; 11am-7.30pm Mon-Sat, 11.30am-5.30pm Sun; bus 7, 105 or 106 from Penang Rd or Orchard Blvd

An interesting gallery offering quirky Mao statues, Ho Chi Minh busts, Indian velvet embroidered cushions and other ephemera.

HOLLAND ROAD SHOPPING CENTRE

Map pp222-3 Art & Antiques

211 Holland Ave; bus 7, 105 or 106 from Penang Rd or Orchard Blvd

This Holland Village stalwart, haunt of hundreds of expatriate women, has three floors of eclectic shops selling everything from Asian crafts and jewellery to furniture, carpets and art. There are also several tailors. **Lim's** (02-01), the centre's largest shop, stocks the widest variety of gifts, furniture and crafts, both beautiful and cheesy. Other notable places for modern and antique furniture, lamps and statues include **Essential Crafts** (03-08), **Esteli Studio** (03-13), **Vista** (02-30) and **Jessica** (02-22). Funky jewellery and general hippy wear can be found at **Angie's Handmade Fashion** (02-14), **Espana** (02-15) and **Shaw Sisters** (02-08). Decent modern art galleries and frame shops include **D'Artist Gallery** (03-24) and **Framing Angie** (03-02).

Sleeping

Sleeping

Whether you're looking for a basic dorm bed, the most decadent suite or even a spa, Singapore offers almost every conceivable kind of accommodation.

Thanks to the peerless public transport system, it doesn't really matter where you stay in central Singapore. Everywhere is less than half an hour from everywhere else. If you're looking for atmosphere and character, we recommend Chinatown or Little India, both of which harbour most of the budget accommodation and boutique hotels in shophouse conversions.

Orchard Rd and its environs are crammed with identikit upmarket hotels (with a few distinctive exceptions), as is the area around Marina Bay, where you'll find the Esplanade complex and Suntec City mall. There are also good options dotted close by the redeveloped quays of the Singapore River.

The demise of the Bencoolen St backpacker hub has spawned better budget options, especially around Little India, the best of which are a world away from the $10-per-night Singapore fleapit of old.

If you want to experience the grittier side of Singapore outside your hotel room, then Geylang is worth considering. Likewise, if you want the sea and a beach close at hand, Sentosa's the go, but avoid weekends, when rates and occupancy are higher.

While Singapore might be the most expensive city in Southeast Asia in which to bed down, top hotels are constantly offering promotional deals, sometimes slashing up to half off the official rates (even throwing in breakfast for good measure). The entire year of 2005, for instance, was declared a 'promotion period' and many exclusive hotels were offering rates not much higher than midrange Chinatown guesthouses.

In this highly competitive atmosphere, it pays to call around or, even better, check the hotel websites or discount websites like www.asiabesthotels.com or www.wotif.com for special deals before you book.

Be aware that reservation desk staff in top hotels usually add a casual (and often barely audible) 'plus plus plus' after the rate they quote you. Ignore this at your peril. The three plusses are service charge, government tax and GST, which together amounts to a breezy 16% on top of your bill.

Price Ranges

Rooms in the cheapest places are cubicle-like, cramped, often windowless and facilities are invariably shared. Most places offer both air-con and cheaper fan rooms. Although basic, these are good places to meet other travellers and share information. Sometimes a simple breakfast is included in the price. Note that both YMCA International House (p169) and YWCA Fort Canning Lodge (p169) also have dorm beds.

We list the published rates for a standard room. (In Singapore hotel parlance, a standard room is often called 'superior'.) Unless otherwise stated, the price will be the same whether the room is single or double occupancy. All these hotels have slightly more expensive 'deluxe' or 'club' rooms, which tend to be larger, have a better view, and include extras such as breakfast or free Internet access. Most also have suites.

Reservations

There are so many hotels in Singapore that you'll almost never experience a problem finding a room. The only exception may be Chinese New Year, when advance booking

TOP FIVE SLEEPS

- **Raffles Hotel** (p52) The ultimate Singapore hotel.
- **Goodwood Park Hotel** (p173) For a dash of 1920s style.
- **Fullerton Hotel** (p166) Elegant and imposing.
- **Ritz-Carlton** (p168) Sumptuous and seductive.
- **Hangout@Mt.Emily** (p172) Just pipping InnCrowd and Sleepy Sam's as best budget option.

is recommended. The best reason to book in advance is that you can often score substantial discounts.

Longer-Term Rentals

For medium- to long-term stays, Singapore has a number of serviced apartments. It is also possible to rent rooms in private flats (check the classified pages of the *Straits Times* for listings). Rents are high, regardless of how near or far from the city centre you are. Note that the prices quoted include all taxes.

METRO-Y APARTMENTS

Map pp226-7 Serviced Apartments

☎ 6839 8100; apartment@mymca.org.sg; 58 Stevens Rd; studios per week/month $1260/2700; Orchard MRT;

Next to the Metropolitan Y, Metro-Y has its own swimming pool, gym and washing machines, a bonus at this price and this close to Orchard Rd. The rooms are OK and come with compact kitchenettes and cable TV.

ORCHARD GRAND COURT

Map pp226-7 Hotel

☎ 6733 1133; www.ogc.com.sg; 131 Killiney Rd; r for 14 days from $158.80; Somerset MRT;

This is actually a hotel (the rooms have no cooking facilities), but its good-value long-term rates and convenient location near Orchard Rd make it a top choice. There's a decent gym and café, too.

PARKLANE SUITES

Map pp226-7 Serviced Apartments

☎ 6730 1811; www.goodwoodparkhotel.com/parklanesuits.htm; 22 Scotts Rd; ste per month $4500-5500; Orchard MRT;

A real dose of style, these 64 split-level luxury suites are in a separate building next to the Goodwood Park Hotel. Immaculately done out with timber louvres, timber floors, black-slate wall panels, curved ceilings, plus your own balcony. Facilities include two swimming pools, gym and launderette.

PERAK LODGE

Map p232 Hotel

☎ 6299 7733; www.peraklodge.net; 12 Perak Rd; r per month $1400-2300; Little India MRT

One of the best budget hotels in Singapore, Perak is also a good bet for long-stay accommodation. Around $1400 a month will get you a comfortable superior room with special laundry rates, while the higher rate gets you a larger room.

TOP FIVE HOTEL VIEWS

- **Swissôtel, The Stamford** (p168) The highest hotel in Singapore; need we say more?
- **Shangri-La's Rasa Sentosa** (p178) Sweeping vistas of container-ship city and the Indonesian islands.
- **Ritz-Carlton** (p168) The sexiest rooms, with equally sexy views.
- **Fullerton** (p166) Perfectly placed to capture the vibe of the quayside.
- **Le Meridien Changi Village** (p177) A surprise entry; the rooftop pool is exquisitely peaceful.

RIVERSIDE VIEW

Map pp224-5 Serviced Apartments

☎ 6428 8262; csq_mktg@fareast.com.sg; 30 Robertson Quay; studio apt per week/month from $1400/4200, 2-bedroom apt from $1600/5000, 3-bedroom apt $2000/5500; Clarke Quay MRT;

A modern, classy place at trendy Robertson Quay, with an enticingly peaceful riverside location. The minimum lease is for one week and the price includes a thrice-weekly maid service, breakfast on weekdays, Jacuzzi, kids' playground and gym.

COLONIAL DISTRICT & THE QUAYS

These two nerve centres of tourist activity contain the widest variety of accommodation in the city. You can splurge thousands on a classy suite with a stunning view or spend less than $20 on a dorm bed in a heritage shophouse just a few minutes' walk away.

ALLSON HOTEL Map p230 Hotel

☎ 6336 0811; allson.sales@pacific.net.sg; 101 Victoria St; r from $260; City Hall MRT;

Fitting its location, the Allson has an old-fashioned feel, despite its modern exterior. Rooms are tastefully done out with dark wood and leather furniture. There are non-smoking floors, and facilities include a pool and several restaurants.

CONRAD CENTENNIAL SINGAPORE
Map p230 International Hotel
☎ 6334 8888; www.conradhotels.com; 2 Temasek Blvd; r $210-310; City Hall MRT;
Despite a slightly odd exterior design, this is an elegant, stylish place, from the sweeping curved staircase and contemporary artwork in the lobby to the warm magnolia of the rooms, some of which have bay views. Recommended.

FULLERTON HOTEL Map p230 Hotel
☎ 6733 8388; www.fullertonhotel.com; 1 Fullerton Sq; r from $572; Raffles Place MRT;
Creating a luxury hotel out of an old GPO doesn't sound too promising unless it happens to be in one of Singapore's most magnificent pieces of colonial architecture (see Historic Hotels, p175). This hotel is perhaps the only one in Singapore that rivals Raffles for elegance. The heritage principles involved in the restoration mean some of the Armani-beige rooms overlook the inner atrium. Spend a bit extra to gain access to the hotel's private Straits Club and upgrade to river- or marina-view rooms, all of which are stunning.

GALLERY HOTEL Map pp224-5 Hotel
☎ 6849 8686; www.galleryhotel.com.sg; 76 Robertson Quay; r with breakfast from $295; Clarke Quay MRT;
From its primary colour fixtures and fittings and hi-tech room facility control panels to its gorgeous lap pool, the Gallery is about as trendy as they come – and wants you to know it. Home to the self-consciously hip **Liquid Room** (p132) dance club, this is a magnet for the club set and architects who want to discuss Post-industrial Minimalist Interactivism loudly without being laughed at.

GRAND COPTHORNE WATERFRONT HOTEL Map pp224-5 International Hotel
☎ 6733 0880; http://millenniumhotels.com; 392 Havelock Rd; s/d from $295/325; bus 123 from Tiong Bahru MRT;
Of the several hotels clustered at the Robertson Quay end of the river (the closest MRT is Tiong Bahru, but it's not walking distance), the fanciest is this imposing place. This is the best of the Copthorne's group of hotels, with light-filled, comfortable rooms.

GRAND PLAZA PARKROYAL HOTEL
Map p230 International Hotel
☎ 6336 3456; www.parkroyalhotels.com; 10 Coleman St; r from $320; City Hall MRT;
It's won an award for its architecture apparently and though the rooms are virtually indistinguishable from many other top hotels, there is an in-house spa that will appeal to frazzled shoppers. Look out for dramatic online discounts.

HOLIDAY INN ATRIUM
Map pp224-5 International Hotel
☎ 6733 0188; www.holiday-inn.com; 317 Outram Rd; s/d from $260/280; Outram Park MRT;
Located in a dazzling 27-storey atrium, the former Concorde has slightly less spectacular rooms but is nevertheless a good choice, located near the Robertson Quay entertainment district and Great World City shopping centre.

HOTEL BENCOOLEN
Map p230 Hotel
☎ 6336 0822; www.hotelbencoolen.com; 47 Bencoolen St; s/d $93/110; Dhoby Ghaut MRT;
Good value. The rooms are as bland as the location, but reasonably sized, with big beds and the full range of facilities. There's

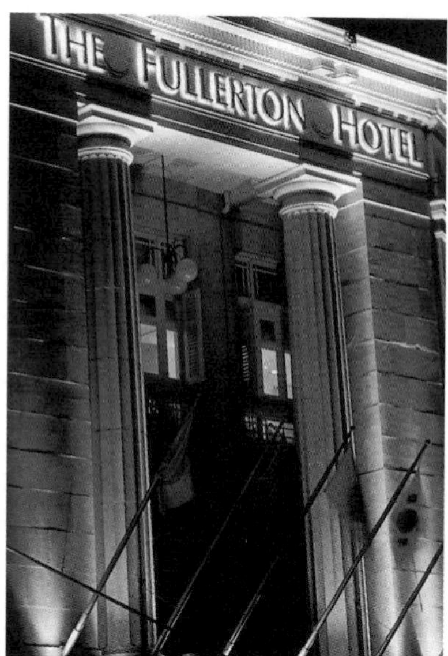

Entrance to the Fullerton Hotel (left)

AIRPORT HOTEL DESK & THE TRANSIT HOTEL

If you arrive in Singapore without a hotel booking, don't despair. The efficient **Singapore Hotel Association** (www.stayinsingapore.com.sg) has four desks at Changi airport, with two at **Terminal 1** (east wing 10am-11.30pm; west wing 24hr) and two at **Terminal 2** (north wing 7am-11pm; south wing 24hr).

There are dozens of hotels on its lists, ranging from $37 a night right up to Raffles Hotel at over $650. There's no charge for the service, and promotional or discounted rates, when available, are passed on to you. You can also book the hotels over the Internet on the association's website.

Also, if you're only in Singapore for a very short time or have a long wait between connecting flights, consider using the Ambassador Transit Hotel. There are branches inside both **Terminal 1** (6542 5538; t1@airport-hotel.com.sg) and **Terminal 2** (6542 8122; t2@airport-hotel.com.sg). For the first six hours, rates start at $40.45 for a comfortable windowless single with shared bathroom, and $57.75/64.70 for singles/doubles with attached bathroom. The Terminal 1 branch has a sauna, gym and outdoor pool. If you just want to nip in for a shower, it will cost you $5.15. Staff members recommend that you reserve a long way in advance, but a planned large expansion should ease the congestion somewhat.

an outdoor spa pool, just big enough for a soak. Rates include breakfast.

HOTEL INTER-CONTINENTAL

Map p230 International Hotel

6338 7600; www.ichotelsgroup.com; 80 Middle Rd; standard r from $440, shophouse r $470; Bugis MRT;

Top class, if you can afford it (though Internet rates can plunge to as low as $170). Decorated in an appealing Peranakan and colonial style, the shophouse-style rooms and suites (wooden floors, oriental rugs, hand-painted lampshades) have a lot of character. Facilities include a fitness centre, a pleasant rooftop pool and several good restaurants.

HOTEL RENDEZVOUS

Map p230 International Hotel

6336 0220; www.rendezvoushotels.com; 9 Bras Basah Rd; s/d from $300/330; Dhoby Ghaut MRT;

Overlooking Bras Basah Park, the rooms here are a little heavy on the pastel, but well worth it if you can get a discount rate. There's an attractive bar next to a cool, imposing courtyard.

METROPOLE HOTEL

Map p230 Hotel

6336 3611; www.metrohotel.com; 41 Seah St; r from $98; City Hall MRT

Suffers slightly from its close proximity to the peerless Raffles, but if you can overcome your envy, this is one of the cheaper Colonial District places, with no-nonsense rooms aimed at businessmen who don't need to show off.

NOVOTEL CLARKE QUAY

Map p230 International Hotel

6338 3333; www.novotelclarkequay.com.sg; 177A River Valley Rd; s/d from $300/320; Clarke Quay MRT;

The no-nonsense approach you expect from the Novotel chain. No bells or whistles, no surprises or extravagant extras; plain, clean, comfortable and professional.

ORIENTAL SINGAPORE

Map p230 International Hotel

6338 0066; www.mandarinoriental.com; 5 Raffles Ave, Marina Sq; r from $410; City Hall MRT;

Recently renovated, the sumptuous rooms here have stunning views, either over Marina Bay and the 'durians' of the Esplanade theatre, or the city skyline. A bonus is the large baths and your own DVD player. Worth every cent.

PAN PACIFIC HOTEL

Map p230 International Hotel

6336 8111; http://singapore.panpac.com; 7 Raffles Blvd, Marina Sq; r from $420; City Hall MRT;

Taking the prize in the flash lobby stakes, the newly refitted Pan Pacific soars up 35 storeys. The rooms are decorated in neutral tones and a contemporary style (the business rooms even have ergonomic Aeron desk chairs); those with a balcony and a view are a bit pricier. Promo rates drop as low as $260.

RAFFLES HOTEL Map p230 Hotel
☎ 6337 1886; www.raffleshotel.com; 1 Beach Rd; ste from $650; City Hall MRT;
Hotels that double as tourist attractions are sometimes a let-down. This one isn't. With its wooden floors, high ceilings, unshakeable colonial elegance and even its famous Sikh doorman, it stands alongside the Peninsular Hong Kong and Oriental Bangkok as one of Asia's truly special hotels. Hopefully its new American owners will keep it that way. Pull out your best togs (yes, some guests do turn up in tennis shoes), lay down your $650 and enjoy.

RAFFLES, THE PLAZA
Map p230 International Hotel
☎ 6339 7777; www.raffles-theplazahotel.com; 80 Bras Basah Rd; r from $330; City Hall MRT;
It shares the same facilities as its twin Swissôtel, but the rooms here are markedly different in design from the usual flowers and magnolia look of many hotels. Stylish and understated, this place is top-notch.

RITZ-CARLTON
Map p230 International Hotel
☎ 6337 8888; www.ritzcarlton.com/hotels/singapore; 7 Raffles Ave; s/d from $465/515; City Hall MRT;
This place was clearly designed with sex in mind, right from the striking entrance dominated by a Frank Stella sculpture. The rooms are an aphrodisiac all their own, with stunning harbour views from the raised beds and even from the bathrooms, which are located, unusually, on the exterior wall. A must for romantic occasions.

RIVER VIEW HOTEL
Map pp224-5 Hotel
☎ 6732 9922; www.riverview.com.sg; 382 Havelock Rd; s/d from $220/240; Clarke Quay MRT;
Excellent value if one of its generous discounts is on offer, this uninspiring off-white tower opposite Robertson Quay has an excellent riverside location and large comfortable rooms. A free shuttle service runs to Orchard Rd, Suntec City and Chinatown. Particularly popular with visiting Chinese.

ROBERTSON QUAY HOTEL
Map pp224-5 Hotel
☎ 6735 3333; www.robertsonquayhotel.com.sg; 15 Merbau Rd; s/d $120/150; Clarke Quay MRT;
This is one of the best-value hotels on Robertson Quay (if you don't mind being next to the expressway). This squat, circular tower has immaculate rooms and an unusual rooftop swimming pool landscaped with large boulders. Best of all is its proximity to both the Robertson Quay and Clarke Quay entertainment areas. Generous Internet booking discounts are often available, too.

STRAND HOTEL Map p230 Hotel
☎ 6338 1866; fax 6338 1330; 25 Bencoolen St; r from $85; Dhoby Ghaut MRT
The stonework and backlit sign marks the Strand out as a bit different from your usual mid-price place. Some imagination has gone into the rooms, which are painted in earthy colours and funky fabrics. If you're really up for it, ask for the 'special rooms', which have funkier décor and glass-walled bathrooms (popular with honeymooners apparently!).

SWISSÔTEL, MERCHANT COURT
Map p230 International Hotel
☎ 6337 2288; www.singapore-merchantcourt.swissotel.com; 20 Merchant Rd; s/d from $285/315; Clarke Quay MRT;
Probably the best located of the quayside hotels, the Swissôtel is opposite Clarke Quay, near the MRT, a stone's throw from Riverside Point and a short walk from Boat Quay. It has a bustling atmosphere at night and its outdoor **Ellenborough Market Café** is a pleasant place to sit with a drink and watch the quay crowds pass by. The rooms are also very classy, as you would expect.

SWISSÔTEL, THE STAMFORD
Map p230 International Hotel
☎ 6338 8585; www.singapore-stamford.swissotel.com; 2 Stamford Rd; r from $270; City Hall MRT;
More like an indoor town than a hotel – it even has its own MRT entrance – the Stamford is massive and the sixth-tallest hotel on earth (it was the tallest when

it was built in 1986). The views are just magnificent, as are the hotel's numerous restaurants and bars, and with more than 1200 rooms, you're unlikely to have trouble getting in.

CHEAP SLEEPS

AH CHEW HOTEL Map p230 Hostel

☎ 6837 0356; 496 North Bridge Rd; rooftop/fan/air-con dm $8/10/12, r with fan/air-con $26/30; Bugis MRT

Above the Tong Seng Coffee shop, with its frontage facing the restaurant/bar strip on Liang Seah St, this dusty old flophouse has a certain dingy charm and the cheapest, noisiest beds in Singapore. Certain to make your stay a memorable one.

BACKPACKER COZY CORNER GUESTHOUSE Map p230 Guesthouse

☎ 6339 6128; www.cozycornerguest.com; 490 North Bridge Rd; dm with fan/air-con $8/15, s/d $28/45; Bugis MRT;

It feels a little like a kindergarten, with its 'museum' and its flags, kitsch reading corner and government-issue paint, but at these rates who's complaining? It's clean, friendly and well located, with free breakfast, free Internet and a rooftop lounging area as well.

SUMMER TAVERN Map p230 Hostel

☎ 6535 6601; www.summertavern.com; 31 Carpenter St; dm/r $22/60; Clarke Quay MRT;

Hard to believe a place like this exists so close to the quays – and not surprisingly it's popular. Dorms are very large (which accounts for the price) but the real draws are the location, the beer lounge and the rooftop lounging area. Rates include breakfast.

WATERLOO HOSTEL Map p230 Hostel

☎ 6336 6555; fax 6336 2160; 4th fl, Catholic Centre Bldg, 55 Waterloo St; dm $23, s with shared/private bathroom $53/68, d $58/69; Dhoby Ghaut, City Hall or Bugis MRT

A clean, well organised place run by the Catholic Church, the Waterloo has single-sex and mixed dorms that are decent value. The private rooms, equipped with TVs, fridges and phones, are also a good bet. It's within reasonable walking distance of Orchard, the Colonial District and Bugis. Breakfast is included.

YWCA FORT CANNING LODGE

Map p230 Hostel

☎ 6338 4222; reservations@ywcafclodge.org.sg; 6 Fort Canning Rd; s/tw from $98.60/115.20, family ste $179.80; Dhoby Ghaut MRT;

This is probably the best of the three Ys, boasting large, comfortable rooms complete with wooden floors and a decent range of facilities including a café, swimming pool and tennis court. It's sandwiched between busy roads, but it's a short walk from both Orchard Rd and the serenity of Fort Canning Park.

YMCA INTERNATIONAL HOUSE

Map p230 Hostel

☎ 6336 6000; www.ymcaih.com.sg; 1 Orchard Rd; s/tw from $92/103.50, family ste $132.25; Dhoby Ghaut MRT;

Like the YWCA, this place has large, clean rooms, a handy location and good facilities, including a fitness centre, rooftop swimming pool, squash and badminton courts, and a billiard room. There's also a restaurant, which offers a cheap set meal daily. All rooms have a telephone.

CHINATOWN & THE CBD

Chinatown has become a centre for boutique hotels in recent years, riding the shophouse restoration wave. Here you'll find everything from elegant old-world charm to funky designer guesthouses, all in close proximity to some of Singapore's best eating and nightlife.

AMARA SINGAPORE

Map pp234-5 Boutique Hotel

☎ 6879 2555; www.amarahotels.com; 165 Tanjong Pagar Rd; r from $320; Tanjong Pagar MRT;

Ultra-stylish with a sleek modern design, from the tasteful black-and-white photos of Singapore in the rooms to the Balinese spa and the stone walls in the swimming pool, the Amara does its best to stand out – and succeeds. The only downside is the location, a bit of a hike from most points of interest, though close to the MRT.

BERJAYA HOTEL SINGAPORE

Map pp234-5 Boutique Hotel

☎ 6227 7678; www.berjayaresorts.com; 83 Duxton Rd; r from $210, ste $290; Tanjong Pagar MRT

If you're looking for a boutique hotel with a bit more luxury, this elegant shophouse conversion is one of your best bets – all wooden fixtures and old-world charm. All rooms are beautifully furnished and the suites have an unusual mezzanine bedroom reached by spiral staircase.

CHINATOWN HOTEL

Map pp234-5 Boutique Hotel

☎ 6225 5166; www.chinatownhotel.com; 12-16 Teck Lim Rd; s/d $88/99; Outram Park MRT

Another of a growing cluster of boutique hotels around Teck Lim Rd. The rooms here are very clean and painted in warm yellow shades, though many have that squeezed-in feeling that some may find uncomfortable. The staff are very friendly and the reception/lounge area has a cosy charm. Rates include breakfast.

DAMENLOU HOTEL

Map pp234-5 Boutique Hotel

☎ 6221 1900; fax 6225 8500; 12 Ann Siang Rd; standard/deluxe r $80/100; Chinatown MRT

There are only 12 rooms in this restored 1920s shophouse, which have all the modern hotel facilities while still retaining their historical character and family-run friendliness. Handily placed for the trendy Club St bars and restaurants, there is also a rooftop terrace with splendid views over Chinatown and the towering CBD beyond. The **Swee Kee** (p108) restaurant is well worth a visit too.

HOTEL 1929 Map pp234-5 Boutique Hotel

☎ 6347 1929; www.hotel1929.com; 50 Keong Saik Rd; s/d $110/130; Outram Park MRT; 💻

Certainly the most fashionable of Chinatown's crop of boutique hotels, Hotel 1929 has tiny rooms that are full of imaginative touches. From the plate glass frontage and the lobby with its eclectic furniture (you can't stay here unless you use the word 'eclectic' a lot) to the flat-screen TVs and outdoor Jacuzzi, this is one of Singapore's more distinctive places, though some would call it plain pretentious.

INN AT TEMPLE STREET

Map pp234-5 Boutique Hotel

☎ 6221 5333; www.theinn.com.sg; 36 Temple St; r $98; Chinatown MRT

Right in tourist Chinatown, the Inn might be a little too close to the action for some, but it is bursting with character. Set in a row of shophouses and filled with semi-antique objects from the colonial era, the rooms are a bit small (ask for one with windows), but otherwise it's thoroughly recommended.

M HOTEL Map pp234-5 Hotel

☎ 6224 1133; www.mhotel.com.sg; 81 Anson Rd; r from $380; Tanjong Pagar MRT; 💻

On the southern edge of the CBD, this is a place for Chanel-handbagged and Armani-suits business types. It oozes chic, from the flat-screen TVs in the rooms to the neon blues of the bar. The only downside is the location, next to the expressway and a fair way from Singapore's main attractions.

ROYAL PEACOCK HOTEL

Map pp234-5 Boutique Hotel

☎ 6223 3522; www.royalpeacockhotel.com; 55 Keong Saik Rd; s/d $161.50/179, with windows from $201.25/218.50; Outram Park MRT

The small rooms, with their dark wood furnishings and red walls, are appealing and the fancy, mood-lit lobby marks this out as one of the more upmarket shophouse conversions in the area. Huge discounts are often available, but otherwise it's a little overpriced for what you get.

CHEAP SLEEPS

A TRAVELLERS' REST STOP

Map pp234-5 Guesthouse

☎ 6225 4812; fax 6225 4813; 5 Teck Lim Rd; dm/s/d $18/35/55; Outram Park MRT

With brightly coloured walls, this lively guesthouse leaves you in no doubt that fun is on the agenda. Clean, safe and well-run, with Chinatown tours and bike rentals on offer, this is the best budget option in the area.

TROPICAL HOTEL

Map pp234-5 Hotel

☎ 6225 6696; fax 6225 6626; 22 Teck Lim Rd; s/d from $70/90; Outram Park MRT

This is a gay-friendly shophouse conversion, but lacks style inside. Some singles are without windows and the larger rooms at the front with balconies go for $100, but they're open to bargaining for longer stays.

YES CHINATOWN HOTEL

Map pp234-5 Hotel

☎ 6222 1218; fax 6222 1220; 68A Smith St; r with/without window $50/39; Chinatown MRT

Renting by the hour (and we all know what that means), this is a shabby but acceptable place to flop if you're running low on options. Rooms are functional and have attached showers, but the toilet is shared.

LITTLE INDIA & THE ARAB QUARTER

You won't find any upmarket swank here, but there's a sprinkling of pleasantly low-key boutique hotels and a few functional two- and three-star places catering mainly to Indian visitors. Little India is now the new budget traveller hotspot, however, and a host of well-run, modern hostels are springing up in the area.

ALBERT COURT HOTEL

Map p232 Boutique Hotel

☎ 6339 3939; www.albertcourt.com.sg; 180 Albert St; standard/deluxe r $200/220; Little India MRT;

At the southern edge of Little India, this is a splendid, colonial-era boutique hotel in a shophouse redevelopment that now shoots up eight storeys. All rooms have the usual mod cons, and include a choice of fan or air-con. The promotional rates go as low as $120.

DICKSON COURT HOTEL

Map p232 Hotel

☎ 6297 7811; dicksonl@magix.com.sg; 3 Dickson Rd; d from $120; Little India MRT

Cobbled together from a row of old shophouses, the lobby and courtyard areas of the Dickson Court Hotel have a touch of elegance about them and the rooms are clean, though some of them are small and dark. There's a restaurant and café as well as a good range of services. There's almost always a promotional rate on offer, which can see prices drop to $89.

FORTUNA HOTEL Map p232 Hotel

☎ 6295 3577; fax 6294 7738; 2 Owen Rd; r from $125; Farrer Park MRT

Looks more like an office building than a hotel, but the rooms are actually quite appealing – and very large – and staff members are very welcoming. If you can get one of the $80 promo rates, snap it up.

GOLDEN LANDMARK HOTEL

Map p232 Hotel

☎ 6297 2828; www.goldenlandmark.com.sg; 290 Victoria St; r from $190; Bugis MRT;

One of the few hotels in the Arab St area, the Golden Landmark has spacious, decent-value rooms, though the ageing shopping centre downstairs is a bit off-putting.

MADRAS HOTEL Map p232 Hotel

☎ 6392 7889; www.madrassingapore.com; 28-32 Madras St; s/d/tr $60/70/90; Little India MRT;

Plainly decorated but clean, this is a good option if you want something reliable with no frills. Ask for a room with a balcony at the front of this attractive Art Deco–style building. You can also rent rooms on a 'transit' basis for $30, if you're not staying overnight. Prices include breakfast.

NEW PARK CENTRA SINGAPORE

Map p232 Hotel

☎ 6291 5533; newpark@plazapacifichotels.com; 181 Kitchener Rd; r from $240; Farrer Park MRT

This towering hotel is where well-to-do Indian families and tour groups stay – observing the melodrama in the lobby as tour groups arrive can fill up hours by itself. Its ambience is nothing special but its simply decorated rooms are pleasant. A free shuttle service runs to Orchard Rd three times daily. Internet bookings can draw huge discounts.

PERAK LODGE Map p232 Hotel

☎ 6299 7733; www.peraklodge.net; 12 Perak Rd; standard/superior/deluxe r with breakfast $70/80/90; Little India MRT;

Pick of the bunch. This tasteful guesthouse is in a renovated Peranakan-style building. There's a quiet communal area where you serve yourself breakfast and use the Internet. Some of the cheaper rooms don't have windows but they're all nicely furnished and the staff is very helpful. This is also a good long-term stay option (see p165).

SOUTH-EAST ASIA HOTEL

Map p232 Hotel

☎ 6338 2394; www.seahotel.com.sg; 190 Waterloo St; standard/superior d $77/88; Bugis MRT

Next to a couple of the area's most colourful temples on one of Singapore's most bustling, lively pedestrian precincts, this hotel is clean, friendly and good value, though you can barely swing a mouse in the bathrooms. Highly recommended, particularly for its location.

SUMMER VIEW HOTEL

Map p232 Hotel

☎ 6338 1122; www.summerviewhotel.com.sg; 173 Bencoolen St; d $154; Bugis MRT

Clean and comfortable, the rooms here are quite large for a midrange hotel and it's handily located. The MRT is a bit of a hike, so the shuttle service to Orchard Rd and Suntec City might come in useful.

CHEAP SLEEPS

BUGIS BACKPACKERS

Map p232 Hostel

☎ 6338 5581; 162B Rochor Rd; dm/d $20/56; Bugis MRT

In the bustling centre of Bugis Village, this clean, functional, appealing hostel (with the usual facilities) is particularly well located to sample the lively night markets and other nocturnal activity in the area – and it's a short walk from Arab St.

CACTUS HOTEL Map p232 Hotel

☎ 6391 3913; cactus98@singnet.com.sg; 407 Jalan Besar; d $55; Farrer Park MRT

Close to Lavender Food Sq and the buses to Malaysia, Cactus offers reasonable rooms with attached bathrooms. In a former incarnation, as the Palace Hotel, it counted among its guests Tony and Maureen Wheeler, who wrote some of the first edition of *Southeast Asia on a Shoestring* here.

HAISING HOTEL Map p232 Hotel

☎ 6298 1223; www.haising.com.sg; 37 Jalan Besar; s/d from $40/50; Little India MRT; 💻

Haising has tiny rooms – the double bed in the cheaper rooms takes up virtually the entire space. The cheaper singles use communal bathrooms and not all rooms have windows. All local calls are free.

HANGOUT@MT.EMILY

Map p232 Hostel

☎ 6438 5588; www.hangouthotels.com; 10A Upper Wilkie Rd; dm $35, s/d $88/76; Little India or Dhoby Ghaut MRT; 💻

Stunning, sleek, trendy boutique hostel set among the leafy glades of Mt Emily a stone's throw from Orchard Rd and Little India. Done out in vibrant colours, with murals done by local art students, the unisex and mixed dorms and private rooms are immaculate, as are the bathrooms. There's also a magnificent rooftop terrace, complete with Balinese sculptures, as well as library, café, free Internet and cosy lounging areas. Knock $10 of the rates for Internet bookings. One of the best budget place in the city. Private room rates include breakfast.

HAWAII HOSTEL Map p232 Hostel

☎ 6338 4187; 2nd fl, 171B Bencoolen St; 4-bed dm $12, s/d $28/35; Bugis MRT

The last of the Bencoolen St hostels, this place has managed so far to survive the redevelopment of the area. The rooms would make a monk flinch, but the kitchen, laundry, great location and friendly owner make it a good bet for budgeteers.

HIVE Map p232 Hostel

☎ 6341 5041; www.thehivebackpackers.com; 269A Lavender St; dm/capsule $16/18; Boon Keng MRT; 💻

Another new top-notch hostel that leaves the old guard in the shade. The Hive's friendliness and cleanliness more than makes up for a slightly inconvenient location. The 'capsule beds' (single beds surrounded by curtains) are a great idea for those seeking a little privacy without having to dig out the dollars for it. There's free breakfast, free Internet and a homely lounge room.

INNCROWD Map p232 Hostel

☎ 6296 9169; www.the-inncrowd.com; 35 Campbell Lane; dm/d $18/48; Little India MRT; 💻

In the heart of Little India and painted in funky colours, this is pitching itself successfully as the ultimate backpacker hostel in Singapore, so popular that it has branched out to a **second location** (73 Dunlop St) nearby. The air-con dorms, common bathrooms and kitchens are spotless and there's even a washing machine. Add to that a sun deck, pub, minimart, free Internet, free breakfast, extremely friendly staff and a branch of the Singapore Visitors Centre and perhaps you do actually have the ultimate hostel.

LITTLE INDIA GUESTHOUSE

Map p232 Hotel

☎ 6294 2866; fax 6298 4866; 3 Veerasamy Rd; s/d/family r with fan $35/40/60, s/d with air-con $40/45; Little India MRT

In the heart of the district, this is yet another very plain, but spotlessly maintained and friendly place. Rooms are stripped to bare essentials – thin metal-frame beds, a chair or two, floor fans, TV – but it's not too bad if you don't mind feeling like a student on campus. Doubles have a bunk bed with a double on the base and single on top.

NEW 7TH STOREY HOTEL

Map p232 Hostel

☎ 6337 0251; www.nsshotel.com; 229 Rochor Rd; dm $17, r with shared/private bathroom $53/76, deluxe r $79; Bugis MRT; 🖳

Sitting in splendid isolation on a patch of cleared land, this well-run, very friendly place has clean dorms with rather spindly bunks and very good-value private rooms. Other good points include delightful garden patios, a games room and bike rental.

PRINCE OF WALES BACKPACKER HOSTEL Map p232 Hostel

☎ 6299 0130; www.pow.com.sg; 101 Dunlop St; dm/d A$14/36; Little India MRT

Australian-style pub and hostel, featuring spit-and-sawdust live music pub downstairs (see p134) with excellent Australian beers and clean dorms upstairs painted in bright oranges and blues. The noise won't suit everyone, but it's a fun place to stay and is deservedly popular.

SLEEPY SAM'S Map p232 Hostel

☎ 9277 4988; www.sleepysams.com; 55 Bussorah St; dm/s/d $25/39/65; Bugis MRT; 🖳

It's not often you'd list a Singapore backpacker hostel as a 'must stay', but Sleepy Sam's qualifies. Looking more like a boutique hotel than a hostel – with its Asian dark wood furnishings and floor cushions – it's located just down from the imposing Sultan Mosque on the historical, burgeoning Bussorah St 'bohemian district', one of the most pleasant streets in Singapore. There are mixed or female-only dorms, private rooms and free Internet.

ORCHARD ROAD

ELIZABETH Map pp226-7 Hotel

☎ 6738 1188; www.theelizabeth.com; 24 Mount Elizabeth Rd; r from $240; Orchard MRT; 🖳

In a quiet spot a short walk north of Orchard Rd, the Elizabeth has an exclusive feel, complemented by a wonderful waterfall-side dining room where staff serve excellent wood-fired pizzas at night. The rooms, accessed by external lifts, are warm and welcoming, with William Morris–style print bedspreads. There's a nifty shortcut to Scotts Rd through the lobby of the York Hotel opposite. Recommended.

FOUR SEASONS HOTEL

Map pp226-7 International Hotel

☎ 6734 1110; www.fourseasons.com/singapore; 190 Orchard Blvd; s/d from $435/475; Orchard MRT; 🖳 🏊

In a quiet, tree-lined street just off Orchard Rd, the Four Seasons has a beautiful lobby matched by elegant antique-style rooms. Among its many facilities are air-conditioned tennis courts. Check out its weekend special, which starts at $248.

GOODWOOD PARK HOTEL

Map pp226-7 Hotel

☎ 6730 1811; www.goodwoodparkhotel.com; 22 Scotts Rd; r from $385; Orchard MRT; 🏊

This historic hotel has an old-fashioned feel but bags of class, from its two swimming pools to the hotel's pet cat roaming the lobby. Nice touches in the rooms include arty black-and-white photos of Singapore, Persian rugs and neatly hidden TVs and minibars. If you have $3000 to spare, treat yourself to a night in the opulent Brunei suite, or for longer stays try the wonderful serviced apartments (see p165).

GRAND HYATT SINGAPORE

Map pp226-7 International Hotel

☎ 6738 1234; http://singapore.grand.hyatt.com; 10-12 Scotts Rd; r from $290; Orchard MRT; 🖳 🏊

Redesigned in 1998 to feng shui principles, this is a very grand place. The lovely rooms, decorated in a soothing lemon colour, have louvred wooden shutters and small patios. An excellent range of facilities is complemented by two tennis courts. For a truly indulgent experience, try the Grand Club rooms, which offer personalised service and use of an exclusive lounge.

HILTON INTERNATIONAL

Map pp226-7 International Hotel

☎ 6737 2233; www.singapore.hilton.com; 581 Orchard Rd; standard r $290, executive-fl r $350; Orchard MRT;

In the heart of Orchard Rd is the Hilton. Although nothing spectacular (apart from the distinctive sculpted exterior wall panels), this is a good choice for business travellers – executive-floor guests have a buffet breakfast, use of the gym and other benefits included in the room cost. Rates can go much higher.

HOTEL PHOENIX

Map pp226-7 Hotel

☎ 6737 8666; www.hotelphoenixsingapore.com; 277 Orchard Rd; r from $280; Somerset MRT;

Inside a gleaming white, not entirely attractive building, Hotel Phoenix is actually a fancy place offering some bargain rates (Internet bookings can effectively halve the price). The rooms are outfitted with multimedia computers with Internet connections and even exercise equipment, while all guests have free access to the nearby California Fitness Centre, which is stocked with 300 exercise machines.

LE MERIDIEN SINGAPORE

Map pp226-7 Hotel

☎ 6733 8855; www.lemeridien-singapore.com; 100 Orchard Rd; s/d from $290/320; Somerset MRT;

The atrium lobby, with its glass-panel elevators and line drawings, is beginning to look dated, but this is still a decent hotel. The rooms are quite pleasant and the Chinese screens on the walls add a distinctive touch.

LLOYD'S INN

Map pp226-7 Hotel

☎ 6737 7309; www.lloydinn.com; 2 Lloyd Rd; standard/deluxe r $70/80; Somerset MRT

Lloyds is less than 10 minutes' walk south from Orchard Rd in a fort-style building on a quiet street surrounded by old villas. The rooms are spread out, motel style, around the reception building. Don't expect anything special from the rooms, but they are clean and tidy and quite spacious. Bookings are advisable, as the low rates mean the place can fill up fast.

Goodwood Park Hotel (p173)

HISTORIC HOTELS

It's not just Raffles that has an illustrious past (see p52): Goodwood Park Hotel (p173), dating from 1900 and designed to resemble a Rhine castle, served as the base for the Teutonia Club, a social club for Singapore's German community, until 1914 when it was seized by the government as part of 'enemy property'. In 1918 the building was auctioned off and renamed Club Goodwood Hall, before it morphed again into the Goodwood Park Hotel in 1929, fast becoming one of the finest hotels in Asia.

During WWII it accommodated the Japanese high command, some of whom returned here at the war's end to be tried for war crimes in a tent erected in the hotel grounds. By 1947 the hotel was back in business with a $2.5-million renovation programme bringing it back to its former glory by the early 1960s. Further improvements in the 1970s have left the hotel as it is today.

The Fullerton Hotel (p166) occupies the magnificent colonnaded Fullerton Building, named after Robert Fullerton, the first Governor of the Straits Settlements. When it opened in 1928 it was the largest building in Singapore and cost over $4 million. The General Post Office, which occupied the three floors of the building, was said to have the longest counter (100m) in the world at the time. Above the GPO was the exclusive Singapore Club, in which Governor Sir Shenton Thomas and General Percival discussed surrendering Singapore to the Japanese.

In 1958 a revolving lighthouse beacon was added to the roof; its beams could be seen up to 29km away. By 1996 the GPO had moved out and the entire building underwent a multimillion-dollar renovation and reopened in 2001 to general acclaim, receiving the prestigious Urban Redevelopment Authority Architectural Award the same year.

MERITUS MANDARIN SINGAPORE

Map pp226-7 International Hotel

☎ 6737 2200; www.mandarin-singapore.com; 333 Orchard Rd; south-/main-tower r from $360/400; Somerset MRT;

An elegant yet informal place. The cheapest rooms are in the south tower, while those in the main tower (the one with the observation lounge and the revolving restaurant **Top of the M**, see p116) are decorated in warm tones with Oriental-themed furniture and fresh orchids in the bathrooms.

ORCHARD PARADE HOTEL

Map pp226-7 Hotel

☎ 6737 1133; www.orchardparade.com.sg; 1 Tanglin Rd; r from $260; Orchard MRT;

One for Manchester United fans, this is an excellent-value place right next to the football club's official Singapore store. The rooms are a good size with huge beds and sofas – the cheapest ones are on the 6th floor and below – and the hotel occupies a pleasant spot facing the greenery of Tanglin, but close to the bustle of Orchard.

SHA VILLA Map pp226-7 Hotel

☎ 6734 7117; www.sha.org.sg; 64 Lloyd Rd; standard/superior r $125/165; Somerset MRT;

In a charming colonial building, Sha Villa has polished teak floors and interior decoration with a Peranakan flavour. The hotel has been taken over recently by the Singapore Hotel Association tourism training college and the staff are all hospitality students (which means they are trying extra hard). Standard rooms don't have windows, but are quite spacious. Rates include breakfast.

REGENT HOTEL

Map pp226-7 International Hotel

☎ 6733 8888; www.regenthotels.com; 1 Cuscaden Rd; r from $350; Orchard MRT;

Walking from the far west end of Orchard Rd, the first hotel you'll come across is one of the best. A classy operation with all the colourful, spacious rooms arranged around the airy central atrium. There are acres of marble and gorgeous furnishings in the lobby, which is a top place for afternoon tea.

SHANGRI-LA HOTEL

Map pp226-7 International Hotel

☎ 6737 3644; www.shangri-la.com/singapore; 22 Orange Grove Rd; Tower Wing deluxe r from $355; Orchard MRT;

This vast, opulent hotel, set in the leafy lanes surrounding the west end of Orchard, boasts a luxurious interior featuring a 15-acre tropical garden and large rooms done out in rich, butterscotch tones with the odd Asian touches. For long-term stayers with plenty of spare cash, there are 127 serviced apartments (at $7500 a month or $315 a day) and 55 private apartments.

SHERATON TOWERS

Map pp226-7 International Hotel

☎ 6737 6888; www.sheraton.com/towerssingapore; 39 Scotts Rd; deluxe/executive r $430/500; Newton MRT;

Oozes opulence and has all manner of facilities. The rooms are decorated in mossy greens with beautiful pictures of flowers, and the service is efficient and pleasant. The grand lobby is a lovely place for tea.

SINGAPORE MARRIOTT

Map pp226-7 International Hotel

☎ 6735 5800; www.marriot.com/sindt; 320 Orchard Rd; deluxe/executive r $280/340; Orchard MRT;

With its pagoda-like tower, this is one of the most distinctive buildings along Orchard Rd; it's located on one of Orchard Rd's busiest corners next to the famous Tang's department store. The rooms are excellent and well decorated and the whole place has a bustling, big city atmosphere. It's also home to one of Singapore's trendiest bars – **Bar None** (p131). The hotel's outdoor **Crossroads Cafe** seems to be a favourite lurking spot for sleazy middle-aged European men.

SLOANE COURT HOTEL

Map pp226-7 Hotel

☎ 6235 3311; sloane@singnet.com.sg; 17 Balmoral Rd; s/d $90/100; Newton MRT

A 10-minute walk north of the main drag, this is an excellent-value mock Tudor–style hotel in a garden setting, with an English pub. Rooms are reasonably sized and have a distinctly English character, right down to the black-and-white tiled bathrooms. Excellent value for its location and, dare we say it, a touch romantic.

TRADERS HOTEL

Map pp226-7 International Hotel

☎ 6738 2222; www.shangri-la.com/singapore/traders/en/index.aspx; 1A Cuscaden Rd; s/d from $290/320; Orchard MRT;

Attached to Tanglin Mall, this hotel has stylish, plush rooms, a decent kidney-shaped outdoor pool and an attractive water wall running the length of its spacious lobby (flowing at peak times only). If you pay the full tariff, extras thrown in include complimentary airport transfers, laundry service, breakfast and free local calls.

CHEAP SLEEPS

METROPOLITAN Y Map pp226-7 Hostel

☎ 6737 7755; www.mymca.org.sg; 60 Stevens Rd; s/d from $90/110; Orchard MRT;

The cheapest rooms have no windows, but they're spacious and well-appointed and the excellent facilities include a gym and pool. It's a good 15-minute walk north of Orchard Rd, but a shuttle bus runs there Monday to Friday. For long-term visitors (see p165), apartments are also available. Booking online knocks $20 off the price.

NEW SANDY'S PLACE Map pp226-7 Hotel

☎ 6734 1431; sandygiam@hotmail.com; 3C Sarkies Rd; s/d with fan $35/38, with air-con $45/50; Newton MRT or bus 170

In a residential home (so there's no sign), this is a couple of minutes' walk from Newton MRT, next to the Alliance Française. It's a simple, friendly place with a scrappy garden. Rooms range from a broom-cupboard single on the 1st floor to a spacious double room with fan and attached bathroom on the 3rd floor (overlooking a playing field). Breakfast is included. Bus 170 to Johor Bahru passes along nearby Bukit Timah Rd.

EASTERN SINGAPORE

Few visitors choose to stay in the eastern part of Singapore, mainly because it's far from the city's main attractions and the Geylang/Joo Chiat area has a reputation for sleaze. It does afford a different perspective on Singapore for those seeking a bit of 'real Asia', however, and the pace is certainly gentler. The East Coast area is also very pleasant – and the main attraction of staying out here would be the chance to bookend every day among the cooling breezes of East Coast Park.

ASTRO HOTEL Map p236 Hotel

☎ 6348 9000; www.astro-singapore-hotel.com; 51 Joo Chiat Rd, Katong; s $45-75, d $55-85; Paya Lebar MRT

A spick-and-span place a short walk from the Malay Village (if that's an advantage), this place bills itself as a boutique hotel, but feels more like a run-of-the-mill motel. Though the place is clean, well-run and friendly, some of the windowless rooms are a little cheerless. Room rates vary according to the time of week.

CENTURY ROXY PARK HOTEL SINGAPORE Map p236 Hotel

☎ **6344 8000; www.centuryhotels.com; 50 East Coast Rd; s/d from $220/240; Eunos MRT**

This hotel has a great location close to both Katong and the East Coast Park and 9km from the airport (the entrance is on Marine Parade Rd). The contemporary Asian design of the rooms is appealing and it has plenty of facilities. Rates include breakfast.

COSTA SANDS RESORT (EAST COAST) Map p236 Chalets

☎ **6442 7955; www.costasands.com.sg; 1110 East Coast Parkway; single-/double-storey chalets $140/170; bus 12, 14 or 32;**

Smack on the beach at East Coast Park, this is a popular spot for Singaporeans to 'escape' for the weekend, offering an attractive, peaceful (except at weekends!) alternative to the usual city centre accommodation, especially for travellers with kids. The chalets are comfortable and clean and there are plenty of facilities, from swimming to bike riding and fishing, plus the popular East Coast restaurants and pubs. Transport hassles into the city are the only downside.

FRAGRANCE HOTEL Map p236 Hotel

☎ **6344 9888; www.fragrancehotel.com; 219 Joo Chiat Rd, Katong; s/d Sun-Thu $58/59, Fri & Sat $68/69**

In fierce competition with the Hotel 81 chain for the 'quickie dollar', Fragrance has eight branches, most of them in Geylang, with gaudy names like Pearl and Crystal. The hotels, including this original branch, are attractive and clean enough, but when you consider that they can turn one room around five times a day at $20 per two hours, you might want to think twice.

GATEWAY HOTEL Map p236 Boutique Hotel

☎ **6342 0988; gwhotel@singnet.com.sg; 60 Joo Chiat Rd, Katong; r $48-148; Paya Lebar MRT**

The Gateway is one of the few boutique hotels in the area. Housed in a vaguely fort-like building with sloping tiled roofs, it offers modern rooms with louvred shutters, though the TV bolted to the ceiling detracts from the general effect. Ask for a room with a window, even though Joo Chiat Rd can get a little noisy.

HOTEL 81 JOO CHIAT Map p236 Hotel

☎ **6348 8181; www.hotel81.com.sg/hotels_joochiat.shtml; 305 Joo Chiat Rd, Katong; r Sun-Fri $49, Sat $69; Paya Lebar MRT**

One of the burgeoning chain of no-nonsense business (and funny business) hotels sprouting up in central Singapore (there were 13 at last count), this one, strung out behind a row of Peranakan shophouses, is among the best-looking, though all branches are identikit inside. It offers specially fitted rooms for the disabled. Check the website for other locations.

LE MERIDIEN CHANGI VILLAGE HOTEL Map pp222-3 International Hotel

☎ **6379 7111; http://changivillage.lemeridien.com; 1 Netheravon Rd; r $160-320; bus 2 from Tanah Merah MRT;**

If you're going to stay out of the city, you may as well go all the way. This plush, stylish, luxurious gem is nestled among some gorgeous gardens with a superb view (especially at night) across to Malaysia and Pulau Ubin, particularly from the wooden deck around its rooftop pool. Close to the Changi Golf Course, the sailing club, beach park, airport and the gentle pace of Changi Village, it's an excellent choice.

SENTOSA ISLAND

SENTOSA SINGAPORE Map p237 International Hotel

☎ **6275 0331; www.beaufort.com.sg; 2 Bukit Manis Rd; r from $380; shuttle from HarbourFront MRT;**

A low-rise, elegantly designed five-star resort with a beautiful cliff-top setting. Contemporary furnishings in the rooms, the pleasant **Terrace** café, very classy **Cliff** seafood restaurant and garden spa with mud pools, Turkish baths and a curious meditation area make this a splendid choice for its target market. The promotional rate takes the price much lower during mid-week.

SHANGRI-LA'S RASA SENTOSA RESORT Map p237 International Hotel

☎ 6275 0100; www.shangri-la.com/singapore/rasasentosa/en/index.aspx; 101 Silosa Rd; hillfacing/sea-facing r from $290/320; shuttle from HarbourFront MRT;

Singapore's only beachfront resort is shaped like a bent cruise ship and is ideal for a short family break. The rooms are very well designed to take maximum advantage of the sweeping views and there's a huge swimming pool for guests who don't quite fancy the Singapore Strait waters. Prices include breakfast.

SIJORI RESORT SENTOSA

Map p237 Hotel

☎ 6271 2002; www.sijoriresort.com.sg/sentosa.htm; 23 Beach View; r from $180; shuttle from HarbourFront MRT;

Despite the appealing setting in a colonial-era mansion at the centre of the island, this is the least fancy of Sentosa's upmarket hotels. The rooms and facilities, including a pool room and video arcade, are not terribly inspiring, but reasonable value and rates include breakfast. Try not to get a room facing the *Merlion*.

CHEAP SLEEPS

COSTA SANDS RESORT (SENTOSA)

Map p237 Hotel

☎ 6275 1034; www.costasands.com.sg; 30 Imbiah Walk; kampong huts from $60, r from $140; shuttle from HarbourFront MRT;

Reasonable budget choice, with 15 small air-conditioned wooden huts sleeping up to three people and using shared bathrooms. Use of the barbecue pit is $5 extra. Scoring a room over the weekend can be near impossible unless you book months ahead; during the week it shouldn't be a problem. Its hotel rooms are quite smart and good value. There's a small pool all guests can use.

Excursions

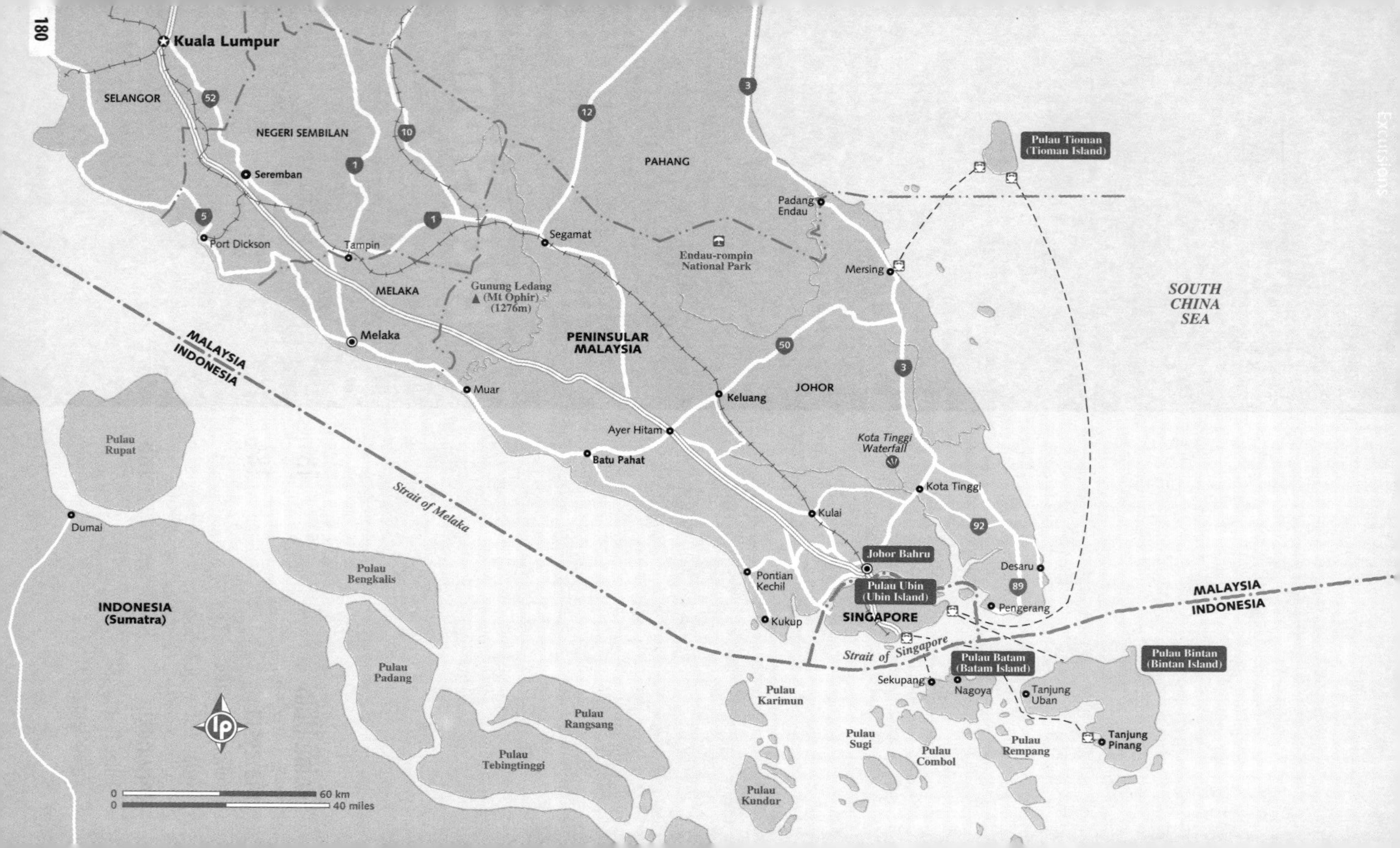
Kuala Lumpur
SELANGOR
52
NEGERI SEMBILAN
10
1
Seremban
5
Port Dickson
Tampin
MELAKA
Melaka
Gunung Ledang
(Mt Ophir)
(1276m)
Muar
12
PAHANG
3
Segamat
Endau-rompin
National Park
Padang
Endau
Mersing
Pulau Tioman
(Tioman Island)
SOUTH
CHINA
SEA
PENINSULAR
MALAYSIA
50
JOHOR
Keluang
Ayer Hitam
Batu Pahat
Kota Tinggi
Waterfall
Kota Tinggi
Kulai
92
Johor Bahru
Desaru
89
Pontian
Kechil
Pulau Ubin
(Ubin Island)
Pengerang
Kukup
SINGAPORE
Strait of Singapore
MALAYSIA
INDONESIA
Pulau Batam
(Batam Island)
Pulau Bintan
(Bintan Island)
Sekupang
Nagoya
Tanjung
Uban
Tanjung
Pinang
Pulau
Karimun
Pulau
Sugi
Pulau
Combol
Pulau
Rempang
Pulau
Kundur
MALAYSIA
INDONESIA
Strait of Melaka
Pulau
Rupat
Dumai
INDONESIA
(Sumatra)
Pulau
Bengkalis
Pulau
Padang
Pulau
Rangsang
Pulau
Tebingtinggi
0 60 km
0 40 miles

Excursions

The same geographical advantages that made Singapore a key port also make it an ideal starting point for trips to the rest of Asia. But the beauty of the island nation is you don't need to get on a plane. Less than an hour away by bus or boat are several popular getaways.

For a touch of rural calm away from the sometimes overwhelming modernity, you don't even have to leave Singapore. Pulau Ubin is one of the last inhabited, untouched parts of the country – often billed as a glimpse into Singapore's past, where quiet kampong life continues much as it has since before WWII. Most visitors come over for a day's walking or cycling, but it's possible to spend a night under canvas, or at the island's lone resort.

In Malaysia, the city of Johor Bahru, just across the Causeway, is a favourite shopping getaway for Singaporeans, who like to scoot over at weekends to tour the malls, stock up on groceries, fill their cars with petrol and maybe buy a few pirated CDs and movies to slip into their bags.

A few hours to the north by road and boat, Pulau Tioman offers the Malaysian east coast's best beaches and some excellent snorkelling and diving.

For a quick beach holiday, most Singaporeans prefer the more convenient trip to Pulau Bintan, located in Indonesia's nearby Riau Archipelago. Home to a large number of swanky resorts, there are also some fascinating historical sites from the days when it was the heart of an empire.

An equally short distance away, but an entirely different proposition, is Pulau Batam, renowned for its gambling dens, prostitution, cheap shopping and entertainment. There's little here to attract the casual visitor except a dose of seediness and a reminder of just how large the contrasts between Singapore and its neighbours are.

Travel in Malaysia is covered in Lonely Planet's *Malaysia, Singapore & Brunei,* and the *Indonesia* and *Bali & Lombok* guides cover the world's largest archipelago.

Lonely Planet's *Indonesian phrasebook* and *Malay phrasebook* may also come in handy.

PULAU UBIN

This small, rural, heavily forested island is a mere 15-minute bumboat ride from the 'mainland', but might as well be in a different country. (If you have a mobile phone, you'll even get a message welcoming you to the Malaysian network!) Home to less than 100 people, Ubin is ringed with mangroves and sprinkled with traditional kampong stilted houses, beautiful abandoned granite quarries, peaceful lanes and tracks, prawn farms, rubber and coconut plantations, curious shrines and temples, camp sites and a lone resort. It's also home to otters, monitor lizards and many species of birds.

A relaxing escape from Singapore's ultramodern bustle, Ubin is particularly popular with nature lovers and, perhaps surprisingly, with the young, who trickle over here at weekends to hike, cycle and camp.

The bumboat from Changi Village's incongruously modern ferry terminal arrives at Ubin's **village**, a ramshackle time capsule of Singapore's past, where fish traps and the skeletal remains of abandoned jetties poke out of the muddy water, docile dogs flop unmolested on the sleepy streets and smiles rarely seem far from local faces.

TRANSPORT

Distance from mainland Singapore 500m

Direction Northeast

Travel time 15 minutes

Boat Getting to Pulau Ubin is easy. A taxi from the city centre to the Changi Village ferry terminal will cost about $15 and take about 20 minutes. Going by public transport, get the MRT to Tanah Merah, then bus 2 or 29 to the Changi Village interchange, a two-minute walk from the ferry terminal. From this spankingly modern terminal, ferries leave whenever there are 12 people to fill a boat and ostensibly run 24 hours a day, though there are unlikely to be regular departures much beyond 8.30pm. The trip each way costs $2 per person.

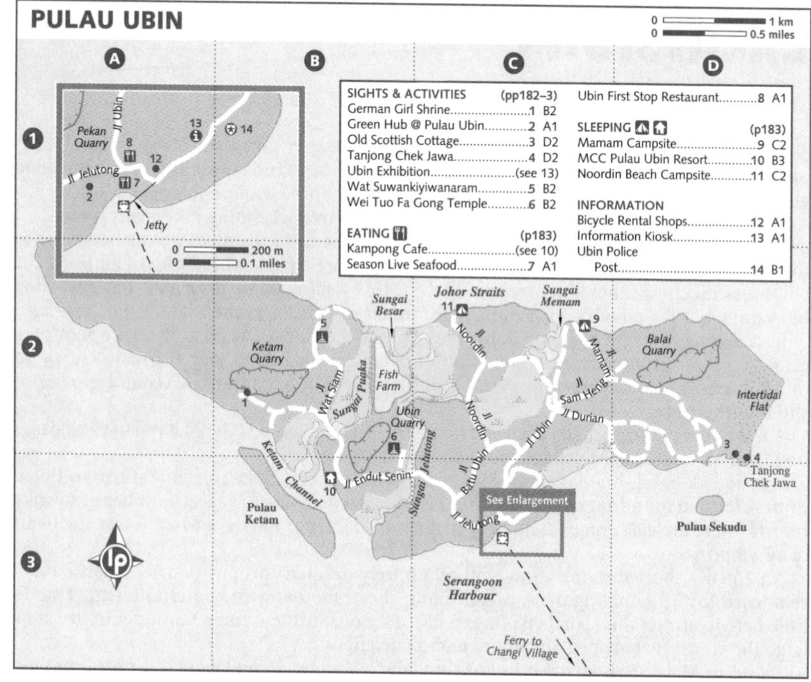

A right turn at the end of the jetty takes you to the **information kiosk**, where you can pick up a half-decent map and visit a small new **exhibition** describing the culture, history and wildlife of the island – a worthwhile introduction for the first-time visitor. This is also the place to arrange guided trips to **Tanjong Chek Jawa**, which cost around $60 for a group. Due to conservation regulations, these tours are the only way to see this mangrove area teeming with marine life at the eastern tip of the island.

Left from the jetty is the tiny village, where a host of **bicycle rental shops** offer bikes in various states of repair for $3 to $10 a day. It is recommended that you go for a test ride and check the gears and brakes are working before you set off; you'll need them on Ubin's undulating hills.

There are plenty of **drink stops** along the way, so don't worry about carrying water.

Turn left when you reach the small village square and after a couple of minutes you'll see a basketball court on your right and the **Green Hub @ Pulau Ubin** – the refurbished community centre that now serves as a base for nature activities, occasional exhibition space and, would you believe, karaoke room.

From the junction at the basketball court, there are two options. Straight ahead takes you to the west of the island; a right turn leads you to the north and east.

Heading west, you'll pass **Pekan Quarry** on the right, a beautiful deep pool ringed with granite cliffs. Sadly, it's fenced off (swimming is strictly forbidden in all Ubin's quarries), but halfway along, the fence has been trodden down and no-one's going to arrest you for taking a look.

After the first bridge, a dirt track on the right leads you to **Wei Tuo Fa Gong temple**, a colourful Chinese temple beside a carp-filled pool.

Back on the main road, after another five minutes and some mildly strenuous uphill cycling, you'll see the chocolate-brown chalets and the impressive climbing wall tower of **MCC Pulau Ubin Resort.** Just after the resort, a dirt track to the right leads you to Ubin Quarry, another impressive deep-blue pool where swimming, sadly, is forbidden.

Just after the resort and another bridge is a fork in the road.

THE GERMAN GIRL SHRINE

Beyond the Ubin Lagoon Resort along a winding gravel track (which is being developed) is the curious **German Girl Shrine**, a yellow shack housing a large white urn next to an assam tree. The shrine is filled with all manner of charms, offerings, folded lottery tickets, a medium's red table and chair, burning candles and joss paper. Legend has it that the young German daughter of a coffee plantation manager, running away from British troops who had come to arrest her parents during WWI, fell to her death into the quarry behind her house. Discovered a day later, she was initially covered with sand, though Chinese labourers eventually gave her a proper burial. Her ghost supposedly haunts the area to this day.

However, somewhere along the way, this daughter of a Roman Catholic family became a Taoist deity, whose help some Chinese believers seek for good health and, particularly, good fortune. A small, devoted collection of Singaporeans regularly make the trek to the shrine seeking her favours. Some reportedly even bring German-speaking mediums along.

Right leads to the **Wat Suwankiyiwanaram**, a large, unattractive yellow Thai Buddhist monastery, fronted with a couple of carved elephant statues and a pair of golden monk figures guarding the door. Inside are images of Buddha's life and some unpleasant depictions of Buddhist hell. The Thai monks are used to visitors (and may try to sell you some trinkets). Free meditation classes are held at weekends. Cycle beyond the temple and you'll reach the north shore; there are views of Johor, Malaysia, and the razor-wire fence used to scare off illegal immigrants.

Left from the fork leads to the German Girl Shrine (see above).

From the village basketball court, a right turn leads north to two choices. At the next fork, take a left turn followed by a right turn and head up past some prawn farms to the camp sites of **Noordin Beach**. Carrying straight on from the fork winds through the island's rubber plantations and best-preserved examples of colourful stilted kampong houses.

Further on are two signposted dirt tracks. The first goes to the large NPCC Campsite, which is for police cadets only. The second heads to the **Mamam Campsite**.

Take either Jalan Durian or, further on, another right turn, to reach Tanjong Chek Jawa (you need to make a booking at the village to visit). Just beyond an old jetty is the **Old Scottish Cottage**, a bizarre former doctor's house that looks like it was transplanted from the British countryside.

For food, you'll have to bring your own (if camping), or head back to the village, where the best of a small crop of eateries are **Season Live Seafood** and **Ubin First Stop Restaurant.** There's also the small **Kampong Cafe** at the Pulau Ubin resort.

How long Ubin will remain in its unspoilt state depends on both government plans – and the not-inconsiderable strength of public pressure to preserve the island in its current state. The government said in its last Concept Plan for the country that it wants to maintain Ubin in its natural state 'for as long as possible', but added the ominous qualifier: 'However…we need to retain the flexibility to review the situation in the future.' There's little doubt the government would like to bring Ubin's transport and facilities into line with Singapore's policy of relentless modernisation. For now, its charm is intact.

Information

Information Kiosk (☎ 6542 4108; ⌚ 8am-5pm)

Ubin Police Post (☎ 6542 8664)

Eating

Kampong Cafe (☎ 6388 8388; ⌚ 8am-9pm) Decent set lunch for $25, inside the Pulau Ubin resort.

Season Live Seafood (☎ 6542 7627; ⌚ 11am-7.30pm) Sea views and seafood, offering Tiger beers ($6), mango fish ($14), fried squid ($8) or black pepper crab ($12).

Ubin First Stop Restaurant (☎ 6543 2489; ⌚ 11am-8pm Thu-Tue) Another top seafood spot in the village square.

Sleeping

MCC Pulau Ubin Resort (☎ 6388 8388; www.marinacountryclub.com.sg; 1-bedroom chalets $120) Chalet resort aimed at the activity junkie – with rock climbing, kayaking, archery and a flying fox.

Noordin Beach & Mamam Campsites Pleasant free camping spots with imported white-sand beaches. Watch out for otters, bats and the odd python! If planning group camping, consult the National Park officers at the Information Kiosk for finer details. Campers are advised to drop by the Ubin Police Post to register, so they know that you are on the island in case of emergencies.

MALAYSIA

JOHOR BAHRU

☎ 07

Connected to Singapore by the 1038m-long Causeway, Johor Bahru (or JB as it's commonly known) inevitably suffers in comparison to its more glamorous neighbour, yet its rough edges are an interesting contrast to Singapore. Some call it 'the real Asia'; others – including, famously, Lee Kuan Yew – call it something else.

JB is almost considered a suburb of Singapore. Thousands of people – Singaporeans included – live there and commute through the crowded Woodlands checkpoint, which handles about 50,000 people a day. Singapore residents flock over here at weekends and public holidays to take advantage of cheaper grocery and petrol prices and stock up on pirated CDs and DVDs.

Unless you have a burning need for any of these items, Johor doesn't have a great deal to offer as a tourist attraction, but there are a few interesting diversions and some excellent eating options.

Motor boat docked by the jetty, Pulau Ubin (p181)

Walking west from the immigration checkpoint along the busy esplanade of Jalan Ibrahim, you'll find JB's main attraction, the **Royal Abu Bakar Museum**. The former Istana Besar (main palace) of the Johor royal family, it was built in Victorian style on a small hill

TRANSPORT

Distance from Singapore 1km

Direction North

Travel time 30 minutes to one hour

Bus Many bus companies run bus services from Singapore to Malaysia. Visit http://plusliner.com for online and off-line ticketing services for Plusliner and NiCE Executive coaches plying between Malaysia and Singapore. The Singapore–Johor Express coach leaves every 15 minutes from the Queen St bus terminal (Map p232) between 6.30am and 11pm and costs $2.40. Alternatively take the public bus 170, also from Queen St terminal, which runs every 15 minutes between 5.20am and 12.10am and costs $1.70. Yet another, quicker, option is to go to Kranji MRT station by train and catch bus 160, which cuts down on your bus time dramatically.

In all cases, when you get to the Singapore checkpoint, take all your belongings and get off. After clearing immigration, you have to wait for the next bus (but don't have to pay again, as long you have your ticket). Repeat the process at the Malaysian side, or simply take a two-minute walk into JB city centre. The public bus stops at the Komtar Shopping Centre and then the Larkin Bus Terminal 5km north of the Causeway, while the coach stops only at the bus terminal.

Coming back, the public bus costs RM1.20 and the coach RM2.40.

If at all possible, avoid crossing at weekends, when it gets infernally busy and the whole process can become a frustrating waste of time. Coming back into Singapore on a Sunday evening is little short of a nightmare.

Taxi A taxi from the city into JB will cost around $24, more if there is a long wait at immigration. Alternatively, you can try to pick up a share taxi from Queen St bus terminal, which will cost $6 to $8 per person.

overlooking the Johor Strait by the Anglophile sultan Abu Bakar in 1866. The palace is now a museum chock-full of the sultan's possessions, furniture and hunting trophies and surrounded by magnificent grounds. There are some superb pieces. Despite the hefty foreigner price (payable in ringgit) it's well worth a visit.

Nearby is a small **zoo**, but with one of the world's best zoos just across the water it's hardly worth the effort.

A little further west, off Jalan Gertak Merah, is the impressive **Sultan Abu Bakar Mosque**; like some of the mosques in Singapore, it features a mish-mash of architectural influences – including Victorian. Also like the mosques in Singapore, it took some time to build (eight years from 1892 to 1900), but you can see why. Hailed in Singapore as one of the most magnificent, it occupies large grounds and, according to its caretaker, can hold up to 2000 people.

If you continue west (you'll have to take a taxi), you can see the real residence of the Sultan of Johor, the **Istana Bukit Serene**, but of course you're not allowed to wander in and say hello.

Temple enthusiasts can head up the east side of the Istana Gardens along Jalan Ayer Molek, which turns into Jalan Yahya Awal. On the right, about 2km from the Istana, is the **Ro Fo Gu Miao** (Old Temple), a beautiful, elaborately painted Chinese temple with a large

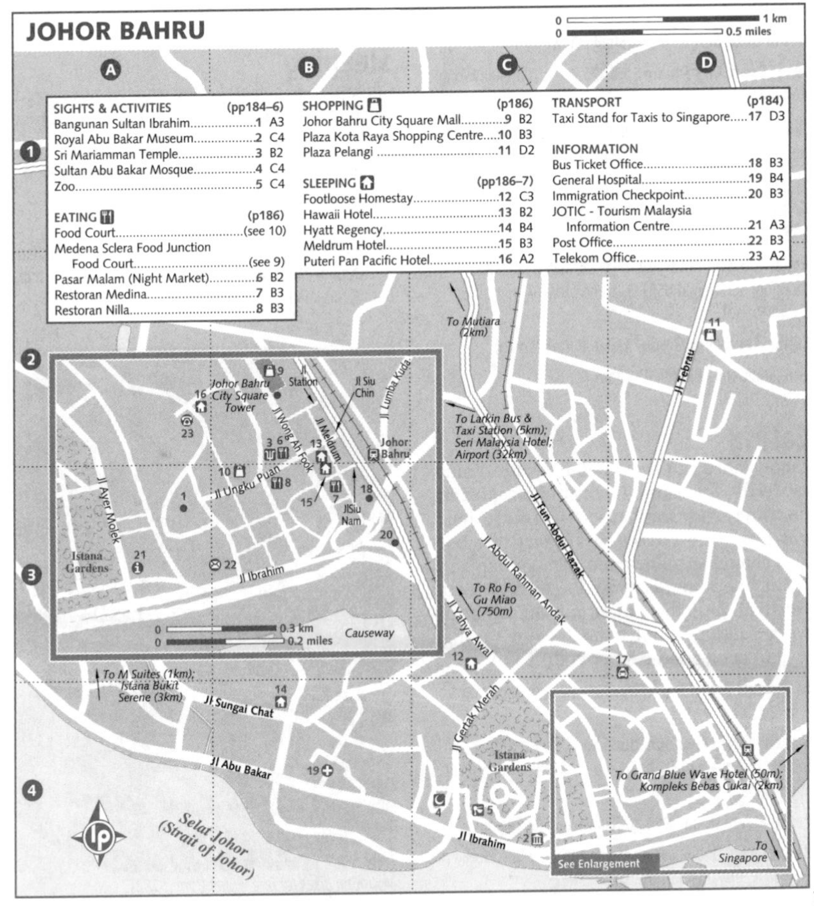

wooden door. It is reputedly the only temple in Johor that survived WWII and is hence a highly sacred place for Chinese Malays.

Back in the city, start your exploration in the city centre, which is overlooked by the **Bangunan Sultan Ibrahim**, an imposing fortress-style building that looks like it was transported from Mogul India – though in fact it was built in the 1940s. Follow Jalan Ungku Puan, which runs away from this building and you'll pass on your left the **Plaza Kota Raya shopping centre**, **Sri Mariamman Temple** and the **Pasar Malam** (night market), a favourite eating spot where you can also find some souvenirs and clothes. Starting at 5.30pm, it is divided into three sections – Chinese, Malay and Indian – and has a great selection of dishes. Try the laksa Johor (hearty noodle dish in a coconut soup) and *mee rebus* (Javanese-style noodles in a thick sauce).

For shopping though, most people head to the big malls like the fancy **Johor Bahru City Square**, along the chaotic, somewhat dirty Jalan Wong Ah Fook thoroughfare just across from the immigration post. **Plaza Pelangi**, an even fancier mall featuring handicrafts, fashion and food, seems to have surpassed City Square in the modernity stakes; while **Kompleks Bebas Cukai duty-free shopping complex**, about 2km east of the Causeway, proudly proclaims itself one of the largest duty-free complexes in the world, with more than 160 shops.

Sights & Information

Bangunan Sultan Ibrahim (State Secretariat Bldg; Bukit Timbalan)

Istana Bukit Serene (Jalan Straits View)

Johor Bahru City Square (☎ 226 3668; 108 Jalan Wong Ah Fook)

Johor Tourist Information Centre (☎ 222 3590; www.tourismmalaysia.gov.my; 2 Jalan Ayer Molek; 🕑 8am-5pm Mon-Fri)

Kompleks Bebas Cukai duty-free shopping complex (☎ 922 2611; Bukit Kayu Hitam)

Royal Abu Bakar Museum (☎ 223 0555; Jalan Ibrahim; foreigner adult/child US$7/3, around RM26/11; 🕑 9am-5pm Sat-Thu)

Sultan Abu Bakar Mosque (Jalan Gertak Merah)

Zoo (adult/child RM2/1; 🕑 8am-6pm)

Eating

Johor Bahru can be a good place for dining, especially for seafood. Lots of Singaporeans do come across the Causeway to eat seafood, but given the hassles of crossing the border, changing money and then getting back again, to our minds it just doesn't really seem worth it (but then these *are* Singaporeans we're talking about, who'll swim through lava to get a good pepper crab).

Food Court (Upper level, Plaza Kota Raya shopping centre) A decent food court.

Medena Sclera Food Junction Food Court (5th fl, Johor Bahru City Square mall) Asian and Western restaurants in abundance.

Pasar Malam (Night Market; Jalan Wong Ah Fook)

Restoran Medina (12 Jalan Meldrum; 🕑 24hr) Excellent *murtabak*, biryani and curries.

Restoran Nilla (3 Jalan Ungku Puan; 🕑 6pm-midnight) Opposite the Sri Mariamman Temple, it specialises in South Indian banana-leaf vegetarian set meals.

Sleeping

Cheap, basic hotels are mostly clustered in the Jalan Meldrum neighbourhood, just east of the railway station.

Footloose Homestay (☎ 224 2881; foot loose_jb2000@yahoo.com; 4H Jalan Ismail; dm/d RM15/35) Nothing flash, but clean and friendly.

Hawaii Hotel (☎ 224 0633; 21 Jalan Meldrum; r with fan & bathroom RM40, with air-con from RM50) A little dismal, but OK for a night.

Mountain bikes for hire, Pulau Ubin (p182)

Hyatt Regency (☎ 222 1234; hyatt@hrjb.po.my; Jalan Sungai Chat; s/d from RM430/450) A stylish, top-end joint, often offering huge discounts, but a bit far out of town.

Meldrum Hotel (☎ 227 8988; hotel_meldrum@po.jaring.my; 1 Jalan Meldrum; r RM70) Smart, clean rooms with air-con and TV; better than the Hawaii.

Puteri Pan Pacific Hotel (☎ 223 3333; fax 223 6622; The Kotoraya; r from RM420) Best top-end bet close to town – also with big discounts.

PULAU TIOMAN

☎ 09

The largest and most spectacular of Malaysia's east-coast islands (though cynics say it's been overdeveloped), Tioman has beautiful beaches, clear water, good snorkelling and excellent dive sites. Its major attraction, though, has to be its diversity. A short walk from the coast and you are in dense jungle on the lower slopes of high mountains.

Tioman is the east coast's most popular destination and can get very crowded, especially weekends and public holidays. The main budget accommodation areas are in **Air Batang** (usually called ABC), **Salang**, **Juara** and **Tekek**, all of which have good beaches and swimming. Of all these, Salang is the most popular, with the highest number of beach chalet operations, the best nightlife on the island, and proximity to the **Monkey Bay** and **Pulau Tulai** snorkelling and dive sites. Tekek is the administrative centre of Tioman, containing the airport, hospital, shops, moneychangers and post office. There's even a small **museum** (admission RM1; 9.30am-5.30pm) displaying mostly Chinese ceramics lost by stricken trading ships.

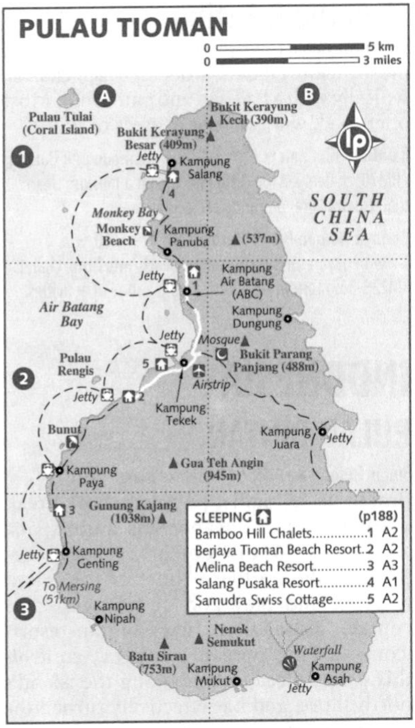

PULAU TIOMAN

SLEEPING	(p188)	
Bamboo Hill Chalets	1	A2
Berjaya Tioman Beach Resort	2	A2
Melina Beach Resort	3	A3
Salang Pusaka Resort	4	A1
Samudra Swiss Cottage	5	A2

TRANSPORT

Distance from Singapore 178km

Direction Northeast

Travel time Air 35 minutes, overland five hours

Air If you have ready cash and not much time, **Berjaya Air** (☎ 6227 3688; 67 Tanjong Pagar Rd; return $268) operates daily flights direct to Tioman's newly upgraded airport from Singapore's Seletar airport, departing at 1.55pm. The flight takes 35 minutes.

Bus/boat Early birds can catch the **Kaiho Coaches** (☎ 607 241 8208; return $35) bus to Mersing in Malaysia, which departs from Newton Circus (Map pp226–7) at 6.30am and takes three to four hours. Alternatively, hop on the **Transnasional bus** (☎ 6294 7034; $26.50), which leaves the Lavender St bus terminal (Map p232) at 9am, 10am and 10pm. When you arrive at Mersing, you have three options. The speedboats (one way adult/child RM45/40; 7.30am, 10.30am, 1.30pm, 3pm) are quickest, taking a bit more than an hour. The speed ferry (one way adult/child RM30/25; 8am, noon) takes between 90 minutes and two hours and drops you wherever you want. The normal ferry (one way adult/child RM30/25; 11.30am) is slowest, taking anywhere from two to three hours and stopping at Genting, Paya, Berjaya Tioman Beach Resort, Tekek, ABC and Salang, in that order. Departures are all dependent on tide, conditions and number of passengers.

Taxi If you're in a group of three or four, a taxi from Johor Bahru's Larkin Bus Station to Mersing will cost about RM80 to RM90 and take about two hours.

Sleeping & Eating

Tioman has a huge range of accommodation, mostly identical basic wooden beach chalets, typically with a bed, fan and bathroom. Most offer food, with varying degrees of skill.

Bamboo Hill Chalets (☎ 419 1339; Kampung Air Batang; r RM70, chalets RM100-120) Perched on a hillside; clean chalets with verandas and spectacular views.

Berjaya Tioman Beach Resort (☎ 419 1000; www.berjayaresorts.com/tioman-beach/info.html; chalets RM275-385) Fancy resort with a huge range of activities.

Melina Beach Resort (☎ 419 7080; s/d with fan RM80/90, with air-con RM149/159) Offers excellent German-run chalets, with a bay all to itself.

Samudra Swiss Cottage (☎ 419 1642; www.samudra-swiss-cottage.com; Kampung Tekek; longhouse/chalet/bungalow r RM65/88/98) Located at the far south of Tekek in a peaceful spot. Samudra Swiss Cottage also offers diving courses.

Salang Pusaka Resort (☎ 419 5317; Kampung Salang; r with fan/air-con RM75/100) Clean, comfortable beachfront chalets in well-kept garden.

INDONESIA

PULAU BINTAN

Bintan Resorts area ☎ 0770, rest of island ☎ 0771

Bintan is a highly popular short-break destination for Singaporeans and expats, who flock to the upmarket beach resorts on the northern shore of the island to relax and play golf at four top-class courses. **Bintan Resorts** (www.bintan-resorts.com), a Singaporean company, controls this prime piece of land along the island's north shore, and has effectively turned the area into an offshore enclave of the Lion City, with reliable power supplies, potable water and decent restaurants. You don't even have to change your Singapore dollars into rupiah.

Not surprisingly, this is where most Singaporeans and other weekenders head (though we had problems with sandflies on the beaches). The Bintan Resorts are divided into four main areas: Nirwana Gardens, Laguna Bintan, Ria Bintan and Bintan Lagoon. They have little that's authentically Indonesian about them (other than the staff), but are more than adequate if you're looking for a stress-free place to kick back, and enjoy some top-class golf, a host of water sports or other activities.

If the resorts are not your bag, then there's the rustic, white-sand beaches of the **east coast** where it's possible to rent a seaside hut from locals for a few dollars.

Outside Bintan Resorts, the island retains some of the sleepy Riau islands' charm that is largely lost on neighbouring Batam. The old town of **Tanjung Pinang** is worth a look, mainly as a jumping-off point for Pulau Penyenget. It's a charming port town, particularly its seafront, where traditional stilted houses jut out over the water, and vessels (from old sampans to large freighters) stream in and out of the harbour. You'll also see what appear to be the town's

TRANSPORT

Distance from Singapore 45km

Direction Southeast

Travel time 45 minutes

Boat This is the only way to get to/from Bintan. The high-speed catamaran departs from the **Tanah Merah Ferry Terminal** (Map pp222-3; ☎ 6542 4369; www.brf.com.sg; peak/off-peak return $47.20/36.20) five times a day between 9am and 8pm from Monday to Thursday, six times between 8am and 8pm on Friday and Sunday and seven times on Saturday. The boat arrives at the Bandar Bentan Telani Ferry Terminal. For Tanjung Pinang, there are three ferries operating from Tanah Merah – and all of them have happily now synchronised their timetables and fares. **Penguin Ferries** (☎ 6542 7107), **Falcon** (☎ 6542 6786) and **Berlian** (☎ 6786 9959) all do the run for $35 return. There are six departures a day between 9.30am and 6.55pm Monday to Friday, and nine departures between 9.15am and 6.55pm at weekends.

Bus The bus terminal is 7km out of Tanjung Pinang. You can catch an *opelet* (small minibus) along the road to Pantai Trikora (500Rp). There aren't many buses and unless you happen to turn up when one is leaving, you'll have to bargain for a driver to take you to your destination.

Ojek Tanjung Pinang is crawling with orange-helmeted *ojek* (motorbike taxi) drivers – it's fine to travel with them for shorter distances.

Taxi Hiring a taxi in Tanjung Pinang is more convenient than travelling by bus and won't cost much more. Count on spending 50,000Rp to get to the east-coast beaches.

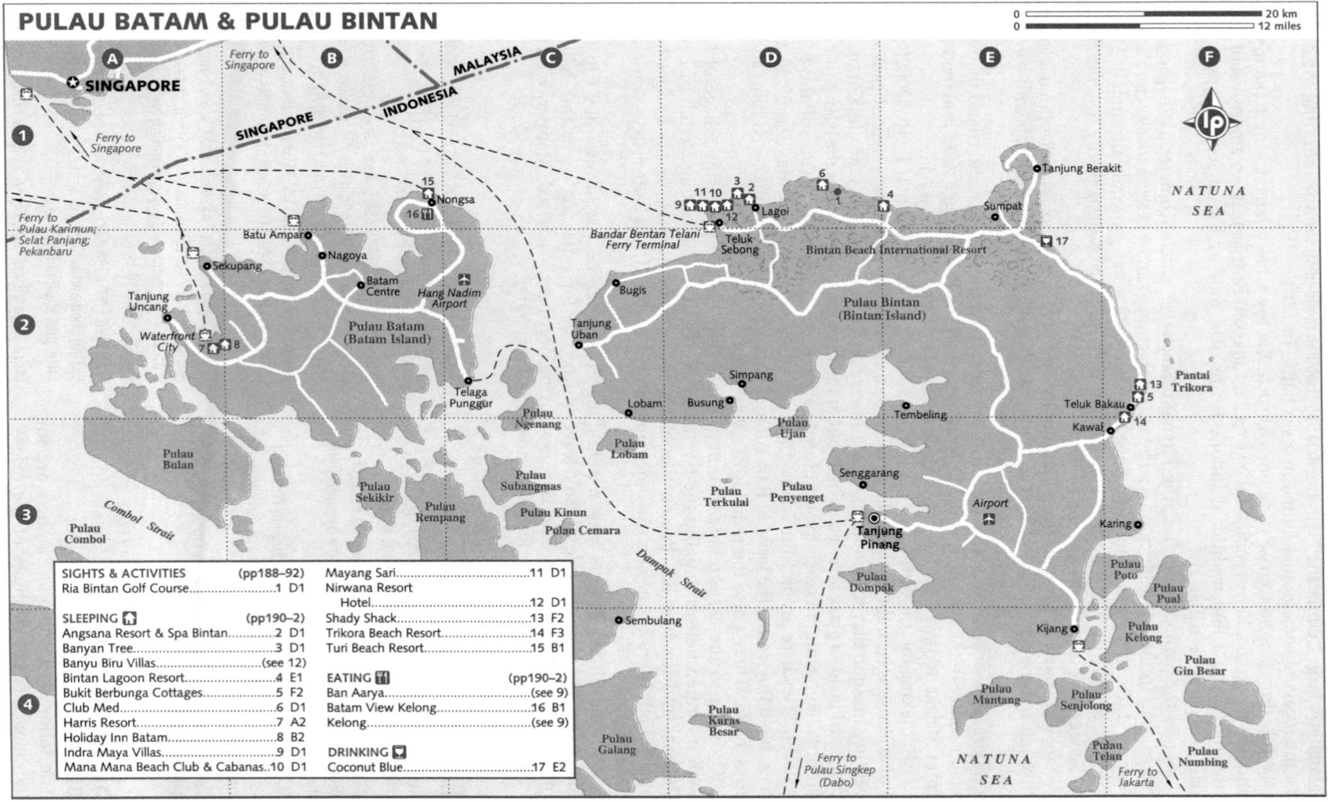

PULAU BATAM & PULAU BINTAN
0 20 km
0 12 miles
A
B
C
D
E
F
1
2
3
4
SINGAPORE
Ferry to Singapore
Ferry to Singapore
SINGAPORE
INDONESIA
MALAYSIA
Ferry to Pulau Karimun; Selat Panjang; Pekanbaru
Batu Ampar
Nagoya
Sekupang
Batam Centre
Hang Nadim Airport
Nongsa
Tanjung Uncang
Waterfront City
Pulau Batam (Batam Island)
Telaga Punggur
Pulau Ngenang
Pulau Bulan
Pulau Sekikir
Pulau Rempang
Pulau Subangmas
Pulau Kinun
Pulau Cemara
Combol Strait
Pulau Combol
Bandar Bentan Telani Ferry Terminal
Teluk Sebong
Lagoi
Bintan Beach International Resort
Sumpat
Tanjung Berakit
NATUNA SEA
Bugis
Tanjung Uban
Pulau Bintan (Bintan Island)
Simpang
Busung
Lobam
Pulau Lobam
Pulau Ujan
Tembeling
Pantai Trikora
Teluk Bakau
Kawal
Senggarang
Airport
Tanjung Pinang
Pulau Terkulai
Pulau Penyenget
Karing
Dampak Strait
Pulau Dompak
Sembulang
Kijang
Pulau Poto
Pulau Pual
Pulau Kelong
Pulau Gin Besar
Pulau Mantang
Pulau Senjolong
Pulau Karas Besar
Pulau Galang
Pulau Telan
Pulau Numbing
Ferry to Pulau Singkep (Dabo)
Ferry to Jakarta
NATUNA SEA
SIGHTS & ACTIVITIES (pp188–92)
Ria Bintan Golf Course 1 D1
SLEEPING (pp190–2)
Angsana Resort & Spa Bintan 2 D1
Banyan Tree 3 D1
Banyu Biru Villas (see 12)
Bintan Lagoon Resort 4 E1
Bukit Berbunga Cottages 5 F2
Club Med 6 D1
Harris Resort 7 A2
Holiday Inn Batam 8 B2
Indra Maya Villas 9 D1
Mana Mana Beach Club & Cabanas 10 D1
Mayang Sari 11 D1
Nirwana Resort Hotel 12 D1
Shady Shack 13 F2
Trikora Beach Resort 14 F3
Turi Beach Resort 15 B1
EATING (pp190–2)
Ban Aarya (see 9)
Batam View Kelong 16 B1
Kelong (see 9)
DRINKING
Coconut Blue 17 E2

symbols, a large helmet shell and the **Raja Haji Fisabillah monument**, commemorating the defeat by the locals of the colonial Dutch in a sea battle in 1784.

While there are no tourist attractions as such, the town has a large Chinese population and a lively atmosphere, typified by its excellent market, **Pasar Baru**. Set in a network of narrow alleys, you'll find traditional Indonesian textiles, food and even some shops selling religious paraphernalia.

Across the harbour from Tanjung Pinang is **Senggarang**, where Chinese first began landing in Riau in the late 18th century. The star attraction is an old **Chinese temple**, close to the pier, held together by the roots of a huge banyan tree that has grown up through it. Half a kilometre along the waterfront is a big square with three **Chinese temples** side by side. Boats to Senggarang leave from the end of Jalan Pelantar II.

You can charter a sampan from Tanjung Pinang to take you up **Sungei Ular** (Snake River) through the mangroves to a Chinese temple, with gory murals of the trials and tortures of hell.

Spare most of your time here for a trip to **Pulau Penyenget**, a tiny, peaceful island that was a major centre in the Islamic world 200 years ago when the Riau-Lingga Kingdom held sway from Melaka to Java. Scholars from Mecca reputedly came here to teach.

After taking the 15-minute ferry ride from Tanjung Pinang's Pelantar I jetty (2000Rp) to Pulau Penyenget, walk straight ahead to reach the **Masjid Raya Sultan Riau**, a magnificent 19th-century mosque that still contains its old library and a beautiful 200-year-old Koran, now displayed inside a glass case. Turn right out of the mosque and go across the island (it's only around 800m wide) to reach the other main attraction, the **Istana Raja Ali** (the sultan's former palace). Elsewhere around the island there are subtler reminders of the island's glorious past, including ruins, the **tombs** of Raja Ali and Raja Hamidah, who preceded him, and old royal baths. There's also the remains of a **Dutch fort**.

Crossing to the eastern side of Bintan you'll find the pretty seaside village of **Kawal**, with its stilted houses hugging the riverbank. North of here is a long stretch of beautiful bays and the best beaches on the island. Accommodation is mainly budget beach chalets, but there is one slightly more upscale place – the **Trikora Beach Resort** – which is a little rundown.

Both the Bintan Resorts area and Tanjung Pinang can be visited on a day trip from Singapore, but the schedule doesn't leave much time for exploring the island, which is more than twice the size of Singapore, so staying overnight is advised. Many travel agents in Singapore offer packages far below advertised rack rates.

Eating

Kelong (☎ 692 557) An excellent seafood restaurant built over the water near the Indra Maya Villas.

Baan Aarya (☎ 692 789; resatria@indosat.net.id) A beautiful villa serving classic Thai cuisine by candlelight in the evenings.

Manak Den (Jalan Bakar Batu 57) In Tanjung Pinang, it serves recommended Padang food such as fish curry or *kare nangka* (jackfruit curry).

Sangkuriang (Jalan Bakar Batu 76) In Tanjung Pinang, it's a decent place for seafood.

Sleeping

BINTAN RESORTS

The following telephone numbers are for the Singapore-based offices of the resorts. All the resorts have a range of decent places to eat.

Angsana Resort & Spa Bintan (☎ 6849 5899; www.angsana.com; r from US$225) Very classy resort with luxury spa – often offers discount rates.

Banyan Tree (☎ 6849 5899; www.banyantree.com; r from S$445) A byword in Singapore for pampered luxury and the favourite spot for romantic weekends.

Banyu Biru Villas (☎ 6323 6636; www.nirwanagardens.com; villas from S$400) Large beachfront villas aimed at families and groups.

Bintan Lagoon Resort (☎ 6226 3122; www.bintanlagoon.com; r from S$250, villas from S$800) Huge resort with excellent rooms and villas, featuring two golf courses and lots of activities.

Club Med (☎ 6738 4222; www.clubmed.com; r from S$300) Food and activities in abundance for all-inclusive price, plus a top golf course.

Indra Maya Villas (☎ 6323 6636; www.nirwanagardens.com; villas from S$900) Very exclusive luxury hillside villas overlooking the sea.

Mana Mana Beach Club & Cabanas (☎ 6339 8878; www.manamana.com; cabanas S$90) Wooden air-con cottages set back from the beach, hosting Bintan's main water-sports centre.

Mayang Sari (☎ 6323 6636; www.nirwanagardens.com; chalets from S$220) This place has newly renovated large wood-and-thatch cottages on a delightful stretch of beach.

Nirwana Resort Hotel (☎ 6323 6636; www.nirwanagardens.com; r from S$220) A large resort with decent rooms, but a bit shabby at the edges.

TANJUNG PINANG

Bong's Homestay (☎ 22 605; 20 Lorong Bintan II; d 30,000Rp) On a small alley off Jalan Bintan (look for the blue Wartel sign) is this spartan place. The rooms are tiny, but the two old blokes in charge are friendly enough.

Hotel Laguna (☎ 31 1555; fax 31 2555; Jalan Bintan 51; r from S$50) In the midrange, this modern hotel is clean, comfortable and in a quiet spot. Rates include breakfast.

Hotel Sadaap (☎ 22 357; 17 Jalan Hang Tuah; r US$20) Peaceful hillside place with clean rooms and gorgeous views. The best choice by far.

Johnny's Homestay (22 Lorong Bintan II; r 15,000Rp) Next door to Bong's Homestay and a good place to get travel info.

EAST COAST

Bukit Berbunga Cottages (cottages 50,000Rp) A laid-back, friendly spot with basic mattress-on-floor huts.

Shady Shack (cottages 70,000Rp) Newly renovated place featuring two-storey beach huts with beds upstairs and excellent local food.

Trikora Beach Resort (☎ 24 452; chalets S$50) Air-con chalets and the most upmarket on the east coast, but overpriced.

PULAU BATAM

☎ 0778

Development has been rampant on Batam since the island was declared a free-trade zone in 1989 and Singaporean companies began building industrial complexes to be served by a ready source of cheap labour. Although Batam has one decent resort and several golf courses, the main reason why you would want to come here is to catch an onward ferry to other parts of Indonesia. The gambling dens that brought Singaporean men here in droves have been shut down (for the moment, at least), but the prostitution remains a big drawcard and ensures that the island's reputation for sleaze remains undiminished. More recently, though, it has developed a small **spa** industry that, with its bargain rates, has pulled in Singaporean women in their thousands. The massive new **Waterfront City** development near the ferry terminal at Sekupang has lent a family edge to Batam entertainment, with **cable skiing**, **go-karting**, **bowling** and even a **Snow World** not dissimilar to Singapore's own Snow City.

From Singapore, most travellers arrive by boat at **Batu Ampar**, the port for the main town of Nagoya, or at **Sekupang**, the primary connection place for boats to Sumatran destinations.

Charmless **Nagoya**, renamed by the Japanese during WWII, is a dusty bustling boom town packed with cheap shopping centres and dodgy massage parlours, though it also offers weekenders activities like tenpin bowling, go-karting and paintball. The nearby town

TRANSPORT

Distance from Singapore 20km

Direction Southeast

Travel time 30 minutes

Boat Ferries leave from the World Trade Centre terminal (Map p237) and take about 30 minutes to get to Sekupang, or 45 minutes to get to Batu Ampar. The main agents are **Penguin** (☎ 6271 4866), **Dino Shipping** (☎ 6270 2228) and **Berlian** (☎ 6272 2192), all with offices at the WTC. Between them they have dozens of departures every day to Batam, at least every half-hour from 7.30am to 8pm. Tickets cost from S$20 return. Ferries dock at Sekupang, where you can take a boat to Tanjung Buton on the Sumatran mainland. From there it is a three-hour bus ride to Palembang. This is a popular travellers' route to Sumatra.

Speedboats to Tanjung Pinang on neighbouring Bintan leave from Telaga Punggur, 30km southeast of Nagoya. There's a steady flow of departures from 8am to around 5pm daily. The trip takes 20 minutes and costs 15,000Rp one way.

of **Batam Centre** is the island's administrative centre with some large public buildings, a huge modern mosque and little else. The **Nongsa** peninsula in the northeast, ringed by verdant golf resorts built with Singapore visitors in mind, is the main draw here.

Eating

Batam View Kelong A restaurant built out over the sea on stilts. The fish are kept live in tanks, and you'll pay for everything by the kilo.

Night markets (Jalan Raja Ali Haji) A cheap, lively spot for evening food and drinks.

Sleeping

Budget accommodation in Nagoya is appalling; the rock-bottom places are little more than brothels. Avoid staying here if you can help it. Better resort options can be found at Waterfront City in the west of the island, where the new Holiday Inn and Harris Resort are located, or on the northeast tip at Nongsa.

Formosa Hotel (☎ 42 6789; formosa@indosat.net.id; r Sun-Fri S$65, Sat S$70) In Nagoya. Upmarket, respectable hotel, with well-kept rooms. Rates include breakfast.

Harris Resort (☎ 38 1888; fax 38 1142; r from S$102) Huge yet friendly, with excellent, brightly decorated rooms, spa and lots of activities.

Holiday Inn Batam (☎ 38 1333; fax 38 1332; r from S$125) Located 500m from Waterfront City ferry terminal. Large, lush and very comfortable.

Hotel Limindo Pasifik (☎ 42 5077; fax 42 5089; Jalan Imam Bonjol, Komplek Ruko, 10 Block N; r from 100,000Rp) Close to Komplek Nagoya Business Centre for shopping. Clean and simple rooms.

Turi Beach Resort (☎ 76 1079; rturi@citratubindo.com; r Sun-Fri from S$120, Sat S$140) The choice place to stay, with thatched and stilted wooden cottages and beachside bar with great views.

Directory

Directory

TRANSPORT

Having invested squillions into its public transport infrastructure, Singapore is without doubt the easiest city in Asia to get around. With a typical mixture of far-sighted social planning and authoritarianism, the government has built, and continues to extend, its Mass Rapid Transit (MRT) rail system and is improving its already excellent roads.

Traffic is minimal as the government controls private cars by a restrictive licensing system and prohibitive import duties that make owning a vehicle primarily a preserve for the rich. Cars entering the central business district (CBD) have to buy special licences.

For getting around, the pocket-size *TransitLink Guide* ($1.50 from MRT ticket offices), listing all bus and MRT rail routes, is a good investment if you will be regularly using public transport. Maps show the surrounding areas for all MRT stations, including bus stops. The *TransitLink Map* ($6) shows the whole island with numbered bus routes and MRT stations. Also turn to the MRT network map (p238) in this book.

SBS Transit (www.sbstransit.com.sg) is an excellent online resource that includes a very useful route planner.

AIR

Singapore's location and excellent facilities make it a natural choice as a major Southeast Asian aviation hub. As a result, cheap long-haul deals are often available. It is the base for four budget airlines, which offer amazingly cheap fares to many cities in the region.

Websites worth checking out for flights to Singapore include the following:

www.cheapestflights.co.uk This site really does post cheap flights (out of the UK only), but you have to get in early to get the bargains.

www.dialaflight.com This site offers worldwide flights out of Europe and the UK.

www.expedia.msn.com A good site for checking worldwide flight prices.

www.lastminute.com This site deals mainly in European flights but does have worldwide flights, mostly package returns.

www.statravel.com This is STA Travel's US website. There are also sites for the UK (www.statravel.co.uk) and Australia (www.statravel.com.au).

www.travel.com.au This is a good site for Australians to find cheap flights, although some prices may turn out to be too good to be true.

www.zuji.com.au This site offers good deals on a range of top-notch carriers, including Singapore Airlines.

www.travelonline.co.nz This is a good site for New Zealanders to find worldwide fares from their part of the world.

www.airtreks.com This American site is good for arranging round-the-world and circle Pacific fares.

Airlines

Following are some of the major airline offices in Singapore. Check the Business Yellow Pages for any that are not listed here.

Air New Zealand (Map pp234-5; ☎ 6532 3846; 24-07/08 Ocean Bldg, 10 Collyer Quay; Raffles Place MRT)

British Airways (Map pp226-7; ☎ 6589 7000; 06-05 Cairnhill Pl, 15 Cairnhill Rd; Orchard MRT)

Cathay Pacific Airways (Map pp234-5; ☎ 6533 1333; 16-01 Ocean Bldg, 10 Collyer Quay; Raffles Place MRT)

Garuda Indonesia (Map pp226-7; ☎ 6250 5666; 12-03 United Sq, 101 Thomson Rd; Novena MRT)

KLM-Royal Dutch Airlines (Map pp226-7; ☎ 6737 7622; 12-06 Ngee Ann City Tower, 391A Orchard Rd; Orchard MRT)

Lufthansa Airlines (Map pp226-7; ☎ 6835 5933; 05-01 Palais Renaissance, 390 Orchard Rd; Orchard MRT)

Malaysian Airlines (Map p230; ☎ 6336 6777; 02-09 Singapore Shopping Centre, 190 Clemenceau Ave; Dhoby Ghaut MRT)

Qantas Airways (Map pp226-7; ☎ 6589 7000; 06-05 Cairnhill Pl, 15 Cairnhill Rd; Orchard MRT)

Singapore Airlines (Map pp226-7; ☎ 6223 8888; Level 2, Paragon Bldg, Orchard Rd; Orchard MRT)

Thai Airways International (Map pp234-5; ☎ 1800 224 9977; The Globe, 100 Cecil St; Raffles Place MRT)

Following are the budget airlines operating in Singapore that, if they stay in business, will have revolutionised Asian travel. They are expanding their networks all the time, so check websites for details. Bookings are made almost entirely online, though

Air Asia tickets can also be bought at post offices. At the time of writing, Jetstar Asia and Valuair had merged, but it wasn't clear what form they were going to take in the future.

Air Asia (☎ 6733 9933; www.airasia.com)

Air Sahara (☎ 6557 4550; www.airsahara.net)

Jetstar Asia (☎ 6822 2288; www.jetstarasia.com)

Tiger Airways (☎ 6538 4437; www.tigerairways.com)

Valuair (☎ 6229 8338; www.valuair.com.sg)

Airports

Airport departure tax, or passenger service charge (PSC), from Changi is $21 and will be included in the cost of your air ticket.

CHANGI AIRPORT

Singapore is a good place to buy air tickets. Practically all international air traffic goes through **Singapore Changi Airport** (Map pp222-3; ☎ 6542 1122; www.changi.airport.com.sg).

Regularly voted the world's best airport, Changi is vast, efficient and amazingly well organised. Among its many facilities you'll find foreign exchange booths, a **post office** (⏲ 24hr), courtesy phones for local calls, free Internet access, **left-luggage facilities** (☎ 6214 0628; suitcase or backpack per 24hr $4.20; ⏲ 24hr), scores of shops, as well as restaurants, fitness centres, saunas, a swimming pool, showers, and business and medical centres (including one that is open 24 hours in the basement of Terminal 2).

Currently Changi has two terminals, of which Terminal 2 is the newer and handles most major international flights. A third terminal dedicated to budget airlines was set to open in 2006. On your way through the arrivals concourse, pick up the free booklets, maps and other guides (including the airport's own magazine) available from stands. Left luggage is in the basement of Terminal 1 and in the arrival hall of Terminal 2.

About 20km from the city centre, the airport is now served by the MRT. Changi Airport to City Hall is a bargain at $1.35 and takes 26 minutes with trains departing roughly every seven minutes.

The most convenient bus is the airport shuttle service – six-seater maxicabs that will take you to your hotel or anywhere in the CBD (adult/child $7/5). The shuttle operates daily from the arrivals halls of both terminals from 6am to midnight, departing every 15 minutes. Bookings can be made at the airport shuttle counters at the arrivals halls in both terminals and you pay the driver.

Public bus 36 leaves the airport for the city approximately every 10 minutes between 6am and midnight. You should have the right change ($2.50) when you board.

Taxis from the airport are subject to a surcharge of about $5 on top of the metered fare, which is around $12 to most places in the city centre. This supplementary charge only applies to taxis from the airport, not from the city.

There's also a limousine taxi service ($35) available between 6am and 2am to the CBD vicinity. You can choose between a Mercedes and a London cab.

SELETAR AIRPORT

The small, modern Seletar airport (Map pp222–3) is more used to corporate flyers and visiting luminaries. You may come here to catch the daily Berjaya Airways flights to Pulau Tioman in Malaysia.

Seletar is in the north of the island, and the easiest way to get there is to take a taxi for around $11; otherwise bus 103 will take you from Serangoon or outside the National Library to the gates of the Seletar Air Force base, from where you change to a local base bus to the airport terminal.

BICYCLE

If you can cope with the heat and sometimes fast-moving traffic, getting around Singapore by bicycle isn't too bad an idea. Cycling up to Changi Village and then taking the bike over to Pulau Ubin (or just hiring a bike on Ubin) is a very popular activity and there's a great mountain-bike track circling the base of the Bukit Timah Nature Reserve.

Hire

In the city centre you can hire bicycles from **Wheelpower Rent-a-Bike** (Map p232; ☎ 6238 2388; 01-09 Sunshine Plaza, 91 Bencoolen St; ⏲ 9.30am-7pm) for $10/28 per hour/day and **Treknology Bikes 3** (Map pp222-3; ☎ 6732 7119; www.treknology3.com; 01-02 Tanglin Pl, 91 Tanglin Rd; ⏲ 11am-7.30pm Mon-Sat, 11.30am-3.30pm Sun) for $35 per 24 hours. Treknology is also a good place to buy a bike.

Bikes can also be rented at several places along East Coast Parkway, on Sentosa Island and Pulau Ubin from $3.

BOAT

You can charter a bumboat (motorised sampan) to tour the Singapore River or to visit the islands around Singapore (see p48).

The big cruise centre at the World Trade Centre (WTC; Map p237), next to HarbourFront MRT station, is the main departure point for cruises and many ferries; a host of agents here handle bookings. Regular ferry services run from the WTC to Sentosa and the other southern island.

The Tanah Merah ferry terminal (Map pp222–3) south of Changi airport handles ferries to the Indonesian island of Bintan. To get to the Tanah Merah ferry terminal, take the MRT to Bedok and then bus 35. A taxi from the city is around $13.

Changi ferry terminal (Map pp222-3; ☎ 6546 8518) and the pier at Changi Village (Map pp222–3), both north of Changi airport, have ferries to Malaysia. Regular ferry services run from Changi Village to Pulau Ubin ($2). To get to Changi ferry terminal, take bus 2 to Changi Village, then walk.

Malaysia

For information on getting to Pulau Tioman, see p187.

TANJUNG BELUNGKOR

The ferry from Changi ferry terminal to Tanjung Belungkor, east of Johor Bahru, is primarily a service for Singaporeans going to Desaru in Malaysia. The 11km journey takes 45 minutes and costs $16/22 one way/return. There are four services daily in each direction. From the Tanjung Belungkor jetty, buses operate to Desaru and Kota Tinggi.

PENGERANG

From Changi Village, ferries go to Pengerang, an interesting back-door route into Malaysia. There's no fixed schedule; ferries leave throughout the day when a full quota of 12 people is reached. The cost is $10 per person or $60 for the whole boat. The best time to catch one is early in the morning before 8am. Clear Singapore immigration at the ferry terminal.

Indonesia

No direct ferries run between Singapore and the main ports in Indonesia, but it is possible to travel between the two countries via the islands in the nearby Riau Archipelago. Most services run to Pulau Batam (p191) and Pulau Bintan (p188) from Tanah Merah ferry terminal. Upon arrival, most nationalities are issued a tourist pass for Indonesia, valid for 60 days, and do not require a visa. The ferries are modern and fast as well as air-conditioned. From Batam, boats go to Sumatra, a popular way to enter Indonesia.

BUS

Singapore's extensive bus service should be the envy of the world. You rarely have to wait more than a few minutes for a bus, and they will take you almost anywhere you want to go. Some even have TVs.

Bus fares start from 60¢ (air-conditioned buses are 70¢) for roughly the first 3.2km, rising to a maximum of $1.20 ($1.50 air-con). There are also a few flat-rate buses. When you board the bus, drop the exact money into the fare box, as no change is given.

Ez-link cards can be used on all buses. Just tap it on the reader as you board, and again when you get off.

Tourist Buses

The SIA Hop-On, run by Singapore Airlines, passes Orchard Rd, Bugis Junction, Suntec City, the Colonial District, Clarke Quay, Boat Quay, Chinatown and the Botanic Gardens. It operates daily (every 30 minutes) between 9am and 6pm and runs on a continuous loop. It's free if you are on a 'Singapore stopover holiday' (show your SSH identification card); it costs $3 for passengers on either Singapore Airlines or Silk Air (show your ticket or boarding card). Other passengers pay $6/4 per adult/child for an all-day pass. Tickets can be bought from the bus driver, hotels or Singapore Airlines offices. Or call ☎ 6734 9923 for bookings.

The **Singapore Trolley** (☎ 6339 6833) is a red bus made up to look like an old-fashioned tram. Its route takes in Orchard Rd, the Colonial District, Clarke Quay, Marina Centre and Suntec City. Fares are $9/7 per adult/child for an all-day ticket.

CityBuzz gives you a chance to explore the city on your own without lagging behind a tour operator and dozens of tourists. For $5, CityBuzz double-decker buses give an unlimited tour of the city, stopping at key attractions like Orchard Rd, Little India, Chinatown, Clarke Quay, Kampong Glam and

Suntec City. Tickets are available at TransitLink, Singapore Visitors Centre offices and authorised agents. The bus operates every 10 to 15 minutes between 10am and 10pm.

Malaysia

For information on getting to Johor Bahru, see p184; for Pulau Tioman, see p187. If travelling beyond Johor Bahru, it's easier to get a long-distance bus straight from Singapore; there's a greater variety of bus services from Johor Bahru and cheaper fares.

In Singapore, long-distance buses to Melaka and the east coast of Malaysia leave from and arrive at the **Lavender St bus terminal** (Map p232; cnr Lavender St & Kallang Bahru). Take the MRT to Lavender, then bus 5 or 61; or it's a 500m walk from the MRT station.

From here, **Transnasional** (☎ 6294 7034) has services to Kuala Lumpur ($15), Mersing ($11.10), Kuantan ($16.50) and Kota Bharu ($35.10). Both **Hasry** (☎ 6294 9306; www.hasryexpress.com) and **Melaka-Singapore Express** (☎ 6293 5915) run regular services to Melaka ($11) taking around four hours.

For destinations north of Kuala Lumpur, most buses leave from the **Golden Mile Complex** (Map p232; Beach Rd). This terminal handles buses to Thailand, and northern destinations on the way such as Ipoh, Butterworth and Penang. Bus agents line the outside of the building; **Gunung Raya** (☎ 6294 7711; www.gunungraya.com) is one of the biggest.

Thailand

The main terminal for buses to and from Thailand is at the **Golden Mile Complex** (Map p232; Beach Rd). Among the travel agents specialising in buses and tours to Thailand are **Grassland Express** (☎ 6292 1166), with buses to Hat Yai ($42); **Phya Travel** (☎ 6294 5415) and **Kwang Chow Travel** (☎ 6293 8977), both with bus services to Hat Yai and Bangkok (around $70). Most buses leave around 6.30pm and travel overnight.

CAR & MOTORCYCLE

Singaporeans drive on the left-hand side of the road and it is compulsory to wear seat belts in the front and back of the car. Unlike in most Asian countries, traffic is orderly, but the profusion of one-way streets and streets that change names (sometimes several times) can make driving difficult for the uninitiated. The *Singapore Street Directory* is essential for negotiating the city.

Driving

If you plan on driving in Singapore, bring your current home driver's licence and an international driving permit issued by a motoring association in your country.

Hire

If you want a car for local driving only, many of the smaller rental operators quote slightly cheaper rates than the major companies. Rental rates are more expensive than in Malaysia – if you intend driving from Singapore to Malaysia and spending time there, it will be better to rent your car in Johor Bahru.

Rates start from around $150 a day, while a collision damage waiver will cost about $20 per day for a small car such as a Toyota Ford Laser or Mitsubishi Lancer. Special deals may be available, especially for longer-term rental. There are hire booths at Singapore Changi Airport as well as in the city. Contact details for the major companies include the following:

Avis (Map pp224-5; ☎ 6737 1668; www.avis.com.sg; 392 Havelock Rd, 01-07; Clarke Quay MRT)

Budget Rent a Car (Map pp234-5; ☎ 6532 4442; 26-01A Clifford Centre, 24 Raffles Pl; Raffles Place MRT)

Hertz Rent-a-Car (Map pp226-7; ☎ 6734 4646; 15 Scotts Rd, 01-01 Thong Teck Bldg; Orchard MRT)

Thrifty (Map p230; ☎ 6338 7900; 80 Middle Rd; Bugis MRT)

Parking

Parking in many places in Singapore is operated by a coupon system. You can buy a booklet of coupons at parking kiosks and post offices; display them in your window.

Restricted Zone

From 7.30am to 6.30pm weekdays, as well as from 10.15am through to 2pm Saturdays, the area comprising the CBD, Chinatown and Orchard Rd is considered a restricted zone. Cars are free to enter as long as drivers pay a surcharge. Vehicles are automatically tracked by sensors on overhanging gantries that prompt drivers to insert a cash card into their in-vehicle unit, which then extracts the appropriate toll. The same system is also in operation on certain major highways. Rental cars are subject to the same rules.

Anyone who does not pay the entry toll is automatically photographed and fined.

MASS RAPID TRANSIT (MRT)

The superb MRT subway system is the easiest, quickest and most comfortable way to get around. It operates from 6am to midnight, with trains at peak times running every three minutes, and off-peak every six minutes. For a map of the system, see p238.

Most of the MRT track runs underground in the inner-city area, emerging overground out towards the suburban housing estates. It has three lines: North South, North East and East West. Construction of a new Circle Line is expected to be finished by 2009.

Fares

Single-trip tickets cost from 80¢ to $1.80, but it's cheaper and more convenient to buy an ez-link card from any MRT station ($15, including $8 credit). A birth certificate or passport (photocopy or original is accepted) must be shown when purchasing a child ez-link card ($8). These cards can be used on all public buses and can be topped up using the ticket machines in MRT stations. Fares with an ez-link card range from 60¢ to $1.65. Otherwise, you have to buy a single trip ticket every time you make an MRT journey, then get your $1 refund at the other end.

TAXI

Singapore has close on 19,000 taxis, but in the city it can often be hard to find one. Major cab companies are **City Cab** (☎ 6552 2222), **Comfort** (☎ 6552 1111), **Premier** (☎ 6363 6888), **Smart** (☎ 6485 7777) and **TIBS** (☎ 6555 8888). Fares start from $2.10 (TIBS off peak) and $2.40 (other companies) for the first kilometre, then 10¢ for each additional 220m. There are various surcharges to note:

Overnight From 11.30pm to 6am, surcharge rises incrementally from 10% to 50% of the metered fare.

Peak hour Surcharge of $1 between 7.30am and 9.30am and 5pm and 8pm.

From the airport A $5 surcharge from 5pm to midnight Friday to Sunday, $3 all other times.

Bookings $2.50 for off-peak telephone bookings, $4 for peak-hour bookings (less than an hour before needed). For advance bookings you'll pay $5 to $5.20.

To/from the CBD Surcharge of $1 on all trips from the CBD between 4.30pm and 7pm on weekdays and from 11.30am to 2pm Saturdays. You may also have to pay another surcharge if you take the taxi into the CBD during restricted hours (see Restricted Zone, p197).

Credit-card payment Add 10% to the fare.

You can flag down a taxi any time. Also look out for the special taxi stands (they have signs) where you can queue. Ordering a taxi by phone is a computerised process that is usually extremely efficient. After telling the operator your name and location, you will be transferred to an automatic message that gives you the numberplate of your designated cab. All you need to do then is wait and watch for the cab with this numberplate.

Share taxis to Malaysia are also available (see Excursions, p184).

TRAIN

Malaysia & Thailand

Singapore is the southern termination point for the Malaysian railway system, **Keretapi Tanah Malayu** (KTM; www.ktmb.com.my). Malaysia has two main rail lines: the primary line going from Singapore to Kuala Lumpur, Butterworth, Alor Setar and then into Thailand; and a second line branching off at Gemas and going right up through the centre of the country to Tumpat, near Kota Bharu on the east coast.

There is a booking office is located at **Singapore railway station** (Map pp234-5; ☎ 6222 5165; Keppel Rd; 🕑 8.30am-2pm & 3-7pm).

Three express trains depart every day to Kuala Lumpur (1st/2nd/3rd class $68/34/19), roughly around 8am, 3pm and 10pm, passing through Johor Bahru en route; check the website or call the booking office for the exact times. The journey takes around seven hours. There are three daily services to Gemas, Kluang and Gua Musang (on the east-coast line to Tumpat). There's also an express train to the far northeastern town of Tumpat (1st/2nd/3rd class $51/41/32), the *Express Timuran*, at 8.20pm, which reaches Jerantut at 3.40am for Taman Negara National Park.

The luxurious **Eastern & Oriental Express** (☎ 6392 3500; www.orient-express.com) departs on alternate Wednesdays, Fridays and Sundays. The sumptuous antique train takes 42 hours to do the 1943km journey from Singapore to Bangkok. Don your linen suit, sip a gin and tonic, and dig deep for the fare: from $3030 per person in a double compartment to $6140 in the presidential suite.

PRACTICALITIES

ACCOMMODATION

In this guide, we have grouped accommodation according to district, then listed midrange and top-end hotels alphabetically, followed by a separate section for Cheap Sleeps. There aren't really noticeable peak or low seasons in Singapore and seasons don't affect accommodation prices. June, July and December see small peaks in arrival numbers, but it doesn't affect prices or availability of rooms. For information on price ranges, checking-in times, reservations and special deals, see p164.

Booking Services

There are dozens of booking services that save you the trouble of trawling through brochures and hotel websites. They include the following:

AsiaBestHotel.com (www.asiabesthotel.com)

AsiaRooms.com (www.asiarooms.com)

Hotels.online Singapore (www.hotels.online.com.sg)

Bookings (www.bookings.net)

Wotif.com (www.wotif.com)

Rental

Probably the best place to start looking for long-term rental in Singapore is **Singapore Expats** (www.singaporeexpats.com), which has detailed information on the different districts, outlines the whole rental procedure and carries an apartment search engine.

BUSINESS HOURS

In Singapore, government offices are usually open from Monday to Friday and Saturday morning. Hours tend to vary, starting at around 7.30am to 9.30am and closing between 4pm and 6pm. On Saturday, closing time is between 11.30am and 1pm.

Shop hours vary. Small shops generally open from 10am to 6pm weekdays, while department stores and large shopping centres open from 10am to 9pm or 9.30pm, seven days a week. Most small shops in Chinatown and Arab St close on Sunday, though Sunday is the busiest shopping day in Little India.

Banks are open from 9.30am to 3pm weekdays (to 11.30am Saturday), while top restaurants open at lunchtime and in the evenings. Bar opening hours vary widely.

CHILDREN

Singapore is a safe, healthy and fun country for children. In addition, Singaporean society is very family-oriented; eating out as a family is considered a normal thing to do and hotels are usually able to provide family rooms, extra beds or cots. Lonely Planet's *Travel with Children* by Cathy Lanigan is packed with useful information for family travel.

For things to see and do, see p50.

Baby-sitting

The **YMCA Metropolitan** (Map pp226-7; ☎ 6839 8385; www.mymca.org.sg; 60 Stevens Rd) runs a crèche that's open to anyone with children on weekdays from 7am to 1pm ($15 per child). For all other times, the best option is to ask your hotel to arrange baby-sitting for you.

Also check out **Gymboree Play & Music** (Map pp226-7; 03-17/18 Tanglin Mall, 163 Tanglin Rd), a playgroup with classes daily for kids from birth up to four years old. A trial class is $30.90 per child.

CLIMATE

Singapore is hot and humid all year round and though it gets regular rainfall, it's usually in the form of heavy tropical showers that last an hour or two and leave clear skies behind them. There's little distinction between seasons (see p8).

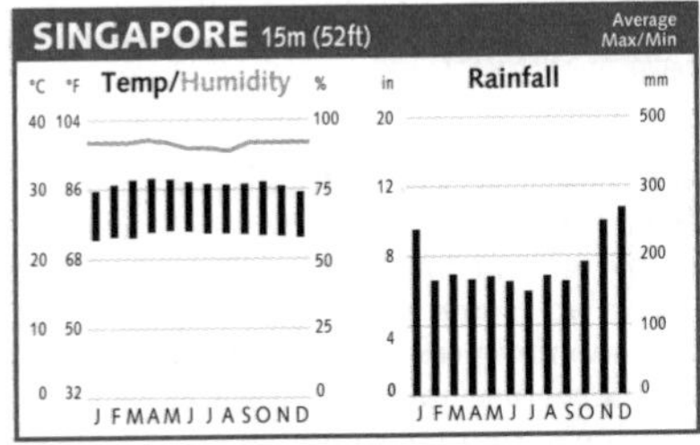

COURSES

Singaporeans are mad on courses, but that is because their town councils provide them at subsidised rates to citizens or permanent residents. For visitors, the most popular short-term courses are in cookery (see p33).

CUSTOMS

Visitors to Singapore are allowed to bring in 1L of wine, beer or spirits duty-free. Electronic goods, cosmetics, watches, cameras, jewellery (but not imitation jewellery), footwear, toys, arts and crafts are not dutiable; the usual duty-free concession for personal effects, such as clothes, applies. Singapore does not allow duty-free concessions for cigarettes and tobacco. Importing chewing gum is banned.

Duty-free concessions are not available if you are arriving in Singapore from Malaysia or if you leave Singapore for less than 48 hours.

Fire crackers, toy currency and coins, obscene or seditious material, gun-shaped cigarette lighters, endangered species or their by-products, and pirated recordings and publications are prohibited. The importation or exportation of illegal drugs carries the death penalty for more than 15g of heroin, 30g of morphine or cocaine, 1.2kg of opium, 500g of cannabis, 200g of cannabis resin, 1000g of cannabis mixture or 250g of methamphetamine. Trafficking in ecstasy (more than 150 tablets) carries a penalty of 30 years' jail and 15 strokes of the *rotan* (a cane made of rattan).

Penalties for trafficking in lesser amounts range from two years in jail and two strokes of the *rotan* to 30 years and 15 strokes of the *rotan*. If you bring in prescription drugs, you should have a doctor's letter or a prescription confirming that they're necessary.

There is no restriction on the importation of currency.

DISABLED TRAVELLERS

If you're confined to a wheelchair, travelling around Singapore will be a chore. There are some ramps leading to hotels and shopping centres, but no coordinated infrastructure to speak of. The sight or hearing impaired should have an easier time. Check out *Access Singapore*, a useful guidebook by the Disabled Persons Association of Singapore, it can be found online at www.dpa.org.sg/DPA/access/contents.htm. The booklet is also available from STB offices (see p205) or from the **National Council of Social Services** (☎ 6210 2500; www.ncss.org.sg).

ELECTRICITY

Electricity supplies are dependable and run at 220V to 240V and 50 cycles. Plugs are of the three-pronged, square-pin type used in the UK.

EMBASSIES

For a list of Singaporean missions abroad, check out www.visitsingapore.com/index_main.html, where you'll also find a full list of foreign embassies and consulates in Singapore. Contact details for some foreign embassies and consulates include the following:

Australia (Map pp226-7; ☎ 6836 4100; www.singapore.embassy.gov.au; 25 Napier Rd; Orchard MRT)

Canada (Map pp234-5; ☎ 6325 3200; www.cic.gc.ca; IBM Towers, 80 Anson Rd; Tanjong Pagar MRT)

China (Map pp226-7; ☎ 6471 2117; www.chinaembassy.org.sg; 150 Tanglin Rd; Orchard MRT)

France (Map pp224-5; ☎ 6880 7800; www.france.org.sg; 101-103 Cluny Park Rd; Newton MRT)

Germany (Map pp226-7; ☎ 6737 1355; www.singapur.diplo.de; 14-01 Far East Shopping Centre, 545 Orchard Rd; Orchard MRT)

India (Map pp226-7; ☎ 6737 6777; www.embassyofindia.com; 31 Grange Rd; Orchard MRT)

Indonesia (Map pp226-7; ☎ 6737 7422; 7 Chatsworth Rd; Orchard MRT)

Japan (Map pp226-7; ☎ 6235 8855; www.sg.emb-japan.go.jp; 16 Nassim Rd; Orchard MRT)

Malaysia (Map p230; ☎ 6235 0111; fax 6733 6135; 301 Jervois Rd; City Hall MRT)

New Zealand (Map pp226-7; ☎ 6235 9966; www.nzembassy.com; 15-06/10 Ngee Ann City, 391A Orchard Rd; Somerset MRT)

Thailand (Map pp226-7; ☎ 6737 2644; fax 6732 0778; 370 Orchard Rd; Orchard MRT)

UK (Map pp226-7; ☎ 6424 4200; www.britain.org.sg; 100 Tanglin Rd; Orchard MRT)

USA (Map pp226-7; ☎ 6476 9100; http://singapore.usembassy.gov; 27 Napier Rd; Orchard MRT)

EMERGENCY

Useful emergency numbers include **fire/ambulance** (☎ 995) and **police** (☎ 999).

GAY & LESBIAN TRAVELLERS

Although you're perfectly free to be homosexual in Singapore, homosexual sex is illegal and you can be sentenced to between 10 years and life if you're caught in the act. Though there are an increasing number of gay bars in the city (see p125), the government's ban on gay parties has sent a strong signal that talk of the country's gay renaissance was a touch premature.

A good place to start looking for information is on the websites of **Utopia** (www.utopia-asia.com) or **Fridae** (www.fridae.com), which provide excellent coverage of gay and lesbian events and activities across Asia. Gay men can also check out www.sgboy.com for local happenings and hang-outs.

Singaporeans are quite conservative about displays of public affection; women and straight Indian men can get away with same-sex handholding, but an overtly gay couple doing the same would attract disapproving attention.

HEALTH

As well as being a healthy place, Singapore has excellent facilities (see Medical Services, p203) that draw 'Medical Tourists' in their thousands, seeking everything from basic check-ups to surgical procedures and cosmetic surgery. For a complete rundown on what's available, see www.singaporemedicine.com.

On a day-to-day basis, you shouldn't encounter any major health problems. Hygiene is strictly observed and the tap water is safe to drink. However, hepatitis A does occur. You only need vaccinations if you come from a yellow fever area. Singapore is not a malarial zone but dengue fever is an increasing concern.

Lonely Planet's *Healthy Travel: Asia & India* is a handy pocket size and packed with useful information including pre-trip planning, emergency first aid, immunisation and disease information, and what to do if you get sick on the road. *Travel with Children* from Lonely Planet also includes advice on travel health for younger children.

Medical Problems & Treatment

Self-diagnosis and treatment can be risky, so you should always seek medical help. Singapore has superior medical facilities, and an embassy, consulate or five-star hotel can usually recommend a local doctor or clinic. Singapore has many pharmacies (see the Yellow Pages).

Dengue Fever

Singapore, like most countries where dengue is endemic, has suffered a sharp rise in cases of this nasty viral disease. Spread by day-biting *Aedes aegypti* mosquitoes – recognisable by their black-and-white striped bodies – it is characterised by sudden high fever, extremely painful joint pains (hence its old name 'breakbone fever'), headache, nausea and vomiting, which peaks and settles after a few days, after which a rash often spreads across the body. The illness usually disappears after 10 years, but the resulting weakness can take months to recover from. The biggest danger is dengue haemorrhagic fever, which causes internal bleeding and can be fatal. If you suspect dengue, seek medical treatment immediately.

Heat Exhaustion

In constantly hot Singapore it is important to avoid dehydration, which can lead to heat exhaustion. Take time to acclimatise to high temperatures; drink sufficient liquids and do not do anything too physically demanding. Salt deficiency, another cause of dehydration, is characterised by fatigue, lethargy, headaches, giddiness and muscle cramps; salt tablets may help, but adding extra salt to your food is better.

Hepatitis A

Hepatitis A can be found in Singapore and is transmitted through contaminated food and drinking water. Symptoms include fever, chills, headache, fatigue, feelings of weakness, and aches and pains, followed by loss of appetite, nausea, vomiting, abdominal pain, dark urine, light-coloured faeces, jaundiced (yellow) skin and yellowing of the whites of the eyes. People who have had hepatitis should avoid alcohol for some time after the illness, as the liver needs time to recover.

You should seek medical advice, but there is not much you can do apart from resting, drinking lots of fluids, eating lightly and avoiding fatty foods.

The hepatitis A vaccine (eg Avaxim, Havrix 1440 or VAQTA) provides long-term immunity (possibly more than 10 years) after an initial injection and a booster after six to 12 months.

Prickly Heat

This is an itchy rash caused by excessive perspiration trapped under the skin. It usually strikes people who have just arrived in a hot climate. Keep cool, bathe often, dry the skin and use a mild talcum or prickly heat powder, or resort to air-conditioning.

Sunburn

In the tropics you can get sunburnt surprisingly quickly, even through cloud. Use a sunscreen, a hat (or umbrella), and a barrier cream for your nose and lips. Calamine lotion or a commercial after-sun preparation is good for mild sunburn. Protect your eyes with good-quality sunglasses.

HOLIDAYS

Public Holidays

Listed are public holidays in Singapore. For those days not based on the Western calendar, the months they are likely to fall in are provided. The only holiday that has a major effect on the city is Chinese New Year, when virtually all shops shut down for two days.

New Year's Day 1 January

Chinese New Year January/February (two days)

Hari Raya Haji February/March

Good Friday April

Labour Day 1 May

Vesak Day May

National Day 9 August

Deepavali November

Hari Raya Pusa December

Christmas Day 25 December

School Holidays

If you want to avoid crowded shopping malls, theatres, theme parks, zoos and other attractions you might want to avoid Singapore school holidays. There are two long breaks; the first is a four-week break in June (roughly 1–25 June) and the second is usually the entire month of December.

INTERNET ACCESS

If you plan to carry your notebook or palmtop computer with you, Singapore uses the three-pronged, square-pin plugs used in the UK.

Every top hotel has Internet access and will help get you set up if you bring your own laptop or palmtop computer. The newer backpacker hostels all offer free Internet access.

Most PCs – and all Macs – have suitable global modems these days and Singapore's island-wide broadband network means you don't have to worry about bringing the right kind of telephone socket. If you need dial-up Internet access, ensure that you have at least a US RJ-11 telephone adaptor that works with your modem. You can almost always find an adaptor that will convert from RJ-11 to the local variety.

For wireless access, Singapore has a network of more than 500 wireless hotspots. See www.wi-fihotspotsdirectory.com for details.

If you intend to rely on Internet cafés, you'll need your incoming (POP or IMAP) mail server name, your account name and your password. Your Internet Service Provider (ISP) or network supervisor will be able to give you these. If you are planning on staying a while, you may want to consider taking out an Internet account with a local ISP; SingTel and StarHub are the two biggest operators.

There are numerous outlets where you can access the Internet in Singapore (from around $5 per hour), though it's worth noting that Chinatown has virtually none. Try the following:

Book Cafe (Map pp224-5; ☎ 6887 5430; 01-02 Seng Kee Bldg, 20 Martin Rd; 8.30am-10.30pm Sun-Thu, 8.30am-1.30pm Fri & Sat; bus 54 from Clarke Quay MRT)

Chills Cafe (Map p230; 01-07 Stamford House, 39 Stamford Rd; 9.30am-midnight; City Hall MRT)

Cyber-Action (Map p232; 01-06 Burlington Sq, 17 Bencoolen St; 10am-9.30pm; Bugis MRT)

Cyberstar ComCentre (Map p230; 15 Beach Rd; 24hr)

I-Surf (Map pp226-7; 02-20, Far-East Shopping Centre, Orchard Rd; 9am-9pm)

Mega Cybernet (Map pp234-5; 04-16 Pearl Centre, 100 Eu Tong Sen St; 11am-11.30pm; Outram Park MRT)

Selegie Cyber (Map p232; 185 Selegie Rd; 10am-midnight; Little India MRT)

LEGAL MATTERS

With Singapore's reputation for harsh laws, many visitors are surprised by the lack of police presence on the streets (though this may change, since Singapore considers itself a target for 'terrorism'). Don't be fooled; if you get caught doing something you shouldn't, don't expect any special treatment just because you are foreign. Police have broad powers and you would be unwise to refuse any requests they make of you. You will be treated well, entitled to legal counsel and contact with your embassy, but the law will treat you harshly.

MAPS

Various maps, many in Japanese as well as English, are available free at tourist offices, the airport on arrival, and at some accommodations and shopping centres. The *Official Map of Singapore*, available free from the Singapore Tourism Board (STB) as well as hotels everywhere, is very good and very easy to follow. Of the commercial maps, Nelles and Periplus maps are good. The *Mighty Minds Singapore Street Directory* ($11.90) is superb and essential if you plan to drive. Also check out Lonely Planet's *Singapore City Map*, a durable, full-colour, laminated fold-out map with a full index of streets and sights.

MEDICAL SERVICES

Singapore's medical institutions are first-rate and generally a lot cheaper than in the West. The medical tourism industry pulls in an estimated $500 million a year. Needless to say, it helps to have insurance cover. Check with insurance providers what treatments and procedures are covered before you leave home.

Alexandra Hospital (☎ 6472 2000; www.alexhosp.com.sg; 378 Alexandra Rd)

KK Women's and Children's Hospital (☎ 6293 4044; www.kkh.com.sg; 100 Bukit Timah Rd)

National University Hospital (☎ 6779 5555; www.nuh.com.sg; 5 Lower Kent Ridge Rd)

Raffles SurgiCentre (Map p232; ☎ 6334 3337; www.raffleshospital.com; 585 North Bridge Rd; 24hr; Bugis MRT) A walk-in clinic.

Singapore General Hospital Accident & Emergency Department (Map pp234-5; ☎ 6321 4311; Outram Rd; 24hr; Outram Park MRT) Located in Block 1 of this big compound.

MONEY

The unit of currency is the Singapore dollar, locally referred to as the 'singdollar', which is made up of 100 cents. Singapore uses 5¢, 10¢, 20¢, 50¢ and $1 coins, while notes come in denominations of $2, $5, $10, $50, $100, $500 and $1000. Singapore also has a $10,000 note – not that you'll see many. The Singapore dollar is, not surprisingly, a highly stable and freely convertible currency. Also see Economy & Costs, p18.

ATMs

Most ATMs will accept Visa, MasterCard and cards with Plus or Cirrus. ATMs can be found in most large shopping centres and MRT stations.

Changing Money

Banks can be found all over the city. Exchange rates tend to vary from bank to bank and some even have a service charge on each exchange transaction – this is usually $2 to $3, but can be more, so ask first. Most banks are open from 9.30am to 3pm Monday to Friday, and to 11.30am Saturday.

Moneychangers do not charge fees, so you will often get a better overall exchange rate for cash and travellers cheques with them than at the banks. You'll find moneychangers in just about every shopping centre in Singapore. Most shops accept foreign cash and travellers cheques at a slightly lower rate than you'd get from a moneychanger.

Apart from changing other currencies to Singapore dollars, moneychangers also sell a wide variety of other currencies and will do amazing multiple-currency transactions in the blink of an eye.

Credit Cards

Major credit cards are widely accepted. The tourism authorities suggest that if shops insist on adding a credit card surcharge (which they should not do), you should contact the relevant credit company in Singapore. Most hotels and car-hire companies will insist on a credit card and may demand full payment upfront without one. Credit card companies in Singapore include the following:

American Express (☎ 6299 8133)

Diners Club (☎ 6294 4222)

JCB (☎ 6734 0096)

MasterCard & Visa (☎ 1800 345 1345)

NEWSPAPERS & MAGAZINES

English dailies in Singapore include the *Straits Times* (which includes the *Sunday Times*), the *Business Times,* the afternoon tabloid *New Paper,* and *Today,* a free paper available at the MRT stations.

The *Straits Times* has something of a stuffy image, which it's trying hard to shake off, but its coverage of Asian and other international news is good and it's by far the best-selling paper in Singapore. A long way behind in circulation and seriousness, but a lot more fun, is the *New Paper*, which offers mildly sensationalised local scandals, gossip and general seaminess, but is often the first to break local stories. If you're into English football, the *New Paper* coverage is obsessively detailed (they devoted 16 pages to a single Arsenal–Manchester United match).

Today looks like a dog's breakfast, but it is a little freer in its criticism and frequently publishes opinions you wouldn't see in other papers.

The foreign media sometimes doesn't know its limits and several have found to their cost that the government will quickly restrict the circulation of foreign publications that do not report to their liking. Nevertheless, many foreign magazines are readily available. Pornographic publications are strictly prohibited, though *Cosmopolitan* and racy lads' magazines like *FHM*, *Ralph* and the locally-produced *Maxim* are allowed.

POST

Postal delivery in Singapore is very efficient. Most post offices are open 8am to 6pm Monday to Friday, and 8am to 2pm Saturday. Call ☎ 1605 to find the nearest branch or check www.singpost.com.sg.

Letters addressed to 'Poste Restante' are held at the **Singapore Post Centre** (Map p236; ☎ 6741 8857; 10 Eunos Rd), which is next to the Paya Lebar MRT. Handy central branches include **Comcentre** (Map pp226-7; 31 Exeter Rd), and **Orchard** (Map pp226-7; 04-15 Takashimaya, Ngee Ann City, 391 Orchard Rd). Terminals 1 and 2 at Changi airport (Map pp222–3) also have branches open 8am to 9pm daily.

Airmail postcards and aerograms cost 50¢ to anywhere in the world. Letters cost 70¢ to $1.

RADIO

The Media Corporation of Singapore (MediaCorp) runs the largest radio network, with 12 local and four international radio stations. It has five English-language stations: Gold 90.5FM, Symphony 92.4FM, NewsRadio 93.8FM, Class 95FM and Perfect 10 98.7FM. International Channel 96.3FM, also run by Mediacorp, specialises in French, German and Japanese programmes. Private stations include Passion 99.5FM, which is an arts and world music station; and Safra Radio's English-language Power 98FM, a 24-hour station aimed at the 18- to 35-year-old market. The BBC broadcasts on 88.9FM.

Most of the island's radio stations have Web streaming if you want to get a taste before you come. For iPod owners, www.podcast.net lists dozens of private broadcasters. One of the most popular commentaries is 'the mrbrown show'.

TELEPHONE

You can make local and international calls from public phone booths. International calls can be made from booths at the Comcentre (Map pp226–7) 24 hours a day, and at selected post offices. Most phone booths take phonecards and some take credit cards, although there are still booths around that take coins. For enquiries, see www.singtel.com. Local phonecards are widely available from 7-Eleven stores, post offices, Telecom centres, stationers and bookshops, and come in denominations of $2, $5, $10, $20 and $50.

Singapore also has credit-card phones – just swipe your AmEx, Diners Club, MasterCard or Visa card through the slot. At the SingTel centres, there are also Home Country Direct phones – press a country button to contact the operator and reverse the charges, or have the call charged to an international telephone card acceptable in your country. The Home Country Direct service is available from any phone by dialling the appropriate code that is listed in the front pages of the phone book.

Useful numbers include the following:

Directory information (☎ 100)

Flight information (☎ 1800 542 4422)

STB 24-hour Touristline (☎ 1800 736 2000)

From public phones, local calls cost 10¢ for three minutes. There are no area codes within Singapore; telephone numbers are eight digits unless you are calling toll-free (☎ 1800).

To call Singapore from overseas, dial your country's international access number and then ☎ 65, Singapore's country code, before entering the eight-digit telephone number.

Calls to Malaysia are considered to be STD (trunk or long-distance) calls. Dial the access code ☎ 020, followed by the area code of the town in Malaysia that you wish to call (minus the leading zero) and then your party's number. Thus, for a call to ☎ 346 7890 in Kuala Lumpur (area code ☎ 03) you would dial ☎ 020-3-346 7890. Call ☎ 104 for assistance with Malaysian area codes.

Mobile Phones

In Singapore, mobile phone numbers start with ☎ 9. As long as you have arranged to have 'global roaming' facilities with your home provider, your GSM digital phone will automatically tune into one of Singapore's two digital networks, MI-GSM or ST-GSM. There is complete coverage over the whole island and phones will also work in the underground sections of the MRT rail network. Rates are variable but quite reasonable compared with other countries in the region.

From post offices and 7-Eleven stores it's also possible to buy SIM cards for one of the three local mobile phone services (SingTel, StarHub and M1), from $20 per card.

TELEVISION

The Media Corporation of Singapore (MediaCorp) is the country's largest terrestrial broadcaster, operating five free-to-air channels: Channel 5 (English); Channel 8 (Mandarin); Suria (Malay language programmes); Central (the arts channel in English, plus a section of children's programming and Indian language broadcasts); and **Channel News Asia** (CNA; www.channelnewsasia.com), a news and information channel.

TIME

Singapore is eight hours ahead of GMT/UTC (London), two hours behind Australian Eastern Standard Time (Sydney and Melbourne), 13 hours ahead of American Eastern Standard Time (New York) and 16 hours ahead of American Pacific Standard Time (San Francisco and Los Angeles). So, when it is noon in Singapore, it is 8pm in Los Angeles and 11pm in New York the previous day, 4am in London and 2pm in Sydney.

TIPPING

Tipping is not usual in Singapore. The most expensive hotels and restaurants have a 10% service charge, in which case tipping is discouraged. Don't tip at hawker stalls or coffee shops, or in taxis (though drivers won't discourage you!).

TOILETS

It will come as no surprise that Singapore's public toilets are widely distributed and immaculate, even those in public parks and train stations. Many places, the zoo for example, even have the latest ultra-fancy 'outdoor' designs. Occasionally you'll need to pay 10¢ to use them – particularly at hawker centres.

TOURIST INFORMATION

Before your trip, the best place to check for information is the website of the **Singapore Tourism Board** (www.visitsingapore.com).

In Singapore, there are several tourism offices offering a wide range of services, including tour bookings and event ticketing:

Liang Court Tourist Service Centre (Map p230; ☎ 6336 7184; Level 1, Liang Court Shopping Centre, 177 River Valley Rd; 🕑 10am-10pm; Clarke Quay MRT)

Singapore Visitors Centre @ Orchard (Map pp226-7; ☎ 1800 736 2000; 1 Orchard Spring Lane; 🕑 8am-10.30pm; Orchard MRT)

Singapore Visitors Centre @ Little India (Map p232; ☎ 6296 4280; 73 Dunlop St, InnCrowd Backpackers Hostel; 🕑 10am-10pm; Little India MRT)

Suntec City Visitors Centre (Map p230; ☎ 1800 332 5066; 01-35/37/39/41 Suntec City Mall, 3 Temasek Blvd; 🕑 10am-6pm; City Hall MRT)

VISAS

Citizens of British Commonwealth countries (except India) and citizens of the Republic of Ireland, Liechtenstein, Monaco, the Netherlands, San Marino, Switzerland and the USA do not require visas to visit Singapore. Citizens of Austria, Belgium, Denmark, Finland, France, Germany, Iceland, Italy, Japan, Korea, Luxembourg, Norway, Spain and Sweden do not require visas for stays of up to 90 days for social purposes.

You'll be given a 30-day visitor's visa if you arrive by air and a 14-day visa if you are arriving by land or sea. Extensions can be applied for at the **Immigration Department** (Map p232; ☎ 6391 6100; 10 Kallang Rd; Lavender MRT).

WOMEN TRAVELLERS

Singapore is probably the safest Asian country in which to travel and sexual harassment is very rare – though we recommend that women avoid Little India in the evenings at weekends. Women are not cloistered in Singaporean society and enjoy much more freedom and equality than in the rest of Asia. Government policy favours sexual equality, and abortion is available on request, though not for 'foreign' (non-Singaporean) citizens.

WORK

Work opportunities for foreigners are limited. While Singapore does have a fairly large expatriate European community, this is more a reflection of the large representation of overseas companies than a shortage of skills in the local labour market. However, the vacancies pages of the *Straits Times* are crammed with job notices.

In the great majority of cases, foreign workers obtain employment before they come to Singapore. One of the main reasons for this is the high cost of accommodation and car ownership, which overseas companies normally cover. The overwhelming majority of locally available positions are for domestic servants and unskilled labourers.

Some foreigners arrive in Singapore and find work. Business experience, economic training and easily marketable job skills are your best bet. Some travellers have picked up temporary work as waiters. Finally, check out **Contact Singapore** (www.contactsingapore.org.sg/home.htm), where jobs are posted; you might find something suited to your talents.

Doing Business

Singapore prides itself on being a dynamic and efficient place to do business. Leaving Barings Bank and a couple of other scandals aside, Singapore has stable financial markets, a stable government and negligible corruption.

Singapore has aggressively attracted foreign capital, and big money from overseas has played a large part in the dramatic rise in Singapore's wealth. As a free-trading entrepôt promoter of foreign investment with minimal restrictions, Singapore is a good place to do business, though it primarily directs its energies and substantial concessions to large investors in export-oriented industries. The domestic economy is very much directed by the government through the auspices of the Economic Development Board (EDB).

Singapore pursues a free-trade policy and, other than the GST for the importation of goods, very few goods are dutiable or restricted for import or export. The **Trade Development Board** (Map p232; ☎ 6337 6628; www.iesingapore.com; 07-00 Bugis Junction Tower, 230 Victoria St), also known as International Enterprise (IE) Singapore, has simplified import and export procedures, and trade documents can be processed through TradeNet, an electronic data system. Check its website for a list of its offices worldwide, usually located at the Singaporean diplomatic missions.

Singapore bookshops are awash with trade and business publications, and there are various chambers of commerce in Singapore, such as the **Singapore International Chamber of Commerce** (Map pp234-5; ☎ 6224 1255; www.sicc.com.sg; 10-01 John Hancock Tower, 6 Raffles Quay).

You may also find the *Business Times* newspaper useful.

Bring plenty of business cards with you – business meetings typically begin with the exchange of cards, which are offered with two hands in a humble gesture signifying that you are presenting yourself to your contact. Expect to be liberally dined and entertained. Establishing personal rapport is important and your business contacts are unlikely to let you languish in your hotel at the end of a working day.

Language

Language

The four official languages of Singapore are Malay, Tamil, Mandarin and English. Malay is the national language, adopted when Singapore was part of Malaysia, but its use is mostly restricted to the Malay community.

Tamil is the main Indian language; others include Malayalam and Hindi.

Chinese dialects are still widely spoken, especially among older Chinese, with the most common being Hokkien, Teochew, Cantonese, Hainanese and Hakka. The government's long-standing campaign to promote Mandarin, the main nondialectal Chinese language, has been very successful and increasing numbers of Singaporean Chinese now speak it at home.

English is becoming even more widespread. After independence, the government introduced a bilingual education policy aimed at developing the vernacular languages and lessening the use of English. However, Chinese graduates found that this lessened their opportunities for higher education and presented them with greater difficulties in finding a job. English was the language of business and united the various ethnic groups, and the government eventually had to give it more priority. It officially became the first language of instruction in schools in 1987. In 2000 the government launched a 'speak good English' campaign to improve the standard of English.

All children are also taught their mother tongue at school. This policy is largely designed to unite the various Chinese groups and to make sure Chinese Singaporeans don't lose contact with their traditions.

SPEAK MANDARIN, PLEASE!

Singapore is a country with many languages and people, but Chinese ultimately predominate.

When their forebears came from China they brought with them a number of Chinese languages and dialects, including Hokkien, Teochew, Hakka, Cantonese and Mandarin. So dissimilar are these dialects that they might as well be separate languages. The British temporarily solved the problem by making English the lingua franca (common language) of its tropical colony, and to a large degree that still remains the case today.

Since 1979 the Singapore government, in an effort to unite its disparate Chinese peoples, has been encouraging minority-language speakers to adopt the language of administration used by Beijing, namely Mandarin. It is hoped that in this way disunity and differences can be eliminated and the concept of a Singaporean nation can be better realised.

The campaign was initially targeted at monolingual Chinese-speakers, but over the years it has spread to English-educated Chinese who have begun to show an increasing willingness to use Mandarin as their main vehicle for communication in business and pleasure. The government is so intent on its 'Speak Mandarin Campaign' that it even has a website where would-be converts can get themselves motivated – it's at www.mandarin.org.sg.

SINGLISH

You're unlikely to spend much time in Singapore without finding yourself at some point staring dumbly at someone, trying to work out what on earth they are on about. Unnecessary prepositions and pronouns are dropped, word order is flipped, phrases are clipped short and stress and cadence are unconventional, to say the least. Nominally English, the Singaporeans' unique patois contains borrowed words from Hokkien, Tamil and Malay.

There isn't a Singlish grammar as such, but there are definite characteristics, such as the long stress on the last syllable of phrases, so that the standard English 'government' becomes 'guvva-men'. Words ending in consonants are often syncopated and vowels are often distorted. A Chinese-speaking taxi driver might not immediately understand that you want to go to Perak Road, since they know it as 'Pera Roh'.

Verb tenses tend to be nonexistent. Past, present and future are indicated instead by time indicators, so in Singlish it's 'I go tomorrow' or 'I go yesterday'.

The particle 'lah' is often tagged on to the end of sentences for emphasis, as in 'No good lah'. Requests or questions may be marked with a tag ending, since direct questioning can be rude. As a result, questions that are formed to be more polite often come across to Westerners as rude. 'Would you like a beer?' becomes 'You wan beer or not?'

You'll also hear Singaporeans addressing older people as 'uncle' and 'auntie'. They are not relatives and neither is this rude, but more a sign of respect.

Following are a few frequently heard Singlishisms. For a more complete exploration, look at the hilarious Coxford Singlish Dictionary on the satirical website **Talking Cock** (www.talkingcock.com).

a bit the
very; as in *Wah! Your car a bit the slow one*

ah beng
every country has them: boys with spiky gelled hair, loud clothes, the latest mobile phones and a choice line in gutter phrases; his fondest wish, if not already fulfilled, is to own a souped-up car with an enormous speaker in the boot, so that he may pick up the cutest *ah lian*

ah lian
the female version of the *ah beng*: large, moussed hair, garish outfits, armed with a vicious tongue; also known as *ah huay*

aiyah!
'oh, dear!'

alamak!
exclamation of disbelief or frustration, like 'oh my God!'

ang mor
common term for Westerner (Caucasian), with derogatory undertone; literally 'red-haired monkey' in Hokkien

ayam
Malay word for chicken; adjective for something inferior or weak

blur
slow or uninformed

buaya
womaniser, from the Malay for crocodile

can?
'is that OK?'

can!
'yes! That's fine.'

char bor
babe, woman

cheena
derogatory term for old-fashioned Chinese in dress or thinking

confirm
used to convey emphasis when describing something/someone, as in *He confirm blur one* (He's not very smart)

go stun
to reverse, as in *Go stun the car* (from the naval expression 'go astern')

heng
luck, good fortune (Hokkien)

hiao
vain

inggrish
English

kambing
foolish person, literally 'goat' (Malay)

kaypoh
busybody

kena
Malay word close to meaning of English word 'got', describing something that happened, as in *He kena arrested for drunk driving*

kenna ketok
ripped off

kiasee
scared, literally 'afraid to die'; a coward

kiasu
literally 'afraid to lose'; selfish, pushy, always on the lookout for a bargain

kopi tiam
coffee shop

lah
generally an ending for any phrase or sentence; can translate as 'OK', but has no real meaning, added for emphasis to just about everything

lai dat
'like that'; used for emphasis, as in *I so boring lai dat* (I'm very bored).

looksee
take a look

makan
a meal; to eat

malu
embarrassed

minah
girlfriend

or not?
general suffix for questions, as in *Can or not?* (Can you or can't you?)

see first
wait and see what happens

shack
tired

shiok
good, great, delicious

sotong
Malay for 'squid', used as an adjective meaning clumsy, or generally not very switched on.

steady lah
well done, excellent; an expression of praise

Wah!
general exclamation of surprise or distress

ya ya
boastful, as in *He always ya ya*

GLOSSARY

Also see the glossaries for Chinese (p30), Indian (p31), Malay and Indonesian (p32) and Peranakan (p34) cuisine.

adat – Malay customary law
akad nikah – Malay wedding ceremony
ang pow – red packet of money used as offering, payment or gift
Asean – Association of Southeast Asian Nations

Baba – male Peranakan
bandar – port
batik – technique for printing cloth with wax and dye
batu – stone, rock, milepost
bendahara – Sultan's highest official
bercukur – Malay haircut
bertunang – to become engaged
bukit – hill
bumboat – motorised *sampan*
bumiputra – indigenous Malays (literally 'sons of the soil')

chettiar – Indian moneylender
chinthes – half-lion, half-griffin figure
chou – clown character in Chinese opera

godown – river warehouse
gopuram – colourful, ornate tower over the entrance gate to Hindu temple
gurdwara – Sikh temple

hajj – Muslim pilgrimage to Mecca; man who has made the pilgrimage to Mecca
hajjah – woman who has made the pilgrimage to Mecca
hantar tanda – family's permission to marry
haveli – traditional, ornately decorated Indian residence
hawker centre – undercover eating area with food stalls; known as hawker market, food court and food centre
HDB – Housing & Development Board; state body responsible for the provision of public housing

imam – Islamic leader
istana – palace

jalan – road

kallang – shipyard
kampong – traditional Malay village
kasot manek – slippers
kavadi – spiked metal frames decorated with peacock feathers, fruit and flowers used in the Thaipusam parade
kebaya – blouse worn over a sarong
kelong – fish trap on stilts
kenduri – important Malay feast
keramat – Malay shrine
kerasong – brooches, usually of fine filigree gold or silver
kiasu – Hokkien word expressing the Singaporean philosophy of looking out for oneself
kongsi – Chinese clan organisations for mutual assistance known variously as ritual brotherhoods, heaven-man-earth societies, triads and secret societies
kopi tiam – traditional coffee shop
kota – fort, city
kramat – Malay shrine
KTM – Keretapi Tanah Malayu (Malaysian Railways System)
kuala – river mouth, place where a tributary joins a larger river

lorong – narrow street, alley

masjid – mosque
merlion – half-lion, half-fish animal and symbol of Singapore
moksha – the Hindu notion of spiritual salvation
MRT – Singapore's Mass Rapid Transit railway system
muezzin – the official of a mosque who calls the faithful to prayer

namakarana – Indian name-giving ceremony
Nonya – female Peranakan

padang – open grassy area; usually the city square
pantai – beach
PAP – People's Action Party; main political party of Singapore
pasar – market
pasar malam – night market
penjing – Chinese bonsai
Peranakan – literally 'half-caste'; refers to the Straits Chinese, the original Chinese settlers in Singapore, who intermarried with Malays and adopted many of the Malay customs
pintu pagar – swing doors seen in Chinese shophouses
po chai pills – traditional remedy for travellers' diarrhoea and minor stomach problems
pulau – island

raja – prince, ruler
Ramadan – Islamic month of fasting
rotan – cane made of rattan used to punish criminals

sampan – small boat
shen – local deities
Singlish – variation of English spoken in Singapore
STB – Singapore Tourism Board
STDB – Singapore Trade Development Board
sungei – river

tanjung – headland
temenggong – Malay administrator
thali – necklace worn by bride during Indian wedding ceremony; buffet of rice, curried vegetables, soup, curries and bread (Indian)
thola – Indian unit of weight
towkang – Chinese junk
towkays – Chinese business chiefs

wayang – Chinese street opera
wayang kulit – shadow puppet play
wet market – produce market
WTC – World Trade Centre

Behind the Scenes

THE LONELY PLANET STORY

The story begins with a classic travel adventure: Tony and Maureen Wheeler's 1972 journey across Europe and Asia to Australia. There was no useful information about the overland trail then, so Tony and Maureen published the first Lonely Planet guidebook to meet a growing need.

From a kitchen table, Lonely Planet has grown to become the largest independent travel publisher in the world, with offices in Melbourne (Australia), Oakland (USA) and London (UK). Today Lonely Planet guidebooks cover the globe. There is an ever-growing list of books and information in a variety of media. Some things haven't changed. The main aim is still to make it possible for adventurous travellers to get out there – to explore and better understand the world.

At Lonely Planet we believe travellers can make a positive contribution to the countries they visit – if they respect their host communities and spend their money wisely. Every year 5% of company profit is donated to charities around the world.

THIS BOOK

This 7th edition of *Singapore* was researched and written by Mat Oakley. The 6th edition was written by Simon Richmond. Christine Niven updated the 5th edition. This guide was commissioned in Lonely Planet's Melbourne office and produced in Melbourne. The project team included the following:

Commissioning Editor Kalya Ryan

Coordinating Editors Susie Ashworth & Kyla Gillzan

Coordinating Cartographer Jacqueline Nguyen

Coordinating Layout Designer Carol Jackson

Managing Cartographer Corie Waddell

Assisting Layout Designer Pablo Gastar

Cover Designer Marika Kozak

Project Manager Chris Love

Language Content Coordinator Quentin Frayne

Thanks to Carol Chandler, Sally Darmody, Michael Day, Ryan Evans, Jennifer Garrett, Mark Germanchis, Victoria Harrison, Kusnandar, Stephanie Pearson, Nick Stebbing and Jane Thompson.

Cover photographs Woman watching a waterfall fountain, Macduff Everton/Corbis (top); Singapore Chinatown shop display, Neil Setchfield/Alamy (bottom); Toys for sale in Changi Village hawker centre, Phil Weymouth/Lonely Planet Images (back).

Internal photographs by Lonely Planet Images and Phil Weymouth except for the following: p2 (#2, #3, #4, #5), p30, p34, p42, p51, p56, p67 (#2, #3, #4), p68 (#2, #3), p69 (#3), p70 (#2, #3, #4), p71 (#1, #4), p72 (#2, #4), p73 (#1, #2, #3), p79, p85, p90, p91, p94, p96, p97, p104, p124, p133, p147 (#1, #3), p148 (#1, #2, #4), p149 (#1, #2, #3, #4), p150 (#1, #2, #3, #4), p151 (#3, #4), p152 (#3, #4), p153 (#1, #2, #3, #4), p154 (#2), p156, p158, p166, p184, p186 Glenn Beanland; p154 (#3) Tom Cockrem; p154 (#1) Veronica Garbutt; p69 (#4) Richard I'Anson.

ACKNOWLEDGMENTS

Many thanks to the following for the use of their content: Mass Rapit Transit System Map © 2005 Land Transport Authority Singapore.

THANKS

MAT OAKLEY

First and foremost, thanks to Shiwani Diwakar, whose patience, help and tips were invaluable. Little Mae, who selflessly tested out all the kids' attractions, comes a close second. Huge thanks also to Andrew Duffy for help with the front-end material and the loan of books, Judith Holmberg and Vidya Heble for tips along the way, and Siti Andrianie at the STB for the necessary stats.

SEND US YOUR FEEDBACK

We love to hear from travellers – your comments keep us on our toes and help make our books better. Our well-travelled team reads every word on what you loved or loathed about this book. Although we cannot reply individually to postal submissions, we always guarantee that your feedback goes straight to the appropriate authors, in time for the next edition. Each person who sends us information is thanked in the next edition – and the most useful submissions are rewarded with a free book.

To send us your updates – and find out about Lonely Planet events, newsletters and travel news – visit our award-winning website: www.lonelyplanet.com/feedback

Note: We may edit, reproduce and incorporate your comments in Lonely Planet products such as guidebooks, websites and digital products, so let us know if you don't want your comments reproduced or your name acknowledged. For a copy of our privacy policy visit www.lonelyplanet.com/privacy.

OUR READERS

Many thanks to the travellers who used the last edition and wrote to us with helpful hints, useful advice and interesting anecdotes:

A Tamer Abolghar, Richard Adams, Jonathan Ayres **B** Helen Badham, Richard Bennett, Franck Bessoles, Nicola Bevan, Karl Birthistle, Luc Blattmann, Audrey & Roy Bradford, Steve Bray, Tor Brendeford, Andy & Claire Brice, Catherine Brinkley, Scott Brown, EJ Butler **C** Martin Caminada, Rusty Cartmill, Jon Casey, Debora Chobanian, Rob & Mieke Choufoer, Noemeier Christian, Paul Clammer, Joanna Clough, John & Maggie Coaton **D** Jason Dance, Sarah Jane Davis, Saskia de Rover, Dave de Villiers, Richard Desomme, Andy Dickinson, Ellie Downes, R Drakeford, Amy Duray **E** Jane Edwards, Isabella Egan, Anas Elgasmi **F** Ian Fair, Anna Fayeg, Marek Feldman, Kevin Ford, Beauchamp Francois **G** Shell & Brian Gare, Lisa Goh, Ronalie Green, Robin Isobel Greenfield, Stefan & Adele Grosse, Jonas Grundstrom, Andrea Gryak, A Salemi Gulec, Katrina Gulliver, Sunita Gupta **H** Kerry Hamill, Loic Harel, Nils Hoefer, Marc Hofstetter, Dominic Holt, Jackie Hoskins, Eveline How, Paul Huckin, Jussi Huhtanen **I** Michael Imbleau, Michelle Imison, Stephen Ireland **J** Neil James, Kyle Johnson **K** Judith Karena, Pius Karena, James & Kasia Kilvington, Catherine Koch, Oliver Krause, Lucas Krezdorn, Marieke Krijnen **L** Diane Leighton, Mun Yi Leong, Steve Lewis, Patrick Lim, Mikkel Lindemark, Jonathon Lindqvist, Rebecca Liu, Patricia Lopez, Jane Ludemann **M** John MacNeil, Chris & Sarah MacQuillan, Rachael Main, Vladimir Marhefka, Haley Marshall, Stephanie Marton, Julian J Matius, Pam McDonald, Margaret McKinnon, Miguel Melo, Andrea Messmer, Michael Mischna, Kwezi Mjumbe, Rana Moayad, Theresa Mun Yi Leong **N** Jessi Nabuurs, Joe Nai, Lukas Nardella, Leni Neoptolemos, Dirk Noldt, Christian Nömeier, Simona Novak **P** Mads Theilade Pedersen, Suzie Peek, Janet Penn, Jonathan Phillips, Lauren Phillips, Tanja Piessens, Lilyanne Price **R** Rishi Ramchand, John Reeves, Geoff Ring, Rosie Rogers, Brian Ross, Alfred Rowe, Ellen Ryan **S** Valter Maria Santoro, Karin Schacknat, Shad Schroeder, Tjeerd Schuit, Berthold Schweitzer, Blandine Sebileau, HW Sheldon, Shabbir Simjee, Mette Sjovik, Jason Smith, Jim Smith, Hyunah Song, Kelli Speller, Jens Sprenger, Nicky Stokes, Pamela Stokes, Emma Stone, C Su **T** Darion Teoh, David Thomas, David Tracy **V** Anne Vallée, Caroline & Herman van den Wall Bake, Martin van Rongen, Maries Villarosa, Giorgio Vintani, Tamas Visegrady, JH Voon **W** Emma Walmsley, Anthony Warren, Jan Wessels, Marjan Willemsen, Holly Williams, Richard Wong

Notes

Index

See also subindexes for Eating (p218), Entertainment (p218), Shopping (p219) and Sleeping (p220).

000 map pages
000 photographs

SHOPPING

SLEEPING

000 map pages
000 photographs

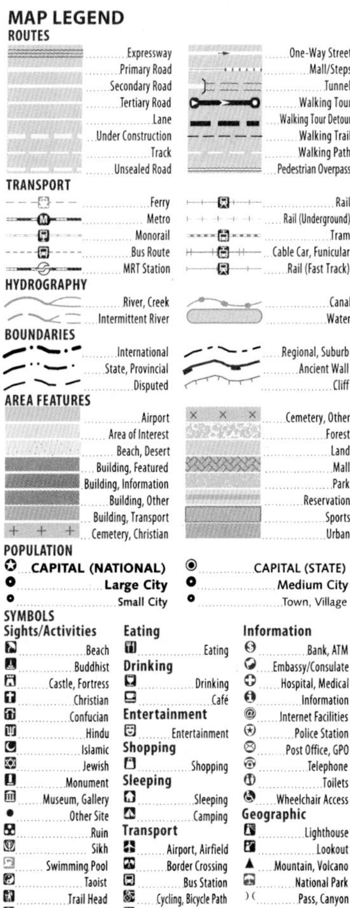
MAP LEGEND
ROUTES
Expressway
Primary Road
Secondary Road
Tertiary Road
Lane
Under Construction
Track
Unsealed Road
One-Way Street
Mall/Steps
Tunnel
Walking Tour
Walking Tour Detour
Walking Trail
Walking Path
Pedestrian Overpass
TRANSPORT
Ferry
Metro
Monorail
Bus Route
MRT Station
Rail
Rail (Underground)
Tram
Cable Car, Funicular
Rail (Fast Track)
HYDROGRAPHY
River, Creek
Intermittent River
Canal
Water
BOUNDARIES
International
State, Provincial
Disputed
Regional, Suburb
Ancient Wall
Cliff
AREA FEATURES
Airport
Area of Interest
Beach, Desert
Building, Featured
Building, Information
Building, Other
Building, Transport
Cemetery, Christian
Cemetery, Other
Forest
Land
Mall
Park
Reservation
Sports
Urban
POPULATION
CAPITAL (NATIONAL)
Large City
Small City
CAPITAL (STATE)
Medium City
Town, Village
SYMBOLS
Sights/Activities
Beach
Buddhist
Castle, Fortress
Christian
Confucian
Hindu
Islamic
Jewish
Monument
Museum, Gallery
Other Site
Ruin
Sikh
Swimming Pool
Taoist
Trail Head
Winery, Vineyard
Zoo, Bird Sanctuary
Eating
Eating
Drinking
Drinking
Café
Entertainment
Entertainment
Shopping
Shopping
Sleeping
Sleeping
Camping
Transport
Airport, Airfield
Border Crossing
Bus Station
Cycling, Bicycle Path
Parking Area
Taxi Rank
Information
Bank, ATM
Embassy/Consulate
Hospital, Medical
Information
Internet Facilities
Police Station
Post Office, GPO
Telephone
Toilets
Wheelchair Access
Geographic
Lighthouse
Lookout
Mountain, Volcano
National Park
Pass, Canyon
River Flow
Waterfall

Maps

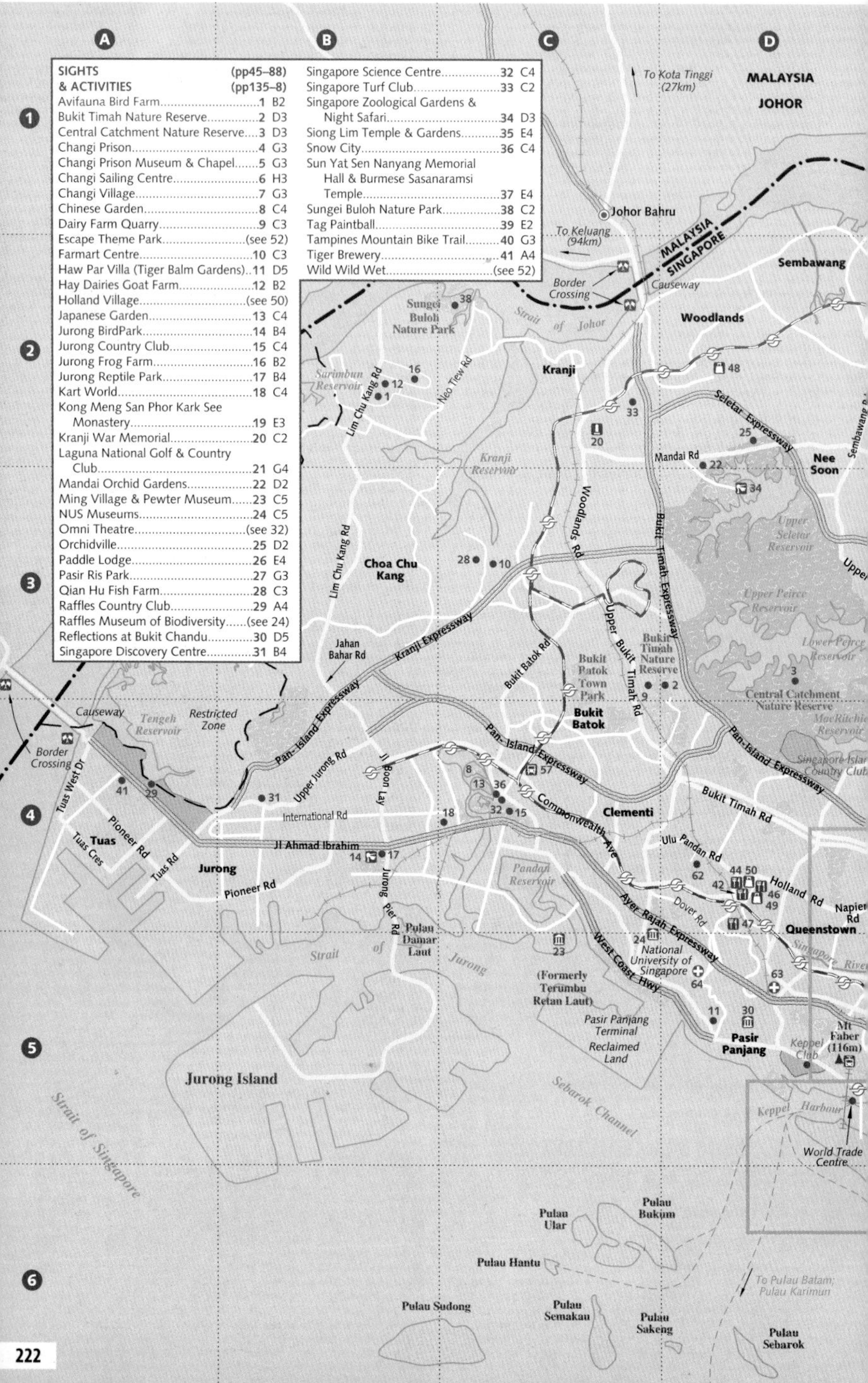
A
B
C
D
1
2
3
4
5
6
SIGHTS & ACTIVITIES (pp45–88) (pp135–8)
Avifauna Bird Farm.....1 B2
Bukit Timah Nature Reserve.....2 D3
Central Catchment Nature Reserve.....3 D3
Changi Prison.....4 G3
Changi Prison Museum & Chapel.....5 G3
Changi Sailing Centre.....6 H3
Changi Village.....7 G3
Chinese Garden.....8 C4
Dairy Farm Quarry.....9 C3
Escape Theme Park.....(see 52)
Farmart Centre.....10 C3
Haw Par Villa (Tiger Balm Gardens).....11 D5
Hay Dairies Goat Farm.....12 B2
Holland Village.....(see 50)
Japanese Garden.....13 C4
Jurong BirdPark.....14 B4
Jurong Country Club.....15 C4
Jurong Frog Farm.....16 B2
Jurong Reptile Park.....17 B4
Kart World.....18 C4
Kong Meng San Phor Kark See Monastery.....19 E3
Kranji War Memorial.....20 C2
Laguna National Golf & Country Club.....21 G4
Mandai Orchid Gardens.....22 D2
Ming Village & Pewter Museum.....23 C5
NUS Museums.....24 C5
Omni Theatre.....(see 32)
Orchidville.....25 D2
Paddle Lodge.....26 E4
Pasir Ris Park.....27 G3
Qian Hu Fish Farm.....28 C3
Raffles Country Club.....29 A4
Raffles Museum of Biodiversity.....(see 24)
Reflections at Bukit Chandu.....30 D5
Singapore Discovery Centre.....31 B4
Singapore Science Centre.....32 C4
Singapore Turf Club.....33 C2
Singapore Zoological Gardens & Night Safari.....34 D3
Siong Lim Temple & Gardens.....35 E4
Snow City.....36 C4
Sun Yat Sen Nanyang Memorial Hall & Burmese Sasanaramsi Temple.....37 E4
Sungei Buloh Nature Park.....38 C2
Tag Paintball.....39 E2
Tampines Mountain Bike Trail.....40 G3
Tiger Brewery.....41 A4
Wild Wild Wet.....(see 52)
To Kota Tinggi (27km)
MALAYSIA
JOHOR
Johor Bahru
To Keluang (94km)
MALAYSIA
SINGAPORE
Border Crossing
Causeway
Sembawang
Woodlands
Strait of Johor
Sungei Buloh Nature Park
Sarimbun Reservoir
Lim Chu Kang Rd
Neo Tiew Rd
Kranji
Seletar Expressway
Mandai Rd
Nee Soon
Sembawang Rd
Kranji Reservoir
Woodlands Rd
Bukit Timah Expressway
Upper Seletar Reservoir
Choa Chu Kang
Upper Peirce Reservoir
Lower Peirce Reservoir
Upper Bukit Timah Rd
Bukit Timah Nature Reserve
Bukit Batok Rd
Bukit Batok Town Park
Bukit Batok
Central Catchment Nature Reserve
MacRitchie Reservoir
Singapore Island Country Club
Kranji Expressway
Jahan Bahar Rd
Causeway
Tengeh Reservoir
Restricted Zone
Border Crossing
Pan-Island Expressway
Upper Jurong Rd
Jl Boon Lay
Tuas West Dr
Tuas
Pioneer Rd
Tuas Cres
Tuas Rd
Jurong
International Rd
Jl Ahmad Ibrahim
Jurong Pier Rd
Pioneer Rd
Commonwealth Ave
Clementi
Bukit Timah Rd
Ulu Pandan Rd
Holland Rd
Napier Rd
Dover Rd
Queenstown
Ayer Rajah Expressway
Pandan Reservoir
Pulau Damar Laut
Strait of Jurong
(Formerly Terumbu Retan Laut)
National University of Singapore
West Coast Hwy
Singapore River
Pasir Panjang Terminal
Reclaimed Land
Pasir Panjang
Keppel Club
Mt Faber (116m)
Jurong Island
Sebarok Channel
Keppel Harbour
World Trade Centre
Strait of Singapore
Pulau Ular
Pulau Bukum
Pulau Hantu
To Pulau Batam; Pulau Karimun
Pulau Sudong
Pulau Semakau
Pulau Sakeng
Pulau Sebarok

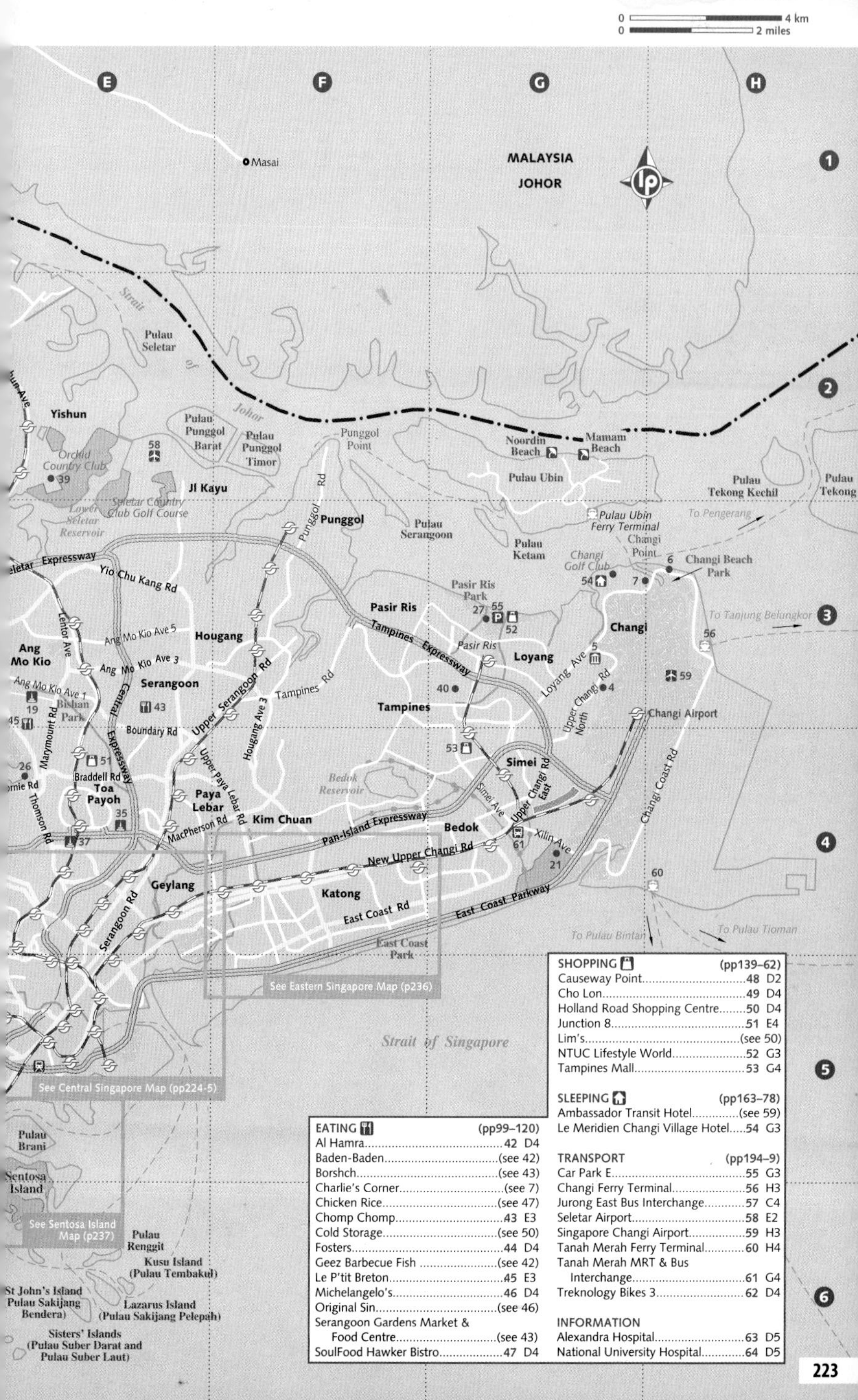

SHOPPING (pp139–62)

Causeway Point	48	D2
Cho Lon	49	D4
Holland Road Shopping Centre	50	D4
Junction 8	51	E4
Lim's	(see 50)	
NTUC Lifestyle World	52	G3
Tampines Mall	53	G4

SLEEPING (pp163–78)

Ambassador Transit Hotel	(see 59)	
Le Meridien Changi Village Hotel	54	G3

EATING (pp99–120)

Al Hamra	42	D4
Baden-Baden	(see 42)	
Borshch	(see 43)	
Charlie's Corner	(see 7)	
Chicken Rice	(see 47)	
Chomp Chomp	43	E3
Cold Storage	(see 50)	
Fosters	44	D4
Geez Barbecue Fish	(see 42)	
Le P'tit Breton	45	E3
Michelangelo's	46	D4
Original Sin	(see 46)	
Serangoon Gardens Market & Food Centre	(see 43)	
SoulFood Hawker Bistro	47	D4

TRANSPORT (pp194–9)

Car Park E	55	G3
Changi Ferry Terminal	56	H3
Jurong East Bus Interchange	57	C4
Seletar Airport	58	E2
Singapore Changi Airport	59	H3
Tanah Merah Ferry Terminal	60	H4
Tanah Merah MRT & Bus Interchange	61	G4
Treknology Bikes 3	62	D4

INFORMATION

Alexandra Hospital	63	D5
National University Hospital	64	D5

CENTRAL SINGAPORE

A B C D
1 2 3 4 5 6

Dunearn Rd
Farrer Rd
Cluny Park Rd
32
Singapore Botanic Gardens
Novena
See Orchard Road Map (pp226-7)
Bukit Timah Rd
Rochel Canal
Stevens Rd
Newton Rd
Dunearn Rd
Nassim Rd
Balmoral Rd
Orange Grove Rd
Stevens Rd
Newton Circus
Newton
Rochel Canal
Kampong Java Rd
Bukit Timah Rd
Scotts Rd
Clemenceau Ave North
Anderson Rd
Singapore Botanic Gardens
Cairnhill Rd
Napier Rd
Napier Rd
Tanglin Rd
Orchard Rd
Cairnhill Circle
Cavenagh Rd
Central Expressway
Tanglin Golf Course
Blvd
Orchard
Paterson Rd
Orchard
Bideford Rd
Orchard
Tanglin Rd
Orchard Blvd
Orchard Link
Grange Rd
Orchard Rd
Penang Rd
Somerset
Grange Rd
Paterson Hill
Grange Rd
Exeter Rd
Eber Rd
Killiney Rd
Oxley Rise
Irwell Bank
Hoot Kiam Rd
River Valley Rd
Alexandra Canal
Kim Seng Rd
Zion Rd
See Enlargement
Singapore River
Robertson Bridge
Clemenceau Ave
Tiong Bahru Rd
Redhill
Delta Stadium
Tiong Bahru Park
Alexandra Rd
Outram Rd
Havelock Rd
Lower Delta Rd
Henderson Rd
Zion Rd
Tiong Bahru
Henderson Park
Tiong Bahru Rd
Jl Bukit Merah
Lim Liak St
12 2 8
Kim Pong Rd
Seng Poh Rd
Guan Chuang St
Tiong Poh Rd
Pearl's Hill City Park
Havelock Rd Area
River Valley Cl
Kim Yam Rd
15 19 17
Mohamed Sultan Rd
16
Unity St
22
Martin Rd
10
Jiak Kim St
21
Mergui Rd
20 29 18 30
Jl Bukit Merah
Central Expressway
Outram Rd
Outram Park
Robertson Bridge
26
Rodyk St
Saiboo St
6
25
14
Robertson Quay
Singapore River
Saiboo Bridge
Clemenceau Ave
28
Havelock Rd
27
Outram Rd
Ayer Rajah Expressway
Kampong Bahru Rd
Neil Rd
Cantonment Rd
0 200 m
0 0.1 miles
Raeburn Park
Spottiswoode Park
Singapore
Ayer Rajah Expressway
Mt Faber Park
3
Mt Faber (116m)
31
Lower Delta Rd
Kampong Bahru Rd

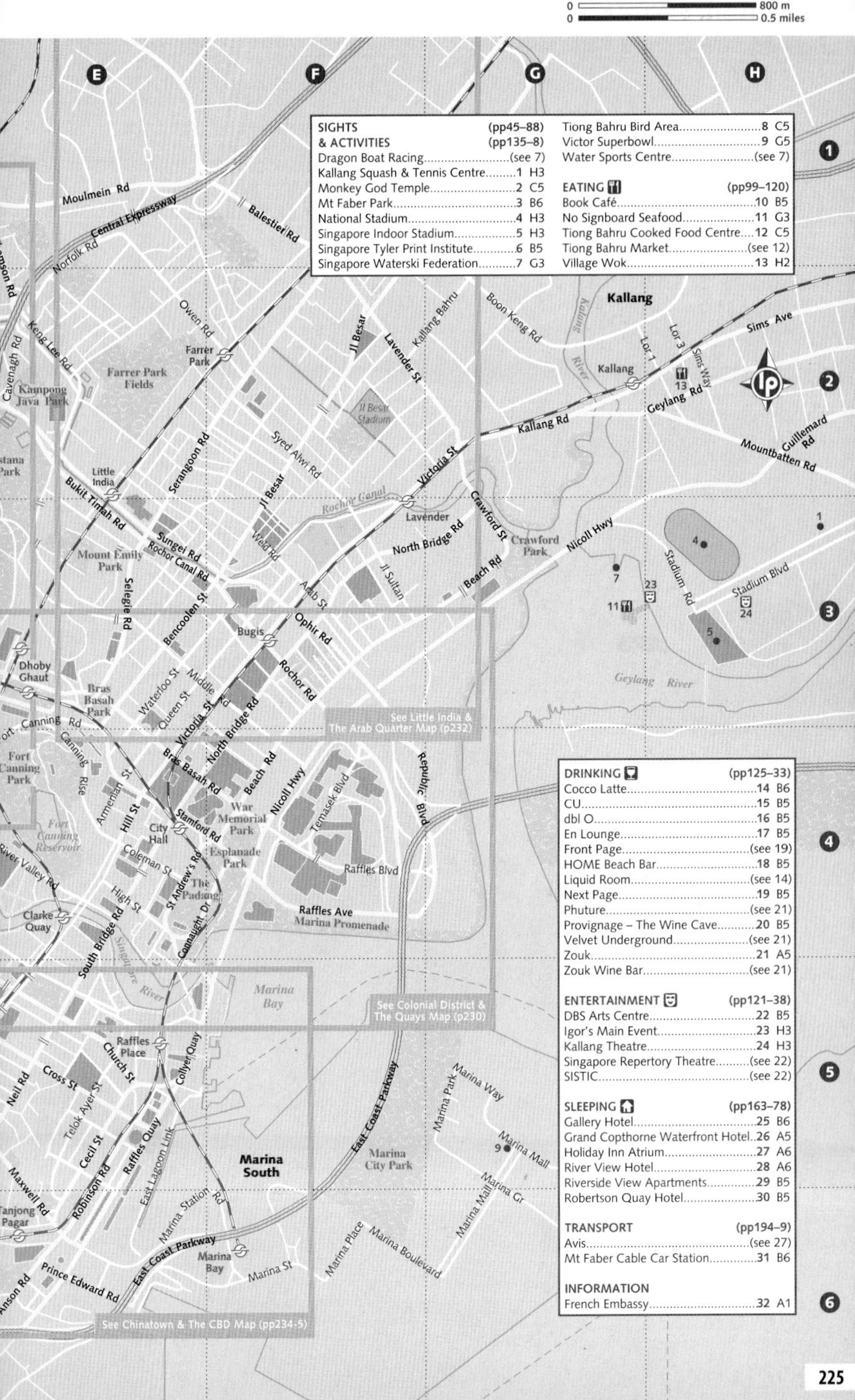
0 800 m
0 0.5 miles
E
F
G
H
1
2
3
4
5
6
SIGHTS & ACTIVITIES (pp45–88) (pp135–8)
Dragon Boat Racing.........................(see 7)
Kallang Squash & Tennis Centre.........1 H3
Monkey God Temple.........................2 C5
Mt Faber Park..................................3 B6
National Stadium..............................4 H3
Singapore Indoor Stadium..................5 H3
Singapore Tyler Print Institute............6 B5
Singapore Waterski Federation...........7 G3
Tiong Bahru Bird Area........................8 C5
Victor Superbowl...............................9 G5
Water Sports Centre..........................(see 7)
EATING (pp99–120)
Book Café..10 B5
No Signboard Seafood.......................11 G3
Tiong Bahru Cooked Food Centre....12 C5
Tiong Bahru Market.........................(see 12)
Village Wok.......................................13 H2
DRINKING (pp125–33)
Cocco Latte.......................................14 B6
CU...15 B5
dbl O..16 B5
En Lounge...17 B5
Front Page.......................................(see 19)
HOME Beach Bar..............................18 B5
Liquid Room....................................(see 14)
Next Page...19 B5
Phuture..(see 21)
Provignage – The Wine Cave...........20 B5
Velvet Underground........................(see 21)
Zouk...21 A5
Zouk Wine Bar.................................(see 21)
ENTERTAINMENT (pp121–38)
DBS Arts Centre................................22 B5
Igor's Main Event.............................23 H3
Kallang Theatre.................................24 H3
Singapore Repertory Theatre..........(see 22)
SISTIC..(see 22)
SLEEPING (pp163–78)
Gallery Hotel.....................................25 B6
Grand Copthorne Waterfront Hotel..26 A5
Holiday Inn Atrium...........................27 A6
River View Hotel...............................28 A6
Riverside View Apartments..............29 B5
Robertson Quay Hotel......................30 B5
TRANSPORT (pp194–9)
Avis...(see 27)
Mt Faber Cable Car Station..............31 B6
INFORMATION
French Embassy................................32 A1
Moulmein Rd
Central Expressway
Balestier Rd
Norfolk Rd
Owen Rd
Keng Lee Rd
Cavenagh Rd
Farrer Park
Farrer Park Fields
Kampong Java Park
Little India
Bukit Timah Rd
Serangoon Rd
Syed Alwi Rd
Jl Besar
Lavender St
Kallang Bahru
Boon Keng Rd
Jl Besar Stadium
Kallang
Kallang River
Lor 1
Lor 3
Sims Ave
Sims Way
Geylang Rd
Kallang Rd
Guillemard Rd
Mountbatten Rd
Victoria St
Rochor Canal
Lavender
North Bridge Rd
Crawford St
Crawford Park
Nicoll Hwy
Stadium Rd
Stadium Blvd
Beach Rd
Jl Sultan
Arab St
Weld Rd
Sungei Rd
Rochor Canal Rd
Mount Emily Park
Selegie Rd
Bencoolen St
Bugis
Ophir Rd
Rochor Rd
Geylang River
Dhoby Ghaut
Bras Basah Park
Waterloo St
Middle Rd
Queen St
Canning Rd
Canning Rise
Fort Canning Park
Fort Canning Reservoir
See Little India & The Arab Quarter Map (p232)
Bras Basah Rd
Republic Blvd
Temasek Blvd
Armenian St
Hill St
City Hall
Stamford Rd
War Memorial Park
Esplanade Park
Coleman St
St Andrew's Rd
The Padang
High St
River Valley Rd
Clarke Quay
South Bridge Rd
Connaught Dr
Raffles Blvd
Raffles Ave
Marina Promenade
Singapore River
Marina Bay
See Colonial District & The Quays Map (p230)
Raffles Place
Church St
Collyer Quay
Cross St
Neil Rd
Telok Ayer St
Cecil St
Raffles Quay
East Lagoon Link
Robinson Rd
Maxwell Rd
Tanjong Pagar
Marina South
Marina Station Rd
East Coast Parkway
Marina Bay
Marina St
Prince Edward Rd
Anson Rd
See Chinatown & The CBD Map (pp234-5)
Marina City Park
Marina Park
Marina Way
Marina Mall
Marina Gr
Marina Place
Marina Boulevard

A
B
C
D
1
2
3
4
5
6
Cluny Park Rd
Evans Rd
Dalvey Estate
Margoliouth Rd
Stevens Rd
Robin
Stevens Dr
White House Rd
74
Robin Rd
Dalvey Rd
Singapore Botanic Gardens
Tyersall Rd
Gallop Rd
10
Nassim Rd
Fernhill Rd
Fernhill Rd
4
13
Lermit Rd
Tyersall Ave
Nassim Rd
80
Orange Grove Rd
Anderson
Nassim Rd
99
Nassim Rd
Singapore Botanic Gardens
7
21
Napier Rd
Napier Rd
Nassim Hill
60
25
38
Minden Rd
St Martin's Dr
Tanglin Rd
48
26
20
Dempsey Rd
91
104
101
47
35
Cuscaden R
Harding Rd
92
23
59
93
78
Tomlinson Rd
84
Tanglin Golf Course
Omni Marco Polo Hotel
Grange Rd
103
Orchard Spring La
Orchard Blvd
Tanglin Rd
Rochalie Dr
One Tree Hill
Loewen Rd
Ridley Park
Chatsworth Rd
Grange Rd
98
42
Bishopgate
Nathan Rd
Margaret Rd
Alexandra Canal
Jervois Rd

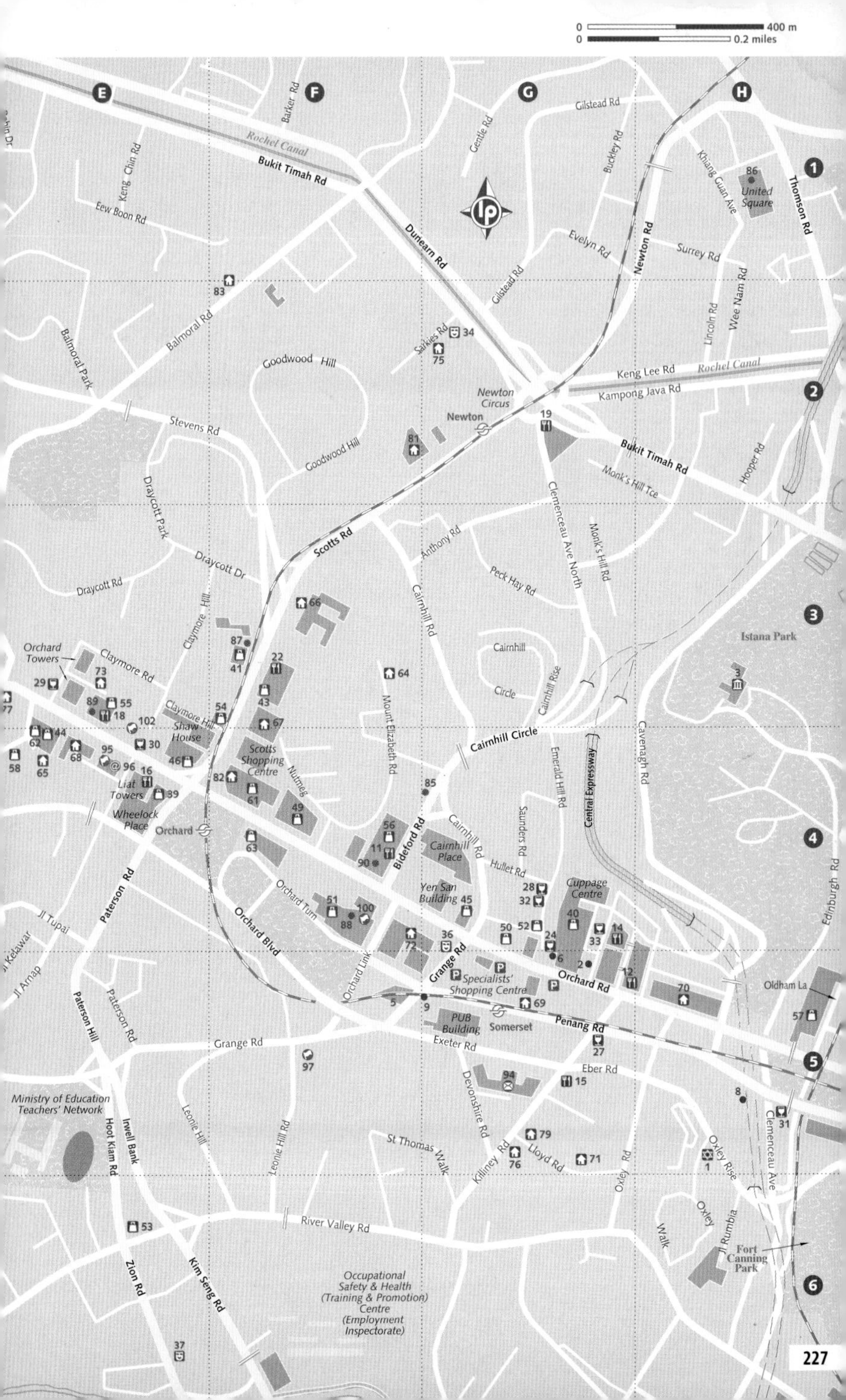
0 400 m
0 0.2 miles
Rochel Canal
Bukit Timah Rd
Barker Rd
Gentle Rd
Gilstead Rd
Buckley Rd
Khiang Guan Ave
United Square
Thomson Rd
Keng Chin Rd
Eew Boon Rd
Dunearn Rd
Evelyn Rd
Newton Rd
Surrey Rd
Wee Nam Rd
Lincoln Rd
Balmoral Rd
Balmoral Park
Goodwood Hill
Sarkies Rd
Keng Lee Rd
Kampong Java Rd
Newton Circus
Newton
Stevens Rd
Monk's Hill Tce
Hooper Rd
Draycott Park
Draycott Dr
Draycott Rd
Scotts Rd
Anthony Rd
Peck Hay Rd
Clemenceau Ave North
Monk's Hill Rd
Cairnhill Rd
Istana Park
Claymore Hill
Orchard Towers
Claymore Rd
Cairnhill Circle
Cairnhill Rise
Mount Elizabeth Rd
Claymore Hill
Shaw House
Scotts Shopping Centre
Nutmeg
Emerald Hill Rd
Central Expressway
Cavenagh Rd
Liat Towers
Wheelock Place
Orchard
Bideford Rd
Cairnhill Place
Saunders Rd
Hullet Rd
Cuppage Centre
Edinburgh Rd
Orchard Turn
Yen San Building
Jl Tupai
Paterson Rd
Orchard Blvd
Orchard Link
Grange Rd
Specialists' Shopping Centre
Orchard Rd
Oldham La
Jl Kelawar
Jl Arnap
Paterson Hill
PUB Building
Somerset
Penang Rd
Grange Rd
Exeter Rd
Eber Rd
Ministry of Education Teachers' Network
Hoot Kiam Rd
Inwell Bank
Leonie Hill
Leonie Hill Rd
Devonshire Rd
St Thomas Walk
Killiney Rd
Lloyd Rd
Oxley Rd
Oxley Rise
Clemenceau Ave
Oxley Walk
Jl Rumbia
River Valley Rd
Fort Canning Park
Zion Rd
Kim Seng Rd
Occupational Safety & Health (Training & Promotion) Centre (Employment Inspectorate)

ORCHARD ROAD (pp226–7)

SIGHTS & ACTIVITIES (pp45–88) (pp135–8)

Chesed-El Synagogue....1 H5
Cuppage Terrace....2 G5
Istana....3 H3
Kenko....(see 59)
National Orchid Garden....4 B2
National Youth Centre Skate Park.5 F5
Ngee Ann Foot Reflexology....(see 50)
Orchard Bowl....(see 36)
Peranakan Place....6 G5
Singapore Botanic Gardens....7 B3
Tan Yeok Nee House....8 H5
Youth Park....9 G5

EATING (pp99–120)

Au Jardin....10 B2
Blood Café....11 F4
Blu....(see 80)
Bombay Woodlands Restaurant....(see 17)
Club Chinois....(see 77)
Din Tai Fung....(see 11)
Gordon Grill....(see 66)
Hachi....12 G5
Halia....13 B2
Izakaya Nirumaru....14 G4
Killiney Kopitiam....15 G5
Lingzhi Vegetarian....16 E4
Magic of Chongqing Hot Pot....17 D3
Marmalade Pantry....18 E3
Mezza9....(see 67)
Newton Circus Hawker Centre....19 G2
Organic Fruit & Vegetable Market....20 A4
Samy's Curry Restaurant....21 A3
Soup Restaurant....(see 41)
Sunflower Vegetarian....22 F3
Tanglin Mall Food Junction....23 D4
Top of the M....(see 72)
Ya Kun Kaya Toast....(see 88)

DRINKING (pp125–33)

Alley Bar....24 G4
Anywhere Music Pub....25 D3
Bar None....(see 82)
Brix....(see 67)
Chinablack....(see 54)
Dempsey's Hut....26 A4
Dubliners....27 G5
Ice Cold Beer....28 G4
Muddy Murphy's....29 E3
Music Underground....30 E4
Planet Paradigm....31 H5
Que Pasa....32 G4
Rouge....(see 6)
Round Midnight....33 G4
Wine Network....(see 26)

ENTERTAINMENT (pp121–38)

Alliance Francaise....34 G2
British Council....35 C4
CalendarOne TicketCharge....(see 44)
Cathay Cineleisure Orchard....36 G4
Golden Village Cinema....37 E6
Lido Cinema....(see 46)
Milieu....(see 24)
Plaza Singapura Cinema....(see 57)
Punchline Comedy Club....(see 82)
SISTIC....(see 63)

ORCHARD ROAD (pp226–7)

SHOPPING (pp139–62)
Apple Centre........(see 39)
Asiatique........38 A4
Best Denki........(see 88)
Borders........39 E4
Centrepoint........40 G4
DFS Galleria Scottwalk........41 F3
Eastern Discoveries........(see 48)
EM Trade & Design........42 D5
Far East Plaza........43 F3
Far East Shopping Centre........(see 96)
Flea Market........(see 59)
Forum - The Shopping Mall........44 E4
Heeren........(see 45)
HMV........45 G4
Isetan........46 E4
Isetan........(see 63)
Jazmin Asian Arts........47 D4
Jehan Gallery........48 A4
Kinokuniya........(see 88)
Linda Gallery........(see 48)
Lucky Plaza........49 F4
Midpoint Orchard........50 G4
Ngee Ann City........51 F4
One Price Store........52 G4
Opera Gallery........(see 51)
Originasia........53 E6
Pacific Plaza........54 F3
Pagoda House........(see 93)
Palais Renaissance........55 E3
Paragon........56 F4
Pasardina Fine Living........(see 48)
Plaza Singapura........57 H5
Project Shop Blood Brothers........(see 90)
Project Shop Blood Brothers........(see 63)
Select Books........(see 60)
Sembawang Music Centre........(see 36)
Shang Antiques........(see 48)
Shanghai Tang........58 E4
Shopping Gallery at Hilton........(see 68)
Song+Kelly21........(see 62)
Sunny Books........(see 43)
Tanglin Mall........59 D4
Tanglin Shopping Centre........60 D3
Tangs........61 F4
Toys R Us........62 E4
Tudor Court Shopping Gallery..(see 93)
Wisma Atria Shopping Centre........63 F4

SLEEPING (pp163–78)
Elizabeth........64 F3
Four Seasons Hotel........65 E4
Goodwood Park Hotel........66 F3
Grand Hyatt Singapore........67 F3
Hilton International........68 E4
Hotel Phoenix........69 G5
Le Meridien Singapore........70 H5
Lloyd's Inn........71 G5
Mandarin Singapore........72 F4
Meritus Negara Hotel........73 E3
Metro-Y Apartments........(see 74)
Metropolitan Y........74 D1
New Sandy's Place........75 G2
Orchard Grand Court........76 G5
Orchard Parade Hotel........77 E3
Parklane Suites........(see 66)
Regent........78 D4
SHA Villa........79 G5
Shangri-La Hotel........80 D3
Sheraton Towers........81 F2
Singapore Marriott........82 F4
Sloane Court Hotel........83 F2
Traders Hotel........84 D4

TRANSPORT (pp194–9)
British Airways........85 G4
Garuda Indonesia........86 H1
Hertz Rent-a-Car........87 F3
KLM-Royal Dutch Airlines........88 F4
Lufthansa........89 E3
Qantas........(see 85)
Singapore Airlines........90 F4

INFORMATION
Australian High Commission........91 C4
British High Commission........92 C4
Chinese Embassy........93 D4
Comcentre Post Centre........94 G5
German Embassy........95 E4
Gymboree Play & Music........(see 59)
I-Surf........96 E4
Indian High Commission........97 F5
Indonesian Embassy........98 D5
Japanese Embassy........99 D3
New Zealand Embassy........100 F4
Orchard Post Office........(see 88)
Post Office........101 D4
Royal Thai Embassy........102 E4
Singapore Visitors Centre @ Orchard........103 D4
US Embassy........104 C4
YMCA Metropolitan........(see 74)

COLONIAL DISTRICT & THE QUAYS

COLONIAL DISTRICT & THE QUAYS (p230)

SIGHTS & ACTIVITIES	(pp45–88) (pp135–8)
Amrita Spa	(see 110)
Armenian Church	1 C3
Asian Civilisations Museum	2 C4
Asian Civilisations Museum	3 C2
At-Sunrice Cooking Academy	(see 78)
Battle Box	4 B2
Caldwell House	(see 87)
Campers' Corner	5 C2
Cathedral of the Good Shepherd	6 C2
Chettiar Hindu Temple	7 A2
City Hall	8 C3
Civil Defence Heritage Gallery	9 C3
Civilian War Memorial	10 D3
Esplanade Jetty	11 D4
Fort Canning Park	12 B2
Fountain of Wealth	13 E2
G-Max Reserve Bungy	14 B3
Lim Bo Seng Memorial	15 C4
Maghain Aboth Synagogue	16 C1
Merlion Park	(see 17)
Merlion Statue	17 D4
Nanyang Academy of Fine Arts	18 D1
National Library	19 B2
Old Parliament House	20 C4
Omar Kampong Melaka Mosque	21 A4
Parliament House	22 C4
Raffles Culinary Academy	(see 109)
Raffles Landing	23 C4
Raffles Museum	(see 92)
River Valley Swimming Complex	24 A3
St Andrew's Cathedral	25 C3
St Joseph's Catholic Church	26 C1
Sculpture Square	27 C1
Singapore Art Museum	28 C1
Singapore Cricket Club	29 C4
Singapore History Museum	30 B2
Singapore Management University	31 C2
Singapore Philatelic Museum	32 B3
Singapore Recreation Club	33 D3
Speakers' Corner	34 B4
Suntec City Fountain Terrace	(see 45)
Supreme Court	35 C3
Tan Kim Seng Fountain	36 D3
Tan Si Chong Su Temple	37 A4

EATING	(pp99–120)
A-Roy Thai	(see 90)
Ah Teng's Bakery	38 D2
Al Dente	(see 43)
Annalakshmi	39 C3
Armenian Kopitaim	40 C2
Café Society	41 C4
Christa & Naomi Café (CAN)	42 D1
Colours by the Bay	43 D3
Coriander Leaf	44 A3
Courtyard	(see 99)
Crystal Jade Kitchen	45 E2
Doc Cheng's	(see 92)
Equinox	46 D2
Food Junction	47 D1
Garibaldi	48 D2
Hai Tien Lo	49 E3
Imperial Herbal Restaurant	(see 104)
Indochine Waterfront	50 C4
Jade	(see 99)
Keyaki	(see 49)
Kopitiam	51 C1
Max Brenner's Chocolate Bar	(see 77)
Mirchi	(see 77)
My Humble House	(see 43)
No Signboard Seafood	(see 43)
Saint Pierre	52 A4
Seah Street Deli	53 D2
Soup Restaurant	(see 45)
Summer Pavilion	54 E3
Teajoy	55 D2
Tiffin Room	(see 92)
Town	(see 99)
Victoria Street Food Centre	56 C1
Wah Lok	57 C2

DRINKING	(pp125–33)
Actors' Bar	58 B4
Attica	(see 44)
Balaclava	59 D3
Bar & Billiard Room	60 D2
Bar Opiume	(see 50)
Bed Room Bar	61 B4
Brewerkz	62 A3
Café Iguana	63 A4
Chihuly Lounge	(see 111)
Crazy Elephant	64 B3
Fabulous Fizz	65 D3
Father Flanagan's	66 C2
Fez Lounge Bar	67 C4
Hideout	68 C4
Insomnia	(see 66)
Introbar	(see 46)
Jazz@South Bridge	69 C4
Live Jazz @ The Green Room	(see 65)
Living Room	70 C4
Long Bar	(see 92)
Lot, Stock & Barrel	71 D2
Molly Malone's	72 C4
New Asia Bar	(see 46)
Paulaner Brauhaus	73 E3
RAV	74 B4
Somerset's	75 C2
Upper Bar	(see 87)
Victoria Bar	(see 102)

ENTERTAINMENT	(pp121–38)
Action Theatre	76 C1
Black Box	(see 78)
CalendarOne TicketCharge	(see 82)
Drama Centre	(see 78)
Esplanade - Theatres on the Bay	77 D3
Fort Canning Centre	78 B2
Guinness Theatre	(see 82)
Jubilee Hall	(see 92)
Marina Square Complex Cinemas	79 E3
Nrityalaya Aesthetics Society	80 C1
Shaw Towers Cinemas	81 E2
Singapore Dance Theatre	(see 78)
SISTIC	(see 84)
SISTIC	(see 94)
Substation	82 C2
Suntec City Cinemas	83 E2
Theatreworks	(see 78)
Victoria Theatre & Concert Hall	84 C4

SHOPPING	(pp139–62)
Art-2 Gallery	85 B3
Aseana	86 E3
Carrefour	(see 83)
Chijmes Complex	87 C2
CityLink Mall	88 D3
Clarke Quay Flea Market	89 B3
Esplanade Mall	(see 77)
Funan – The IT Mall	90 C3
Gajah Gallery	(see 85)
Harvey Norman	(see 94)
Marina Square Complex	91 E3
MITA Building	(see 85)
Pagoda House	(see 92)
Peter Hoe Evolution	(see 87)
Raffles Hotel Arcade	92 D2
Red Sea Gallery	93 A2
Soobin Art Gallery	(see 85)
Suntec City	94 D2
Tower Records	(see 94)

SLEEPING	(pp163–78)
Ah Chew Hotel	95 D1
Allson Hotel	96 C1
Backpacker Cozy Corner Guesthouse	97 D1
Conrad Centennial Singapore	98 E2
Fullerton Hotel	99 C4
Grand Plaza Parkroyal Hotel	100 C3
Hotel Bencoolen	101 C1
Hotel Intercontinental	102 D1
Hotel Rendezvous	103 B1
Metropole Hotel	104 D2
New 7th Storey Hotel	105 D1
Novotel Clarke Quay	106 A3
Oriental Singapore	107 E3
Pan Pacific Hotel	108 E3
Raffles Hotel	109 D2
Raffles, The Plaza	110 D2
Ritz-Carlton	111 E3
Strand Hotel	112 C1
Summer Tavern	113 B4
Swissôtel, Merchant Court	114 A4
Swissôtel, The Stamford	115 D2
Waterloo Hostel	116 C1
YMCA International House	117 B1
YWCA Fort Canning Lodge	118 B1

TRANSPORT	(pp194–9)
Malaysian Airlines	119 A1
Thrifty	120 D1

INFORMATION	
Chills Cafe	121 C2
Cyberstar Comcentre	122 D2
Liang Court Tourist Service Centre	123 A3
Malaysian Embassy	124 C2
Small Claims Tribunal	125 A4
Suntec City Visitors Centre	(see 94)

LITTLE INDIA & THE ARAB QUARTER

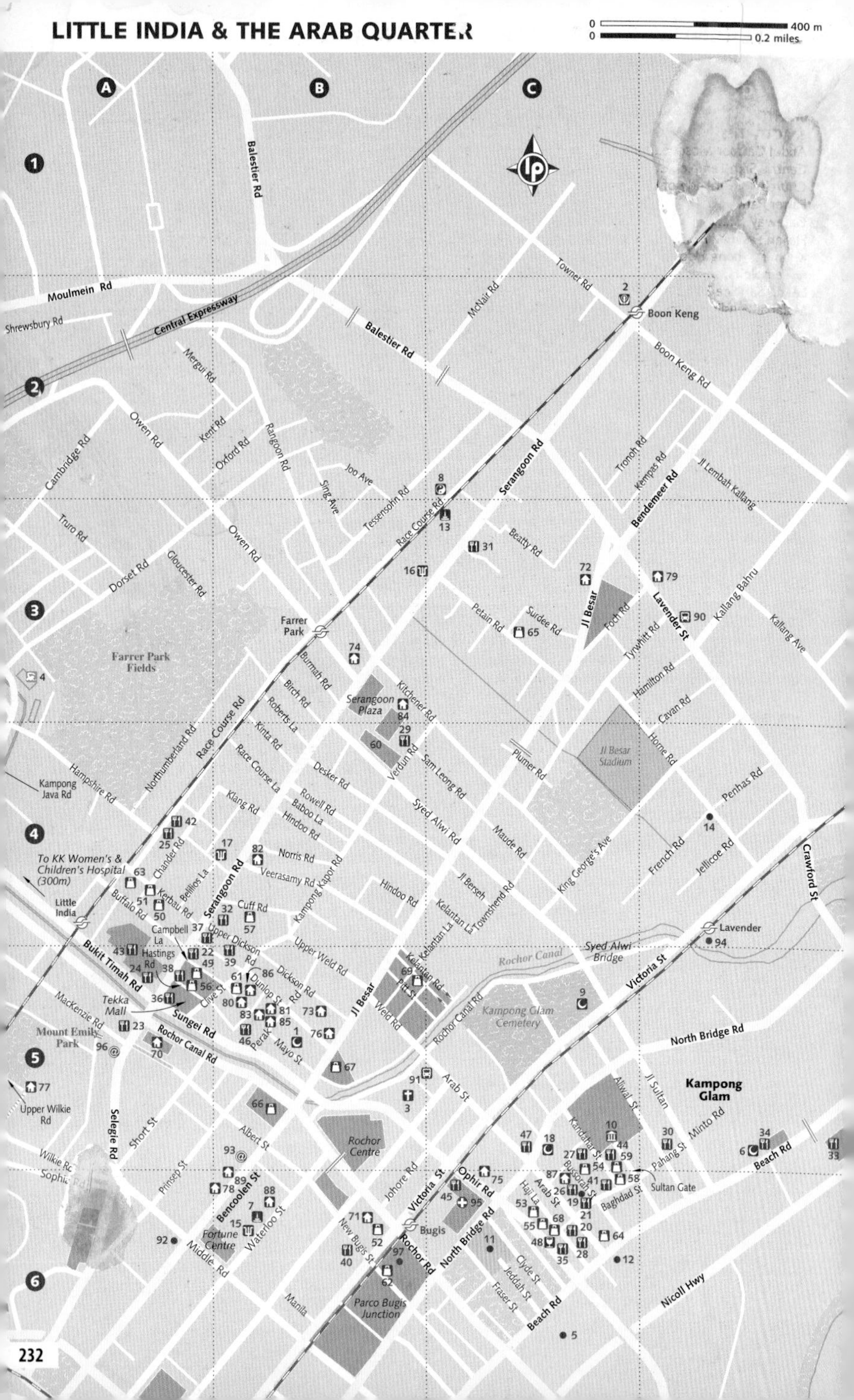

LITTLE INDIA & THE ARAB QUARTER (p232)

[illegible] (pp45–88)

[illegible] (pp135–8)

[illegible] 1 B5
[illegible] 2 C2
[illegible] Lourdes 3 B5
[illegible] Pool 4 A3
[illegible] 5 C6
[illegible] Mosque 6 D5
[illegible] d Cho [illegible] 7 B6
[illegible] Temple 8 C2
[illegible] Muslim Jama-Ath Mosque 9 C5
Malay Heritage Centre 10 C5
Parkview Square 11 C6
St Gregory Javana Spa 12 C6
Sakaya Muni Buddha Gaya Temple (Temple of 1000 Lights) 13 C3
Scuba Corner 14 D4
Sri Krishnan Temple 15 B6
Sri Srinivasa Perumal Temple 16 B3
Sri Veeramakaliamman Temple 17 B4
Sultan Mosque 18 C5
Wayan Retreat 19 C6

EATING (pp99–120)

Al-Tazzag 20 C6
Ambrosia Café 21 C6
Ananda Bhavan 22 A5
Ananda Bhavan 23 A5
Ananda Bhavan 24 A5
Banana Leaf Apolo 25 A4
Blue Oasis 26 C6
Bumbu 27 C5
Café Le Caire (Al Majlis) 28 C6
CLE African Restaurant 29 B4
El-Sheik 30 D5
French Stall 31 C3
Ganges 32 B4
Golden Mile Complex 33 D5
Golden Mile Food Centre 34 D5
Kaki Gallery & Cafe 35 C6
Kerala Cuisine 36 A5
Komala Vilas 37 A4
Little India Arcade 38 A5
Madras New Woodlands 39 B5
New Bugis St 40 B6
Samar 41 C6
Spice Mela 42 A4
Tekka Centre 43 A5
Tepak Sireh 44 C5
Ya Kun Kaya Toast 45 C6
Yogi Hub 46 B5
Zam Zam 47 C5

DRINKING (pp125–33)

BluJaz Cafe 48 C6

ENTERTAINMENT (pp121–38)

Shaw Bugis Complex Cinema (see 97)
SISTIC (see 62)

SHOPPING (pp139–62)

A Jaffar Spices Centre 49 A5
Ansa Store 50 A4
Bhaskar's Art Academy 51 A4
Bugis Village 52 B6
Comme des Garcons Guerrilla Store 53 C6
Grandfather's Collections 54 C5
House of Japan 55 C6
Indian Classical Music Centre 56 A5
Khan Mohamed Bhoy & Sons 57 B4
Khim's Collections 58 C6
Melor's Curios 59 C5
Mustafa Centre 60 B4
Nalli 61 B5
Parco Bugis Junction 62 B6
Plastique Kinetic Worms 63 A4
Samra 64 C6
Shoma Studio 65 C3
Sim Lim Square 66 B5
Sim Lim Tower 67 B5
Straits Records 68 C6
Sungei Rd Thieves Market 69 B5

SLEEPING (pp163–78)

Albert Court Hotel 70 A5
Bugis Backpackers 71 B6
Cactus Hotel 72 C3
Dickson Court Hotel 73 B5
Fortuna Hotel 74 B3
Golden Landmark Hotel 75 C6
Haising Hotel 76 B5
hangout@mt.emily 77 A5
Hawaii Hostel 78 B6
Hive 79 D3
InnCrowd (at Campbell) 80 B5
InnCrowd (at Dunlop) 81 B5
Little India Guest House 82 B4
Madras Hotel 83 B5
New Park Centra Singapore 84 B3
Perak Lodge 85 B5
Prince of Wales Backpacker Hostel & Pub 86 B5
Sleepy Sam's 87 C6
South-East Asia Hotel 88 B6
Summer View Hotel 89 B6

TRANSPORT (pp194–9)

Lavender St Bus Terminal 90 D3
Queen St Bus Terminal 91 B5
Wheelpower Rent-a-Bike 92 A6

INFORMATION

Cyber-Action 93 B5
Immigration Department 94 D4
Raffles SurgiCentre 95 C6
Selegie Cyber 96 A5
Singapore Visitors Centre @ Little India (see 81)
Trade Development Board 97 B6

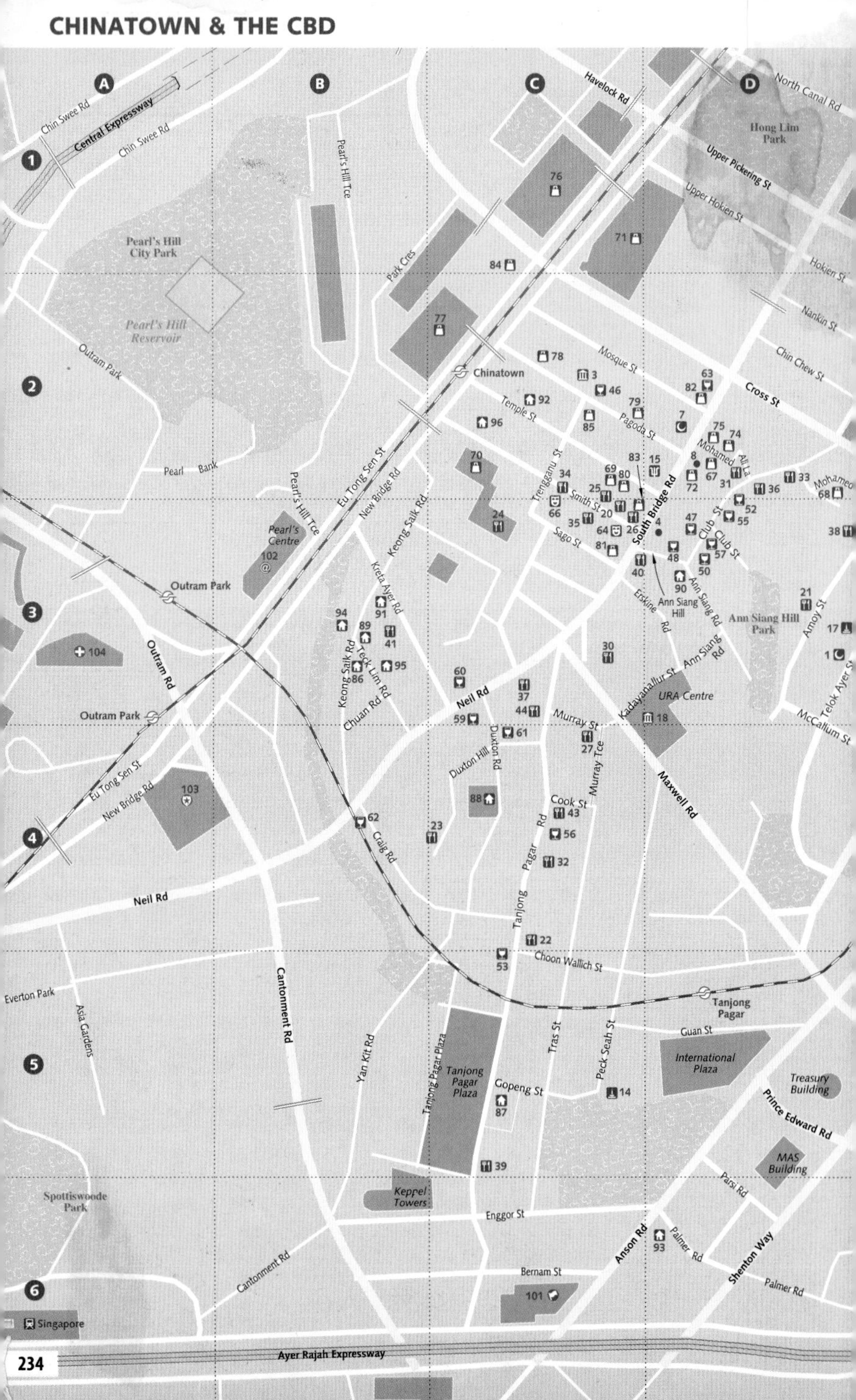
A
B
C
D
1
2
3
4
5
6
Chin Swee Rd
Central Expressway
Havelock Rd
North Canal Rd
Hong Lim Park
Upper Pickering St
Upper Hokien St
Hokien St
Nankin St
Chin Chew St
Cross St
Pearl's Hill Tce
Pearl's Hill City Park
Pearl's Hill Reservoir
Outram Park
Park Cres
Chinatown
Mosque St
Temple St
Pagoda St
Mohamed Ali La
Trengganu St
Smith St
Sago St
South Bridge Rd
Club St
Ann Siang Rd
Ann Siang Hill
Ann Siang Hill Park
Erskine Rd
Amoy St
Telok Ayer St
McCallum St
Pearl Bank
Eu Tong Sen St
New Bridge Rd
Keong Saik Rd
Pearl's Centre
Kreta Ayer Rd
Teck Lim Rd
Chuan Rd
Outram Rd
Neil Rd
Duxton Hill
Duxton Rd
Murray St
Murray Tce
Kadayanallur St
URA Centre
Maxwell Rd
Cook St
Tanjong Pagar Rd
Craig Rd
Choon Wallich St
Tanjong Pagar
Everton Park
Asia Gardens
Cantonment Rd
Yan Kit Rd
Tanjong Pagar Plaza
Gopeng St
Tras St
Peck Seah St
Guan St
International Plaza
Treasury Building
Prince Edward Rd
MAS Building
Parsi Rd
Spottiswoode Park
Keppel Towers
Enggor St
Anson Rd
Palmer Rd
Shenton Way
Bernam St
Singapore
Ayer Rajah Expressway
1 3 4 7 8 14 15 17 18 20 21 22 23 24 25 26 27 30 31 32 33 34 35 36 37 38 39 40 41 43 44 46 47 48 50 52 53 55 56 57 59 60 61 62 63 64 66 67 68 69 70 71 72 74 75 76 77 78 79 80 81 82 83 84 85 86 87 88 89 90 91 92 93 94 95 96 101 102 103 104

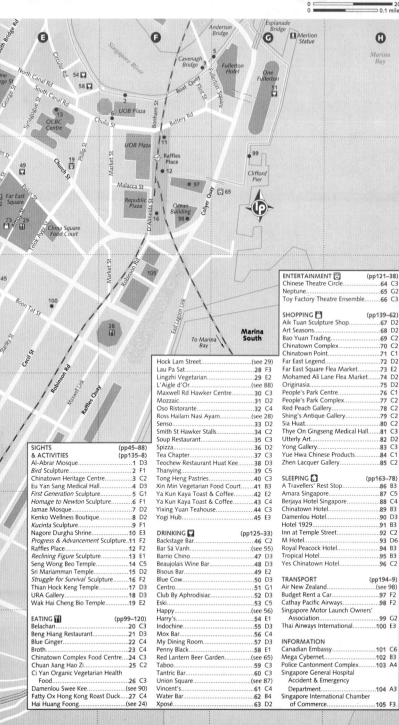

SIGHTS & ACTIVITIES (pp45–88) (pp135–8)

- Al-Abrar Mosque 1 D3
- *Bird* Sculpture 2 F1
- Chinatown Heritage Centre 3 C2
- Eu Yan Sang Medical Hall 4 D3
- *First Generation* Sculpture 5 G1
- *Homage to Newton* Sculpture 6 F1
- Jamae Mosque 7 D2
- Kenko Wellness Boutique 8 D2
- *Kucinta* Sculpture 9 F1
- Nagore Durgha Shrine 10 E3
- *Progress & Advancement* Sculpture 11 F2
- Raffles Place 12 F2
- *Reclining Figure* Sculpture 13 E1
- Seng Wong Beo Temple 14 C5
- Sri Mariamman Temple 15 D2
- *Struggle for Survival* Sculpture 16 F2
- Thian Hock Keng Temple 17 D3
- URA Gallery 18 D3
- Wak Hai Cheng Bio Temple 19 E2

EATING (pp99–120)

- Belachan 20 C3
- Beng Hiang Restaurant 21 D3
- Blue Ginger 22 C4
- Broth 23 C4
- Chinatown Complex Food Centre 24 C3
- Chuan Jiang Hao Zi 25 C2
- Ci Yan Organic Vegetarian Health Food 26 C3
- Damenlou Swee Kee (see 90)
- Fatty Ox Hong Kong Roast Duck 27 C4
- Hai Huang Foong (see 24)
- Hock Lam Street (see 29)
- Lau Pa Sat 28 F3
- Lingzhi Vegetarian 29 E2
- L'Aigle d'Or (see 88)
- Maxwell Rd Hawker Centre 30 C3
- Mozzaic 31 D2
- Oso Ristorante 32 C4
- Ross Hailam Nasi Ayam (see 28)
- Senso 33 D2
- Smith St Hawker Stalls 34 C2
- Soup Restaurant 35 C3
- Spizza 36 D2
- Tea Chapter 37 C3
- Teochew Restaurant Huat Kee 38 D3
- Thanying 39 C5
- Tong Heng Pastries 40 C3
- Xin Min Vegetarian Food Court 41 B3
- Ya Kun Kaya Toast & Coffee 42 E2
- Ya Kun Kaya Toast & Coffee 43 C4
- Yixing Yuan Teahouse 44 C3
- Yogi Hub 45 E3

DRINKING (pp125–33)

- Backstage Bar 46 C2
- Bar Sá Vanh (see 55)
- Barrio Chino 47 D3
- Beaujolais Wine Bar 48 D3
- Bisous Bar 49 E2
- Blue Cow 50 D3
- Centro 51 G1
- Club By Aphrodisiac 52 D3
- Eski 53 C5
- Happy (see 56)
- Harry's 54 E1
- Indochine 55 D3
- Mox Bar 56 C4
- My Dining Room 57 D3
- Penny Black 58 E1
- Red Lantern Beer Garden (see 65)
- Taboo 59 C3
- Tantric Bar 60 C3
- Union Square (see 87)
- Vincent's 61 C4
- Water Bar 62 B4
- Xposé 63 D2

ENTERTAINMENT (pp121–38)

- Chinese Theatre Circle 64 C3
- Neptune 65 G2
- Toy Factory Theatre Ensemble 66 C3

SHOPPING (pp139–62)

- Aik Tuan Sculpture Shop 67 D2
- Art Seasons 68 D2
- Bao Yuan Trading 69 C2
- Chinatown Complex 70 C2
- Chinatown Point 71 C1
- Far East Legend 72 D2
- Far East Square Flea Market 73 E2
- Mohamed Ali Lane Flea Market 74 D2
- Originasia 75 D2
- People's Park Centre 76 C1
- People's Park Complex 77 C2
- Red Peach Gallery 78 C2
- Shing's Antique Gallery 79 C2
- Sia Huat 80 C2
- Thye On Gingseng Medical Hall 81 C3
- Utterly Art 82 D2
- Yong Gallery 83 C3
- Yue Hwa Chinese Products 84 C1
- Zhen Lacquer Gallery 85 C2

SLEEPING (pp163–78)

- A Travellers' Rest Stop 86 B3
- Amara Singapore 87 C5
- Berjaya Hotel Singapore 88 C4
- Chinatown Hotel 89 B3
- Damenlou Hotel 90 D3
- Hotel 1929 91 B3
- Inn at Temple Street 92 C2
- M Hotel 93 D6
- Royal Peacock Hotel 94 B3
- Tropical Hotel 95 B3
- Yes Chinatown Hotel 96 C2

TRANSPORT (pp194–9)

- Air New Zealand (see 98)
- Budget Rent a Car 97 F2
- Cathay Pacific Airways 98 F2
- Singapore Motor Launch Owners' Association 99 G2
- Thai Airways International 100 E3

INFORMATION

- Canadian Embassy 101 C6
- Mega Cybernet 102 B3
- Police Cantonment Complex 103 A4
- Singapore General Hospital Accident & Emergency Department 104 A3
- Singapore International Chamber of Commerce 105 F3

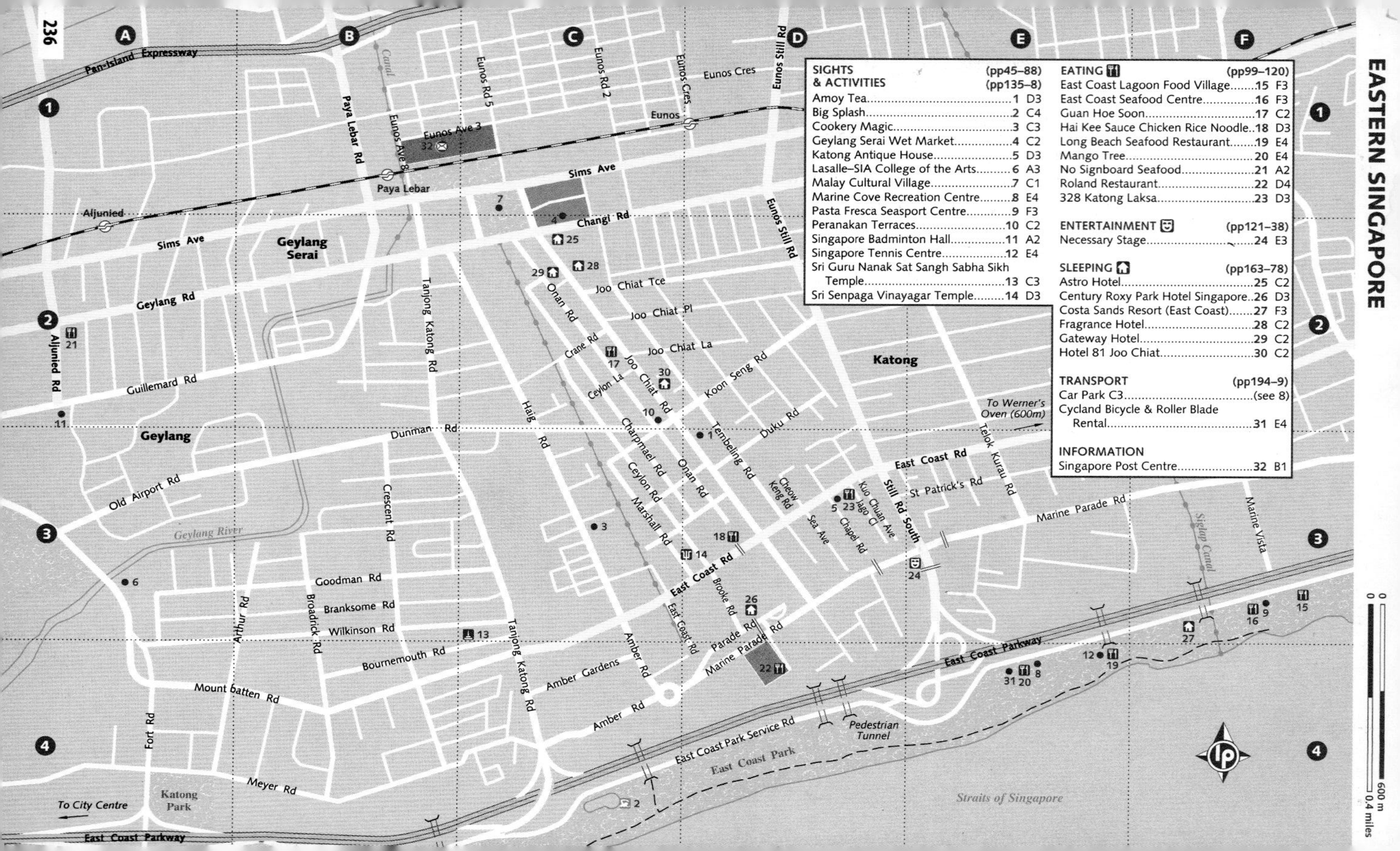
0 600 m
0 0.4 miles
SIGHTS & ACTIVITIES (pp45–88) (pp135–8)
Amoy Tea 1 D3
Big Splash 2 C4
Cookery Magic 3 C3
Geylang Serai Wet Market 4 C2
Katong Antique House 5 D3
Lasalle–SIA College of the Arts 6 A3
Malay Cultural Village 7 C1
Marine Cove Recreation Centre 8 E4
Pasta Fresca Seasport Centre 9 F3
Peranakan Terraces 10 C2
Singapore Badminton Hall 11 A2
Singapore Tennis Centre 12 E4
Sri Guru Nanak Sat Sangh Sabha Sikh Temple 13 C3
Sri Senpaga Vinayagar Temple 14 D3
EATING (pp99–120)
East Coast Lagoon Food Village 15 F3
East Coast Seafood Centre 16 F3
Guan Hoe Soon 17 C2
Hai Kee Sauce Chicken Rice Noodle 18 D3
Long Beach Seafood Restaurant 19 E4
Mango Tree 20 E4
No Signboard Seafood 21 A2
Roland Restaurant 22 D4
328 Katong Laksa 23 D3
ENTERTAINMENT (pp121–38)
Necessary Stage 24 E3
SLEEPING (pp163–78)
Astro Hotel 25 C2
Century Roxy Park Hotel Singapore 26 D3
Costa Sands Resort (East Coast) 27 F3
Fragrance Hotel 28 C2
Gateway Hotel 29 C2
Hotel 81 Joo Chiat 30 C2
TRANSPORT (pp194–9)
Car Park C3 (see 8)
Cycland Bicycle & Roller Blade Rental 31 E4
INFORMATION
Singapore Post Centre 32 B1
Katong
Geylang Serai
Geylang
Straits of Singapore
East Coast Park
Katong Park
Pedestrian Tunnel
Siglap Canal
Geylang River
Canal
East Coast Parkway
Pan-Island Expressway
East Coast Park Service Rd
Marine Vista
Marine Parade Rd
Telok Kurau Rd
East Coast Rd
St Patrick's Rd
Still Rd South
Kuo Chuan Ave
Jago Cl
Chapel Rd
Sea Ave
Cheow Keng Rd
Duku Rd
Koon Seng Rd
Tembeling Rd
Onan Rd
Joo Chiat Rd
Joo Chiat Tce
Joo Chiat Pl
Joo Chiat La
Crane Rd
Ceylon La
Ceylon Rd
Charpmael Rd
Marshall Rd
Brooke Rd
Amber Rd
Amber Gardens
Haig Rd
Changi Rd
Sims Ave
Eunos Still Rd
Eunos Cres
Eunos
Eunos Rd 2
Eunos Rd 5
Eunos Ave 3
Eunos Ave 8
Paya Lebar
Paya Lebar Rd
Tanjong Katong Rd
Dunman Rd
Crescent Rd
Goodman Rd
Branksome Rd
Wilkinson Rd
Bournemouth Rd
Broadrick Rd
Arthur Rd
Mount batten Rd
Meyer Rd
Fort Rd
Old Airport Rd
Guillemard Rd
Geylang Rd
Aljunied
Aljunied Rd
To Werner's Oven (600m)
To City Centre